Alice Munro *Country*

ESSAYS on HER WORKS I

ESSENTIAL WRITERS SERIES 51

Guernica Editions Inc. acknowledges the support
of the Canada Council for the Arts and the Ontario Arts Council.
The Ontario Arts Council is an agency of the Government of Ontario.
We acknowledge the financial support of the Government of Canada.

Alice Munro *Country*

ESSAYS ON HER WORKS I

Edited by J.R. (Tim) Struthers

GUERNICA
EDITIONS
TORONTO • CHICAGO • BUFFALO • LANCASTER (U.K.)
2020

J.R. (Tim) Struthers, editor
Michael Mirolla, general editor
Joseph Pivato, series editor
Cover and Interior Design: Rafael Chimicatti
Cover Art: Derived from a painting,
Levels (2017), by Ron Shuebrook

Guernica Editions Inc.
287 Templemead Drive, Hamilton (ON), Canada L8W 2W4
2250 Military Road, Tonawanda, N.Y. 14150-6000 U.S.A.
www.guernicaeditions.com

Distributors:
Independent Publishers Group (IPG)
600 North Pulaski Road, Chicago IL 60624
University of Toronto Press Distribution,
5201 Dufferin Street, Toronto (ON), Canada M3H 5T8
Gazelle Book Services, White Cross Mills
High Town, Lancaster LA1 4XS U.K.

First edition.
Printed in Canada.

Legal Deposit – First Quarter
Library of Congress Catalog Card Number: 2019946616
Library and Archives Canada Cataloguing in Publication
Title: Alice Munro country : essays on her works I / edited by J.R. (Tim) Struthers
Names: Struthers, J.R. Tim, 1950-
Series: Essential writers series ; 51.
Description: Series statement: Essential writers series ; 51
Includes bibliographical references.
Identifiers: Canadiana (print) 20190164905 | Canadiana (ebook) 20190164913
ISBN 9781771834353 (softcover) | ISBN 9781771834360 (EPUB)
ISBN 9781771834377 (Kindle)
Subjects: LCSH: Munro, Alice, 1931-—Criticism and interpretation.
Classification: LCC PS8576.U57 Z515 2020 | DDC C813/.54—dc23

Alice Munro Country: Essays on Her Works I
and
Alice Munro Everlasting: Essays on Her Works II
are dedicated to Alice Munro
with admiration, with gratitude, and with love
for a lifetime spent working so ardently
in devotion to the form of the short story.

Contents

Douglas Gibson

Alice Munro: Not Bad Short Story Writer *1*

Jack Hodgins

Looking, Imagining *23*

Judith Thompson

The Boy with the Banana in His Mouth *29*

John B. Lee

Einstein's Hammer and the Painting Pachyderm:
Reading Alice Munro in the Digital Age
(every day is trying to teach us something) *35*

James Reaney

An ABC to Ontario Literature and Culture *49*

Reg Thompson

All Things Considered: Alice Munro First and Last *59*

J.R. (Tim) Struthers

Remembrance Day 1988: An Interview with Alice Munro *65*

Dennis Duffy

Too Little Geography; Too Much History:
Writing the Balance in Alice Munro *87*

Alec Follett
"The Region That I Know":
The Bioregional View in Alice Munro's
The View from Castle Rock *115*

Coral Ann Howells
Intimate Dislocations: Buried History
and Geography in Alice Munro's Souwesto Stories *139*

John Weaver
Society and Culture in Rural
and Small-Town Ontario: Alice Munro's
Testimony on the Forty Years from 1945 to 1985 .... *155*

Ian Rae
Alice Munro and the Huron Tract as a Literary Project *181*

George Elliott Clarke
Alice Munro's Black Bottom;
or Black Tints and Euro Hints
in *Lives of Girls and Women* *207*

W.R. Martin and Warren U. Ober .
Alice Munro as Small-Town Historian:
"Spaceships Have Landed" *237*

William Butt
Killer OSPs and Style Munro in "Open Secrets" *255*

Shelley Hulan
Not for Entertainment Purposes Only:
Ethnicity and Alice Munro's "Powers" *263*

Ailsa Cox

Thoughts from England:
On Reading, Teaching, and Writing Back
to Alice Munro's "Meneseteung" *281*

Louis K. MacKendrick

Giving Tongue: Scorings of Voice, Verse,
and Flesh in Alice Munro's "Meneseteung" *303*

Marianne Micros

"Pearl Street ... is another story":
Poetry and Reality in Alice Munro's "Meneseteung" *323*

J.R. (Tim) Struthers

A Bibliographical Tour of Alice Munro Country *345*

About the Writer *382*
About the Artist *383*
About the Editor *384*
Contributor Biographies *385*
Acknowledgements *397*

Alice Munro: Not Bad Short Story Writer

Douglas Gibson

When I reach the Pearly Gates, I know that I have the perfect password to get in. Even if St. Peter is at his grumpy, bureaucratic worst – "So what have you ever done in your miserable, selfish life to deserve getting into Heaven?" – I can waltz in simply by saying: "I kept Alice Munro writing short stories."

And he, if his English is any good, will rush to wave me through, maybe even making a saintly exclamation like "Holy smokes, Alice Munro!"

I even have the documents to prove it. When Robert Thacker was hard at work researching his masterful biography entitled *Alice Munro: Writing Her Lives* (2005, since revised and updated, and published in 2011), he came upon a letter that Alice wrote in March 1986. The situation was this: I had just left Macmillan of Canada to set up Douglas Gibson Books at McClelland & Stewart, and Alice was keen to join me there, with her book *The Progress of Love* that I had signed up for Macmillan. Linda McKnight, the new head of Macmillan, was less keen on this idea. So Alice wrote her the following letter, asking to be set free from her contract, in order to join me:

> Doug first talked to me about publishing with Macmillan in the mid-seventies. I was very discouraged at that time. Ryerson had done nothing to promote or even distribute my first book. McGraw-Hill Ryerson had published the second with expressed reluctance and the third without enthusiasm – merely, I believe, to keep a Canadian fiction writer on their list. Every publisher I had met had assured me that I would have to grow up and write novels before I could be taken seriously as a writer. No one in Canada had shown the least interest in taking on a writer who was going to turn out book after book of short stories. The result of this was

that I wasted much time and effort trying to turn myself into a novelist, and had become so depressed that I was unable to write at all. Doug changed that. He was absolutely the first person in Canadian publishing who made me feel that there was no need to apologize for being a short story writer, and that a book of short stories could be published and promoted as major fiction. This was a fairly revolutionary notion, at the time. It was this support that enabled me to go on working, when I had been totally uncertain about my future.

I came to Macmillan because of Doug, and his respect for my work changed me from a minor, "literary" writer who sold poorly into a major writer who sold well. I hope that you will understand how I have felt, from that time on, that I owe him a great deal, and that I want him to have charge of any book I publish. I am not making a judgment against Macmillan – my relations in the house have always been good – but for Doug Gibson.

In the end, thanks to Avie Bennett's generosity in paying Macmillan a fee to free Alice, it all worked out. In fact it worked out so well that the *Toronto Star* reported that I had "scored a coup by acquiring Canadian publishing rights to the work of Alice Munro from Macmillan." *The Globe and Mail* reported the story, which included the news that Hugh MacLennan and W.O. Mitchell were also coming with me, under the agreeable headline: "CanLit Luminaries Stick with Gibson."

It was priceless publicity for my new line. In the next few years, so many Macmillan authors chose to follow me to M&S that Macmillan simply stopped publishing fiction. And *The Progress of Love* sold far better than even our highest hopes had predicted, handsomely recovering our investment.

This is a good place to pay tribute to Avie Bennett, a good friend of Alice, and of mine. It was typical of Avie that he would take the gamble of paying out what I call a large "ransom" to Macmillan (despite which my former employer, sadly, went downhill and disappeared) in order to let Alice's new book start off my new imprint with a bang. He had used that same daring gambler's instinct to make a fortune as a developer, and then, fairly late in his life, after joining the M&S board to help it through bad times, had used it again to buy the company in 1986. He soon lured me there to start my imprint, and from September 1988 until he sold the company in mid-2000, he and I were in and out of each other's office for hours every day, and I got to know him very well.

Michael Levine, the entertainment lawyer, agent, and ubiquitous man-about-town, called us "the Odd Couple," exulting in the many differences between me, the fancy-pants literary guy, and Avie, the businessman from the school of hard knocks who, among many other differences, did not share my aversion to alcohol. Avie used to complain publicly that I was "stubborn" (a charge I'll fight to my dying day), and I would roll my eyes at his passion for doing things differently, for "trying something new." I learned that it was a terrible mistake ever to propose a solution by saying: "Well, here's what we usually do in publishing...." But I also learned that he was such a bright guy that his new ideas were often good ones, and that they were motivated by the same love of books – and of doing a good job for our authors, and selling lots of copies – as my own, more traditional, plans.

For his dedicated (often very expensive) support of McClelland & Stewart over the years, Canada's writers – and their readers – owe him a great deal. His support of many other good causes is impossible to quantify, because he preferred to do so much of his good work secretly, as an "Anonymous Donor."

Editors, too, are usually fairly anonymous (unless they shamelessly blazon their own imprint all over their books) and it is always a magical thing for editors to find a book dedicated to them by the author. That is what happened to me with Alice's very personal 2006 book, *The View from Castle Rock*, which is a fiction collection based on the history of her own family, the Laidlaws. Her dedication at the front of the book is pure Alice. "Dedicated to Douglas Gibson, who has sustained me through many travails, and whose enthusiasm for this particular book has even sent him prowling through the graveyard of Ettrick Kirk, probably in the rain." (As I check the exact wording, I find that Alice has corrected these words in my personal signed copy, adding: "For Doug, who is even more loyal and admirable and funny than this indicates.")

Let me explain the Ettrick Kirk reference, by accounting for the (*rain-free!*) research trip that I took with my wife Jane who is – almost by defi-nition – a patient woman. She has always cheerfully accompanied me on the routine social occasions, and even the more unusual expeditions, that a book publisher's life provides. Yet a raw winter morning spent poking around unglamorous streets in the east end of Montreal, following the career of Yves Beauchemin's bold young hero, Charles Thibodeau, once moved her to ask: "Let me get this straight. We're tracing the life – finding the high school, and the church where they buried his mother, and so on – of a *fictional* character?"

It was more a comment than a complaint, you understand, and she listened politely, shivering only slightly, while I explained the need to catch just the right atmosphere on the cover for *Charles the Bold* and the rest of the series, and how vital it is for an editor to fully understand a character's life, blah, blah, blah, blah.

But these things even out. She was much keener when we interrupted a visit to Scotland in order to explore the setting for the first chapters of Alice's then-forthcoming book, *The View from Castle Rock*. We knew that Alice's ancestors, the Laidlaws, came to Canada in 1818 from the Scottish Borders. We had also learned from the first version of the manuscript that the earliest known Laidlaw relative, born around 1700, lived at the very end of the Ettrick Valley, at a farm named Far-Hope. We were sure that we could find it.

The Ettrick River flows roughly from west to east into the North Sea about halfway between Edinburgh and the English border. From the town of Peebles we drove south until we met the Ettrick Valley. On the way we passed Tushielaw. (Alice, I remembered from the manuscript, on her own exploration had caught a bus from Tushielaw – not a name you forget.)

Following the river west we were among wild, lonely, bare hills, sheep country for many generations, ever since the medieval forest that once sheltered William "Braveheart" Wallace's guerilmas was felled, leaving no trace but the name "Ettrick Forest." The only place that had even a cluster of houses, and a small grey school, was Ettrick itself. There, in the graveyard by the Kirk, we found the grave of William Laidlaw of Far-Hope, locally called "Phaup." The tombstone memorably declares: "Here lyeth William Laidlaw, the far-fam'd Will o' Phaup who for feats of frolic, agility and strength, had no equal in his day."

Beside it lay the grave of the man who wrote the epitaph, Will's grandson, James Hogg, author of *The Private Memoirs and Confessions of a Justified Sinner* (1824), and a great literary figure in his day. I copied the wording down carefully for Alice's book. Inside the spare Presbyterian church I noted that the first man from the parish to die in the First World War was a Robert Laidlaw, who shared a name – and, no doubt, bloodlines – with Alice's Canadian father.

Jane and I returned to the car and headed west with mounting excitement. Now the Ettrick River was narrowing to the point that we could imagine Will O' Phaup trying one of his legendary leaps (encompassing "frolic, agility and strength") across it. Soon the farms were falling away, the road becoming a track. We parked the car and started to walk in to Potburn, the farm that lies before Far-Hope. To our relief, Potburn proved to be deserted, occupied only by sparrows and finches, although the curtains in the windows hinted at recent occupancy. Now the buildings of Far-Hope were in plain sight.

"Far-Hope" indeed. It was supposedly the highest farm in Scotland, a designation that held no prospect of rich land. Our map told us that the hills that rose right behind the low stone house were the spine of Scotland. Just over their tops the rainwater drained west into the Solway, and the Atlantic, a fact that I was able to pass on to Alice.

The old farm buildings were a surprise and a delight. Usually a visit to a 300-year-old farm site will produce either a heap of rubble showing only bare outlines or, perhaps worse, a working farm, where literary intruders are not routinely welcomed, by man or dog. Miraculously, Far-Hope is preserved in something close to its original state, and is unoccupied, yet at the same time open to all comers as a "bothy" (a rough sleeping hostel) on the walking trail known as the Southern Upland Way.

Inside, a literary tourist can pace the rough stone floor, seeing the original kitchen layout around the fireplace, and can easily imagine the old family's straw bedding in place. A stroll around the silent outbuildings reveals where the horse was stabled, and the milk-providing cow. Sheep pens, the farm's raison d'être, are prominent, and the Ettrick provides running water at the door.

Before we left, I wrote in the bothy visitor's book an account of Alice Munro's career, and its links to this small, humble place. I hope that many Canadians familiar with Alice's work, especially *The View from Castle Rock*, will tear themselves away from the fleshpots of Edinburgh and make the pilgrimage to Far-Hope.

Failing that, there is another Alice Munro pilgrimage, one much closer to home. Roughly an hour outside Toronto, just north and west of the town of Milton, lies the Boston Church. It is named after Thomas Boston, the minister of, yes, Ettrick Kirk, because so many of his former parishioners chose to come to this area, to settle in this heavily Scottish part of what was then called Canada West. A plaque outside the grey Gothic Revival building notes that the first service was held in 1820, while the handsome building itself was "designed and constructed in 1868 by Charles Blackwood, Thomas Henderson and congregation volunteers from Esquesing's Scotch block."

The setting, on a road lined with old maple trees running northwest towards Halton Hills, is idyllic, with the property itself adorned by maples, cedars, lilacs, and a great weeping willow, with few other buildings in sight. As you approach the church door, turn to the nearest corner on the left, and there you will find the graves devoted to the Laidlaws, Alice's ancestors. Several of these graves have ancient tombstones giving details of the lives of those interred beneath them, including old James Laidlaw Senior, born in Ettrick Forest, Scotland, in 1763, who came to Esquesing in 1818, and died in 1829. And all of this history is to be found, as Alice writes, "almost within sight, and well within sound, of Highway 401 north of Milton, which at that spot may be the busiest road in Canada."

Alice's ancestors moved farther west from here, as pioneers, into the uncleared forest and bush of Southwestern Ontario's Huron County. We get a very clear picture of what life was like for them in Alice's story, "A Wilderness Station," where after a tree-felling incident one character ends up in the Goderich jail. That ancient jail still stands, as a tourist attraction, in the town that anchors the county at the Lake Huron shore. The huge lake has allowed travel industry copywriters to go wild with descriptions of "Ontario's West Coast," complete with dramatic photos of a summer sun sinking into its wide waters. But it is the undramatic landscape stretching east of Goderich – a flat, partly wooded stretch of farming country with no striking natural features – that has become known to numberless readers as "Alice Munro Country."

The word "undramatic" also applies to the history of the area, settled in the nineteenth century by immigrants from Scotland, England, and Ireland, as shown by place names like Dunlop, Clinton, and the ominous

Donnybrook. (My old friend Harry J. Boyle grew up near there, admired by young Alice as he walked to work at the Wingham radio station, on his way to a career at the CBC, and to another as the author of many books including *The Luck of the Irish*, and – because he was willing to go along with my mischievous title idea – as the author of record of *The Great Canadian Novel*.) There are other Irish traces in this heavily Scottish area. The nearby community of Dublin has a tiny river running through it. The local blend of sentiment and realism is reflected in the name given to that watercourse, "The Liffey Drain." This is not a land of Great Expectations.

No wars were fought with the Native people who lived here, no great battles with American invaders. Instead it was the scene of countless small heroic family battles, to fell the trees and clear the land, to build a cabin, to get the crops in; in short, to survive. To survive enough winters, in fact, to replace the cabin with a house, and in time to build the little towns with mills, and churches, and schools that dot today's settled landscape. These early struggles are neatly caught, I think, in the C.W. Jefferys drawing of brawny settlers straining to clear away giant tree trunks that I chose to put on the cover of an informative historical novel that I published about these pioneer days. It was called *The McGregors*, and it was written by Alice's father, Robert Laidlaw.

For today's literary tourist the points of special interest in Huron County are *Clinton*, where Alice now lives, her privacy protected by kindly neighbours (although I, as a privileged visitor, can tell you that this woman who once wrote in A Laundry Room of Her Own, still has no writing room of her own where she can shut her door on a ringing phone, or on the general business of the household – which has become quieter, sadly, since her husband Gerry Fremlin passed away); *Goderich*, where she still prefers to meet visitors (although her favourite restaurant on the hexagonal central square was destroyed, as if singled out, by a tornado in 2011 – a literary as well as a culinary loss, since the staff were only too happy to tell a visiting publisher, decisively, which potential book cover should be chosen for Alice's next work) and where she and Gerry used to enjoy strolling down by the harbour, her silver hair blowing in the wind off the lake; or *Blyth*, where her father had strong links, and where she plans to be buried alongside Gerry, and where, as Val Ross's perfect story showed, she could be counted on to roll up her sleeves and pitch in as a waitress to help raise funds for the local theatre, where, amazingly, she once played a small part onstage; or the lakeside town of *Bayfield*, where she enjoys the little bookstore, where she once staged a "Long Pen" event to help her friend Margaret Atwood; or, above all, *Wingham*, her birthplace, where the main street is graced by the Alice Munro Literary Garden. In Wingham you will also find a leaflet that will help visitors to follow an Alice Munro walking tour that begins at the house where she grew up. In an ideal world that house will eventually be bought by sensible authorities aware that for the next century it can be a well used tourist centre for the many people from around the world who will wish to see "Alice Munro Country" for themselves.

The day in 2002 that the attractive little literary garden was opened in Wingham, Jane and I cut short our honeymoon (are you feeling sorry for her yet?) in order to attend the happy festivities. Speeches were given by old friends like David Staines and Alice's effervescent agent, Ginger Barber, in the grand old Victorian Opera House across Josephine Street from the garden, while Alice, who knew her expected role, smiled serenely beneath a large, flowered hat. It was the only time in my life when I earned a warm round of applause simply by revealing that my middle name is – Maitland! The audience knew that the Maitland River, and its many branches, dominates the Huron County landscape. I knew that not every publisher is lucky enough to have a mother whose uncommon surname was sure to strike Alice as a link with home.

The fine Canadian literary critic Philip Marchand concisely explained the importance of these settings to Alice and her work – and vice versa – in a 2009 review of *Too Much Happiness*:

> If Alice Munro had never existed, part of the soul of Canada would have remained inarticulate, forgotten, submerged. The locus of this Canadian scene rendered so powerfully in her fiction is rural Southwestern Ontario, settled by Scotch Presbyterians, Congregationalists and Methodists from the north of England. … everything in her world comes back to that small-town milieu of pokey little stores, dull Sunday-afternoon dinners with aunts and uncles, a mentality made up of respect for hard work, resentment of show-offs and dim memories of Calvinist terrors.

Hmm – resentment of show-offs.

The point of a stroll through these little towns, or a drive along the placid roads dotted with mixed farms (with patches of bush still preserved in the background as a source of firewood or maple syrup) is that what you see around you is so *ordinary*. It's a dull, everyday landscape. And Alice Munro the magician has waved her wand over this undramatic scene, and made it the setting for some of the most astonishing and thrilling short stories ever seen. She has made the lives of people like a chambermaid at the Blue Spruce Inn in Huron County the stuff of world literature. For Alice Munro knows Huron County in her bones. She has been determined to catch it on paper, just as her character Del in *Lives of Girls & Women* hoped: "What I wanted was every last thing, every layer of speech and thought, stroke of light on bark or walls, every smell, pothole, pain, crack, delusion, held still and held together – radiant, everlasting."

Robert Thacker's splendid biography makes it unnecessary for me to run through Alice's life story in any detail, beyond the main points. She was born in the summer of 1931, in Wingham, which was then a town of about 3,000. Her father had a failing fox farm on the wrong side of town, and her mother, a former teacher, fell ill early with Parkinson's Disease and died young. Alice was a bright girl who did well in school and went on to The University of Western Ontario, in the conservative, yellow-brick city of London, the regional centre. After two penny-pinching years that saw Alice selling her blood for cash, lack of funds forced her to drop out. But she had met James Armstrong Munro, a fellow student, and soon moved to Vancouver with him as his wife. Jim and she raised three daughters (Sheila, Jenny, and Andrea) there and in Victoria, where the two established a fine bookstore, still going strong.

Sheila Munro's memoir, *Lives of Mothers & Daughters*, tells us a lot about Alice the mother. We know from Thacker's careful account that she started trying her hand as a short story writer in 1953, and after years of contributing stories to little magazines and to the CBC (where a producer named Robert Weaver was her mentor, and her first link with the writing world) she became "an overnight sensation" when her first book, *Dance of the Happy Shades*, came out in 1968 and won the Governor General's Award. A local paper greeted that book with a headline: "Housewife Finds Time To Write Short Stories."

When her marriage broke down, Alice returned home to Southwestern Ontario, where she soon met a contemporary, Gerry Fremlin, who remembered her fondly. They lived together, until Gerry's death in the spring of 2013, in Clinton, only thirty kilometres away from Wingham. Robert Thacker sees huge significance in the fact that, after brief spells in London and Toronto (where at York University she tried her hand at teaching writing, and had the courage to quit when she realized that she was not a good teacher), Alice moved *all the way home*, to Huron County. Certainly, although she has written a number of fine stories set on the West Coast (or in Miles City, Montana, come to think of it), it is Southwestern Ontario that has most reliably inspired her writing.

My own contact with Alice – so generously described by her in the letter I quoted earlier, a letter I only got to see when I published Thacker's brilliantly researched biography – began with a fan letter from me, followed by a meeting for lunch at the London downtown Holiday Inn. (I recently revisited it on a research trip, and must report that no plaque records our meeting, and even the name of the hotel has changed.) Alice has always been such a beautiful woman that I use the word "courtship" cautiously, but I was certainly courting her professionally, to assure her that she would be comfortable working with me (which took a few meetings), and to promise explicitly that I would never, ever, ask her for a novel.

You know the rest.

Before I came on the scene Alice had brought out *Lives of Girls & Women* (1971), which was unwisely published as a novel. (It's always better to under-claim and try for a Yes-And response, rather than the Yes-But response that the book received from people who liked it, yes, but felt that it wasn't really a novel.) Then came a fine short story collection called – in a typical Munro phrase that foretells trouble – *Something I've Been Meaning To Tell You* (1974). I recall an academic conference on Alice's work where I was used by Alice as an observer who could report to her what was being said about her work. I remember her genuine shock and outrage at the waste of an intelligent teacher's time when I reported that one speaker, a well-paid professor, had spent much ingenuity and effort proving that *Something* ... was really, secretly, a novel!

The very first book we worked on together was *Who Do You Think You Are?* (1978). Usually in those days all Canadian fiction titles had a cover produced by a commercial artist who was instructed to break out a new set of crayons and do a nice picture of the book's most exciting scene. I exaggerate, slightly. It was time, I thought, to change all that for Alice, by seeking out, and paying for, a fine, existing work by a recognized Canadian artist. Our cover, graced by the art of the magic realist Ken Danby, showed a reflective young woman, sitting on a patch of grass, hugging her knees. It went wonderfully well with Alice's stories about a girl growing up, and the double-edged title, *Who Do You Think You Are?*.

A note about that title. As I've mentioned, the book's later publishers in the U.S. and the U.K. were alarmed that Malcolm Bradbury had recently used the same title (although book titles are not protected by copyright). So despite the perfect double meaning of the Canadian title, in the other editions the book came out under the feeble name *The Beggar Maid*. Under its proper title it won the Governor General's Award and smashed all existing sales records for a Canadian short story collection. And we never looked back.

The proud roll call of titles continued through the eighties and nineties. *The Moons of Jupiter*, *The Progress of Love* (the ransomed story collection), *Friend of My Youth*, *Open Secrets*, *The Love of a Good Woman*. In the new century the nine- or ten-story collections continued with *Hateship, Friendship, Courtship, Loveship, Marriage*, then *Runaway*, then *The View from Castle Rock*, then *Too Much Happiness*, followed by her 2012 collection *Dear Life*. My own role in all this was very easy. Basically I was hanging on for the ride, whooping.

I did the odd useful thing, like finding wonderful paintings by people like Alex Colville, Christopher and Mary Pratt, and Paul Peel to give the books the right, elegant look. I knew that we had succeeded when other Canadian publishers started using Canadian magic realist paintings on their covers, as if waving and shouting, "Hey, this author's kind of like Alice Munro!" without the embarrassing business of having to state the claim openly, in words.

On occasion, I found a good title lurking inside a story. The final story in her 2009 collection was originally entitled "To the Danish Islands." I suggested to Alice that the main character's dying words, "Too much happiness," would make a fine title. Then with that installed as the title of the longest story, I suggested that it made an ideal title for the whole book. And so it proved.

And I did try to keep track of all the prizes Alice was winning, all over the world, and the acres of ecstatic reviews that she was receiving. Soon my hardest editorial task was choosing which prizes and which review quotes I should use in my flap copy describing the book. As for my editing, actually working on the stories, that role shrank over the years (from the days, when, as Robert Thacker reminds me, I helpfully cut a long story into two) as Alice became such a popular writer in *The New Yorker* that all of the stories reached me carefully pre-edited. They also were benefitting from the wise editorial attention given by Ann Close, Alice's editor at Knopf in New York.

In fact, often my most useful role was twisting Alice's arm at two stages. First, to get her to agree that, oh all right, we really do have enough stories now to bring out a new collection. (This is a great joke between us, since Alice is famously reluctant to start the publicity windmill yet again. This means that when the issue is whether we should plan to publish a new collection, she has been known to say, "Oh, I guess there's no getting out of it," knowing that the arrival of another new book will complicate her life, even if she does no publicity.)

Then, once we've got the manuscript going through the publishing process, my main arm-twisting role is to stop Alice from trying to rewrite the book, compulsively polishing the proofs as they go to her for what we hope will be purely formal approval. There is a history here, of course. When our first book together, *Who Do You Think You Are?*, was at the printers (carrying along with it our hopes for a successful fall season), I returned home from Saturday shopping to find the phone ringing in the kitchen. It was Alice. Following what she once described as "country manners," she asked how I was, and the family. Then she asked how far advanced her new book was.

"Ah, I've got good news for you there, Alice," I said, "it's at the printers. They start printing on Monday."

"Well," said Alice, "I'd like to change the second half of the book. Is there time to change it all, from the first person to the third person, and add a new story?"

I was speechless. But we arranged that she would come in to the Macmillan office on Monday morning early to discuss it with my bosses while we stopped the printing. The Monday meeting, dammit, ended with everyone agreeing that Doug would read the revised version (including the new story, "Simon's Luck," which Alice felt altered the whole narrative structure) and see if it was such an improvement that it was worth redoing the whole book – and losing weeks, possibly months, of valuable selling time.

We reassembled at 2:00 and I agreed that, yes, Alice was right, and this *was* better, so we should scrap the second half, re-typeset it (including "Simon's Luck") and publish the book later, and damn the torpedoes. As it happened, the printers were so thrilled by this historic high drama that we only lost about ten days of selling time. So it all worked out, and the world got a wonderful, prize-winning book. And Alice, as I had warned her, had to pay the financial penalty for making excessive late changes.

"You made Alice Munro pay a penalty?" scandalized readers may ask. Yes, that was the deal. And I know that Alice expected nothing less, true to her Calvinist Presbyterian background, which does not favour anyone expecting special treatment in this world. I had a flash of similar awareness once when I was visiting Alice in Comox, her B.C. summer home. Our planned dinner was cancelled when Alice had to be taken to the local emergency ward. I tracked her down there, and we chatted as she lay on a bed, awaiting the doctor. When he arrived, I got up from my seat and made to leave. I was just starting to joke with the doctor that I hoped he'd do a good job, since this was a pretty important patient, when I stopped, aware that Alice would not want that. I clapped her on the ankle, and left. Years later, in 2005, when Alice graciously spoke at the Scot of the Year Award ceremony, she complained that I was so physically undemonstrative that she had come that evening in the hope of getting her first hug from me.

When people ask me what Alice Munro is really like, I try to deal with the two halves of the complete Alice. One is the frowning, concerned good citizen, determined to do The Right Thing, and worrying her way towards it. That's the Alice who some years ago quietly put me under pressure to make sure that her next book was printed on recycled environmentally friendly (and more expensive) paper. And this, I should note, was at a time when using recycled paper in books was still rare, and associated with new fringe books by small publishers, not major best-sellers by major writers published by major houses. So her choice had a huge impact. She's still following that idealistic instinct, most recently by having a special edition of *Dear Life* printed on paper made from recycled straw, *pour encourager les autres*.

That's the same Alice who travelled for hours to appear onstage at Massey Hall in Toronto at a rally supporting CBC workers who had been, in effect, locked out. Alice spoke simply and directly about what CBC Radio had meant to her as a young girl with ideas growing up in a small town. Then she spoke affectionately about what the support of Robert Weaver, the producer of CBC's *Anthology*, had meant to her in the early, lonely years. Echoes of the ovation she received still ring around the corners of the old hall.

And that, of course, is the same Alice Munro who in 2009 withdrew her new book from the Giller Prize competition, on the grounds that she had won the prize twice already, so she wanted to step aside to make room for a younger writer. This selfless decision – which in the role of selfish, greedy publisher I fought against for weeks, until I saw that Alice's mind was made up – meant that the book lost not only potential prize money, but potential sales and publicity worth hundreds of thousands of dollars. With an earlier book Alice had put herself out of the running for these rewards by agreeing to become a Giller Prize juror that year. "Alice," I said, aghast, "why didn't you ask me about this?"

"Because I knew what you'd say," she replied, and laughed happily.

That's the other side of the complete Alice: she is very funny, and we spend a lot of our time together, on the phone or in person, laughing. I think people catch that when they hear her read her stories, in person or on tape; the stories are much funnier than expected and attract a lot of laughter when she reads them with all the right Huron County emphasis. But Alice in person is also very good company, and it's significant that in the fractious world of Canadian writing she has no enemies. W.P. Kinsella, reviewing *Too Much Happiness* in *BC Bookworld*, described that world as "rife with jealousies, feuds and petty backbiting." Yet he notes that "I have never heard anyone say anything unkind about Alice Munro, personally or professionally. When Alice wins a prize other writers and critics are not lined up to name ten books that should have won." Even her famous reluctance to tour to promote a new book is based not on a reluctance to meet, and enjoy meeting, new people. On the contrary, it's because her frail health makes travel hard on her, especially when her day involves her in, say, solving the marital problems of the taxi driver who takes her to the radio station.

Our relationship is based on a long-running joke, to see who can "understate" the other, by being more dramatically low-key. For example, when she wins another prize, I'll pass on the news as "not bad," and she'll agree, saying, "I suppose it's all right." A wiser head than mine might see this as significant, allowing this woman who grew up from birth believing that "showing off," to use Philip Marchand's phrase, was the ultimate sin ("Who Do You Think You Are?"), to cope with her success. Because, except in the very rare cases of writers whose work is torn away from them, and published against their will, writers are indeed in the business of "showing off." They're all saying: "Look at me! Here's what I've written, I think you should pay attention to it!"

I'm the right partner for the low-key game. When Alice won a Giller Prize, I was sitting beside her. When the winner was announced – "ALICE MUNRO!" – there was a blare of triumphant music (possibly the theme from *Rocky*), searchlights caught and held us at the table, and everyone expected the usual Oscar-style ritual of publisher and author and agent hugging and air-kissing interminably for the cameras before the dazed winner ascends the stage. What Alice got from me was "Up you go," and she was on her way to the stage.

A sort of pinnacle of understatement was reached when Alice was nominated for a prize along with several other writers, and told me that she hoped that her friend X would be the one to win. When I heard the results, I phoned her to say that I had good news and bad news. The good news was that her friend X had won the prize. This was greeted with great pleasure on the Clinton end of the line. The bad news was that he had to share the prize ... with you, Alice.

"Oh well," she said, "if he has to share it with someone, I guess it might as well be me."

It's hard to beat her at this game. She even plays it, for fun, in her stories. In "Fiction," for example, in her 2009 collection, *Too Much Happiness*, the central character is horrified to find that she appears as a manipulative adult in a former pupil's new book: "A collection of short stories, not a novel. This in itself is a disappointment. It seems to diminish the book's authority, making the author seem like somebody who is just hanging on to the gates of Literature, rather than safely settled inside."

On the subject of disappointment, I have developed a flourishing career as the man who disappoints audiences by standing in for Alice when she wins awards. This has happened so often that at any event when I hear the words, "Unfortunately, Alice Munro ..." I start to move towards the stage. It's a terrible thing to see a roomful of heads slump in sorrow, even something approaching disgust, as you approach the microphone. Sometimes it's more personal. Once at a Royal York Hotel event for the nation's booksellers, Stuart McLean, the MC, excitedly announced Alice as the winner. When I emerged out of the bright lights to mount the stage, Stuart said nothing about "my old friend Doug Gibson," although I had provided him with weekly movie reviews for three years on the CBC program, *Sunday Morning*, that he produced. Instead, with obvious dismay, he said, in sinking tones: "Awww ... it's Doug."

Much more enjoyable are the times when I'm able to see Alice attend to receive an award. Until 2013, the most exciting such event was in Dublin (the one with the full-size Liffey) in 2009 when Alice won the worldwide prize awarded for a body of work, the Man Booker International Prize. Since M&S was going through the financial hard times endemic to Canadian publishing, and decided that it could not afford to send me to see Alice win, I transformed myself into a journalist covering the event for *The Globe and Mail*. Typing on my hotel bed, this *Globe* correspondent reported, after a suitable opening:

> London's *Observer* believes that, when compared with the Nobel, this prize (presented Thursday for only the third time) "is rapidly becoming the more significant award." And although the thirteen other nominees include Peter Carey, E.L. Doctorow, James Kelman, Maria Vargas Llosa and V.S. Naipaul, there is a general sense of pleasure in the literary world that Alice has received this recognition. James Wood, the Atlantic-spanning critic who writes for *The Guardian* and *The New Yorker*, is wise in the ways of literary juries; at the Griffin Prize in Toronto he quietly expressed his approval of Alice's win. "Sometimes," he said, "they get it right."
>
> Getting it right this year involves choosing the perfect city for a literary prize-giving. As a bookish bastion, Dublin needs no defense....

What remains is a matchless literary setting. En route to the opening reception, the dazzled partygoers find themselves lingering over *The Book of Kells*, arguably the Western world's most beautiful illuminated manuscript. It was rescued from the Scottish island of Iona when the Celtic world was both tight-knit and afflicted by Vikings, who had no use for books, unless they wanted to get warm.

Upstairs the 200-strong crowd moves into one of the world's great temples to the book, the Long Room in the Old Library, a jaw-dropping sixty-five metres of tall barrel-vaulted glory, all rich brown wood and gilded paint and marble busts and 200,000 ancient books.

At the champagne reception in the library, Alice sits quietly, her silver hair matched by a slim silver gown. ... Somehow she has mastered the art of shy vivacity, and people enjoy meeting her. Tonight she prefers to reserve her energies until the award ceremony is over.

In truth, I was appalled to find her sitting alone while the party in her honour twittered on around her. Would she like to meet anyone? No, she said, she was just taking it easy. And then, a flash of Huron County. "They might change their mind," she said, darkly.

They did not change their mind, and in accepting the award Alice rose to the occasion. She recalled being seven years old, pacing in her backyard, trying to find a way to make Hans Christian Andersen's story *The Little Mermaid* have a happy ending. She spoke of a writing life since then spent "always fooling around with what you find. ... This is what you want to do with your time – and people give you a prize for it!" Everyone beamed, Canadians most of all.

The *Globe* story ends: "The hours race by until 'Carriages' are due at 11:00. Mindful of Cinderella's fate, Alice leaves early. We move out into the eighteenth-century night, reflecting that, as Oscar Wilde might have said, sometimes nice writers do finish first."

"Shy vivacity" is good, I think. Anyone who has seen Alice at a literary party – or even at a book-signing session – will know what I mean. The usual pattern at book signings is for bright, articulate people to spend twenty minutes lining up to meet Alice when she signs their book. I, hovering helpfully, know what happens next. They reach Alice, and their carefully prepared speech becomes "I just ... oh, your stories,

I mean – it's so wonderful, I really ..." And Alice kindly rescues them from more blurting, and the book is signed, and they float off.

By now, as Robert Thacker's biography shows, Alice's work has been studied and dissected by hundreds of scholars around the world. One of the best studies to reach my eyes is the introduction to *Alice Munro's Best* by Margaret Atwood. She begins by telling us flatly that "Alice Munro is among the major writers of English fiction of our time. ... Among writers themselves, her name is spoken in hushed tones."

To me, one of her most perceptive points is how often the stories deal with sex. In Atwood's words, "Pushing the sexual boundaries is distinctly thrilling for many a Munro woman." As Exhibit A, I would propose the story "Differently," in which a working mother accepts a ride home on a motorbike from a dangerously attractive man, and ends up tussling in the scrubby bushes at the edge of a Victoria waterfront park. She returns home, telling the babysitter that she's late because her car wouldn't start. "Her hair was wild, her lips were swollen, her clothes were full of sand."

What fascinates many scholars and reviewers about Alice's stories is how her work keeps changing. Her collection *Dear Life*, for instance, is full of a range of traditional stories, and proved to be very popular with readers and reviewers. Yet Thacker was not alone in singling out the last four stories, "The Eye," "Night," "Voices," and "Dear Life," as something new and special. Alice describes them as "not quite stories" and they bring her home, literally. As she writes: "I believe they are the first and last – and the closest – things I have to say about my own life." Dear life, indeed.

One of the hardest sentences for a writer to complete is one that begins, "All Alice Munro stories...." Over the years, Alice's stories have tended to get longer and, one by one, she has demolished all of the barriers to where the short story supposedly cannot go.

Think about it. Alice Munro's individual stories may range across generations and span a century, and they may involve several narrators. These storytellers may be shy teenagers or fierce grandmothers or any age in-between, and they may be men or women. Or the storyteller may be a third-person narrator, more or less omniscient. The stories may seem to proceed backwards in an artless sort of way that somehow works. Some readers will laugh out loud at some shaft of delicious, comic irony, while others will thrill to the sudden, shuddering horrors that are revealed. Some of the incidents clearly spring from the author's own life, others do not.

The setting will usually be "Alice Munro Country," or the Canadian West Coast. Then, as if to defy all categories, as if to say, "I'll show you!", Alice will set a story in Australia, or Scotland, or even in the mountains of Albania almost a century ago. Or she will devote over fifty pages (in *Too Much Happiness*) to the life of a nineteenth-century female Russian mathematical genius.

All this range of material and styles is, of course, populated by characters who become real people, whether they are chambermaids at the Blue Spruce Inn, professors, music teachers, carpenters, librarians, or farmers growing beans in Huron County. No wonder the London *Times* recently reviewed one of her books with the words: "When reading her work it is difficult to remember why the novel was ever invented." The jury for the Man Booker International Prize struck the same note. "She brings as much depth, wisdom and precision to every story as most novelists bring to a lifetime of novels."

Comparisons with Chekhov, Flaubert, and other greats of short fiction abound, as reviewers run out of superlatives. It's clear that in the future the single word "Munro" will be used like "Austen" or "Dickens" in literature courses. Some years ago a reviewer for *The Atlantic* stated, with a confidence that would impress St. Peter: "Alice Munro is the living writer most likely to be read in a hundred years."

And then, in October 2013, came the annual whispers of a Nobel. I should make it clear that the Nobel Committee operates in conditions of the greatest secrecy. For the Prize in Literature – as for all of the Nobel Prizes – there is no short list. But each year there are rumours. Enterprising bookmakers even give odds on various candidates, and the world's press sits up and takes notice.

I know this because every year for the past five years hard-working Canadian journalists have tracked me down at home to ask if I could be available for a comment at 6 a.m. the morning of the announcement. And I would arrange with Alice for a just-in-case statement, and then I'd set the alarm to get up and sit there in my bathrobe in the dark, scowling at the silent phone. Then, when the radio told me the news of that year's winner, I'd go back to bed. Some of us are not morning people.

This year, however, seemed different. With no short list, I had no objective reason to feel confident. But when I met my friend (and witness to this story) Gilbert Reid on the street, I told him that I thought that the next morning Alice Munro was going to win the Nobel Prize. I prepared for the morning announcement differently, too. Instead of playing the yawning bathrobed figure by the phone, I got into my triumphant publisher role. The previous evening I had a late-night shower and shave, and on the morning of October 10, I dressed confidently in full blazer-and-tie interview gear.

And it worked! After the usual ten minutes spent sitting looking at the silent phone, it rang. And rang and rang and rang. Because Alice was at a hotel in Victoria, where she was spending the winter, and on Pacific time, the media was desperate to interview someone and, often, I was it. I was lucky enough to be part of a national celebration as it was happening. I knew, of course, that this was all reflected glory from Alice, but I was enjoying the glow, and almost getting a tan from it.

Later, thanks to the Munro family, Jane and I were lucky enough to be invited to go to the Nobel Prize Week in Stockholm. On the day of the award ceremony, in mid-afternoon the darkening streets were full of men in formal white tie and tails escorting ladies in long dresses towards the Concert Hall. They looked, Jane suggested, like a convention of conductors, but although an orchestra would be involved that afternoon, it was not a musical event. It was the formal ceremony for the presentation of the Nobel Prizes.

It is hard for anyone outside Stockholm to realize what a hugely important event this is. There, Nobel Prize Day is different. There is a Graduation Day feeling about the city. We were startled – admittedly at the Nobel Museum – by a loud trumpet fanfare at midday. But the public fascination in general is so strong (a little like a local Oscar night), that Swedish SVT (the Swedish equivalent of the CBC) devoted *one entire channel*, the Nobel Channel, to the events throughout the day. They were all carefully recorded, minute by minute, up to the end, including the banquet in the evening. Cameras (carried by Swedish cameramen also wearing white tie and tails) intruded on the diners who gave wise interviews. Every so often, of course, in the middle of the flow of mysterious Swedish we could make out the words "Alice Munro."

To say that Alice Munro was a popular Nobel choice is a huge under-statement. She was everywhere. SVT ran a documentary, in prime time, about her. I had a modest hand in this film, having taken the Swedish crew to the Boston Church near Milton, Ontario (where the earliest Laid-laws from Scotland are buried, and where I spoke learnedly about young Alice Laidlaw and her family). Later I took them to Wingham (where the Alice Munro Literary Garden showed up well), and to Clinton (where Alice's local friend, Rob Bundy, took them into Alice's house, noting how seriously they composed themselves, before entering the actual room where Alice wrote). They even posed me for an interview high above the Maitland River near Goderich as we talked about the universal appeal of Alice's work. Best of all, the crew went on to Victoria and recorded a fine interview with Alice, and her daughter Sheila.

During these many Nobel Week events, Alice's daughter Jenny rep-resented her mother, who, with great regret, had decided not to attend in person. Jenny handled her role with poise and charm throughout and made many friends. Her great moment is the Award Ceremony at the Concert Hall. After the entry of the King of Sweden, the prize-giving ceremony soon becomes predictable as it rolls through the formalities of the citation being read by a member of the Swedish Academy, presen-tation of the prize by the king, then general applause.

But in Jenny's case, two remarkable things happen. Right on cue, in her elegant navy blue gown, she moves to stage centre. Then, instead of the usual "Congratulations, well done" brief conversation from the king, he really talks to her, at some length. Then, prepared by her rehearsal (the Swedes may be a friendly, democratic people, but they value careful formality, and the arriving crowd included some gentlemen wearing top hats), she carries off the three bows ... and the applause from the audi-ence goes on and on, even after she returns to her seat. It is noticeably longer and warmer applause than that received by the other, very wor-thy, Nobel Laureates. There are Canadian whoops and cheers, assisted by some American allies – and there are damp eyes in our party.

I said earlier that Alice Munro is hugely popular in Sweden. Two examples. First, after a celebratory lunch at the Canadian Embassy (and the lively Ambassador Kenneth Macartney and his wife, Susan – a former employee of Munro's Books in Victoria! – were keenly aware of the importance of this win for Canadian-Swedish relations), an event was arranged at the largest Stockholm bookstore for that afternoon. Alice's Swedish publisher, her translator, a prominent reviewer, and I were the attractions, but Alice Munro was the real draw. It was standing room only! And every bookstore in this well-supplied city of great culture, many museums, and many, many readers, had mounds of prominently displayed books by Alice Munro, in Swedish and in English. Every window seemed to have the familiar photo of silver-haired Alice in her white blouse looking out thoughtfully from her Clinton porch at passing browsers in Stockholm.

The final proof of Alice Munro's hold on this city came two days after the awards ceremony. The Royal Dramatic Theatre, where Ingmar Bergman ruled for so many years, is the great, ornate downtown theatre, reminiscent of Toronto's Royal Alexandra Theatre. The Thursday evening show was devoted to a dozen actors reading from the work of Alice Munro. In Swedish. On a bare stage. Only two bouquets of flowers set off the line of static chairs on which the actors sat before taking their turn at the reading microphone. Alice Munro's photo was blown up to fill the whole backdrop. Occasionally it was replaced briefly by a photo of the Goderich Harbour or a snowy Huron County scene. But as a drama, the whole attraction was in the words. *And all eight hundred seats were sold out*, as the people of Stockholm flooded in to hear the words of Alice Munro. Their Alice Munro. The world's Alice Munro.

When Alice and I finally got to speak on the phone, after the Nobel publicity explosion that followed the announcement, we both stayed in character, as low-key as ever.

"Hey, Alice," I said, "this Nobel thing ... not bad, eh?"

"No, really not bad at all ... pretty good," she said.

And we both laughed.

Looking, Imagining

Jack Hodgins

Nanaimo, 1969

The headline above an item in the *Nanaimo District Free Press* read: "Victoria Housewife Wins Award." The accompanying black-and-white photo was of a dark-haired young woman named Alice Munro who had won the 1969 Governor General's Award for her first book of short stories, *Dance of the Happy Shades*. The tone of the article was one of excitement, and seemed to imply that she had sprung, in full-bloom, out of nowhere.

Because the newspaper had identified this new prize-winning author as the wife of the respected Victoria bookseller Jim Munro, the next time my wife Dianne and I drove down to Victoria we stopped in at Munro's Books – pure curiosity – and decided the dark-haired young woman moving about to straighten up the books on the shelves, adding more books where there was space, must be the Governor General's Award-winning writer helping her husband in their shop. Although there was nothing about her that seemed intimidating, of course I did not approach her. What could I have said? What if she'd asked me if I was a would-be writer, or if I had published anything – when I'd had only a couple of stories published in literary magazines? This woman had published a book that had won the country's most important prize for fiction.

Nanaimo was a two-hour drive north from Victoria. I was teaching senior English courses at the District Senior Secondary School, and one of my Grade 12 classes included several students who were especially interested in literature and the writing process. In retrospect it may seem a bit presumptuous, but at the time I believed there was little to be lost by writing to ask Alice Munro if she would consider paying a visit to my classroom.

She wrote back in response, accepting the invitation – to visit my classroom but not to give a talk, only to answer questions. By way of payment, "Bus fare would be all I deserve, since I won't be giving a speech."

Of course my motives were mixed. While I was genuinely excited about the opportunity for these enthusiastic students of literature to meet a real "living writer," I was also anticipating the pleasure of meeting the woman who had written those wonderful stories – a woman, moreover, who lived and wrote her fiction on Vancouver Island. Since I had not yet published a book, I wouldn't tell her I had been writing short stories myself. Yet I took much encouragement from the success of her collection. Her protagonists had grown up in or near a rural area as I had. If Alice Munro had grown up in the countryside, as I suspected she had, perhaps there was still hope for me. Her fictional people certainly had plenty of distant "cousins" in the world of my Comox Valley childhood.

The dust jacket flap had promised that in her stories "you'll notice some of the profound though probably unpalatable truths about yourself." This sounded like something that would appeal to high-school students.

For one hour Ms. Munro sat behind my desk and responded to the students' questions. They ranged from "How did you get started writing?" to "Where do you write?" ("In the laundry room" was the answer, "with the door shut") and "Do you write every day?" It seemed that she did. ("You *have* to, even if it is only a page or two.") "Where do you get your ideas?" Whatever the question, the intent, it seemed, was always to discover the secret that had made this woman not only a published writer but the winner of a national award for her book of stories.

Like Eudora Welty, William Faulkner, and Flannery O'Connor, she had the magic touch – despite the fact that she lived just two hours down the highway and had grown up on a back-road fox farm in the Ontario countryside. And, apparently, living on Vancouver Island had not destroyed her talent, undermined her accomplishments, or made it impossible for her to find a national publisher.

As she was leaving the school she told me that this had been her first invitation to visit a classroom as a writer. The students had been respectful and interested (though perhaps a little in awe). It was clear she had enjoyed the experience. In fact, I felt certain of this when, a few months later, she knocked on my classroom door just to say "Hello," interrupting a drive that she and her husband were making for somewhere farther up-Island.

London, Ontario, 1973

When one of my earliest short stories, published in *Wascana Review*, won the President's Medal from The University of Western Ontario, Dianne and I were invited to fly to London, Ontario for the presentation at a faculty dinner. Because I knew that Alice had moved to London, I sent a brief note to indicate we would be in the area – just in case she remembered her visit to my classroom. She responded by inviting us to stop in for tea.

It was impossible not to wonder, while driving our rented car into her neighbourhood, how many of the houses we passed by were lived in by people we already knew, or thought we knew. Did any of them even know who she was – who she *really* was?

Adding another dimension to the experience was the fact that while visiting the writer in her original "territory" I was aware that we were in the area where my paternal grandfather's family had lived in the eighteenth and nineteenth centuries. Old Joe Hodgins had grown up in Lucan, Ontario, and later told his family stories about dramatic encounters with the infamous feuding family known as "The Black Donnellys." He had used some words and phrases that I assumed were peculiar to Back East people – including some expressions I've noticed in the dialogue of Alice Munro's characters.

Of course I would not find any references to the Donnellys in Alice's work. She had no need for violent feuding families to create drama in stories where longings, frustrations, and disappointments had the power to draw the reader into a sense of identifying with – or at least sympathizing with – quieter and more internalized tensions.

Comox Valley, Vancouver Island, early twenty-first century

We were living in Victoria now, but making occasional trips up-Island to visit my folks and other members of the family. Alice and her husband of many years Gerry Fremlin had begun to spend part of each winter in a condo on the road to the village of Comox, overlooking the bay. On more than one occasion they invited Dianne and myself for lunch or tea while we were in the area to visit relatives.

On one of our visits north, Alice asked me to show her "my" world, by which I assumed she meant the real world that had inspired locations and landmarks in my fiction. I drove her the few miles north to Merville, my childhood community, a rural settlement founded by veterans of the First World War and named after a village in France called *Merville-au-bois* (which I would visit several years later). We drove to Kitty Coleman Beach (named after a mysterious woman who'd lived there alone in the nineteenth century); to the Merville General Store; past the house and farm of my childhood near Nurmi Road off what is now the "old" highway to Campbell River. Then we visited the original family homestead on Hodgins Road where my father had often implied he had spent his whole childhood clearing land and picking rocks, and where the rock piles in the corners of hayfields were the size of small houses, overgrown with blackberry vines.

We stopped in at the large log house built by my sister and brother-in-law on one section of the original Hodgins land – approximately where a little two-room tarpaper shack had been my home for the first two years of my life. That small building was now a mere storage shed, moved over against a side fence.

Hay grew in the fenced-in fields of the Hodgins farm. In the uncultivated pastures beyond the fields, cattle found grass to eat amongst the large stumps left standing by the logging company and later charred by a forest fire that had gone through in the early part of the twentieth century. Many of these black stumps were three or four feet across and five or six feet high – the trees having been felled well above the pitch. The well here was the well my father's whole family (including Granny Hodgins with her caged canary) had climbed down inside in order to survive the fire when it was clear there was no other way to escape.

There was little reason to drive farther inland to what had once been the community of Headquarters – the literal headquarters for the Comox Logging Company – since it had been long deserted and everything "gone back to bush." Company offices, a school, two rows of Company-owned houses, and even a small hotel had all disappeared, torn down for the (free) lumber to build new houses in other parts of the Valley.

I imagine that once we were out on the highway again, I pointed out the "stump-ranch" that had been my childhood home, and the farm once owned by my maternal grandparents, who had left their families in the Ottawa Valley, and their own first home in Alberta, to move all the way West to the Comox Valley. The Merville Store hadn't changed much in recent years, nor had Smiths' turkey farm, nor had the original two-storey part of the Tsolum School that I and my parents and almost everyone else in that rural district had attended – the school where my brother had slugged the principal for referring to our father as "just a logger."

It was clear that Alice enjoyed this sort of poking into out-of-the-way corners of the world. I suspect she has always had her own way of inhabiting them, whatever a "local" like myself might have reported. I imagine that some of what I had said, some of what I'd shown her, had already been moved aside to make room for stories the place may have evoked in her own imagination, possibly set in the Comox Valley but just as likely transported to her own more familiar landscape Back East. I had no way of knowing whether the landscape of my world had felt as familiar to her as the landscape of her stories had felt to me.

The Boy with the Banana in His Mouth

Judith Thompson

I have been reading ravenously since I was about six years old, starting, like everybody of my generation, with the Dick and Jane series, then moving through thousands of authors. I have fallen deeply in love with so many books. I have lived inside them and they have saved my life.

Alice Munro has disturbed and awakened me more than any other writer. She triggers me; she reminds me of what I have always known but didn't know I knew. I would never never never be so bold as to write academically about her writing, but because I have been asked I will respond to a story in *Who Do You Think You Are?* with my playwright mind and fingers, the only way I know how.

The story "Spelling" especially speaks to me at this time in my life. It begins: "In the store, in the old days, Flo used to say she could tell when some woman was going off the track. Special headgear or footwear were often the first giveaways. ... Mothers and daughters often the same way. Waves of craziness, always rising, irresistible as giggles, from some place deep inside, gradually getting the better of them."

I am sixty-four and I sometimes wear my sweaters inside out. The other day a student followed me out of the women's dressing room at the gym and whispered to me that my dress was stuck in my underwear in the back. I have double-booked meetings and then forgotten about both. At these moments I do fear that this older lady craziness Alice speaks of is getting the better of me. In some ways, it got the better of my mother. In other ways, she outsmarted all and anything old age could throw at her.

My mother, Mary Therese Forde, grew up in diplomatic circles and had a perfect outfit for every occasion – chiffon, and wool and silk, and intricate lace. Long white gloves with pearl buttons. She and her sisters had to be perfectly turned out for every ball at Australia House in Ottawa.

When she taught at Queen's, she had lovely wool and cashmere green and purple sweater and skirt sets which she wore with pearls.

After my mother stopped teaching, something shifted. She didn't seem to care what anyone thought of the way she dressed. In fact her taste became, well, appalling. After my Dad died, she wore the same grey pantsuit with a pink tie every day for a year. Not only did she not care what people thought, but there was a large part of her that wanted to disgust them, to send them away screaming.

Once when my aunt was visiting from Australia, and several of the neighbours were there, she appeared in her nightgown, so that they would know she wasn't well, and then at the height of our friendly conversation, mostly focussed on the Queen's Dean of Law Dan Soberman's daughter Julie's new baby, Mum took out her false teeth and licked them, as a way to clear the room. It did the trick. Another time she pretended to fall asleep when her best friend, Maria, was telling me about her childhood in Germany. Later, when I asked why, she said: "I've heard that story before."

My mother died two years ago, in 2016, a day after my sixty-second birthday. She had been mostly razor-sharp and as mean as a snake, even meaner than Rose's stubborn old stepmother, Flo, in Alice's story, right until her urinary tract infection acted like a hallucinogen and she became demented, believing that her hand was the remote and she was changing channels with it, and giggling when the doctor examined her in the emergency room, which, mercifully, she thought was her nursing home room. When I arrived from work, breathless and worried, and said: "I'm here, Mum!" she laughed and said: "What? Why?" This memory was triggered by the moment in "Spelling" when Rose drives two hundred miles through blizzards, having had a fit of worry about Flo, and arrives at her door after not seeing her for months and Flo merely looks up and says: "'You can't park there!'"

I am a playwright and director and Rose, who seems to be the narrator of the story, is also a theatre maker of some sort, travelling around promoting plays. Rose goes home after not seeing Flo for almost two years and cleans the filthy house, finally coaxing her into moving into a nursing home. That's not our story: my mother's mid-century Scandinavian coffee table did have old copies of *Ladies Home Journal* spilling out of it, and her couch had three piles of magazines and newspapers on it, with room for only one person to sit, and she did collect little jars which she would pour my leftover tea into so that when I next visited, six weeks later, she could hand it to me and tell me to finish it – but she wasn't really a hoarder.

My mother had a housekeeper named Priscilla who was really her best friend. Priscilla loved Mum and when Mum was being particularly mean-spirited Priscilla would apologize and say: "I don't know why she's being a brat today." They would have quiet conversations while going carefully through my mother's junk mail and utility bills.

I saw my mother a lot more than Rose saw Flo: at least once every six weeks or so, until she gamely decided to move to Toronto to be near us. In the story Rose observes that "Flo felt her death moving in her like a child, getting ready to tear her." That is why, in Rose's mind, Flo suddenly became compliant, packing her things and declaring herself ready to go. My Mum likewise left Kingston suddenly. She didn't tell a single friend in her book club, or her Faculty Women's club, or at the pool; she simply left in an ambulance and arrived at the Belmont House nursing home in Toronto on a freezing January first. She said she wanted to be closer to me and my husband and our five kids, but I think she came here to die.

Like the nursing home in the story, Belmont House had painting lessons, and concerts, and healthy if unappetizing meals. Many of the residents would be passed out at the dinner table, reminding me of the sleeping mouse at the Mad Hatter's dinner party in *Alice's Adventures in Wonderland*, but others, the sentient ones, seemed to be having a great time, singing, flirting, praying. My mother had a big crush on a small Hungarian man who had made a fortune in baskets. When the son of Rosy, their tablemate, cracked one of his awful jokes, the Hungarian would say: "I can't stand his bullshit a second longer." Mum would cackle her appreciation.

Rose has a brother and so do I, but the similarity ends there. My brother lives in Australia, and he would come to see Mum once a year, for about a month. She adored him. When he was in the room, she wanted me out.

There is mention of seven coffins in the story. A man who shot and killed his wife and five kids. An ordinary house. There is mention of an old woman getting a haircut after many years without, and there being burrs and leaves, and a dead bee, and, strangest of all, a hat half rotted that had adhered somehow to her scalp.

It is these very disturbing details that stay with me.

Just as the many disturbing things my mother told me stay with me.

The most disturbing thing my mother ever told me was about the boy with the banana in his mouth. She told me that a boy was found dead in the neighbours' pool, face up with a banana in his mouth. This was around 1965 in Middletown, Connecticut, before we moved back to Canada. Another disturbing thing she told me about Middletown was that at one of my parents' famous cocktail parties, my best friend Rachel's father, Will Lockwood, a publisher who always wore a colourful bow tie and had a sneaky grin, implored her to meet him out back in the kids' pup tent. My Mum said: "Sure, Will. You go ahead and when you are there, lying in the pup tent, just whistle for me." So Will went out to the pup tent and he whistled. He whistled and whistled but Mum never came. She told this story time and time again when company was over. Another disturbing thing: when she had broken her arm she said to me: "Damn, I can't hit you, I'll have to kick you now."

There are so many disturbing things she said and they are like hundreds of splinters that have stayed under my skin for all these years.

Most of them don't bother me at all but a few do. Maybe the worst happened when I was about seventeen and I was running from the shower to get something in the living room. I was wearing a giant towel wrapped around me. Mum followed me to my room and whispered: "Why are you running around in a towel? Are you trying to arouse your father?" This memory was triggered by the part in the story when Flo writes a letter to Rose in response to seeing her in *The Trojan Women* on television with one breast bare. The first word in the letter, written in Flo's shaky handwriting, is "*Shame.*"

For me, the most disturbing Flo moment is when Rose is getting an award in Toronto and Flo, surprisingly, makes the trip. She wears an ill-fitting wig and a polyester pant suit, and when a man who is not white is accepting an award Flo exclaims: "'Look at the N...!'" Clearly she has come all that way only to humiliate Rose because she obviously hates her, even though Rose is the only one who cares at all about Flo.

This reminds me of the time my mother read an interview I did with her local paper about a play of mine that was being performed there. The play features a character who is badly bullied, so I told the journalist how I was bullied almost to death when I attended the Catholic high school, Regiopolis-Notre Dame. A group of ignorant, sadistic thugs made my life unbearable for almost two years. As soon as I changed schools, everything was fine, but we don't forget our nightmares.

After reading that article, my mother told me that "her friend" Tony was horrified and ashamed. They had worked so hard to make a Catholic high school possible – how could I think of jeopardizing all that they had worked for. Only after reading about Flo's racist attack, which was clearly an attack on Rose, did I fully understand my mother's comment to be a hate crime against me.

When Mum was still alive and living in Kingston, my greatest fear was that I would somehow lose everything – my family, my job, my friends, and have to go crawling back to 158 Fairway Hill Crescent. I would have to beg her to let me live in my brother's old room in the basement. I imagined how her friends would regard me: her book club, her Newman House friends, her swimming friends. I feared this more than I feared pain or death or large snakes. Whenever my husband and I and our five kids drove to Kingston to visit, I felt I was going back in time. A mixture of dread and the comfort of the familiar churned in my stomach. The limestone and the light filled me with joy; the Lucerna Housekeeping motel and the Aunt Lucy's restaurant on the edge of town made me want to die. I wonder why Rose feels the need to return to Flo. To make up for her perceived sins? For the sake of her deceased father, who is barely mentioned?

When my mother died in a Toronto hospital I phoned several of her friends on Fairway Hill Crescent in Kingston, where she had lived since 1967, to let them know. Mariella Morrin cheered. She told me how lucky my mother was to be dead. She said her arthritis had made her life a misery for the last forty years and she would give anything to drop dead.

Even after her death two years ago, my mother continues to repeat the disturbing things she said. I remember being in her room in Belmont House and asking her what the best time in her life had been. I was shocked when she said it was boarding school. She had been sent to boarding school at the age of seven because her father was a very busy politician. I knew that her younger sister had found it very painful and lonely. I asked her why boarding school. She said that she had been the most popular girl in the school, that "Everyone wanted to be my fag."

Last November we were gathered at my Dad's grave in the Cataraqui Cemetery in Kingston to inter Mum's ashes with Dad's body, or what was left of it after forty years. Me, my husband, and our five grown children. We had hired a priest to say whatever it is they say because I knew that is what my devoutly Catholic mother would have wanted. The priest was clearly unprepared, his vestments falling off his shoulders as we walked up the hill to my father's grave. Even as we stood around the grave with the freshly dug opening for my mother's ashes, he was desperately searching through the pages of the big book he had brought, unable to find the page for graveside prayers.

Finally, he began. He was mumbling the words in what we thought was the appropriate passage when I caught a reference to an infant death. I turned to him, saying: "Excuse me, my mother was eighty-nine. She was not an infant." He stuttered and blathered, and we basically told him to forget it. We would each pour a teaspoon of dirt into the small grave they had dug at the end of my father's grave. Afterwards we drove him, as requested, to the Kingston psychiatric hospital, feeling sorry for anybody he was going to counsel. My mother had been a lifelong unquestioning Catholic despite her fierce intellect and her cynicism; however, I am sure she would have found this hilarious and made a feast of it as a storyteller.

For me, reading Alice Munro is like walking over a dark minefield. Explosions of memory, one after the other, but with no shrapnel or nails. Instead, each explosion illuminates the field, making my journey as clear as it will ever be.

I am not sure why Alice Munro included in "Spelling" the brief passage about the man who had killed his whole family. Was she exploring Rose's shock at seeing the seven coffins, or her surprise at the ordinariness of the house where the massacre took place? That man and his family were not even minor characters in the story.

This reminds me of my continued struggle to understand why my mother told me about the boy with the banana in his mouth: "Oh, did you hear? They found a boy drowned in the neighbours' pool yesterday, dead, his face midnight blue, with a banana in his mouth." I don't understand exactly why she wanted me to know about that boy, or why Alice wanted us to know about the seven coffins. I think both stories will stay with me until I do.

Einstein's Hammer
and the Painting Pachyderm:
Reading Alice Munro in the Digital Age
(every day is trying to teach us something)

John B. Lee

"It was a great party until someone found a hammer."
— **Neil Innes, Bonzo Dog Band**

April 8, 2009, the day eight-year-old schoolgirl Victoria Elizabeth Marie "Tori" Stafford vanished, seemed an otherwise inauspicious day. For me it began in my home on Strathcona Avenue in Brantford on the Grand, performing my ablutions, shaving a stranger, noshing a modest breakfast of porridge laved in milk purpled by brambleberries. I was slated to read poetry to the students at College Avenue Secondary School at the corner of College Avenue and Fyfe Avenue in Woodstock, Ontario. Due at my destination at 8:30 a.m., I departed at 6:45 a.m. expecting to walk into the main office ready to begin my first session in the library with thirty minutes to spare.

I have always prided myself on being punctual. So, there I was driving west along Highway 403 with time on my hands. I'm often nervous before a performance, so I practised my craft as I drove, reciting from memory a poem I meant to present as the first poem of the day. As I spoke the words aloud behind the wheel, I imagined the promise of student amazement. Driving and declaiming, time ticking past, road signs blurring by, when suddenly I began to wonder as to my whereabouts. I hadn't been paying attention to the road. Had I blown past the

Woodstock exit? Was I well on my way to London, the school of the day in my rearview mirror?

Panic set in. My face flushed and my body began its anxious perspiration. I could feel the lather trickling down my rib cage drenching my shirt so it stuck to my spine like the clammy dampening of flop sweat. I glanced at the green sign on the road. "Princeton." I didn't recognize the name of the town. Is Princeton before or after Woodstock? The terrain around me flashed foreign. *Foreign!* I didn't recognize a single landmark. Nothing to do but exit, turn around, and retrace my route.

I pulled off the highway, re-entered by way of the ramp heading east, hoping to glimpse just one familiar feature. When I arrived at my starting point, I realized how foolish I had been. I exited at Brantford, re-entered the highway going west, having lost an hour. I hadn't been a daydreamer rhapsodizing in a warm window seat. No, I'd lost my way like a stranger on a lonesome highway and now I was guaranteed to be late.

When I arrived, Mr. Bryan Smith and his class were already waiting in the library. Had been there since 8:15. I'd been wrong about the starting time as well. I ran in, apologized, and told the students my sad tale. Trapped in the lustrum of secondary-school adolescence, they were amused to have the myth of the absent-minded writer confirmed by this sweaty, slightly dishevelled, wild-haired fellow standing before them with his pathetic explanation of tardiness for stock and trade.

Without missing a beat, I began the day reading poems, reciting, answering questions, selling a few books, before finishing, packing up, and saying farewell.

Meanwhile, only a block away from where I was visiting, eight-year-old Victoria Elizabeth Marie "Tori" Stafford was spending her last day alive on the earth. She and her classmates were doing what schoolchildren do. She was studying, playing, talking, and dreaming of a future that would be denied her by a chance encounter with the monsters who would abduct her as she departed from the schoolyard of Oliver Stephens Public School on Fyfe Avenue making her way home through familiar streets. Of course, I did not know anything about her existence, nor did I observe her being enticed into an automobile by the girlfriend of the man on the hunt for a child to molest. Neither did those predators figure in my consciousness as I walked from the front door of College Avenue Secondary School to my car, parked in the turn-around on Fyfe Avenue.

I do have a vague recollection of young students thronging the street as they gathered in bunches, jostling and running and laughing along on their way going home from school. I remember noticing the elementary school students spilling over the sidewalk as I waited for an opportunity to depart. This youthful energy was peripheral to my primary attention – as, without my noticing, the woman in the white coat, the one on the hunt for a child to snatch as a gift for her 28-year-old boyfriend, was there close at hand, teasing little Tori with the promise of seeing newborn puppies – for Tori knew her abductor. She was there while I was there: *she* tantalizing the doomed youngster, *I* waiting patiently for a clear path to make the turn off Fyfe onto the main road home.

The Brantford *Expositor* would record that Tori was seen for the last time at about 3:32 p.m. on Wednesday, April 8, 2009 on Fyfe Avenue, walking past the high school up the street. She was wearing a black Hannah Montana jacket with white fur-lined hood, a green shirt, a denim skirt, black and white shoes and carrying a purple and pink Bratz bag. She was walking with "a person of interest." On May 20, only forty days after Tori vanished, police charged Michael Thomas Rafferty, age 28, with first-degree murder and charged Terri-Lynne McClintic, age 18, as an accessory to murder. Tori's mutilated remains were discovered in July. And I was haunted by the fact that I was present on the day of the abduction. I realized as I read about it in the paper that I had been only a few feet away when this horrifying abduction had occurred.

***

Fifty-nine years ago to the very day, in the early hours of an uncommonly cold and rainy spring morning, April 8, 1950, my older sister Georgina Emily Lee was born. The farm lane was flooded, and Dad's car would not start. Rather inconveniently for all concerned, my mother went into labour in the middle of the night. Dad phoned local mechanic Spike McPhale. Spike owned a reliable car. He would meet them at the end of the lane and drive the thirty miles to the hospital in Chatham. I imagine George and Irene Lee wading knee deep in the chilly runoff flowing over the lane coming down from the house through deep country darkness of those early hours, down from the farm on the hill with the waters of the east and west muck joined in the middle. My grandfather Herb had joked

about those fields: "Now I know how Moses felt fleeing Egypt." All worked
out well in the end. And slightly less than a year later, I was conceived.

My mother, now in her ninetieth year, remembers nothing. A widow,
suffering from dementia, she has forgotten us all.

In a recent conversation I said to her: "Mom, do you know who I am?"

"No."

"I'm your son, John."

"I don't know you."

"Do you remember your husband, George Lee?

"I was married?"

"Yes, you were married for nearly sixty years to George Lee."

"What happened to him?"

"He died."

"Well, why would he do that?"

"Do you know who George Lee was?

"My father?"

"No. He was your husband. That's why your name is Lee. You used to
be a Busteed from Mull."

"Busteed? Busted. Mull's dull."

"Do you remember your children, Georgina and Johnny?"

"No."

"Do you remember Herb Lee? He lived in the other house on the farm."

"No."

"Do you remember Stella, his wife? You loved her and always called
her the sweetest woman who ever lived."

"No."

"Do you remember Uncle John? He lived in the bedroom upstairs
across the hall from your daughter Georgina. Sometimes we called him
Redhocks because his hair was red. You and he did not get along, at least
not until Dad died."

"No."

"Do you remember your sisters, Ruth and Dorothy?"

"No."

"So you don't remember your husband. You don't remember your
children. You don't remember Grandpa or Grandma Lee. You don't
remember Uncle John. You don't remember your sisters. Do you remember Tom Malott, the hired man?"

"Well, who could ever possibly forget Tom Malott?"

"Do you remember his dog, Wacky?"

"Of course I remember Wacky."

So, my mother has forgotten her husband of sixty years, both of her children, all of her closest relatives, yet she remembers the hired man. And she remembers his dog. Tom and Wacky remain vivid in her mind. Her face lights up in recalling these two. In the end, she stares at me for the longest while, saying: "I don't know you, do I?" When I say: "I'm your son, I'm John," she dismisses me with a wave of her hand. "No you're not. You can't be." We talk briefly of Tom and Wacky and she smiles to recall.

When first I read the Alice Munro story "The Bear Came Over the Mountain" from her book *Hateship, Friendship, Courtship, Loveship, Marriage*, about a woman losing her mind to Alzheimer's, and then when I saw the movie based on that story, *Away from Her*, I had no idea as to how I would find comfort and consolation in literature inspired by dementia. Great literature broadens our knowledge, deepens our understanding, clarifies our emotions, and connects us to the inner wells of the self where deep need is served. In great literature we also find a meaningful connection with our fellow humans. That essential empathy abides in well-written stories and poems.

***

I suppose as a writer I would have to say that I cherish memory over all other powers of the imagination. I once wrote: "We must imagine the past and remember the future." I say this because reliable memory is an act of the imagination. I also said in an interview: "It's memory that keeps us sane." I think I'm correct in this. And so I grieve the loss of my mother's memory, not for my own sake but for hers. Her personal past is vanishing one image at a time. Irene Lee is no longer a widow, no longer a mother, a grandmother, or a great-grandmother. She is simply an old woman sitting in a chair experiencing vague flickers of recognition concerning what it means to be Irene Lee.

For quite a while her short-term memory has been completely lost. I compare her recollection of immediate experience to the early morning tabula rasa of an empty schoolroom. Imagine someone writing on a blackboard being followed by someone with a chalk brush who is being followed by someone with a wet cloth. As the writing appears, it is being dusted to a white blur, and then washed away to leave only a black slate. As soon as someone is out of her field of vision, they vanish as though they had never been there. She might see my grandson and say: "Oh, look. A baby. Isn't he cute?" She looks away, then turning her head catches sight of him again repeating her remark: "Oh, look. A baby. Isn't he cute?" She says this as though he had only just arrived, though he'd been there for the whole visit.

When I teach writing I remind aspiring writers of the importance of memory, most especially old memory. Memory aged in the mind and deepened by time. The most evocative of all our five senses is the sense of smell. An uncapped fragrance can excite the most profound recollection of the past. And in writing of the present, as it is informed by the past, authors who attend to the olfactory in writing and who are masters of memory can write the smell of varnish, the perfume of apples, the pong of fresh-mown hay, the high sweet rose garden stink of manure, and the diesel burn of the city at the height of the day.

When I think of the great passages in literature that capture experience, I often reconsider a passage from Alice Munro's short story "Floating Bridge" from her book *Hateship, Friendship, Courtship, Loveship, Marriage*. A woman suffering from breast cancer finds herself on a farm at the edge of a field. She leaves her car and walks into the corn. Munro writes:

> The cornfield was the place she wanted to get to. The corn was higher than her head now, maybe higher than Neal's head – she wanted to get into the shade of it. She made her way across the yard with this one thought in mind. The dogs thank God must have been taken inside.
>
> There was no fence. The cornfield just petered out into the yard. She walked straight ahead into it, onto the narrow path between two rows. The leaves flapped into her face and against her arms like streamers of oilcloth. She had to remove her hat so they would not knock it off. Each stalk had its cob, like a baby in a shroud. There was a strong, almost sickening smell of vegetable growth, of green starch and hot sap.
>
> What she'd thought she'd do, once she got in here, was lie down. Lie down in the shade of these large coarse leaves and not come out till she heard Neal calling her. Perhaps not even then. But the rows were

too close together to permit that, and she was too busy thinking about something to take the trouble. She was too angry. ("Floating Bridge" 71)

The line "There was a strong, almost sickening smell of vegetable growth, of green starch and hot sap" sings of memory reified and celebrated and true. I grew up on a farm and I know how profoundly moving it is to experience something in writing that has both the quality of personal familiarity and the ability to connect the inner world with the outer world. The cornfield is internalized, thereby evoking a connection to the character's past, all the while being a melancholy reminder of what is lost to us when we confront our own mortality. The smell is "almost sickening." Nostalgia, false memory, and every sentimental recollection of a world that never existed are unavailable to the reader. We remember. We lament. We experience the nausea of being cloyed by the sweet sap of nature.

For your consideration I offer a few examples of olfactory writing having simply combed through the stories appearing in Munro's book *Friend of My Youth*:

When they walk side by side, she can smell his shaving soap, the barber's oil, his pipe tobacco, the wool and linen and leather smell of his manly clothes. The correct, orderly, heavy clothes are like those she used to brush and starch and iron for her father. She misses that job – her father's appreciation, his dark, kind authority. Jarvis Poulter's garments, his smell, his movements all cause the skin on the side of her body next to him to tingle hopefully, and a meek shiver raises the hairs on her arms. ("Meneseteung" 60)

Her jeans had the smell jeans get when they've been worn a while without being washed – a smell not just of the body but of its labors. He could smell cleaning powder in them, and old cooking. And there was flour that she'd brushed off on them tonight, making the pastry for the pie. The smell of the shirt was of soap and sweat and perhaps of smoke. Was it smoke – was it cigarette smoke? ... His mother's clothes would never smell this way, of her body and her life. ("Oranges and Apples" 131-32)

In wet weather Karin could smell pig, and always she smelled another smell that she thought was blood. ("Pictures of the Ice" 143)

Because she's got that coat, and is willing to wear it every day of the year, Mrs. Carbuncle never has to change her dress. A smell issues from her – camphorated, stuffy. ("Oh, What Avails" 189)

Her smell was like something sweet cooking – spicy jam. ("Wigtime" 249)

***

After having been lost on the road on the way to Woodstock, I think of the importance of paying attention to the landscape going on without me. One of my mentors, poet/professor James Reaney, would sometimes interrupt a student in full flight as he or she was rhapsodizing in an academic exegesis of a poem. Reaney would compliment the aspiring scholar and then redirect his or her attention with this caution: "That's all very good, but what does this have to do with what is going on outside of the window?" The poem wasn't born in a library, and you won't unlock its deep mysteries with purely scholarly concentration. Reaney also encouraged his students to learn the name of everything between their front step and the city sidewalk. He also championed maps, geological surveys, anthropology, archaeology, and generally everything that contributes to a deep appreciation of place.

There is a wonderful passage in Alice Munro's short story "Wild Swans" from her book *Who Do You Think You Are?*, wherein the central character Rose is taking a journey by train to Toronto. It is very clear that Munro has paid studied attention to the landscape. She sees the environment through the filter of her character's point of view – that of an adolescent girl on her way from a small town to the big city. I take up Munro's description beginning in Brantford, the city where I began my own journey west to Woodstock as described at the outset of this essay. Munro writes: "The train was filling up. At Brantford a man asked if she would mind if he sat down" (59). Rose allows him to sit next to her as "She went on looking out the window at the spring morning. There was no snow left, down here. The trees and bushes seemed to have a paler bark than they did at home. Even the sunlight looked different. It was as different from home, here, as the coast of the Mediterranean would be, or the valleys of California" (59).

The man observes that the windows are filthy. He tells Rose that he is a United Church minister. The scene evolves. Rose pretends to fall asleep. The man pretends to read the paper. His hand creeps up her inner thighs crossing the line of the top of her stockings. Seemingly against her will her legs open. And Munro's description of the passing landscape continues:

> As the train crossed the Niagara Escarpment above Dundas, as they looked down at the preglacial valley, the silver-wooded rubble of little hills, as they came sliding down to the shores of Lake Ontario, she would make this slow, and silent, and definite, declaration, perhaps disappoint-ing as much as satisfying the hand's owner. He would not lift his eyelids, his face would not alter, his fingers would not hesitate, but would go powerfully and discreetly to work. Invasion, and welcome, and sunlight flashing far and wide on the lake water; miles of bare orchards stirring round Burlington.
>
> ... she was borne past Glassco's Jams and Marmalades, past the big pulsating pipes of oil refineries. They glided into suburbs where bed-sheets, and towels used to wipe up intimate stains, flapped leeringly on the clotheslines, where even the children seemed to be frolicking lewdly in the schoolyards, and the very truckdrivers stopped at the railway crossings must be thrusting their thumbs gleefully into curled hands. Such cunning antics now, such popular visions. The gates and towers of the Exhibition Grounds came to view, the painted domes and pillars floated marvelously against her eyelids' rosy sky. Then flew apart in celebration. You could have had such a flock of birds, wild swans, even, wakened under one big dome together, exploding from it, taking to the sky. (63)

In the next instant Rose "bit the edge of her tongue" (63). Difficult not to infer the strong connection between Rose's physical response to the man's hand and Munro's selective attention to what is occurring outside the window of the train as it comes shuddering to a halt at Union Station in Toronto.

Munro's use of precisely the right word at the right moment, her sense of the *mot juste*, sets a standard to which all writers might aspire. Her description of children "frolicking lewdly," or of the truckdrivers "thrusting their thumbs gleefully into curled hands," or the impossible to miss double meaning of the phrase "cunning antics," and that final image of wild swans "wakened ... exploding ... taking to the sky" amount to an accumulation of detail connecting what is occurring as Rose climaxes with exactly what is going on in the external world outside of that filthy train window. Memory and imagination allow for selective recollection of appropriate detail in service of the story and of the character's perspective within the story. And what a brilliant story "Wild Swans" is. Almost everyone who lives in Southwestern Ontario has taken the train that runs between Windsor and Toronto. This passage quoted here is something of an object lesson in the value of knowing everything there is to know about the world you inhabit so that you might call upon the essential details of the world in order to erase the barrier between the inner and the outer world.

***

I read a story in my local newspaper today. The article concerned the publication of a book by a woman who began writing in order to cope with a difficult life. She referred to poetry writing as *therapeutic*. She claimed to have written her way out of sorrow and to have struggled through adversity by putting pen to paper. As a result of her private crisis, she produced a small volume of poems called *Down Memory Lane*. Although I contend that as a writer, and as a teacher of writing, one should never steal anyone's joy, and although I have argued in the past that it is better to write a bad poem than it is to make a good bomb, what sometimes shakes my confidence in the future of serious literature arises from the fact that there are so few contemporary readers who recognize the difference between a 'real' book and a purely self-serving project.

When I was in second year as a student of English literature at The University of Western Ontario, I had the good fortune to meet poet Margaret Avison. She had been appointed Writer in Residence and, as an aspiring young author, I visited her office during the second half of her residency. It had taken me most of a school year to work up the courage to show her my work. To my great delight, she saw a quality in my writing worth encouraging. I have written often about her excellence as a mentor. I have written how much I learned simply by noting the very first question Margaret Avison asked me before allowing me to show her a single piece of my own writing. She set my small folder of poems aside and inquired of me: "Whom do you read?"

After listening to me gushing for nearly an hour, she promised to read my poems. The next time I visited her, she left me with two pieces of advice that have stood me in good stead as a writer. "Mind your prepositions," she said. "Everything can turn on the smallest of words." And she added: "Figure out what your taboos are, and then – break them all." To cap off my day, she produced a poem she had written, inspired by the reading of my work. That poem, "To John Lee: Groundhog Day 1973," written in her hand, hangs framed on my office wall to this day.

Over the years, we stayed in touch. My wife and I visited her often in Toronto. I had the pleasure of reading with her on many occasions. And several of those times she spoke to me about certain poems of mine she cherished, ones she claimed to have shared with people she referred to as "real readers." And it is these "real readers" who concern me now.

In my book on writing, *Building Bicycles in the Dark: A Practical Guide to Writing*, I use the phrase "ideal readers" to describe the people for whom I write. These ideal readers, these "real readers" (to use Avison's phrase), know when they are in the presence of real writing. If I dare to suggest that *Fifty Shades of Grey* is not a real book, all I need do to confirm this caveat concerning the exploitative and awful erotica of this risible novel is draw the reader's attention to the aforementioned passage from Munro's story "Wild Swans." Or to this description of sex from the title story of *Friend of My Youth*:

> What made Flora evil in my story was just what made her admirable in my mother's – her turning away from sex. I fought against everything my mother wanted to tell me on this subject; I despised even the drop in her voice, the gloomy caution, with which she approached it. My mother had grown up in a time and in a place where sex was a dark undertaking for women. She knew that you could die of it. So she honored the decency, the prudery, the frigidity, that might protect you. And I grew up in horror of that very protection, the dainty tyranny that seemed to me to extend to all areas of life, to enforce tea parties and white gloves and all other sorts of tinkling inanities. (22)

Phrases like "gloomy caution," "dainty tyranny," and "tinkling inani-
ties" abound in Munro's writing. A reader might not only luxuriate in the
beauty of such phrases, but also consider how they plumb the depth and
stir the murky complexity of human existence. A character might think
of her life as having changed and yet not understand the nature of the
change. A question may seem rhetorical on the surface, but it may also
be an admission of confusion as in this question asked in "Goodness and
Mercy" from *Friend of My Youth*: "How did you learn to be so stubborn
and insistent and to claim your turn?" (161).

The reader of Munro's stories lingers in a moment, reads and re-reads
a single phrase or observation or self-reflection or contemplation without resolution, remaining speculative and uncertain as in her comment
on dreaming as it occurs in the title story of *Friend of My Youth*: "I used
to dream about my mother, and though the details in the dream varied,
the surprise in it was always the same. The dream stopped, I suppose
because it was too transparent in its hopefulness, too easy in its forgiveness" (3). That pivotal verb, that word "suppose," withholds certainty of
conviction, yet the character – and, through the character, the reader
– is allowed insight.

***

When I mentioned to my friend Bryan Smith that I was writing this essay
beginning with the reminder that I had been there the day that Victoria
Elizabeth Marie "Tori" Stafford vanished from Fyfe Avenue in front of the
high school where he taught, his face clouded over, his eyes saddened,
his mouth turned down at the corners, and he said: "The community has
never recovered from that, you know. I'm not sure it ever will. Everyone
is still suffering."

I wondered for a moment if he thought my decision to use this horrifying event in my essay was a violation of basic human morality. Perhaps
he is right. I don't know. I sometimes feel Atwood's words from her poem
"Their attitudes differ" in *Power Politics* goading me on: "Please die, I
said / so I can write about it." At least I am not in the camp of those
life-shallowing pop culture shills who champion the painting pachyderm
as though he were the next slapdash Picasso splashing paint on a piece
of paper with a brilliant brush tucked into the curl of his trunk. And the

monster intent on murder and mayhem who stopped at a hardware store to buy garbage bags and a hammer reminds us all that we may never understand the depravity of certain human beings and by comparison the abiding quality of others.

Consider the axiom: "To a man with a hammer everything looks like a nail," and then imagine that hammer in the hand of a genius. Imagine then Einstein's hammer, and what the hammer, what the nail – as you also might consider Alice Munro, pen in hand as she wrote: "They are driving between walls of corn. The stalks are eight or nine feet high. Any day now the farmers will start to cut them. The sun is low enough even by midafternoon to shine through the cornstalks and turn them to coppery gold. They drive through an orderly radiance, mile after mile" ("Oranges and Apples" 113).

Let me conclude this essay with a poem written the day I first read of the fate of young Tori Stafford. I confess I do not understand. But this is what we writers do. We write towards the light.

She Stops

she stops
the woman in the white coat
she stops
at the hardware
to purchase
a small bag of green bags
and one claw hammer
for her boyfriend, the ghoul
the ogre, the fiend, the monster
who bruised
the little girl's body
who broke
the bone of her skull

what is it that the thin radio waves sing from space
from the starry drumbeat
of dying pulsars
or what the weird

melancholia of lost whales
deep notes
peeping under water
where the sharp clack, clack sound
of struck-together rocks
might startle a silver school
of minnow shoaling away
in murky swirls of milting and gill-breathed water
a quickening galaxy of ugly gulps

I have also heard the static buzz
from mayfly swarms
smouldering above the alders of summer
and over
the lithe-waist poplars and thick-trunk beech
like the low hum of nightfall burning into darkness
all of these ephemeral blue and woeful songs of grace
gather into one profoundly sorrowful ululation
a singular lamentation for

the last Neanderthal
the last Beothuk
the last Taíno Arawak
toiling in the silver mines
of Hispaniola
listening for a greater grief than this

in the soft-hearted suffering
of each new dawn
I hear the voice of God
and whisper back
who stops the woman in the white coat
the one with the red hammer
in her hand
who stops her ...

An ABC to Ontario Literature and Culture

James Reaney

Eyebrows are raised and facial muscles reach for the "sneer" contortion if I happen to mention the fact that sometimes at Western I teach a graduate course with the above title. Possibly giving readers the chance to join in with this activity, I would like in a magazine published near one of the oldest settled parts of Ontario to put forth the "how's" and the "why's" of such a course; as world culture becomes more and more standardized, surely an attempt by a native of a much-hated and much-neglected province or region to show that this region nevertheless has an individual tradition worth affection, surely this attempt might be worth some attention.

To start with here's an outline of the way this course proceeded some years ago at Summer School.

JULY 4: I. *The Physiography of Southern Ontario, The Ontario Leaf Album*, Maps.
I started off with a discussion of Fred Armstrong's *Handbook of Upper Canadian Chronology* as a source for discussion of the fascinating early names for the districts: you may be living in the old Hesse District or the Home District. You probably know that you are living in Essex County and that beside it is Kent County so that when you get to Lincoln County you can see that Simcoe is making the coastline of Ontario into the coastline of England. The name, the motto, and the heraldry of where you live is important; even the scruffiest street gang knows that much. *The Ontario Leaf Album* was useful to enable students to take time to look around themselves at leaves and bark; there's a great deal of mooning about forested landscapes but precise knowledge shows real love and

49

breeds the same quality. Tree worship is to be encouraged. Mile to an inch maps have a similar effect, similar to the tree-leaf worship already mentioned. Chapman and Putnam's great book was my first glimpse of just how you talked about the landscape around my birthplace other than to mumble such imprecise words as "kind of flattish" or "gravel ridge" or "swamp." "Till plain" and "kame" and "aquifer" are much better and enable you, since we have a rather thin two hundred years, to think about mile-high glaciers breeding landscapes in their bottoms. There's a huge granite boulder near Harmony in South Easthope the kids at school used to talk about; until I read Chapman and Putnam's book I did not know, nor was anyone able to tell me, just why it was so exciting and so unlike the limestone rocks that obviously underpinned the ground we stood on.

JULY 5: II. *Sacred Legends of the Sandy Lake Cree*, Lawson Site, Jesuit *Relations*, Father Lafitau's *Customs of the American Indians Compared with the Customs of Primitive Times*.

It takes a jolt, but you should try and see where you live as the original Adams and Eves saw it and you should try and get inside their bodies and minds too. Less than a mile away from Western is the site of a prehistoric Attawandaron village and Wintemberg's pamphlet on its excavation has such suggestive phrases as "The Neutrals are known to have practised tattooing." Selwyn Dewdney's book on pictographs, Trigger's on Huron society, both stimulated me greatly. Why? To the Indians the outer world means very little; it is the inner world of dreams and visions that is *all*. This creates good sources for painting and poetry although I wouldn't want for a moment to live in the taboo-ridden world of *Sacred Legends*; but the legends live in me quite comfortably and the more I explore this day of the course, the more I feel that Ontario is not just a heap of topsoil, parking lots, mineshafts, and stumps, but a sacred place, a place that if it had been left alone with the Indians for some more centuries would have started to look like Ming Dynasty China not President Taft's Ohio, some of whose counties, I understand, have been swallowed up by strip mining.

JULY 6: III. *Wacousta, The Canadian Brothers, Westbrook the Outlaw*.

At last in 1832, our first novelist, or rather prose fictioneer, appeared and the romances about cover the Pontiac Conspiracy, or what the

Wallaceburg Centennial issue of their *News* called "The Surprise of the Forts," in the mid-eighteenth century, the War of 1812, and the death of Tecumseh. Richardson's works are beginning to be available again and both his personality and his work are extremely valuable keys to getting our tradition firmly rooted. To begin with, he's part Ottawa, part Canadian, part Scots-Canadian – representing the sort of families the Border lands turned out at the end of the French regime and the beginning of the British. This means that he's able to see back into the Indian culture, go to Paris and Montreal and survive, balance Jacobite Scots rebel blood against the English snobs and Tories who wanted to make Ontario into a land of forelock-tuggers. The three above romances, if read quickly enough, can quite knock you out with their eroticism, sadism, intricate plotting, and nightmarish devices.

Right now, the recently discovered novella *Westbrook* is my favourite. It concerns a local Middlesex "hero" who stood six feet with red hair and fell afoul of Colonel Talbot who did not commission him for the militia company formed here to combat the Yankees invading in 1812, but instead chose the more genteel son of a local retired British major. Westbrook decides on vengeance, particularly after his daughter marries the chap, AND revenge is what he gets; first of all, he steals his newborn grandson and feeds him to the inhabitants of a wolf den by the River Thames. Unbeknownst to Westbrook, however, the mother wolf brings the babe up. Next, he spies for the Yankees. Then he attempts to rape the chap's sister – have I got this right? – when driving her back from her Montreal convent school in his wagon. A priest manqué had fallen in love with her there, and catches up to Westbrook's wagon just in time, BUT by the time Anselmo gets to Delaware Township with his beloved, Westbrook has freed himself from his bonds and eventually shoots the priest. Westbrook confines Emily for a full year in a small cabin and makes love to her every night therein until trapped by locals. The mother wolf kills him, babe cries, Yankees walk away muttering, "Thank Gawd, he's not won of us," and Canadians do the same on the other side. The baby is described as being "inhumanized."

How's that for an archetypal vision of our province's cultural problems? But by the time Richardson wrote this remarkable blood-curdler (it would make an excellent "sensational" film) he was starving and had no time to elaborate. The other romances take similar plots and articulate them more deeply.

JULY 10: IV. *Salvation! O the Joyful Sound, The Man from Glengarry, The Scotch, The Weekend Man.*
This was a lesson in *White Anglo-Saxon Protestant* folkways, and with the first of these books you can go all the way from a young Methodist who watches cannonballs skating down the lane at Niagara during the Yankee invasion in 1812-14 to his much later being far more terrified at whether trees in Etobicoke (The Place of the Black Alders, explains Peter Jones) will fall on him for taking a journey on the Sabbath.

Next, there's the son of the kirk whose mother on horseback is pursued by wolves. Connor's book is a basic for understanding Bay Street – all that girding up of loins and focussing of spirit ends up in the chapters writ in praise or at least acceptance of plutocracy at the sell-out end. But before they departed to make money, Glengarry-men were apt to snap your backbone in two.

Galbraith takes Dunwich Township and riddles it, thus riddling Ontario, particularly the worship of the schoolmarm: "Every community must have some form of social conflict. ... faction is what people really enjoy." The acerbity about our world is a tonic; one wishes he'd stayed and been our premier.

Instead we turned into weekend men – masturbating, atomic, unable to get along with wife, unable to couple with ladies sheathed in impenetrable foundation garments &c. In other words, the innerness of the Protestant experience in Ontario can just lead to a dying death (patriotic, name on cenotaph spent defending plutocracy) or the living death of the last-named book set in an Oakville where they used to make ships, but now buy Dole Pineapple for their hydrogen bomb shelters.

JULY 11: V. This was a much happier lesson: *The Mackenzie Poems*, David Willson, Atwood and Beckwith's *Trumpets of Summer* (a record).
Mackenzie is all right as a rebel figure I guess, although it seems to me that the label "rebel" doesn't necessarily mean everything you do is patriotic; he could have dumped us into the Yankee fire out of the admittedly hot Tory frying pan. It's Willson I see increasingly as the real revolutionary: his books are hard to get hold of, but a week or two spent with his Koran – *The Impressions of the Mind*, as well as his primitive looking hundreds of hymns, is a fortnight very, very well spent. He's the

only visionary we have who built a community, communistic, artistic, gentle, and loving, and made it work for more than half a century with after effects like the Temple at Sharon, still standing, and the most beautiful building in our province. "I wish to build upon mine own reason, and not merely believe a thing is so because it is written, but come at the real sense of the word, to confirm my understanding in the things of God." Take the insight here, or that contained in "The stone that Israel sought to find / Is deeply buried in the mind," and remember that he also headed a commune of three hundred souls who had the first organ built in Ontario, played and sang a new hymn every Sunday, managed their commercial affairs with great success, but oppressed no one AND our philosophy departments might give him, rather than (fill in the blank), a twirl. If any poet or writer has the sense of what the real community Ontario could be, then it is this man; for a start, go to Newmarket north of Metro and ask how you get to see David Willson's Temple at Sharon.

JULY 12: VI. *Roughing It in the Bush*, *The Journals of Susanna Moodie*, the paintings of David Milne.
Since Milne painted downtown Toronto of the late thirties as well as landscapes in the more Group of Seven country, he's as central as Willson in a way to your seeing what it's like to just sit still in Ontario and listen and watch. The Moodie titles have obvious value since they deal with all the cobwebs you have to get rid of in order to listen and watch here. I'll never forget the thrill of finding that *The London Free Press* had actually reviewed Mrs. Moodie's book when it came out: "Throughout the work, the country, the climate and the neighbours are all blamed for the want of forethought ... the drudgery which the lady suffered in descending to the washtub." So you may find if you start reading your local newspaper files as you would read a novel that, as I did for April 22, 1852, a culture with cross-reference was long ago slowly getting underway: people saw things, but other people saw what they saw and commented on it. Richardson complains about Upper Canada that no one reads books, he might just as well have published *The Canadian Brothers* in Kamschatka. Although this situation is by no means righted, still it did begin to change at the aforementioned date.

JULY 17: VII. *The Bias of Communication*, the Ontario poems in the Smith anthologies, bp nichol.

Innis talks of small countries (Latvia, Albania?) being identified sometimes by nothing more than an anthology of their native poetry. His mother had his father build the house on top of a moraine for the superior view; by looking at a nut, as a boy, Harold Innis could tell what tree it came from on his father's farm. His book proved to be the most difficult and challenging book on the course.

JULY 18: VIII. *Through the Years in West Nissouri*, Miller, Duncan, Munro. This was local history into fiction day since Alice Munro in *Lives of Girls and Women* has an historian uncle whose idea of writing is to pile up droplets from the parish pump (Who was the reeve in 1901? When did the school trustees put in cement platforms around the porch?) and never try to drive a line through them. Eventually, the tin box with his research in it is thoroughly drowned by the Maitland River in flood. Since Sara Jeannette Duncan's novel about Brantford is our first successful realist novel, you should read it to see how these things *should* be done; what is frequently depressing about the run-of-the-mill novel about us nowadays is the imprecision of the viewpoint; all right, you're not going to tell us much of a story, but could you have dug out some photographic details just a tiny bit less clichéd than these?

JULY 19: IX. Confederation Poets – Lampman and Scott. Lampman has a narrative poem, "The Story of an Affinity," that I'd like to read two more times at least; it's about a Lincoln County giant who can't read – he prefers tearing up birch trees by their roots. He is challenged by a girl he loves who has a book he can't read, and off he goes to Trinity College and Toronto to develop something other than his thews. Both Lampman and Scott, of course, break open the Northern Ontario scene which hasn't been touched since the Sandy Lake Cree stories.

JULY 24: X. *Nineteenth-Century Narrative Poems* such as Crawford's "Malcolm's Katie."

Crawford had read Longfellow's *Hiawatha*, a great poem, greater than anything else by Longfellow because he's using Indian myths which crystallize subject-object soul-problems in a far more exciting way than nineteenth-century progress theories do. See Crawford's "Grasshopper Papers" in ms. for her very early handling of the Indian Summer myth; at last a poet who is not content with Mrs. Moodie's "Cobos! Cobos!" but wants to get inside the Ontario forms and use their visionary possibilities.

JULY 25: XI. *Cosmic Consciousness, White Narcissus*, autobiographies. Bucke, born in London, Ontario, foresaw a day when religion would "absolutely dominate the race." He worked out a theory for this which sees evolution as a tree whose branches are tipped by visionaries who lead twigs onward into mighty branches who eventually take over. The fire vision he had in a cab in London, England is the subject of a famous triptych by Greg Curnoe, local regionalist painter. It's interesting to look at the Group of Seven paintings after reading Bucke since he's a big influence. Take Lawren Harris's last painting – "Two Suns"? Harris, by the way is a Brantford boy.

Knister's Essex County novel is about an Adonis whose inability to express his passions and genius comes out in the way the surface of the novel is so clumsy; but a sub-text thunder of erotic mythical landscapes warns the reader that the book isn't about a soybean farmer's difficulty in freeing a girl from her silent, thwarted parents in their Gothic farmhouse at all, it's about a young god who refuses to die.

By this time my students were Ontario up to the eyebrows and I think with a glance at *Two Little Savages*, *Five Legs* (about their own *alma mater*), *Crestwood Heights*, and perhaps *Fortune and Men's Eyes*, we stopped reading and began to listen to their papers on the culture of counties: i.e., Huron, Lambton, Oxford, Frontenac – who wrote, who painted, who sang, who expressed.

Since this course was taught, by the way, the tradition it was seeking to define has become a great deal clearer, and the results of life in Northern Ontario begin to arrive; a book confirming both parts of the previous clauses is, of course, Atwood's *Surfacing*. Anyway, try the reading list and see what happens: as *The London Free Press* said in 1853 in discussing a fledgling organization called The Ontario Literary Society – "a country that makes another's literature, soon makes its laws as well." This was a reference to Yankee school texts and both reference and thought are still relevant today; so much so that I decided to do something about it in the form I have been describing.

Essential Handbooks

Chapman, L.J., and D.F. Putnam. *The Physiography of Southern Ontario.* Toronto: University of Toronto Press, 1951.

Logan, Ila. *Through the Years in West Nissouri 1818-1967.* Privately printed, undated.

Urquhart, F.A. *The Ontario Leaf Album.* Toronto: University of Toronto Press, undated.

Four Maps: Lucan 40 P/3 West Half & East Half; St. Thomas 40 1/14 West Half & East Half. Ottawa: Department of Mines and Technical Surveys, undated.

Essential Texts

Atwood, Margaret. *The Journals of Susanna Moodie.* Toronto: Oxford University Press, 1970.

Bucke, Richard Maurice. *Cosmic Consciousness.* New York: E.P. Dutton, 1969 [1901].

Carroll, John. *Salvation! O the Joyful Sound: The Selected Writings of John Carroll.* Edited by John Webster Grant. Toronto: Oxford University Press, 1967.

Connor, Ralph. *The Man from Glengarry.* Toronto: McClelland and Stewart, 1960 [1901].

Galbraith, John Kenneth. *The Scotch.* Baltimore: Penguin, 1968.

Innis, Harold A. *The Bias of Communication.* Toronto: University of Toronto Press, 1964 [1951].

Knister, Raymond. *White Narcissus.* Toronto: McClelland and Stewart, 1962 [1929].

Lampman, Archibald. "The Story of an Affinity." *The Poems of Archibald Lampman (including At the Long Sault).* Toronto: University of Toronto Press, 1974.

Mackenzie, William Lyon, and John Robert Colombo. *The Mackenzie Poems.* Toronto: Swan, 1966.

Moodie, Susanna. *Roughing It in the Bush.* Toronto: McClelland and Stewart, 1962 [1852].

Munro, Alice. *Lives of Girls and Women.* Scarborough, Ontario: The New American Library of Canada, 1974 [1971].

Richardson, John. *The Canadian Brothers.* Toronto: University of Toronto Press, 1976 [1840].

Richardson, John. *Wacousta.* An abridged edition. Toronto: McClelland and Stewart, 1967 [1832].

Richardson, John. *Westbrook the Outlaw.* Montreal: Grant Woolmer, 1973 [1853].

Sinclair, David, ed. *Nineteenth-Century Narrative Poems.* Toronto: McClelland and Stewart, 1972.

Smith, A.J.M., ed. *The Book of Canadian Poetry.* Third edition. Toronto: W.J. Gage, 1957.

Smith, A.J.M., ed. *Modern Canadian Verse.* Toronto: Oxford University Press, 1967.

Sons of Captain Poetry. Directed by Michael Ondaatje. Performed by bp Nichol. Mongrel Films, 1970.

Stevens, James R. *Sacred Legends of the Sandy Lake Cree.* Toronto: McClelland and Stewart, 1971.

The Trumpets of Summer. Music by John Beckwith. Text by Margaret Atwood. The Festival Singers of Canada. Conducted by Elmer Isler. Toronto: CBC/Capitol Records, 1969. 33 1/3 LP.

Willson, David. *Selections.* Mimeographed.

Wright, Richard B. *The Weekend Man.* Scarborough, Ontario: The New American Library of Canada, 1972 [1970].

Other Available Books

Armstrong, Frederick H. *Handbook of Upper Canadian Chronology and Territorial Legislation.* London, ON: Lawson Memorial Library, The University of Western Ontario, 1967.

Atwood, Margaret. *Surfacing.* Markham, Ontario: PaperJacks, 1973 [1972].

Crawford, Isabella Valancy. *Collected Poems.* Toronto: University of Toronto Press, 1972.

Dewdney, Selwyn, and Kenneth E. Kidd. *Indian Rock Paintings of the Great Lakes.* Toronto: University of Toronto Press, 1962.

Duncan, Sara Jeannette. *The Imperialist*. Toronto: McClelland and Stewart, 1961 [1904].

Fowke, Edith, ed. *Traditional Singers and Songs from Ontario*. Don Mills, Ontario: Burns & McEachern, 1965.

Gibson, Graeme. *Five Legs*. Toronto: House of Anansi, 1969.

Glazebrook, G.P. deT. *Life in Ontario*. Toronto: University of Toronto Press, 1968.

Herbert, John. *Fortune and Men's Eyes*. New York: Grove, 1968 [1967].

Lafitau, Father Joseph François. *Customs of the American Indians Compared with the Customs of Primitive Times*. Edited and translated by William N. Fenton and Elizabeth L. Moore. 2 volumes. Toronto: Champlain Society, 1974, 1977.

Mealing, S.R., ed. *The Jesuit Relations and Allied Documents*. Toronto: McClelland and Stewart, 1963.

Miller, Orlo. *The Donnellys Must Die*. Toronto: Macmillan of Canada, 1967 [1962].

Ross, Malcolm, ed. *Poets of the Confederation*. Toronto: McClelland and Stewart, 1960.

Seeley, John R., Alexander Sim, and Elizabeth W. Loosley. *Crestwood Heights*. Toronto: University of Toronto Press, 1963 [1956].

Seton, Ernest Thompson. *Two Little Savages*. New York: Dover, 1962 [1903].

Trigger, Bruce G. *The Huron: Farmers of the North*. New York: Holt, Rinehart, and Winston, 1969.

Warkentin, Germaine, ed. *Stories from Ontario*. Toronto: Macmillan of Canada, 1974.

Willson, David. *The Impressions of the Mind*. Privately printed, 1835.

Wintemberg, W.J. *Lawson Prehistoric Village Site, Middlesex County, Ontario*. National Museum of Canada, Bulletin No. 94. Ottawa: Department of Mines and Resources, undated.

All Things Considered:
Alice Munro First and Last

Reg Thompson

Thursday, October 10th, 2013

I was getting ready for work in the early morning dark, thinking of my cousin Helen Stewart in Toronto, because it was her birthday, and I was wondering if she had seen my e-mail greetings yet, and the man on CBC Radio One announced that Alice Munro had won the Nobel Prize in Literature. I shouted "Alice!" and laughed and cheered. In that moment something in the world changed.

The Nobel Prize. It had really happened. Finally. I hung on every word as the CBC phoned Alice and interviewed her at some ungodly earlier hour in Victoria. I was some impressed with her responses. How many of us can give a coherent interview when awakened in the middle of the night? Oh, Alice Munro can.

As I drove to work that morning they were harvesting soybeans in the fields in Huron County, combines roaring along at great speed, the familiar clouds of dust drifting across the landscape. Soybeans are lifted when the plants are brown and dead and quite dry. This creates a lot of fine dust. You remember when you live here to close your windows and air intake vents in the car as you drive by the fields in harvest. There was some late corn standing yet, in the middle of it a ruined stone house smothered in grapevine.

Above the fields, circling high, a few turkey vultures, eyes peeled for dead things. Another week or two, they would depart for the South. They stay later and later in recent years, cottagers who can't bear to give up summer. Suddenly one day we will think, hey, haven't seen any lately, and try to remember the last one.

And on part of my route I was meeting the usual gravel trucks, because along this road there are gravel pits, scooped out of the glacier's deposit that for several thousand years lived invisible beneath the forest, then beneath the newly cleared flat fields after 1830 and European settlement. Gravel is a limited crop that runs out as a mine does. A few years, no more harvest there. Probably the extinct pit will form another shallow lake, edged with alders and home to waterfowl.

And in the sky, the Canada geese were practising. Several V formations crisscrossing airspace with that characteristic up and down jogging movement geese make when the flight is casual and local, not serious actual migration. Some unorganized geese scattered here and there, randomly winging, restless, not yet picked for anybody's team, but feeling they should be flying too.

This is a scene that can make you weep, for the familiarity and the bittersweetness of it, the loneliness it reminds us of, every fall. The common life and events, the ordinary landscape that by incidental mention Alice Munro has made quietly famous to the world. "Alice Munro Country."

But I was not weeping. I was elated. This is such a perfect Alice Munro scene, an Alice Munro mood – and Alice Munro has just won the Nobel Prize. What a great day!

It was quite a day. The news spread of the Nobel coming to a Canadian, a well-known one. There was pleasure and delight. People were talking. Here was a Nobel winner you might have actually read. It opened a conversation that people do not often get a chance to have, about reading, about writing. (This is different from asking somebody socially if they have read the new Grisham or Patterson, Evanovich or Woods. This is a different thing.)

People who know me and know that Alice and I are friends were congratulating me. This felt odd, like being congratulated on becoming a grandparent. The honour is somewhat indirect. But the admiration for Munro was genuine and the goodwill generous.

In addition to being longtime friends with Alice, I have helped her with research – sometimes specific details she needs, more often general information. The sort of social information people have about history, characters, odd events. Her late husband Gerald Fremlin was a respected local historian. The three of us shared this interest. Many enjoyable lively talks we have had at their kitchen table.

Writer David Helwig in reviewing the collection *Open Secrets* for the Montreal *Gazette* described Munro's writing as "gossip informed by genius." I would turn that around: genius informed by gossip. I am pleased if my contribution has been useful to Alice. But I would like the world to understand that she needs very little in the way of outside research. The research that truly matters is right inside that amazing head.

Something else that might be noted is this: Alice Munro does not drive. All the years of their life together Gerry was the driver, and Alice rode shotgun, free to look and observe and absorb as they explored the countryside. We should not underestimate this teamwork. The driver should be remembered too. It was a fine partnership. When I heard the Nobel news on the radio, my first thought was great joy for Alice, and the next was a pang of sorrow for Gerry, who had died in April and was not here to share this great moment with her.

Well, gathering raw material from observed life is one thing. What is made of it quite another. We admire the great skill and vision with which Munro has crafted her stories, gradually building this amazing inventory of a lifetime.

The media people scrambled to get something together within hours. I am a constant listener to CBC Radio, and was pleased to hear show after show mention the Munro Nobel win. In following days all the newspapers ran features. *Maclean's* gave her the cover.

The Nobel Prize is a big deal. It impresses even those with no prior knowledge of the recipient. Some woman from Canada has won the literature prize. The first Canadian writer to do so. Who is she? What does she write?

A nice outcome of the prize attention will be that those who have not read Munro before may do so now, out of curiosity or just wanting to keep up. These Nobel people mean business. Their approval may be taken as a recommendation.

This brings up the matter of where one should start. My suggestion to anyone beginning Munro is to start with the early stories. She was an eye-opener for me. Nothing like the Short Stories served to us in English courses. Here was someone giving us our own life, our own people, in a piece of the world we recognized.

There is a tendency now to concentrate on the later stories. Well, Alice Munro built her reputation from the very beginning on her portrayals of familiar landscape and ordinary people. Her first book, *Dance of the Happy Shades*, won the Governor General's Award. No one should miss "Walker Brothers Cowboy" – the very first story in that first book. Everything we have come to esteem in her writing was evident right there at the start.

Munro herself has said that her later stories get "more disjointed and demanding and peculiar." Yes, and the subject matter gets tougher, I think. So start with the early stuff and progress through. After all, that's what the writer has done. Working through a lifetime of experience and observation of the human condition.

Readers who want to know how she does it, where the stories come from, how she works, should get hold of the softcover edition of her *Selected Stories*. The book was published in 1998, two years after the hardcover; it includes stories from her first seven collections. It's a great gathering – though one should still read each collection, for there are always fine stories that have to be left out for space considerations.

But the main thing is that this particular later edition (republished in 2015 as *A Wilderness Station*) has an introduction by the author. In nine pages Alice Munro tells us really the essence of her work. Never mind all the critical analysis by academics, the explanatory essays by other writers. This statement from the author herself is all we need. It cannot be improved upon.

Munro's work has received much study and detailed analysis. There are many in the academic world to whom such analysis and density must be life and breath, and there is usefulness in this thorough examination, but I like to imagine someone who has never read Alice Munro, who has perhaps never heard of her, picking up one of her books at a friend's cottage in a solitary and empty afternoon, and beginning to read a Munro story, being drawn in slowly, into that world that so many of us have come to know and to recognize. I like to think of that reader who has no expectation, no awareness of reputation, or awards, or the opinion of critics – just someone ready to read a story and see what it says.

I remember my early reading of Munro, and I would like other people to be able to have that experience. This is one of the reasons I have some misgivings about the fact that the main book that people have had access to since all the Nobel publicity is *Dear Life*. I think Munro's later work ("more disjointed and demanding and peculiar") is not the best starting point for new readers, and I was dismayed to see a display in the small book section of a Target department store, with copies of *Dear Life* bearing a cover sticker that said "Teen Pick." Really? A tough enough book for grown-ups, it seems to me, and hardly an item to be urged on the young. People get a lot more out of Alice Munro when they have had some of life's wear and tear.

That said, after reading a reasonable amount of Munro as preparation, no enthusiast should miss the title story in the last collection. It's "Dear Life." Although marketed now in a fiction collection, when it ran originally in *The New Yorker* it was tagged as "Personal History." It now appears as the last story in the book, in a section of four special personal stories titled "Finale." In a small introductory note preceding these stories, the author says: "I believe they are the first and last – and closest – things I have to say about my own life." This last story takes us back to the beginning in Munro's childhood, and as you might expect, leaps ahead, giving us a telescoped lifetime with wisdom too late gained and a tinge of regret, apologies that will never happen.

She has said she is finished writing. If that proves to be the case, then the bookends of Munro's writing career would be the stories "Walker Brothers Cowboy" – first in the first book – and "Dear Life" – last in the last book. All the stories, all the books, all the years compacted, we come down to these two wonderful stories, stories that seem to me strikingly similar. The landscape, the parent and child history, the ghosts of thwarted dreams, the inevitable passage of time, and what it takes with it.

When she won the Trillium Prize again in the spring of 2013, for *Dear Life*, she was asked about more stories. What should her eager fans do? She suggested people should go back and reread the old stories. "There's lots of them." My experience in doing this leads me to predict that we will be rewarded in finding things we had forgotten and things we didn't notice before.

She also said of winning the Trillium for what was stated to be her final book: "It's nice to go out with a bang."

And then a few months later – the Nobel Prize. Now *that's* a bang.

If "Dear Life" turns out to be the last story she ever publishes, it would be a perfect lingering chord. It all ends in forgiveness and understanding. It is as good as any word Alice Munro has ever written. We cannot ask for more.

Remembrance Day 1988:
An Interview with Alice Munro

J.R. (Tim) Struthers

TS: I seem to get some things wrong about our region – even possible train arrangements. I've been laughing at myself, thinking of how myopic my upbringing in London, Ontario was – or maybe you could say it was focussed, though I suspect that myopic is closer to the truth – since we spoke about you coming here to Guelph to participate in this four-day conference of writers and critics that I've organized in honour of John Metcalf's fiftieth birthday. I had spent the first thirty-five years of my life in London, Ontario, before getting my teaching position here at the University of Guelph, and I therefore figured that if anyone was going to travel to Guelph by train from somewhere over in that part of South-western Ontario it would have to be from London. And you said: "No, no, no. Gerry will drive me from Clinton to Stratford and I'll take the train from there. That's what I always do when I go to Toronto and so forth to visit friends." I found myself thinking about that and laughing at how short-sighted I was. But then maybe there's a positive side to it in terms of the richness and the depth such a perspective can allow.

Your own experience, Alice, was to grow up in Wingham, Ontario, a small town of 3,000 people about seventy-five miles north of London on Highway 4, to head down to London from 1949 to 1951 to study at The University of Western Ontario until your two-year scholarship ran out, then to move out to the West Coast for twenty years, to Vancouver and later Victoria, right after you first got married, to Jim Munro, and now once again to live back in your home region for the past decade and a half, in Clinton, with your second husband, Gerald Fremlin. What I want to ask you about is your sense of the differences within this region

65

that London, Ontario painter Greg Curnoe, writer and professor James Reaney, and others call "Souwesto." Because I think that variety and particularity are terribly important to you in terms of things like the topography of the region and your favourite places in the area.

AM: Well, you know, as I child I never went very far from home. About once a summer we went to Goderich, to the Lake, and that was a big expedition. London was my first city. I don't think I went there until I was probably fifteen. I still remember the splendours of the Capitol Theatre, where I saw *The Secret Life of Walter Mitty* [laughter]. I had never been in such a gorgeous place in my life – we didn't go to Toronto, we didn't go anywhere. So I had this sense of this very limited world which was the town of Wingham and the countryside, maybe five, six miles around, as far as I could ride my bike. And there were great differences.

This is a landscape that most people think is dull. It's not dramatic in any way, it's not even a dramatically rolling countryside, and it's not tremendously rich-looking. There isn't any easily visible wilderness. But if you know it intimately, there are all these small differences. I know, for instance, that the farmland north of Wingham, which locally is called "The Alps" because it's hilly [laughter], is very different. To me, it was. It was, you know. I'd go out there and I'd think *Wuthering Heights*-ish thoughts [laughter]. I got very stirred up by that landscape. The landscape south of Wingham is sort of flat and practical. That was down towards London and things started to get more prosaic the further south you went. East was interesting because there were a lot of very shacky little villages and the social mix seemed to be different and there were scandalous things always happening in those places. So there was a lot of variety and it was a kind of social variety. You perceived very small differences – they were small, but they seemed very important – between different parts of the area.

Now, of course, because my husband Gerry is a geographer, I've learned to look at the landscape in a totally different way and I see its history over time. This is really wonderful. I love it. I love going out and looking for moraines and where the borderline is between one kind of landscape and another and knowing what happened, what the glacier did there to make this difference in the country. It's a whole new way to look at landscape. It's not the way I used to look at it at all. I used to look and I would get a feeling from landscape. Now I have that feeling but I also have this knowledge, which makes it fun.

TS: I'm interested in a kind of historical sense, too, that seems to be have become stronger in your writing in recent years.

AM: That's because I've lived longer [laughter].

TS: Well ...

AM: Seen a lot of changes, I have [laughter].

TS: But there's a kind of curiosity involved in that. And a use of detail – not necessarily just your own personal and family history but more general oral and cultural history. There seem to be more stories of yours, lately, that draw on that. Most impressively "Meneseteung," published earlier this year in the 11th of January 1988 issue of *The New Yorker*. So I was wondering what your feeling for that is at this stage.

AM: I seem to want to do very complicated stories in terms of time. And intertwining stories. I think this is just because of the stage of my life that I'm at when I remember all this. When I lived in British Columbia, from 1952 to 1972, I wrote a lot about Ontario. And in a way I wrote out of memory. But it was a special kind of memory. There were a lot of things that were left out of that kind of memory. And I don't know how to describe it. I haven't got a word for the kind of memory it was. I guess I left Ontario with the sorts of things that a girl of twenty would have noticed. They seemed to be things about, oh, the more extraordinary turns life can take, people on the fringes of things, people who would be called, I suppose, eccentrics. There was a starkly dramatic colouring to this – I didn't give it to the material – it was what I felt was there.

And then I came back. I came back to live in the area in 1975 and I noticed all sorts of things that I hadn't been interested in before. A lot of these things had to do with very ordinary lives and the ordinary things that happen in people's lives. Of course everyone says I always write about the most ordinary things anyway. But I was more interested in money, for instance. How people make their money and how people think about it. And I was terribly interested then in social distinctions. There's a whole range of such distinctions in a town of 3,000 people. And material things, possessions. How people would set a table and what this would say about them. I started writing about the same country again, just going at it from different angles. And this may well go on all my life. When I'm in the nursing home, I'll get a fresh look at what the community is like. And so I do seem to go on, you know, mining the same thing. But it seems new to me.

TS: Whether it's in the story "Walker Brothers Cowboy" that opens your first book, *Dance of the Happy Shades*, or in the memoir about your father and mother, "Working for a Living," that was published in the first issue of the American literary journal *Grand Street* in 1981, I think of the young girl there taking those car rides, with things beginning to take shape in her imagination, and transformations taking place.

AM: The car rides were very important for me. It was a big thing: Would the car break down? Would we ever get there? So there was this great sense of drama [laughter] involved in going out in the car. It was a risky venture [laughter].

TS: Just over a month ago, on the Thursday afternoon before Thanksgiving Weekend, my wife, Marianne Micros, and our younger daughter, Joy, and I drove over to Bayfield to celebrate my Mom's birthday, having arranged for my parents to come up from London to visit together for the evening. Funny thing, when I was interviewed for my job here at the University of Guelph in the spring of 1985, I was asked if I would be comfortable moving from a larger place like London, Ontario to a smaller place like Guelph and I laughed and said, "I'd be happy in Bayfield." Since then I've realized that in moving to Guelph I was in some sense returning to the London, Ontario of my early childhood, that is, moving to a small city of around 100,000 people or roughly the same size London, Ontario had been when I was born there in the summer of 1950 – right between your first year and your second year of university there at Western.

In any event, Marianne, Joy, and I travelled over to Bayfield on a Thursday afternoon and then returned to Guelph the next morning because all three of us had different responsibilities to keep – I had to pick up the first set of proofs for the book *What Is A Canadian Literature?* by John Metcalf that I'll be publishing imminently with my small press, Red Kite Press. But interestingly, too, in terms of our trip across Souwesto, we passed through different towns at different stages of change, including Seaforth.

AM: All those towns are different, you know.

TS: How? Tell me about Seaforth.

AM: Well, I don't know the history of Seaforth. I just know the way it looks. There's a difference in the houses there. The houses are very pretty if you go along the back streets. You see that almost every builder had some interesting idea of decoration. These would be houses built maybe in the 1860s, 1870s. It looks like a town with a notion of itself as picturesque. I don't know where that would have started. Wingham, on the other hand, had an idea of itself as a factory town, a no-nonsense town. You could see by the number of people who belonged to the different churches the way the town would go. If you get a town with a lot of Methodists, that's going to be a town like Wingham [laughter]. It's going to be a town with factories.

Oh. You know when the Carnegie people came around with their money and said: "Here, take some money and build yourself a library," Clinton and Goderich and Seaforth all said: "Yes, please," and Wingham said: "No, we don't need it" [laughter]. They said: "We don't need a library" because, I don't know, it was probably going to cost them money to keep it up. And taxes – they would probably lose something in the taxes on the property. Even though they would get money to have a library, they weren't going to bother with one. So our library in Wingham was in the Town Hall, with letters on the window. It said "Public Reading Room" and some of the letters had fallen away – I'm not telling you which [laughter]. That's the kind of town you get where there's a strong feeling about people's duty to make money.

And then there were other towns. Goderich was a very classy town where there was a grammar school and there were all sorts of people who belonged to the Anglican Church [laughter], which was like a cathedral, and there was high society. Clinton was somewhere in-between. Clinton had a military aristocracy. And they had – was it called the 199th Battalion? These retired military men would lead this battalion and they marched around town and they trained and were in parades and everything. I think they went overseas at the beginning of the Second World War and found out they were going to have to fight and a lot of them came home [laughter]. I don't know how they managed this. Maybe they were overaged – I think they possibly were. Some of them stayed over there and became firefighters in the air raids. Anyway, this was the military tradition in Clinton [laughter].

Even Bayfield, which you were talking about, was very unlike the rest of the county because it was always a genteel tourist place. People who taught at Western had their vacation homes there. There was this slightly snotty tradition about Bayfield. There was always this feeling about it. Grand Bend was the no-class tourist place – it was further down.

I was telling you about the little places east of Wingham where there were dreadful things going on and these scandalous stories would erupt. I remember once something about a girl being abducted and it got in *The London Free Press* and everybody came out to look for her and then it turned out that she had run off with a man and put the story around, you know. There was always that kind of thing going on east of Wingham. I'm rambling on about all this gossip, but there were different kinds of gossip in each place.

TS: Writer and professor Lawrence Garber once told a graduate course I was attending at Western – one of six eight-month-long graduate courses I audited while writing my Ph.D. dissertation – that he thought gossip was one of the most underrated elements of fiction [laughter].

AM: Oh, yes. Yes. That and the dirty joke [laughter], I think.

TS: Do you know any you might share [laughter]?

AM: Sure [laughter]. But no. I listen to people telling stories all the time. There are a lot of storytellers around where I live. It's this organization of experience. And that shows how people value stories. I'm not talking now about jokes – that's another literary form. There will be the good joke-tellers and the not-so-good joke-tellers. But the people who organize life into anecdotes know a whole lot of fictional tricks. There was a man – he's dead now – who lived across the road from us who was doing this all the time. He knew how to manage suspense. He knew how not to keep you dangling too long, but just long enough. He knew how to lead you down a false path to a dead end and then bring you back. So I thought: All these tricks have been going on for a long time. I don't know if people learn them. A good storyteller, I think, picks them up very quickly.

TS: One of the places, I suppose, where you would hear these kinds of things would be at special gatherings, festivals, and so on. Earlier I mentioned Thanksgiving Weekend. And of course there's Thanksgiving Dinner. And you have a story called "Labor Day Dinner." I was wondering, therefore, if you could just quickly take us through the calendar in terms of the special days, today being Remembrance Day, that people nowadays in Clinton and earlier in your hometown of Wingham would celebrate.

AM: Well, there were a couple of days that nobody celebrates anymore. There was Empire Day. Do you remember that?

TS: No, I don't. Tell me.

AM: That was the 23rd of May, the day before the 24th.

TS: The 24th being Victoria Day. The Queen's Birthday. In honour of Queen Victoria, "The twenty-fourth of May / is the Queen's birthday. / And if you don't give us a holiday, / we'll all run away" [laughter].

AM: Yes. And on the 23rd of May we all remembered that we were part of the British Empire. This was in school. And I think there was also a day we planted trees. But then there was the big festival that nobody talks about now: the 12th of July.

TS: Orangemen's Day.

AM: Yes. And that's in my stories quite a bit because I remember it as, really, the big public day of the year when all the Orange Lodges would collect in one of the towns and they would march down the street with their banners and their fife and drum bands led by King Billy on a white horse. All the Orange Order ladies wore white for purity and they walked with white parasols. Then there was the open Bible and that was paraded, too. This was a great big event.

The last one I saw was about ten years ago. Everybody, I think, was over sixty and they couldn't march anymore. They had to be brought on flatbed trucks [laughter]. And they had the step-dancing, and I think they had the fife and drum contest, but there were only a couple of contestants [laughter] and everybody was ancient. Oh. And even the banners were all faded and tattered.

TS: That's only a day or two after your birthday, isn't it?

AM: That's right.

TS: 10th of July?

AM: 10th of July. Yes. So maybe that's why I always felt it was special.

TS: Well, I know one of the days on the calendar that was special for me was New Year's Eve 1974, when you were Writer-in-Residence at Western and brought your husband-to-be, Gerry Fremlin, out to my apartment on Kipp's Lane in London on your first date [laughter].

AM: That's right. Yes [laughter]. And see where it went from there.

TS: Also the first New Year's Eve of many that I've now celebrated with Marianne. So that occasion can be pretty special [laughter]. But to continue talking about the intensifying of our sense of the passing of time and the deepening of our feeling for history and for changes in experience: What is the emotional response when you see different things changing and this begins to enter into how you write something like "Working for a Living"?

AM: You mean what is my emotional response? I was thinking of my response to everything being: It's interesting. You know, I think this is a writerly response. I suppose there's also this sense of loss and all those other things. But mostly it's so interesting. I just want to keep penetrating and uncovering more and thinking what this is about. "Working for a Living" is a little different because it's the only major piece I've written that isn't fiction. And it was maybe a more conscious attempt just to write about my father and his life and through that about my parents and their life.

I'm interested now in doing some more nonfiction. I want to do a book of nonfiction pieces. There are times when I get, well, all the time I get fed up with fiction. I get tired of trying to do it. I always feel constrained by it, dissatisfied with it. I always think I'm on the verge of finding a better way to do it. But sometimes I back right off and think the better way to do it is to abandon it altogether and write nonfiction. That is, to write out of the concerns I have, though I can't easily specify what they are, but without any of the tricks. You think you'll get rid of the tricks and you get a new set of tricks. Then you think you'll get rid of them and so on. This seems to be what my history of writing fiction has been. Always trying to break out. So sometimes nonfiction appears to be very enticing.

TS: Sometimes.

AM: Yes.

TS: I have a memory of being told about a man who wrote some sort of history of Huron County or perhaps Ontario. I think literary historian and professor Carl F. Klinck told the graduate course that I took from him in the summer of 1974 when I first began writing about your work that this man had come down to London in order to teach creative writing at Western at some point.

AM: He taught creative writing when I was at Western. His name was James Scott. He was from Seaforth. Yes.

TS: Did you visit with him at that time?

AM: No. I couldn't get into his class [laughter]. I wasn't rejected. I think it was for third- and fourth-year students and I was only in first and second year.

TS: Earlier when I spoke about the intensifying of our sense of the passing of time and the deepening of our feeling for history and for changes in experience, I was also thinking about coming into one's inheritance. For example, the honour that you paid your father, Robert E. Laidlaw, by seeing his book *The McGregors: A Novel of an Ontario Pioneer Family*, into print soon after he died. And the honour that you have paid him with those lovely tributes to this person who tells stories and makes up songs and tells jokes, as in "Walker Brothers Cowboy" – or who recalls snippets of poetry, as in "Royal Beatings."

AM: That isn't entirely my father. I mean, I have made another character there. But my father was wonderful in that here I was writing this stuff and he had to live there and he had to have people come up to him on the street about it. You know, when I first started publishing the stories and I would have a first-person narrator and people would come up to my father and say: "Gee, Bob, I never knew that ..." [laughter]. And somebody said: "Bob, I never knew that you travelled for the Watkins people" [laughter]. That was after "Walker Brothers Cowboy" and my father, of course, never did sell from door to door. But things were taken that literally and he showed grace under pressure, I think. He really did [laughter]. He was great about it.

TS: Wasn't there a story that you told me once about somebody arriving at his house with a shotgun on account of a completely fictional but all too seemingly factual description of yours portraying the sort of personal situation that anybody involved in it would want to keep private?

AM: Oh, yes. That's true. That's true. It really wasn't funny. This is funny when people talk about it. It seems hillbilly-like. But in the area where I live there's still a great deal of feeling like this.

TS: For a writer, there's a sense of an environment that exists in actuality. But there's also a sense of an environment that you want to create for yourself. And there are choices that you have to make in order to be the writer you want to be, to create the room, "the soundscape" as Canadian composer R. Murray Schafer calls it, that you need.

AM: Oh, you mean choices in my life to be a writer?

TS: The care that you have to take to make a special place for yourself.

AM: In order that I can write? I don't think I've ever made those kinds of choices too much. I write wherever I can, however I can, whenever I can. And now I have some opportunity to think of myself as a writer all the time. When I started writing – this was in high school and I took my lunch – I got the janitor to lock me into the classroom at noon. I don't know why I had to be locked in. But if you wanted to be in the classroom at noon, you had to be locked in [laughter]. So I was locked in and I was writing this novel and that's what I did all through grade twelve. I guess I found a place that way. But I never had at all ideal conditions to write in and it didn't make that much difference. Later on I had children and I sort of fitted the writing around them.

TS: I'm very interested in the question of a writer's education. And more broadly, of course, in the education of everyone. Clearly, I've had an extensive formal education – which I've survived, I guess I could say [laughter]. For more and more I find myself getting my real education from writers.

AM: You mean from writers telling you how to read their work? Is that what you're saying?

TS: From writers describing in personal conversation or interviews or essays what interests them as they write, as opposed to quite different matters discussed in much academic criticism. But also, as Hugh Hood's and my friend professor Robert Beckett astutely observed the other evening, from the way a writer's work teaches you how to read that work.

AM: I always feel this problem when people are asking me to talk about writing. I feel that I have a choice, in a way, between trying to sound intelligent and being truthful [laughter]. Being truthful often involves saying just deadly things like "Well, I don't really know" or "Well, I never thought about that." I sometimes feel that people think I'm being frivolous to give such answers. But they will, in fact, be the truth. Many other writers are much better at talking about writing. But I think it maybe doesn't hurt, once in a while, to hear a writer like me [laughter] come up against this sort of dead end, this being inarticulate, this inability to explain things very well. It's very hard often for people to accept that, to think that you haven't worked it out, that you haven't got a handle on what you're doing. Of course, it just means that you don't know what you're doing in terms that they understand. I know what I'm doing, but I can't explain it.

TS: Do you have a favourite lie [laughter]?

AM: No! Because I never even was smart enough to think up the good old lies [laughter]. But I do want to say something about what John Metcalf was talking about earlier, about the Canadian writer having this great problem of no tradition and not thinking that writing could be done in Canada. This never occurred to me! I think I was living so far from any centre of education or literature or anything that I didn't know what were the right attitudes to have. I didn't know that you couldn't be a writer because you were a Canadian. I didn't know that you couldn't be a writer in my generation because you were a woman. None of this, which apparently other people of my age thought, got through to me at all. It just was not there. It didn't occur to me whether or not we had a Canadian literature. Or whether or not women were being published either. I didn't think about that. I guess, supposing I had been in Toronto, I might have, because other people might have been thinking about it. But for me there was this great isolation of never, never talking to anyone about writing. Or even about reading. This is supposed to be, you know, a very deprived position to be in, but actually I think it was probably very good.

TS: If I were to ask readers and students to look back at three Canadian short story writers from the earlier part of the twentieth century, the three writers whom I would ask them to consider, and whom I'm interested in studying more myself, would be Raymond Knister, Morley

Callaghan, and Ethel Wilson. I know that one of these three is a special favourite of yours: Ethel Wilson. But I'll start with the earliest, Raymond Knister. Only a few months ago I recorded an interview with his daughter, Imogen Knister Givens, at her home in Waterford. And Imogen said that you two knew each other.

AM: Yes. Yes.

TS: What's that story?

AM: We were at the United Church camp for young girls, on Lake Huron, when we were about, I would say, thirteen or fourteen. And I discovered that she was an actual writer's daughter. That was a tremendous thing. What I thought wasn't that this had been a Canadian writer, but that there really were writers. I knew about books [laughter]. But to meet a writer's daughter was just wonderful. I can't remember what we talked about exactly, but we talked about being writers. I think she wanted to be a writer, and I wanted to be a writer, but I wasn't about to tell anybody. This was the Wingham protection, you know, that you learn so well. So I don't think I told her. No [laughter].

TS: Would you have gone out, in due course, and hunted for any of her father's work? Do you have any memory of that?

AM: My father had read her father's work. So he was read by reading people of – they would have been about the same age, I expect.

TS: The novel *White Narcissus*, probably?

AM: No. A story called "Mist-Green Oats."

TS: Oh. Yes. That's very interesting.

AM: My Dad told me about that and I don't know whether I found it then or found it later. Sorry, I can't remember. I don't think I could have found his work in the library, which wasn't a bad library either, even though we didn't have a building [laughter].

TS: I want to ask you as well about Morley Callaghan. Clearly, there's a writer whom some younger writers were quite close to and looked up to – Hugh Hood being the most obvious instance. As for the response of others, I was struck by the dual nature of a comment Norman Levine made, when he said that as a young writer he admired Callaghan for the international stature Callaghan had achieved, but then added, very significantly I thought, that he didn't think he had actually read Callaghan at the time. And even Hugh Hood has told me that he views Callaghan as an artist whose creative intuitions exceeded the craft he possessed for representing them.

AM: I hadn't read him when I was in high school. I did when I got to university. Not through any class, but I made friends with people who knew about him. That's when I started.

TS: In terms of the last of this group of three writers – Raymond Knister, Morley Callaghan, and Ethel Wilson – you mentioned to me several years ago, in 1981, during our first recorded interview published in Louis K. MacKendrick's collection *Probable Fictions: Alice Munro's Narrative Acts*, that when you moved to Vancouver it was a great delight to you to know that Ethel Wilson was living there.

AM: That's when I read her for the first time. I found a book in a store in Vancouver containing two longer pieces, "Lilly's Story" and "Tuesday and Wednesday."

TS: *The Equations of Love.*

AM: *The Equations of Love.* Yes. And I found her writing more exciting to me than Callaghan's or Knister's at that time. I can't think how to describe what I felt about it. It was cool and elegant in a way that just was enormously pleasurable to me.

TS: I enjoy the way her sentences move.

AM: Yes.

TS: And the way something quite unexpected will follow something else.

AM: And she was witty.

TS: The humour in the style, somehow. Even if a fairly painful situation is being described.

AM: There was a neat bit of dialogue, I remember, in "Tuesday and Wednesday." The women are talking about a party and one of them recalls a friend asking "Are you going short or long?" I just liked that a lot [laughter].

TS: Do you remember *The Innocent Traveller*?

AM: I didn't read that until later, I don't think.

TS: In *What Is A Canadian Literature?*, John Metcalf, in the process of vigorously contesting arguments for the importance of Duncan Campbell Scott's 1896 story cycle *In the Village of Viger*, quotes you as saying: "Tell them that the book that influenced me was *Winesburg, Ohio*." That is, Sherwood Anderson's 1919 story cycle *Winesburg, Ohio*.

AM: I believe I did say that [laughter]. And [addressing John Metcalf, seated in the audience] you're publishing this in your book? Confidential conversation [laughter]. Well, it did. It's true. It's true [laughter].

TS: Didn't writer and broadcaster Harry Boyle, who is also from the Wingham area but about fifteen years before you, have a scene near the end of his book *Memories of a Catholic Boyhood* where the protagonist, "Harry," was reading, or was told he should read, Sherwood Anderson?

AM: I haven't read *Memories of a Catholic Boyhood*. So I can't say.

TS: I seem to remember that he comes up there, too. What impressed you about Sherwood Anderson's book?

AM: All the bleakness and the dimness. You know, all those things that are so attractive to an adolescent [laughter]. When I think about it now, what I get is a feeling about certain rooms and a quality of lives which I imagine in those rooms – the kinds of rooms you would have over the hardware store on the main street. And something about a kind of light you would have. Those things gave me – the only way I can describe it is enormous excitement. That was the response I would have, when I was young, reading that sort of book. It wasn't that I thought "Oh, yes. This is the way people's lives are in Wingham." Because, in fact, I don't suppose I did think that. I just responded to this quality, which I can't be any more definite about, because of course that's what I wanted to write about, too. I didn't want to make any kind of record. I just wanted to get this thing which is like the light in the room.

TS: Another early-twentieth-century writer whom I want to ask you about is Katherine Mansfield.

AM: Oh, yes. I've read Katherine Mansfield.

TS: What are your favourite stories by her?

AM: I like "The Daughters of the Late Colonel" a lot. And "Prelude" I like very much, still. And "At the Bay." Yes.

TS: What strikes you as special about these?

AM: Well, the point of view of childhood is very wonderful in "Prelude."

TS: I want to ask you about the kinds of challenges that you encounter while writing stories: in particular, the stories in your two most recent collections, *The Moons of Jupiter* and *The Progress of Love*. When I came to study your preceding book, *Who Do You Think You Are?*, for a long chapter on it in my Ph.D. dissertation on the Canadian story cycle, which I finished in December 1981, the story that excited me the most was "Simon's Luck." Lawrence Mathews has written very ably about what, echoing phrasing from "Simon's Luck," he calls "Alice Munro's Art of Disarrangement" in that book. Interestingly, that story was the last one you wrote for that book, though it was a rewrite of an earlier piece, I believe.

AM: "Simon's Luck" was three stories. There were three women in Simon's life. And one of the stories was even published, I think.

TS: "Emily"?

AM: Yes. And then how it got from that to the final version – oh, I wish I could tell you. I remember having terrible trouble with it. I remember seeing it at first as these three stories. Simon has been the lover of each woman and they all had their different story of him and I thought that was going to be perfectly all right. Then it didn't work. It must have worked well enough so that I could sell one, but I was very dissatisfied with it. I can remember the time when the organization of it came clear: it was when I was driving back in a pickup truck across Canada. My husband Gerry and I had been out to Victoria and we got my youngest daughter and we were driving back and I remember that the way to do the story came to me in Manitoba [laughter]. I don't know why, but it had been bothering me for a couple of months before that. And then I could see how it was all going to have to go together.

TS: I want to ask you about the newer stories in *The Moons of Jupiter* and in *The Progress of Love*. Perhaps you could comment on some specific stories in terms of personal favourites or the challenges, formally, in the development of particular stories, the structure of particular stories, that you faced writing them.

AM: I think almost every story in *The Progress of Love* was difficult. There were some that were difficult in different ways. "Fits" was probably the most almost-impossible story. "White Dump" gave me a lot of trouble. The title story gave me a lot of trouble. I'm trying to think how I resolved them. I know that in the story "White Dump" the part about the grand-mother swimming came to me earlier than any of the rest. I was fooling around with that maybe ten years before the book. Then the rest sort of branched out from there. That often happens.

It's odd. When I finish a story, I blank my mind to it completely and it's hard for me to remember how I did it. I can just remember the ones that were the hardest. They're sort of my favourites, the ones that I work so hard at. "Fits" is really my favourite story in *The Progress of Love* because I never really pulled it off, I never really got that story. So in a way that's more interesting to you than the story that you get immediately or fairly immediately. What did you want me to say [laughter]?

TS: In terms of the development of your stories, I know that regularly when I start to read them I have this amazing feeling because the first sentence will make sense to me and then I'll move to the second one and it will be wonderful but I can't imagine how you got to that [laughter].

AM: [Laughter] I'm not going to be much good here. I wish I could be better.

TS: We're not talking about some kind of academic logic here.

AM: No. I know. I wish I could even remember one story so that I could talk about it. But always my mind is full of what I'm doing now. I can tell you that now I'm tackling a story – it's another three-part story and I'm doing a simple chronological thing – and I'm already getting intimations that I'm not going to be satisfied with this. I'm going to have to go back and mess it all up and I don't know how I will do it. I do that mainly just by feel and keep on doing it until I've got it the best way I can. And I don't do it with a word processor either [laughter].

TS: They can teach you a lot, you know!

AM: So I hear [laughter]. Someone said to me last summer: "If you would just get yourself a computer, you could be on your next book by now" [laughter]. I thought: "This is the most extraordinary idea [laughter]. If I could just get through the pages a little faster, then I could get on to my next book. But who knows if I've got an idea for my next book?" All this chopping and rearranging I do could conceivably be done with a computer. They say that with a computer you can stick a little paragraph in. You can look down this page and say: "I've got to get a bit of dialogue in here" or "I've got to do some little change there" – and then you can just do it without having to type the whole page over. But if you're going to do this and you start typing, you always discover that putting that one line in changes the balance. There's a ripple effect all the way back and you are going to be changing little things all around that you wouldn't know about if you didn't go through the actual typing. That's my theory, anyway [laughter].

TS: There are two other stories that I want to ask you about. One is from *The Moons of Jupiter*: the story "Bardon Bus."

AM: That's a choppy one for you.

TS: In an earlier collection, *Something I've Been Meaning To Tell You*, you open up stories with space breaks and a repeated symbol marking the breaks. But with "Bardon Bus," there's a numerical arrangement of thirteen parts. At what point would you have decided to do that?

AM: I can't remember. I can't remember when I numbered the parts and I'm not sure why. Maybe I just wanted to make it look more orderly or something. It's so disarranged. And I can't remember in what order I wrote them. Or anything. I do know that I wrote so many endings to that story over and over and over and over again – just the last little bit. And I couldn't get it. Sometimes you do really lose your sense of a story. And so eventually I just chopped it. Like they say you do with a *New Yorker* story: take off the last two paragraphs and you've got the story [laughter]. Well, I sort of did that with that story and just let it go.

TS: Often will you begin with an image or an impression?

AM: You mean, What starts the story? Different stories, different ways. Some stories start from an anecdote. And they're usually the stories that aren't so great. They work, they're easier to do, but they're not as interesting. Other stories do start with an image. The sort of thing that I was calling the *Winesburg, Ohio* feeling, which I can't really describe any better. And those are the stories that I most want to do. There are all sorts of different ways they start. Others perhaps start with some problem I'm trying to work out. Not a literary problem, more an investigation.

"Fits" was that kind of story. It was a case of: How can you write a story about this? I wanted to write a story around a dead centre and keep going around and around like this. Sometimes I see stories in shapes. In fact, very often I see them in shapes and in physical terms like weight. That's what I feel about them when I'm doing them and I've got a kind of tension, firing on all cylinders, a kind of weight that is the way I feel it should be.

TS: Once the stories have been written, there's the important matter of how to arrange them in a particular collection – deciding what would be a good beginning and what you want later on. This order clearly would be quite different, I would assume, from the order in which the stories were written. Could you comment on this matter of how best to arrange a collection?

AM: Well, the arrangement is usually just a more practical business of not putting first-person stories one after the other. But I have a bit of a feeling about that, too. I want to start off with and end up with what I feel to be strong stories. Bury the ones that I don't feel are so strong where they won't be too much noticed, maybe, or where they will be in-between a couple of stronger stories. That's almost like a rhythmical thing. But I don't have a very strong feeling about this because I never read, or feel a book of short stories should be read, one story after the other. I think you should go into it and pick a story and read that story. So I don't have a very strong feeling about what should be on either side.

TS: And in your brief essay "What Is Real?" written for John Metcalf's anthology *Making It New*, you also explained that as a reader you often start reading in the middle of a story.

AM: I usually start reading in the middle of a story. Yes. And to me that seems perfectly reasonable. Everyone says this is surprising. But what happens is the least of what I'm interested in – you know, getting from A to B to C. So this way, what I'm going to know about the story or feel about the story I can get right away. And then I sort of work back from there to find out what peg this is hung on as far as what happens in the story.

TS: The last two stories in *The Progress of Love*, "Circle of Prayer" and "White Dump": Do you have any recollections of how they began?

AM: "Circle of Prayer" began with the image of the funeral parlour scene and the girls throwing their jewellery into the coffin. That was perhaps more a story from something that really did happen. "White Dump" began with the old woman going down for her morning swim and having her clothes ripped and thrown into the water and then coming up to the house naked. The naked old woman coming across the grass as a picture – not something anybody ever told me or that really happened. And then, as I say, the story grew out around that with the different generations. "Circle of Prayer" sort of grew out in the same way, but it came much more from the community I live in where there was, in fact, a funeral like this and where the women do have a circle of prayer. So in a way that was a more superficial story. I like it, but I was taking things off the top.

TS: And then that would affect the final decision about which story might best be put second-last and which might best be put last.

AM: That's right.

TS: With you wanting to have an especially strong story first and last in each collection. May I ask if you're a collector? Do you have favourite things that you like to collect?

AM: You mean things, not books? Ah. No.

TS: Some people collect paintings.

AM: No. No. How should I say this? Anything interests me quite a lot, but not in terms of whether it's beautiful or whether I own it. I mean, I think I could live fairly happily in a motel room [laughter]. I'm indifferent to surroundings to a considerable extent. And indifferent to having myself reflected in the things around me.

TS: And a last question: Because you've travelled a fair amount of late, what would you say has been special about that for you?

AM: It hasn't much to do with writing, I notice. I can't get much sense of other places. Oh, this is interesting. I've written a story about Scotland. I was there about a year ago now for a while and I got this story. I got all the ideas and everything sort of works well about it but it doesn't satisfy me at all. There's something that isn't there. And the reason it isn't there is because of my lack of deep commitment to the place. Even though this seems to work, it doesn't. So obviously I'm not going to benefit greatly as a writer by travel. Philip Larkin didn't travel, did he? When he went on holiday, Philip Larkin went to some awful seaside resort in England. He didn't think you should go to Spain, or anywhere like that, where you might get new ideas. I don't think I respond on any very deep level to other places. Just as a person, I have a wonderful time. But the writer doesn't seem to get much out of it.

TS: Well, all of us have certainly gotten a lot out of this. Can we thank Alice for all of this? [Applause.]

Guelph, Ontario, Canada
11 November 1988

Too Little Geography; Too Much History: Writing the Balance in Alice Munro

Dennis Duffy

... if some countries have too much history, we have too much geography....
— The Rt. Hon. William Lyon Mackenzie King, speech, Canada,
House of Commons Debates, 18 June 1936 (3868)

The past is full of contradictions and complications,
perhaps equal to those of the present,
though we do not usually think so.
— Alice Munro, "No Advantages," *The View from Castle Rock* (17)

The Munro Tract is a written-over district in Ontario bounded by Lakes Huron and Erie on the west and south, the town of Goderich in the north and the city of London in the east. A transparent overlay of the Munro Tract would largely match the boundaries of the Huron Tract, first developed by the Canada Company in 1826. My name for Munro's fictional territory stems from its resemblance to the historical origins of White Canadian settlement.

Gazing into the cold waters of the lake of time past reveals such names as "Tiger" Dunlop, John Galt, Colonel Thomas Talbot, and Will Donnelly. Those names and many others are printed on the wrecks below, all subject to the temporal version of the accretive force producing the northern coral reef at Tobermory. Those names, we might say, label history. The country of the mind that painter Greg Curnoe and others such as playwright James Reaney have called "Souwesto" – that is, the region bounded by Ontario's southwestern peninsula – is plotted by imaginative markers as well. Think of Wilfred Campbell's creaky *A Beautiful Rebel* (1909) and Reaney's powerful Donnelly trilogy (1973-75). And then there are the canvases of Jack Chambers, conveying with such unexpected power the apparently boring flatness of the district. One of them graces the cover of the 1991 Penguin paperback reprint of *Friend of My Youth*, the collection in which Alice Munro's "Meneseteung" appears.

Those last three names – Campbell, Reaney, Chambers – bear on my topic, but understanding their relevance requires background. Since John Richardson's *Wacousta* appeared in 1832 (with a Souwesto setting), Canada's historical novelists have sought to balance Mackenzie King's material ratio, adding an imaginative overlay to the geographical and political mappings. Alice Munro's *The View from Castle Rock* (2006) indicates that her own excursions into historical fiction are not in fact sidebars to her work, despite its usual emphasis on the roughly contemporary.

Campbell, Reaney, and Chambers outline the nature of her historical subject matter, and explain why it forms a major preoccupation within her fiction. Wilfred Campbell – like Munro, an Ontario Scot – wrote historical fiction, the kind of novel originating in the work of Sir Walter Scott. It is a mode of fiction overtly preoccupied with the way in which cultural change works itself out in the lives of obscure individuals. Mentioning the Donnellys brings to mind the melodrama – the neighbourly mass murders that engrossed Canada in 1880 and after, those sporadic upheavals of the magma boiling beneath newcomer settlements that belie the district's placid appearance. The so-called magic realism of Jack Chambers' paintings denotes a technique that in fact compresses meaning in the way that an archer bends a bow. The release of tension generates a torque shooting the bolt into the viewer's heart, smashing through the cuirass of familiarity. Transforming the banal into the momentous – spelunking through those "deep caves paved with kitchen linoleum" (*Lives of Girls and Women* 253) – has long since become Munro's stylistic marque.[1] Jack Chambers spotted that in the landscape, and made us see it too.

Munro's work functions as another offensive launched against what Mackenzie King saw as Canadian geography's unending attrition of Canadian history. Her mapping of the Munro Tract transmutes geography and history into an allegory giving them both their due. That space she now views through a car windshield (Thacker 374, 443, 473),[2] in journeys pausing at every roadside puzzle that teases out the researcher in her. Munro's country drives – her back-concession crawls with her learned husband, geographer Gerald Fremlin, as chauffeur – appear to feed a glutton's appetite for mysterious objects that cry out for definition. She has performed a version of this site-seeing earlier, and through a fictional creation. Blaikie Noble figures in the title story of *Something I've Been Meaning To Tell You* (1974). A yarn-spinning tour guide, he tweaks his territory into resembling a Gothic fantasy through his spurious legendary layering. Profoundly imaginative though she may be, Alice Munro offers a serious version of Blaikie's trip lore.

Accompanying her along one of these apparent meanders offers the most convincing approach to the meaning of "Meneseteung." It will not do to label the story a historical fiction, regaling readers with a series of footnotes indicating the facts that it is based upon. That variety of antiquarianism ignores the story's complexity. To track the story without presenting a conceptual background risks a reader's bewilderment. Think of this: Munro's development of her Tract piles up greater depth and density over the period of her imaginative explorations. My approach begins with an overview of the social thrust of the project of writing historical fiction, but then proceeds to speculate on what her fiction – especially its narrative technique – insinuates about Munro's own personal and even ancestral role in that project.

I

Let us begin with *The View from Castle Rock*, Munro's most heterogeneous collection of narratives. *Castle Rock* melds fiction, personal experience, and historical reconstruction, in turn exposing a sensibility that will not shunt the past along some shelf of archived documents. The narrative voice behind the collection is that of the storyteller rather than of the writer. That voice "intrudes" upon the supposedly fictional narrative, throwing in what are at times facts, at times suppositions, that appear part of an ongoing meditation about the tangled relationship between historical *fact* and historical *understanding*.

Telling the story lodges fact and understanding alike within a dynamic that the author controls. But somewhere an ancestral voice is murmuring also. "Walker Brothers Cowboy" opens Munro's earliest col-lection, *Dance of the Happy Shades* (1968). It deals with her father's job, and depends upon the recounting done by that character representing him. A storyteller himself, Robert Laidlaw presented in *The McGregors* (1979) a succession of vignettes about pioneering in Ontario's South Bruce and North Huron region. During the final three weeks of his life, Robert Laidlaw produced a second draft of his book that Munro has said, "'I read with astonishment after his death'" (Munro in Thacker 315).

His daughter then arranged for the publication of the book (Thacker 284, 337-38, 350). Its reliance upon historical anecdotes and sketches reminds us of the sort of basic building-blocks of material that appear in Munro's manuscripts of this period (Thacker 294-301). Can we con-sider that Robert Laidlaw's storytelling in his *own* voice (for if "Walker Brothers Cowboy" began as his story, it was retold by Alice and turned into *hers* about *him*) became a bequest to his daughter? What was her thrusting of his work into print following his death but an act of filial piety that acknowledged her inheritance?

Of course, that bequest came retroactively, like some newly-discov-ered missing will that corkscrews a Victorian plot. In fact, Munro had been meditating on history's role in the construction of fiction at least since *Lives of Girls and Women* (1971). Del Jordan's scornful rejection of Uncle Craig's antiquarian project presents Munro's earliest announce-ment of a poetic: that her fiction will illuminate rather than attempt to reproduce literally the life around her (*Lives of Girls and Women* 60-63). Yet at the same time, the very inclusion of Uncle Craig and what lan-guishes in his hands as an endless, pointless project denotes that the stuff of fiction can lie anywhere. Mining the past as a genius rather than as a pedant can transmute antiquarianism into the visionary.

As anyone who has ever tried to teach it realizes, *Lives* at times presents itself as a novel, at times as a collection of linked stories. It's a Gombrich-like argument about whether the silhouette outlines a rabbit or a duck (Gombrich 4-6). But that never-to-be-settled question of how we label the book permits this extrapolation: it is possible to view Munro's fictional *oeuvre* as a sustained, varied, episodic, and highly intense *roman fleuve*. Such an endless novel – that is, my critical fiction that such a novel exists – strives to adumbrate how consciousness extends itself not through a new self-definition, but instead through mastery of a sense of place. It is a familiar Romantic quest, with the 'scape serving as a stand-in for the soul. The straitened chamber of maiden thought admits only the facts and times that directly and immediately shape one's personal experience. Maturity, however, delivers the power to express the experiences of others, distant from us not only in their personhood and social milieu but in their temporality.

Fine, except that the first such novel was written in blank verse, never finished, and called *The Prelude* (1805, 1850).[3] Could it be that the historical novel is the logical vehicle for continuing this project of enacting consciousness-in-place-and-in-time? I suggest that this genre offers the surest guide to what Munro is up to in "Meneseteung." When successful, the historical novel displays the power to evoke something greater than antiquarianism, or a nostalgia-driven curiosity about how those who came before us managed their lives. When it falters, then the historical novel is no more than recreational, another version of the presentist thinking that has conned its way into many a museum's display case.

A hidden presentist teleology lurks behind too many pioneer museums, for example. Their appeal rests upon their construction of a moral arc that always peaks with a vision of an era's glory. *Our* era's glory. "Look! Those past midgets evolved into giants like us." We enjoy thinking that our restorations shed light upon the past. Often they simply light a fuse setting off a fireworks display that celebrates our own greatness. The more difficult task – one achievable only through the creative imagination – lies in the construction of a felt continuum and the retelling of how one got there. That makes for the sort of progress engaging an audience's sense of kinship over time with enduring struggles and defeats. That, I submit, is the sort of effect that Munro strives for in "Meneseteung."

Does this strike you as naïvely realistic, like someone persisting in representational painting when the mode seems played out? Like animal art? Like hockey paintings? Think of Canada's Vimy Memorial. What is it but a *grande machine* whose allegorical obsessions will not let us be until it throttles us into believing that the random, often senseless deaths it commemorates are in fact part of a sacrifice made on our behalf? Is that what "Meneseteung" is after? Genius, however, makes its own rules. Carried out by a master like Alice Munro, the creation of a body of work plumbing time's depths within a single setting distills experience. It extends the grace of meaning beyond a single era. The still sad music of humanity reaches its audience polyphonically; its hearers either follow the various temporal parts as they weave in and out, or surrender to the grandeur of the achieved blending into a unified melodic structure. But we have to listen very hard to what she has been meaning to tell us.

We have to listen because Munro's distinctive historical fiction is not fully congruent with classical historical fiction. That literary product – as practised from its inception in 1814 (Scott's *Waverley*) until Modernism sidetracked the form into what is largely pop genre fiction at some point after 1914 – lay in bringing before its readers some realization of social and cultural continuity. This is why we may see that this aspect of the historical novel's tradition – a preoccupation not with being, but with being-in-time – culminates with the triumph of Proust, an unlikely figure in the discussion of historical novels. Has any other novelist – even Tolstoy – so inextricably melded the idea of being with the actual experience of being-in-time? No one to my knowledge has read *Remembrance of Things Past* as historical fiction, yet it brings home as no other imaginative narrative has the scoring of our features that weathering time etches. Psychology and the inner life – rather than the outer, public one – preoccupied Proust's imagination. Yet the core samples that he brought back from his mining of the imagination seem, in hindsight, versions of what a century of historical fiction at its best had been discovering: the dizzying prospect that comes from understanding that we are one with and yet at the same time alien from those preceding us.[4]

Traditional historical fiction created its readers' sense of continuity with the past through a process that couldn't quite shake an essential reductionism. From the forefather Scott onward, the historical novel as he and others following him conceived it strove for two goals. First, it sought to fabricate a continuous and teleological narrative out of the chaos of the perceivable past. Then, it aimed at propelling that narrative toward both the completion of a private romantic quest, and toward discernment of a historically progressive movement (often conceived as a moment in a national genesis) to which the romantic couple contributed and which in turn defined their significance.

Historical fiction from that classic period and in its bestseller mode today deals with such subjects as obscure Romans caught up in the drama of the unfolding Christian Church (*"Quo Vadis"* [1896]), medieval bell-ringers entangled in the intrigues of clerics struggling with royalist nationalists (*Notre-Dame of Paris* [1831]), and Englishmen and women swept into sanctioned and unsanctioned social violence leading to the extinction of Scottish culture and the rise of British nationality (*Waverley* [1814], the genre's originator). Characters furnish their minor role within a greater, evolutionary process, and swim easily amid whatever tide of agency engulfs them. Love or some version of it triumphs. Love's triumph is continuity's too: the permanence, the inescapability, and the infinite volcanic pressures that time stamps upon the bedrock of desire link disparate historical periods within a vision of mutual relevance. Thus is the charm wound up.

History, in those traditional novels (often bestselling) that are with us still, flourishes within a time warp. It gently refrains from chewing up helpless individuals and spitting them out into the random currents of experience. It coats them with meaning instead. Not so in our present-day, postmodern canonical texts. For example, R.C. Harris as a historical figure embalmed within Michael Ondaatje's *In the Skin of a Lion* first drinks from the water tap connecting him to the system whose construction he has supervised. He then spits it back out, where it will pass down the drain and back into the lake, ready for re-consumption (*In the Skin of a Lion* 111). Harris at that moment is a metonymy for a process at once vast, impersonal, and arbitrary, beyond the control of any individual. It is no accident that Ondaatje located this image of circularity and alimentation in one of his historical, rather than imaginatively created actors.

That's history, as we understand it now, a kind of nemesis thundering out of our dystopian machineries and into our image-laden lives. The counter-reality, the para-reality forming the staple of dystopian speculative narrative from *Nineteen Eighty-Four* (1949) to *The Children of Men* (1992) can also be a stand-in for history itself. The romantic interests – with distinguished exceptions like *The Temptations of Big Bear* – remain. *Kamouraska*, *The Wars*, *The Colony of Unrequited Dreams*, *The Stone Carvers*, *Three Day Road*: none offers a reassuring vision of historical or public experience, yet all rely on some version of the erotic quest to drive their plots. Why? We still seem stranded on some contemporary version of Dover Beach. We mutter assurances of love, while the *tsunami* slams into us in the act of grabbing at the cellphone camera that captures our obliteration.

II

We have been focussing on the cultural landscape that surrounds Munro's very usage of the historical fiction apparatus in her story. "Meneseteung" clearly distances itself from that "classic" tradition that I have described. Yet we cannot simply pigeonhole it among the other post-1970 novels that I have mentioned, since it tells its tale in a way that the others do not. That is to say, "Meneseteung" is an instance of literature seeking also to reproduce the effects of orature. That doubleness of effect is what I want to consider now. This discussion entails another excursion into ancestral imaginings, specifically the Scottish oral tradition. But first, we must recall the story's bare bones.

As an Ontario small-town local poetess and spinster living in her dead parents' house in the 1880s and 1890s, Almeda Joynt Roth leads a life in accord with the tragic arc that her culture assigns to "old maids." Shyness leads to her extreme caution in encountering the ritual overtures of local magnate (salt mines) Jarvis Poulter. Delicacy, sexual as well as moral, drives her retreat from the possibilities of marriage with him. She is repelled by his offhanded disposition of the inert form of a lower-class woman who has been sleeping off a binge. This setback is followed by a drift into marked eccentricity that in turn perhaps hastens her death. The local paper speculates that a swarm of teasing boys drove the vulnerable outsider, who had become an object of mockery, into a wetland. The subsequent chill provoked a deadly illness. The story is told in different voices, among them excerpts from Almeda's poetry, clippings from the local newssheet, *The Vidette*, and most importantly, by an anonymous, self-confident narrator – our contemporary – who lacks inhibition about attributing motives and dispositions to the figures in her story.

The romantic quest drives the plot of traditional historical fiction. Though treated ironically, it remains a prominent feature of "Meneseteung." The complex relationship between bumptious narrator and repressed central character stands as Munro's most intense and successful imagining of the angular welds that bind two disparate beings in differing times. Yet the romantic quest figures there, though it concludes with an act of renunciation. Almeda renounces love in the manner of a Jamesian heroine like Fleda Vetch in *The Spoils of Poynton* (1897) because she senses that her suitor lacks her own moral refinement. Like so much else in the story, that gesture bears an ambiguous outcome. It confirms Almeda's marginalization. Is her marginality heroic or foolish? Her moral stance does not stop Almeda from devolving into a kind of dartboard, with the swarm of boys acting out the town's hostility and contempt toward people of her kind.

Critical opinion can idealize Almeda's renunciation. Some readers' admiration for Almeda in fact nudges the story in the direction of a traditional historical fiction, with its teleology of moral progress. Douglas Glover places Almeda in excellent company when he implicitly compares her rejection of married confinement to that of a bedraggled yet heroic Quixote (*The Enamoured Knight* 169-81). Dermot McCarthy's Almeda intuits that the peripheral world of the Pearl Street Swamp stands as "the centre for her life that she ... had been unconsciously seeking" (2). Pam Houston plants Almeda amid the generative springs of vitality itself: "A story, a poem, a history, a life, a river: 'Meneseteung' becomes all things female, all things generative, all things that can never be absolute" (91). To a Christian critic like John C. Van Rys, Almeda experiences a moment of revelation – good men are hard to find – that compels her to immerse herself in life's messiness (353-56). But ask yourself: do affirmatives as ringing as these strike you as typical of Munro? Isn't her memorable phrase from "Royal Beatings" – "He *is* acting and he means it" (16; emphasis added) – a gnomic summary of the way her fiction portrays experience? Glover views Almeda from the perspective of the Don; wouldn't it be just like Munro to use the Sancho Panza viewpoint in the other lens of the binoculars? And wouldn't she insist on her viewers peering through both, however crazed the focus? Is Almeda the disaster-in-waiting that – like Leacock's *Mariposa Belle* – never quite reaches its tragic potential?

The history behind one of Munro's admitted historical models for Almeda, Eloise A. Skimings, explains why heroism sits so awkwardly on this figure ("Contributors' Notes" 322-23). Keep in mind, for example, the period photo of Skimings, frontispiece to her 1904 *Golden Leaves* poetry collection. The Reuben R. Sallows Digital Library's curatorial notes on Sallows' studio photograph of 1902 state that the "Poetess of Lake Huron" is garbed in a "Coronation Costume, Coronation Day, 9th August, 1902, Goderich, Ontario, Canada." Costume it may be; an outlandish one at that. The "long-sleeved floral dress with plaid insets," the bouquet of flowers, the whole capped by the gothic arch of the lace bonnet: she resembles Mrs. Tiggy-Winkle *en fête*, exactly the sort of eccentric that the town rowdies would be licensed to have their way with. In her near-death by water, amid the masses of flowers both live and floral, Skimings seems a stand-in for J.E. Millais's well-known portrait of Hamlet's victim, Ophelia. In Millais's portrait, the foregrounded flowers form a painterly version of the panels on Skimings' dress. Munro knew enough about Pre-Raphaelite painting to allude to an example of it in entitling a story – "The Beggar Maid" – that her American publisher insisted on choosing as the title of the collection that most of us know as *Who Do You Think You Are?* (Thacker 358-64). And that snide question is one that Eloise Skimings' Goderich neighbours likely slung her way, along with much else.

Say that one lacked all indirect evidence, and knew nothing about the writer's typical ironic stance toward her material. Even then, an observant reader would note that "Meneseteung"'s narrative framework denies any ethical (or even ontological) consistency to events. The anonymous narrator – and it is she who layers time into an opaque lens, who afflicts the story's vision with cataracts – busily constructs her own version of Almeda's life and its meaning. She lacks any scruples about ordering a past life according to a presentist template and jelling speculation into fact. Munro's final, hardbacked version of a story often differs from its original appearance in *The New Yorker*. When we compare "Meneseteung"'s final form with its periodical version, we see excised from the earlier version the narrator's final admission of her own limitations: that she herself could no more than guess that Almeda took laudanum and made grape jelly. That excised finale nudges into wakefulness a reader who hasn't yet understood the function of that cavalier narrator. Munro's abdication of omniscience underlines her fiction's partiality, its admission of her hovering presence over events, historical or imaginative in origin.

Munro's *authorial* voice cannot resist "intruding." *Castle Rock*'s title story holds to the absent omniscient narrator for fifty-seven of its sixty-one pages, only to break the spell with the admission about a letter written by a historical character that "I can look it up today" (83). She has already made a similar entry into her story in *Castle Rock*'s opening narrative, "No Advantages" (17). Yet at times, as in "Meneseteung," it is the fictive, *narrator's* voice that intrudes. This throws the narrative into two time paths. Then that voice, which cannot resist having the last word, converts these streams from parallel discourses into a single-edged Möbius strip that lacks a defined beginning or conclusion.

That busy narrative voice simply cannot distinguish between what has happened and what she wanted to have happen: "I thought that there wasn't anybody alive in the world but me who would know this, who would make the connection. ... But perhaps this isn't so. People are curious. ... You see them going around with notebooks, scraping the dirt off gravestones, reading microfilm, just in the hope of seeing this trickle in time, making a connection, rescuing one thing from the rubbish" (73). Here is a narrator a-tingle with a sense of mission, eager to supply connection, anxious to rescue. Lacunae bother her; through supposition, she anneals present to past. The narrative voice turns Almeda's tale into our contemporary obsession, trying to iron past time into an unwrinkled version of the present. A reader beholds the heroically tragic Almeda that the narrator wants to see.

This is why another set of critical readers – Morgenstern, Heller, Stich – avoids the triumphalist view. They offer instead a nuanced position summed up by Gayle Elliott's assertion about the title story of *Friend of My Youth* (1990) that a variety of feminist meta-narratives dwell at the story's heart. *There*, a reader might exclaim, lies the ultimate meaning of "Meneseteung." In this way, readings of the individual story swing back to Magdalene Redekop's apt generalization of 1992: "The pleasure of reading Alice Munro is, in the last analysis, that we catch ourselves in the act of reading" (*Mothers and Other Clowns* 25). To that, I would add "and in the act of listening."

III

We could stop here, with a sense of how Munro has once again performed a narrative act that she has been perfecting for years. We could then link that narrative destabilization with a feminist agenda – what Howells, speaking of the wilderness, terms an attempt to re-appropriate "Canada's most popular cultural myth as the elusive site of the female imagination" (113). Is that the trendy purpose that drove Munro to produce this story? Only a considerable effort can produce that detailed sense of the past that makes this story. Why bother, if one wishes only to display an ironic sense of a narrator's pretensions? Can we assume that questioning historicity inevitably leads to a superior mode of understanding? Or does something more complex lie behind Munro's bossy narrator? Briefly, Munro's narrative play takes the stuff of literature and twists it into a version of orature. Clarifying how that happens will occupy the remainder of my space here, and will compel me to investigate some of Munro's ancestry, actual and cultural.

Let me begin this exposition by considering the story in itself, and what it tells us about those whom Munro has chosen as her local ancestors. What sets "Meneseteung" apart from other Canadian fictions that recount past events through an admittedly partial and flawed narrator?[5] This: its protagonist is herself possessed of an active historical consciousness. Almeda – unlike the historical women writers she is based on – seeks deliberately to evoke whatever history her region holds. Her volume *Offerings* opens with an account of her ancestors' immediate arrival in the district. Almeda's poetry, as Munro constructs it, roams further back in time. Almeda meditates on both the history – "'Champlain at the Mouth of the Meneseteung',' based on an admittedly "popular, untrue belief" – and the geography – "'The Passing of the Old Forest'" – that have shaped her country (52). She wants to write a poem – "'The Meneseteung',' she calls it – encompassing those facts and others, enfolding them within the flow of the river that entitles her poem (70). The verses themselves that Munro produces – pastiches of Elizabeth Barrett Browning and Christina Rossetti – layer the story's costumery.

Munro's narrator dots her own remarks with brief accounts of local history, contrasting then with now: Almeda's "house is there today; the manager of the liquor store lives in it" (53). Details of both setting and overall narrative voicing juxtapose past with present in ways that violate the barriers between them. This strategy's visual equivalent forms a *mise en abyme* in which the outside narrator's historical consciousness is matched by Almeda's. Both attempt to regale their respective audiences with the pasts that they have summoned up. If Almeda's efforts strike us as hackneyed, and inaccurate, rest assured that time will discard our own contemporary speculations in a similar way.

Yet scrutinizing our own assumptions cannot blind us to the weaknesses of Almeda's. Munro rubs her readers' noses in the failings of her historical subjects. Believe me, the writers whom Munro has identified, Eloise A. Skimings and Clara H. Mountcastle ("Contributors' Notes" 322), have well earned their obscurity. More compelling examples of nineteenth-century Canadian women writers neglected during their lifetime than these – Isabella Valancy Crawford, for example – can be found. Why these two? We can only conclude that the facts of geography and history alike brought them to Munro's attention.

Location, location, location: Thacker defines "Meneseteung" as the culmination of a process whereby Munro "was able from August 1975 on to create in her fiction a new imaginative relation with Huron County" (294). He cites a phrase from Munro's manuscripts of this period that finally ends up in "Meneseteung" (298). The recycling underlines how personally engaged Munro is with her project of imaginative relocation. Had Eloise Skimings of Goderich and Clara Mountcastle of Clinton never existed, then Munro would have had to have invented them, not only because of *who* they were, but because of *where* they were. At that point, the *when* of where they were comes into play.

Pioneers, ancestors, "foremothers" as Lorraine McMullen terms them (1) present Munro with an instant family tree. Class distinctions matter deeply in Munro's fictions; her small towns fester with snobbery. "Royal Beatings," one of her finest stories, features the character Flo's savage takes on her social superiors. The title story of the *Open Secrets* volume revels in recounting the misbehaviour of the town's professional class. "Spaceships Have Landed," from the same collection, pulls up the carpet of rural pastoral and discloses the shebeens that cocoon the countryside's lowlife. But even *arrivistes* like Alice Laidlaw own a pedigree. Women writers struggled before them, and her progress in some way fulfills their broken dreams. Place and time alike in "Meneseteung" firmly locate the author within the Munro Tract and place her on a literary family tree.

For she *has* captured the sweep of local history. More than one observer has noted "Menseteung"'s mastery of historical fact and process. Douglas Glover's contention that "Poulter's landscape is industrial, pragmatic, and realistic, while Almeda will always be imagining the sweep of history, changes in environment, and the romance of Indians and early explorers" (*The Enamoured Knight* 180) rightly assumes that Munro reflects upon events in the manner of an imaginative social historian. An Italian critic, Gianfranca Balestra, views the story from a similar discursive viewpoint, noting how it commands "the intersection of history, geography and poetry" (136). Munro herself appears to agree, to want her audience to get the message. Her "Contributors' Notes" to the story's appearance in *The Best American Short Stories 1989* lists an authorial agenda that any traditional historical fictionist could recognize:

> So I thought, What about imagining one of these women and giving her some talent..., just enough to give her glimpses, stir her up? Then put her in one of those towns and see what will happen. ... I wanted to see what she would do about poetry, sex, and living, in that town, that time, when so many sturdy notions were pushing up together – the boisterous commercialism and austere hard-hearted religion, the tenacious gentility hungering for class distinction. (322-23)

Thus, the story is at once historical and contemporary. Historical in subject matter, contemporary in a narrative technique that restates what has become a trope of Munro's stories: the instability of narrative observation. Further, the story implants this vision within a specific time and place of considerable relevance to Munro's *oeuvre*. We could even conclude that this "foremothering" and foreshadowing replicate the aims of classic historical fiction, disclosing a past era's relevance to the readers'. One task remains: that of discovering how the shape of the story's narrative medium throws us into another version of story. Considering some transoceanic ancestry, beginning with the inventor of the historical novel, compels an understanding of "Meneseteung"'s affinities with orature.

IV

When Sir Walter Scott sought in retrospect to explain the onset of the historical in his imaginative life (or, less elegantly, the discovery of new material to exploit for the marketplace), he wrote that "the ancient traditions and high spirit of a people, who, living in a civilized age and country, retained so strong a tincture of manners belonging to an early period of society, must afford a subject favourable for romance" (General Preface 8).[6] Munro's remarks about her subject and purpose couch themselves in the social-science discourse of our own time. Yet in the broadest sense of the term, that strong "tincture of manners belonging to an early period of society" describes her preoccupation as well. And yes, the Matter of Huron did provide "a subject favourable for romance," using the term both in the sense of a fictional narrative, and in that of a love interest.

What we call "Scott" sums up the story's historical bent, its interest in representing a past. The adjective "Scottish" pushes my discussion toward its conclusion. "Scottish" denotes the particular tradition that Munro accesses in her work by way of giving her own twist to what I call "Scott." This Scottish influence surfaces in the very placement of the stories in *Friend of My Youth*, which interweaves her Ontario historical fiction with other, ancestral ones. The collection's title story concludes with a historical anecdote about an extreme religious sect in seventeenth-century Scotland, the Cameronians ("Friend of My Youth" 26). The Cameronians' best-known fictional appearance occurs in Scott's *Old Mortality* (1816). "Meneseteung" in turn immediately precedes "Hold Me Fast, Don't Let Me Pass," a story set in Scotland revolving around the recitation of a folk ballad about bewitchment. "Hold Me Fast" opens with an excerpt from a notebook kept by the story's narrator that contains a laconic reference to Scott. The presence in the collection of "Scott" and the "Scottish" alike testify to Munro's debt to the writer whose contemporaries termed "The Wizard of the North."

The northern excursion doesn't stop here.[7] A literal (rather than literary) ancestor of Munro dealt with similar material. James Hogg used the Cameronians as a subject for a historical novel, claiming that his conception of *The Brownie of Bodsbeck* (1818) antedated that of *Old Mortality* (Mack xii-xix). So long-past a literary set-to holds little interest for anyone but specialists now, and no single writer owns the body of historical material he or she chooses to exploit. Yet the Cameronian allusion's power reinforces Munro's associations with a writer who was a lineal ancestor.

Even now, *Castle Rock* demonstrates Munro's deep interest in that ancestral connection. "The Ettrick Shepherd" was Hogg's literary persona, a successful, Robbie Burns-like way of concocting his humble beginnings into a grab at his metropolitan audience's attention. Munro places herself within that ancestral Ettrick district; the two opening narratives in *Castle Rock* feature that location and its lore. "No Advantages," her first story, tells of Will O'Phaup, a legendary figure who was in fact a grandfather of James Hogg and a bard reputed to have enjoyed close ties to the fairy world. Will O'Phaup knew from the inside the world of oral story-making that a literate culture could only label as fairyland.

Hogg's *Brownie*, with its emphasis on "a world of vision and terror" (9), was an attempt to capture the metropolitan audience enthralled by the Scottish material that Scott had first literarily exploited. Rougher in style and structure than any of Scott's productions, *Brownie* shoves its readers into a world that the metropolis would find even more peculiar and parochial than Scott's. Munro's version of this occurs in her ballad about malevolent fairies – it could have come from Will O'Phaup – that stands at the centre of the story "Hold Me Fast." Munro's story takes a woman aware of gaps in her understanding of her dead husband and thrusts before her a group of crazies who embody the remnants of an attenuated Scottish ballad tradition. A tourist is thus forced to confront the dark actuality underpinning the bleached tourism postcard shot. Munro's use of her Scottish material allows her to create her own version of Blaikie Noble from her long-ago fiction and his Laurentian "Gothick" tourism shtick.

"Scott" in "Meneseteung" summons up the "Scottish." The pale, clichéd folkloric appearing in Almeda's poems exhales the last gasp of what had once been a living sensibility and world view.

> *The Gypsies have departed.*
> *Their camping-ground is bare.*
> *Oh, boldly would I bargain now*
> *At the Gypsy Fair.*
> . . . .
> *I sit at the bottom of sleep,*
> *As on the floor of the sea.*
> *And fanciful Citizens of the Deep*
> *Are graciously greeting me.* (62, 68)

Behind "Meneseteung" loom three sets of ancestors, cultural and actual. First we find the author's father, who himself (*The McGregors*) recalled the historical Huron matter. Then stand those two past, little-known, provincial women writers, Mountcastle and Skimings, while in deepest background swirl the ghosts of the wildly imaginative shepherds and peasants whose world Munro's *Castle Rock* now revisits.

This storied lineage extends back beyond James Hogg even. Before his novels birthed him into knighthood, Walter Scott had first successfully netted for metropolitan audiences the ancient oral ballads that he then reworked into literary poems. Many of those value-added, finished goods that proved so tempting to the literary marketplace had come from the lips of Margaret Laidlaw. She was James Hogg's spunky mother, and Alice Munro's ancestor whose last name she bore at birth. Margaret Laidlaw took considerable issue with Scott's opportunistic transcription/translation of her oral poetry into literature (Hogg, "Memoir of the Author's Life" 61-62).[8] Hers is a dying culture's lament at the commercial acumen capable of packaging her imaginative world into a harmless, beguiling spectacle of itself. She could be Sitting Bull denouncing Buffalo Bill.

What about this Scottish material that I have outlined? Does it recall nothing more than a long-past quarrel of no widespread current interest? Hardly. "Meneseteung"'s cultural authority relies upon more than a set of allusions that a curious reader can trace back to an ancestral myth. The story's fictional weight rests instead upon the foundations that its narrative mode composes, a way of storytelling reminiscent of the devices of orality.

Who is that intrusive, know-it-all narrator but a storyteller, fudging detail in order to strengthen her point, interpolating her own obsessions into the story in order to reshape whatever she feels needs to be said? "Meneseteung"'s pseudo-direct cultural quotations (the gossip sheet *The Vidette*, Almeda's poems) may both be competing voices, but it is the narrator who (literally) gets the last word. Perhaps she would offer in her defence an echo of Hogg's mother, Margaret Laidlaw: another storyteller's version of "Meneseteung" might have spoilt the material altogether. The final effect, however, of that narrative intervention spoils any critical attempt to establish a simple, linear relationship between "Meneseteung" and other Canadian historical fictions, traditional or postmodern. Because Munro wants it all! She has produced a story which appears to follow the agenda set by the traditional, continuous, and pointed historical novel but which finally slams through those guardrails, crosses the median, and drives away in the other direction of the postmodern, de-centred, and diffuse fiction familiar to us now.

Lengthy commentary elsewhere explains how traditional Canadian historical fiction emphasizes the moralization of Canadian space in time, presenting a continuous action that asserts implicitly the continuous nature of the Canadian polity (Duffy, *Sounding the Iceberg* 11-18). Briefly, two representative nineteenth-century novels – William Kirby's *The Golden Dog* (1877) and Sir Gilbert Parker's *The Seats of the Mighty* (1896) – conceived the national destiny in avowedly moralistic terms. Both asserted that moral rather than material factors brought about New France's fall. A convenient moral progress gives these narratives a teleology, Canada an unbroken history, and Canada's role within the British Empire moral significance.

You may wonder what these masculinist, imperialist, and moralistic versions of Canadian history have to do with "Meneseteung," whose implications appear the opposite. However counterintuitive this similarity, the feminist readings of the story that I have cited support my sense of kinship. For Munro also admits to an estimation of her material, ultimately moral in nature, that she wants her readers to share: Munro's two obscure women poets are "conventional, silly. Just the same, they're paying attention, they're making something. ... // ... I ended up with the poetess half mad but not, I thought, entirely unhappy in the midst of this" ("Contributors' Notes" 322-23). A writer saying that is not writing a story without a message.

Almeda Roth at her story's end has a poem in mind: "The Meneseteung." She never writes it. It has to include too much: the history, the pre-history, the climate, the mineral wealth, the exploitation of that wealth. And finally, the mess left by pressed grapes, her own menstrual blood, "and the sweat of her body that has sat all day in the closed hot room" (71). She is a woman in a masculinist culture. Her intuitive repulsion at Jarvis Poulter's manly nudge with his foot of the passed-out lower-class woman who has disturbed Almeda's rest condemns her to spinsterhood. Poulter's bloodshot eyes, which so easily take in a situation, are part of the male gaze that makes Almeda flinch. The reminder of her own sexuality, the menstrual flow that the setting grape jelly recalls to her, leads her to her renunciation. What drives her to her death? Her society's licensing of adolescent boys' casual cruelty toward undefended, solitary, eccentric females, what *The Vidette* terms "*the boldness and cruelty of some of our youth*" (72; emphasis in orig.). The feminine shivers in the blast of a culture's masculinity.

Yet this moralization of experience rubs the narrative fabric in the wrong way, against the bias as it were. That chatty narrator bleeds air from the story's message, flattening ideology's pressure. "Meneseteung" is about even more than Almeda's unwritten "The Meneseteung." Rather than fulfilling Howells' (and Munro's) feminist agendas, "Meneseteung" instead discloses only a telling anecdote about a lone woman writer who experienced what could have been either an epiphany or a drug-addled fit. As an emblem of Victorian Gothic put it, "'There's more of gravy than of grave about you'" (Dickens, "A Christmas Carol" 14). This dissolution of certainty – the sort of effect marking such blatant anti-narratives as George Bowering's *Burning Water* (1980) and Douglas Glover's *Elle* (2003) – has become a commonplace in what we can no longer call "historical novels," but rather contemporary fictions with historical settings. The problem remains: "Meneseteung" cannot be easily filed under either label.

Castle Rock's first half (3-170) and "Meneseteung"'s placement in *Friend of My Youth* immediately before "Hold Me Fast, Don't Let Me Pass" disclose what "Meneseteung" is about: using literature to ape orature. "Hold Me Fast" featured the impish balladeer Maggie Dobie. That anonymous voice of "Meneseteung"'s narrator presents a version of Maggie. "As for what was on Miss Dobie's mind, that seemed to be picked out of the air, all willfulness and caprice" ("Hold Me Fast, Don't Let Me Pass" 96). And Maggie Dobie herself? Who is she but a stand-in for the ancestral Margaret (Maggie) Hogg, the woman who flyted at Sir Walter, contemptuous of any scribbler's reduction of her wholly particularized performance to the impersonality of print? The recitation by a writer as oral storyteller that dominates the first half of *Castle Rock* dazzles its audience with her virtuosity, her ability to have it all. Call it "Some *way* I've been meaning to tell you." That way is the way of the storyteller, unabashedly intervening, shamelessly inventive, about as trustworthy as a real estate agent spiking a "For Sale" sign into a bog.

"Meneseteung" spins our historical fiction toward its origins, back into the oral transmission of the past that was there before the scribes and the sculptors – Ozymandias' thralls – began having their way with it. The job has its drawbacks. "The Father of History," that is the man who invented the history *book*, got called "the father of lies" for his pains. All Herodotus did to earn that obloquy was to jot down the tales of the peoples he so painstakingly visited and thus carry their voices over the gap between their tellings and his writings. His critics can never forgive him this.

There is a Lachine Canal in Montreal because Cartier hoped that China lay right over the horizon. He got the white water of the Long Sault instead. Munro's call to her readers to pay their respects to her foremothers emerges from a bullhorn distorting that call and focussing a hearer's attention upon the medium rather than the message. Her narrative play keeps the message at bay. In doing so, she offers an alternative version of history, another way of expressing the angularity of being-in-time. Call it a written version of oral history. Better, call it conversation.

Notes

1. John Cooke (81-85) surveys the tangled question of just what sort of painting style parallels Munro's literary work. See also Magdalene Redekop's "Alice Munro's Tilting Fields."
2. Munro's "Working for a Living" (140-41) describes one of these road trips.
3. At some point in the early 1970s, novelist Hugh Hood told me of a visit that Munro had made to his house, during which he read to her passages from *The Prelude* that moved them both to tears.
4. I am recalling such masterpieces of historical fiction as H.F.M. Prescott's *The Man on a Donkey* (1952), Marguerite Yourcenar's *Memoirs of Hadrian* (1954), and Zoé Oldenbourg's *The World Is Not Enough* (1948). Is it a coincidence that all these works, which immediately sprang to mind when I searched for examples of successful and noteworthy historical fiction, have been written by women?
5. Rudy Wiebe's "Where Is the Voice Coming From?" – with its bland, final statement that "I do not, of course, understand the Cree myself" (143) in a story that purports to set the reader straight about an incident in the life of a Cree – presents a classic instance of this contemporary strategy in Canadian historical fiction.

6. For a detailed examination of a primal novelist's turn from poetry to historical fiction, see Jane Millgate's *Walter Scott: The Making of the Novelist* (3-57).

7. Magdalene Redekop's generous, insightful reading of an earlier draft of this essay thrust me into considering the import of Munro's homage to James Hogg; that in turn forced my rethinking of my earlier interpretation of "Meneseteung." See also Redekop's "Alice Munro and the Scottish Nostalgic Grotesque."

8. "'[T]here was never ane o' my sangs prentit till ye prentit them yoursell, an' ye hae spoilt them a'thegither. They war made for singing, an' no for reading; and they're nouther right spelled nor right setten down'" (Hogg, "Memoir of the Author's Life" 62).

Works Cited

Arnold, Matthew. "Dover Beach." *The Poetical Works of Matthew Arnold.* Ed. C.B. Tinker and H.F. Lowry. London: Oxford UP, 1950. 210-12.

Balestra, Gianfranca. "Alice Munro as Historian and Geographer: A Reading of 'Meneseteung'." *Intersections: la narrativa canadese tra storia e geografia.* Ed. Liana Nissim and Carlo Pagetti. Bologna, It.: Cisalpino, 1999. 119-36. Quaderni di Acme 38.

Bowering, George. *Burning Water.* Don Mills, ON: Musson, 1980.

Boyden, Joseph. *Three Day Road.* Toronto: Viking Canada-Penguin, 2005.

Browning, Elizabeth Barrett. *The Poetical Works of Elizabeth Barrett Browning; with Two Prose Essays.* London: Oxford UP, 1916.

Burne-Jones, Sir Edward Coley. *King Cophetua and the Beggar Maid.* 1884. <http://www.tate.org.uk/art/artworks/burne-jones-king-cophetua-and-the-beggar-maid-n01771>.

Burns, Robert. *Burns: Poems and Songs.* Ed. James Kinsley. London: Oxford UP, 1969. Oxford Standard Authors.

Campbell, Wilfred. *A Beautiful Rebel: A Romance of Upper Canada in Eighteen Hundred and Twelve.* Toronto: Westminster, 1909.

Cervantes, Miguel de. *The Ingenious Gentleman Don Quixote de La Mancha.* Trans. and introd. Samuel Putnam. New York: Modern Library, 1949.

Chambers, Jack. *Summer Behind the House.* 1963. *Friend of My Youth.* By Alice Munro. Toronto: Penguin, 1991. Front cover.

Cooke, John. *The Influence of Painting on Five Canadian Writers: Alice Munro, Hugh Hood, Timothy Findley, Margaret Atwood, and Michael Ondaatje.* Lewiston, NY: Edwin Mellen, 1990. Canadian Studies 10.

Crawford, Isabella Valancy. *The Collected Poems of Isabella Valancy Crawford.* Ed. J.W. Garvin. Toronto: William Briggs, 1905. Rpt. as *Collected Poems.* Introd. James Reaney. Toronto: U of Toronto P, 1972. Literature of Canada: Poetry and Prose in Reprint.

Dickens, Charles. "A Christmas Carol." *Christmas Books.* 1892. London: Macmillan, 1928. 1-73.

Duffy, Dennis. "'A Dark Sort of Mirror': 'The Love of a Good Woman' as Pauline Poetic." *Alice Munro Writing On....* Ed. Robert Thacker. *Essays on Canadian Writing* 66 (1998): 169-90. Rpt. in *The Rest of the Story: Critical Essays on Alice Munro.* Ed. Robert Thacker. Toronto: ECW, 1999. 169-90.

---. *Sounding the Iceberg: An Essay on Canadian Historical Novels.* Toronto: ECW, 1986.

Elliott, Gayle. "'A Different Tack': Feminist Meta-Narrative in Alice Munro's 'Friend of My Youth'." *Journal of Modern Literature* 20 (1996): 75-84.

Findley, Timothy. *The Wars.* Toronto: Clarke, Irwin, 1977.

Glover, Douglas. *Elle.* Fredericton: Goose Lane, 2003.

---. *The Enamoured Knight.* Ottawa: Oberon, 2004.

Gombrich, E.H. *Art and Illusion: A Study in the Psychology of Pictorial Representation.* New York: Pantheon, 1960. Bolingen Ser. XXXV·5.

Hébert, Anne. *Kamouraska.* Trans. Norman Shapiro. Toronto: Musson, 1973.

Heller, Deborah. "Getting Loose: Women and Narration in Alice Munro's *Friend of My Youth.*" *Alice Munro Writing On....* Ed. Robert Thacker. *Essays on Canadian Writing* 66 (1998): 60-80. Rpt. in *The Rest of the Story: Critical Essays on Alice Munro.* Ed. Robert Thacker. Toronto: ECW, 1999. 60-80.

Herodotus. *The Histories.* Trans. Aubrey de Sélincourt. New ed. Rev. John Marincola. London: Penguin, 1996.

Hogg, James. *The Brownie of Bodsbeck.* Ed. Douglas S. Mack. Edinburgh: Scottish Academic, 1976.

---. "Memoir of the Author's Life." *Memoir of the Author's Life* and *Familiar Anecdotes of Sir Walter Scott.* Ed. Douglas S. Mack. Edinburgh: Scottish Academic, 1972. 1-81.

Houston, Pam. "A Hopeful Sign: The Making of Metonymic Meaning in Munro's 'Meneseteung'." *The Kenyon Review* ns 14.4 (1992): 79-92.

Howells, Coral Ann. *Alice Munro.* Manchester, Eng.: Manchester UP, 1998. Contemporary World Writers.

Hugo, Victor. *Notre-Dame of Paris.* 1831. Trans. and ed. John Sturrock. London: Penguin, 2004.

James, Henry. *The Spoils of Poynton.* 1897. Harmondsworth, Eng.: Penguin, 1963.

James, P.D. *The Children of Men.* London: Faber and Faber, 1992.

Johnston, Wayne. *The Colony of Unrequited Dreams.* Toronto: Alfred A. Knopf Canada, 1998.

Keats, John. "To J.H. Reynolds: 3 May 1818." *The Letters of John Keats: 1814-1821.* Ed. Hyder Edward Rollins. Vol. 1. Cambridge, MA: Harvard UP, 1958. 275-83. 2 vols.

King, The Rt. Hon. William Lyon Mackenzie. Speech. Canada. *House of Commons Debates.* 18th Parliament, 1st Session: Vol. 4. 18 June 1936: 3862-73.

Kirby, William. *The Golden Dog (Le Chien d'Or): A Romance of Old Quebec.* 1877. Toronto: Musson, 1925.

Laidlaw, Robert. *The McGregors: A Novel of an Ontario Pioneer Family.* Toronto: Macmillan of Canada, 1979.

Leacock, Stephen. *Sunshine Sketches of a Little Town.* 1912. Afterword by Jack Hodgins. Toronto: McClelland & Stewart, 1989. The New Canadian Library.

Mack, Douglas S. Introduction. *The Brownie of Bodsbeck.* By James Hogg. Ed. Douglas S. Mack. Edinburgh: Scottish Academic, 1976. ix-xix.

McCarthy, Dermot. "The Woman Out Back: Alice Munro's 'Meneseteung'." *Studies in Canadian Literature / Études en littérature canadienne* 19.1 (1994): 1-19.

McMullen, Lorraine. Introduction. *Re(Dis)covering Our Foremothers: Nineteenth-Century Canadian Women Writers.* Ed. and introd. Lorraine McMullen. Ottawa: U of Ottawa P, 1990. 1-4. Reappraisals: Canadian Writers 15.

Millais, Sir John Everett. *Ophelia.* 1852. <http://www.tate.org.uk/art/artworks/millais-ophelia-n01506>.

Millgate, Jane. *Walter Scott: The Making of the Novelist.* Toronto: U of Toronto P, 1984.

Morgenstern, Naomi. "The Baby or the Violin?: Ethics and Femininity in the Fiction of Alice Munro." *LIT: Literature Interpretation Theory* 14.2 (2003): 69-97.

Mountcastle, Clara H. *The Mission of Love; Lost; and Other Poems, with Songs and Valentines*. By Caris Sima. Toronto: Hunter, Rose, 1882.

Munro, Alice. "The Beggar Maid." *Who Do You Think You Are?* Toronto: Macmillan of Canada, 1978. 65-97. Rpt. in *The Beggar Maid: Stories of Flo and Rose*. New York: Alfred A. Knopf, 1979. 68-100.

---. *The Beggar Maid: Stories of Flo and Rose*. New York: Alfred A. Knopf, 1979.

---. "Contributors' Notes." *The Best American Short Stories 1989*. Ed. Margaret Atwood with Shannon Ravenal. Introd. Margaret Atwood. Boston: Houghton Mifflin, 1989. 322-23.

---. "Friend of My Youth." *Friend of My Youth*. Toronto: McClelland & Stewart, 1990. 3-26.

---. *Friend of My Youth*. Toronto: McClelland & Stewart, 1990.

---. *Friend of My Youth*. Toronto: Penguin, 1991.

---. "Hold Me Fast, Don't Let Me Pass." *Friend of My Youth*. Toronto: McClelland & Stewart, 1990. 74-105.

---. *Lives of Girls and Women*. Toronto: McGraw-Hill Ryerson, 1971.

---. "Meneseteung." *The New Yorker* 11 Jan. 1988: 28-38. Rpt. in *The Best American Short Stories 1989*. Ed. Margaret Atwood with Shannon Ravenel. Introd. Margaret Atwood. Boston: Houghton Mifflin, 1989. 247-68.

---. "Meneseteung." *Friend of My Youth*. Toronto: McClelland & Stewart, 1990. 50-73.

---. "No Advantages." *The View from Castle Rock*. Toronto: McClelland & Stewart, 2006. 3-26.

---. "Open Secrets." *Open Secrets*. Toronto: McClelland & Stewart, 1994. 129-60.

---. "Royal Beatings." *Who Do You Think You Are?* Toronto: Macmillan of Canada, 1978. 1-22.

---. "Something I've Been Meaning To Tell You." *Something I've Been Meaning To Tell You*. Toronto: McGraw-Hill Ryerson, 1974. 1-23.

---. "Spaceships Have Landed." *Open Secrets*. Toronto: McClelland & Stewart, 1994. 226-60.

---. "The View from Castle Rock." *The View from Castle Rock*. Toronto: McClelland & Stewart, 2006. 27-87.

---. *The View from Castle Rock*. Toronto: McClelland & Stewart, 2006.

---. "Walker Brothers Cowboy." *Dance of the Happy Shades*. Fwd. Hugh Garner. Toronto: Ryerson, 1968. 1-18.

---. *Who Do You Think You Are?* Toronto: Macmillan of Canada, 1978.

---. "Working for a Living." *The View from Castle Rock*. Toronto: McClelland & Stewart, 2006. 127-70.

Oldenbourg, Zoé. *The World Is Not Enough*. Trans. Willard R. Trask. New York: Pantheon, 1948.

Ondaatje, Michael. *In the Skin of a Lion*. Toronto: McClelland and Stewart, 1987.

Orwell, George. *Nineteen Eighty-Four*. London: Secker & Warburg, 1949.

Parker, Sir Gilbert. *The Seats of the Mighty: Being the Memoirs of Captain Robert Moray, Sometime an Officer in the Virginia Regiment and Afterwards of Amherst's Regiment*. 1896. New York: Scribner's, 1913. Vol. 9 of *The Works of Gilbert Parker*. Imperial Ed. 24 vols. 1912-23.

Potter, Beatrix. *The Tale of Mrs. Tiggy-Winkle*. London: Frederick Warne, 1905.

Prescott, H.F.M. *The Man on a Donkey: A Chronicle*. 2 vols. London: Eyre & Spottiswoode, 1952.

Proust, Marcel. *Remembrance of Things Past*. Trans. C.K. Scott Moncrieff and Terence Kilmartin et al. 3 vols. London: Chatto and Windus, 1981.

Reaney, James. *The Donnellys: A Trilogy*. With Scholarly Apparatus by James Noonan. Victoria: Porcépic, 1983. Rpt. as *The Donnellys: Sticks and Stones; The St. Nicholas Hotel; Handcuffs*. Introd. Alan Filewod. Toronto: Dundurn, 2008. Voyageur Classics.

Redekop, Magdalene. "Alice Munro and the Scottish Nostalgic Grotesque." *Alice Munro Writing On...*. Ed. Robert Thacker. *Essays on Canadian Writing* 66 (1998): 21-43. Rpt. in *The Rest of the Story: Critical Essays on Alice Munro*. Ed. Robert Thacker. Toronto: ECW, 1999. 21-43.

---. "Alice Munro's Tilting Fields." *New Worlds: Discovering and Constructing the Unknown in Anglophone Literature: Presented to Walter Pache on the Occasion of His 60th Birthday*. Ed. Martin Kuester, Gabriele Christ, and Rudolf Beck. München, Ger.: Ernst Vögel, 2000. 343-62. Schriften der Philosophischen Fakultäten der Universität Augsburg 59.

---. *Mothers and Other Clowns: The Stories of Alice Munro.* London: Routledge, 1992.

The Reuben R. Sallows Digital Library: A Collection of Historic Photography. The Reuben R. Sallows Gallery, Goderich Public Library, Goderich, ON. <www.sallowsgallery.ca>.

Richardson, John. *Wacousta: or, The Prophecy; A Tale of the Canadas.* 1832. Ed. Douglas Cronk. Ottawa: Carleton UP, 1987. Centre for Editing Early Canadian Texts Ser. 4.

Rossetti, Christina. *Poems and Prose.* Ed. and introd. Simon Humphries. Oxford, Eng.: Oxford UP, 2008. Oxford World's Classics.

Scott, Sir Walter. General Preface. *Waverley.* Pref. James C. Corson. London: J.M. Dent & Sons, 1969. 5-20. Everyman's Library.

---. *Minstrelsy of the Scottish Border.* Ed. Thomas Henderson. London: George G. Harrap, 1931.

---. *Old Mortality.* 1816. Edinburgh: Adam & Charles Black, 1886. Vol. 5 of *Waverley Novels.* Centenary Ed. 25 vols. 1886-87.

---. *Waverley; or 'Tis Sixty Years Since.* 1814. Edinburgh: Adam & Charles Black, 1886. Vol. 1 of *Waverley Novels.* Centenary Ed. 25 vols. 1886-87.

Shakespeare, William. *Hamlet.* Ed. Harold Jenkins. London: Methuen, 1982. The Arden Edition of the Works of William Shakespeare.

Shelley, Percy Bysshe. "Ozymandias." *The Complete Poetical Works of Percy Bysshe Shelley.* 1904. Ed. Thomas Hutchinson. London: Oxford UP, 1960. 546. Oxford Standard Authors.

Sienkiewicz, Henryk. *"Quo Vadis": A Narrative of the Time of Nero.* Trans. Jeremiah Curtin. Boston: Little, Brown, 1896.

Skimings, Eloise A. *Golden Leaves.* Goderich, ON: Signal, 1904.

Stich, Klaus P. "Letting Go with the Mind: Dionysus and Medusa in Alice Munro's 'Meneseteung'." *Canadian Literature* 169 (2001): 106-25.

Thacker, Robert. *Alice Munro: Writing Her Lives: A Biography.* Toronto: McClelland & Stewart, 2005.

Tolstoy, Leo. *War and Peace.* Trans. Constance Garnett. New York: Modern Library, 1931.

Trofimenkoff, Susan Mann. *The Dream of Nation: A Social and Intellectual History of Quebec.* Toronto: Macmillan of Canada, 1982.

Urquhart, Jane. *The Stone Carvers.* Toronto: McClelland & Stewart, 2001.

Van Rys, John C. "Reclaiming Marginalia: The Grotesque and the Christian Reader." *Christianity and Literature* 44 (1994-95): 345-57.

Wiebe, Rudy. *The Temptations of Big Bear.* Toronto: McClelland and Stewart, 1973.

---. "Where Is the Voice Coming From?" *Where Is the Voice Coming From?* Toronto: McClelland and Stewart, 1974. 135-43.

Wordsworth, William. "Lines Composed a Few Miles above Tintern Abbey." *The Poetical Works of Wordsworth; with Introductions and Notes.* Ed. Thomas Hutchinson. New Ed. Rev. Ernest de Selincourt. 1936. London: Oxford UP, 1950. 163-65.

---. *The Prelude; or, Growth of a Poet's Mind: An Autobiographical Poem.* [1850 version.] *The Poetical Works of Wordsworth; with Introductions and Notes.* Ed. Thomas Hutchinson. New Ed. Rev. Ernest de Selincourt. 1936. London: Oxford UP, 1950. 494-588.

---. *The Prelude; or, Growth of a Poet's Mind (Text of 1805).* Ed. Ernest de Selincourt. 2nd ed. Rev. Helen Darbishire. London: Oxford UP, 1960.

Yourcenar, Marguerite. *Memoirs of Hadrian.* Trans. Grace Frick in collaboration with the author. New York: Farrar, Straus and Young, 1954.

"The Region That I Know":
The Bioregional View in Alice Munro's
The View from Castle Rock

Alec Follett

Elizabeth looked out over southern Ontario, the land beneath them,
oddly misshapen squares of dark green, black and yellow.
Here and there were farmhouses and barns.
To one side, there were the woods.
And beyond, the crab shape of a small town....
This was who she was.
— André Alexis, *Pastoral* (157)

Souwesto is not flat!
— James Reaney, "Souwesto" (37)

... making our way to Chatham,
Buxton, waiting as they once waited for Black travellers like us,
blanketed, tracked in this cold shimmering.
— Dionne Brand, "Islands Vanish" (74)

Want a different ethic? Tell a different story.
— Thomas King, *The Truth about Stories: A Native Narrative* (164)

I am still partly convinced that this river – not even the whole river,
but this little stretch of it – will provide whatever myths you want,
whatever adventures. I name the plants,
I name the fish, and every name seems to me triumphant,
every leaf and quick fish remarkably valuable.
This ordinary place is sufficient, everything here
touchable and mysterious.
— Alice Munro, "Everything Here Is Touchable and Mysterious" ([33])

On a spring weekend you may find me standing on the shore of Point Pelee National Park, with binoculars in hand and neck craned, witnessing an otherworldly display in which over three hundred species of birds gather to rest before continuing north to their summer breeding grounds. And yet, this wonderful event is of this world. More specifically, it is of this region known as Southwestern Ontario, or "Souwesto." This migratory phenomenon occurs because of the unique combination of a kilometres-long peninsula, a comforting Carolinian forest, a recent attempt at conservation, and the birds, of course. Spring migration could not happen, as it does at Point Pelee, in any other place in the world. In Souwesto, wonder is found in such sublime natural events. It is also found in the mundane, if you know how to look for it.

Because "everything here," as Alice Munro writes about her Souwesto home, is "touchable and mysterious" ("Everything" [33]), my drive to and from Point Pelee is as important as any miraculous encounters I may have on The Point. My journey southwest on Highway 401 from my home in Guelph past Cambridge, Ingersoll, London, the Chippewas of the Thames First Nation and Munsee-Delaware Nation communities, Thamesville, and Chatham allows me to break free of the immense gravitational pull of the Greater Toronto Area and provides me with an opportunity to wonder about my present surroundings. I wonder, in both senses of the word: I am amazed and I am curious. As I move across Southwestern Ontario I wonder at the often violent, yet sometimes generative, confluence of human and environmental histories shared across the region. I also wonder at the many differences within the region.

While I think my way across this agricultural region dotted with towns and cities, and farms and forests, I find myself recalling four other pieces of Southwestern Ontario literature besides individual pieces by Munro: André Alexis's novel *Pastoral,* James Reaney's poem "Souwesto," Dionne Brand's poem "Islands Vanish," and Thomas King's Massey Lectures *The Truth about Stories.* These works, among others, help me appreciate this region nestled between two Great Lakes. When I layer Alexis's story onto farmhouses and fields, I understand that beneath any idyllic views are individuals working through complicated interpersonal relationships and even more complicated relationships with the land. Nevertheless, I am wary about treating as uniform the region's various peoples and environments: for as Reaney asserts, "Souwesto is not flat!" (37).

Indeed, there are important, if often subtle, cultural and environmental shifts between the region's eastern and western points. Roadways reduce from three lanes to two, there are fewer forests and fewer coniferous trees, and there are larger plots of farmland. Many of these fields are fallow; some are topped with greenhouses, while others are topped with pumpjacks or wind turbines. There are also important differences among the ways in which people relate to the region, depending on such factors as race, gender, and class. For the Black characters in Brand's poem, the snowstorm that may worry some travellers is of little concern in comparison to the police officer who stops their car and unfairly questions their presence in the region. Daily life in Souwesto is ordinary and far from that. Rather than suppressing the region's complexities, attempts to be attentive and open to its peoples, histories, and surroundings can do much to help us live well, or dwell, in relation to each other and the environment in Souwesto.

Finding wonder in the mundane requires attentive observation and honest reflection, at least in part. Yet while this approach can help us develop our relationship with our immediate environments, whether or not we are amazed and curious about our surroundings depends a great deal upon the narratives that we embrace. The stories that we are told, tell ourselves, or tell others change the ways we relate to our surroundings, for better or for worse. Discussing North Americans' suspect environmental ethics, Thomas King explains: "We've created the stories that allow them to exist and flourish. They didn't come out of nowhere. They didn't arrive from another planet. // Want a different ethic? Tell a different story" (164). Although narratives are powerful, we have the ability to create, or turn to, "a different story" with "a different ethic." While a great many narratives are needed to represent and to sustain the myriad peoples and landscapes of Southwestern Ontario, in this essay I want to turn to one important Souwesto narrative: Alice Munro's semi-fictional family history, *The View from Castle Rock*. I find special promise in this volume because it encourages readers to adopt a different environmental ethic by finding wonder in their ordinary lives.

The View from Castle Rock provides a detailed exploration of how stories influence the relationship characters have with their surroundings. The first section of the book presents a semi-fictional history of Munro's ancestors who emigrate from Scotland to North America in the early nineteenth century, but struggle to dwell in their new homes because of beliefs or narratives that distance them from their environment. In the second half of the book – a set of semi-autobiographical stories that draws on Munro's life – a young woman grapples with this intellectual inheritance and as she matures she becomes a writer who learns to craft her own stories about how to live well in the region. Despite the protagonist's development, this second group of stories is not a depiction of a region moving from an unjust past to a just future or a how-to guide; it is far from linear or didactic. Rather, Munro is inquisitive, ambiguous, even ironic, thereby continuing her longstanding effort that in the words of critic Ajay Heble "acknowledges the importance of examining *how* it is that we can claim to know something" (14). Indeed, Munro's emphasis on *how* the people of Huron County came to know their surroundings gives *The View from Castle Rock* its environmental import.

Most of the characters in the volume are satisfied with simply knowing; yet although confident, these characters know less about their region than they believe they do. In contrast, Munro, as a character, narrator, and writer, probes *how* we know. Accordingly, Munro constructs an environmentally engaged worldview in which her relationship to her region is always developing. In sum, Munro *wonders*. She challenges restrictive narratives that limit one's ability to dwell and instead develops her own narratives that portray the area around her hometown of Wingham in Huron Country as an ordinary place full of wonder. Presenting daily life with wonder is an important aspect of the story "The View from Castle Rock" according to Corinne Bigot, who states that the narrative "challenges the divide between the sacred and the profane" (33). Extending Bigot's argument, I would propose that such an approach is central not only to the title story but to the volume as a whole. Through her amazement and curiosity about the mundane, Munro offers encouragement to people living in what is now affectionately known as "Alice Munro Country," in the whole of Souwesto, and beyond to treat their intertwined human and environmental surroundings as unique locations worthy of wonder, and therefore value, care, and respect.

Writing, like Munro's, that encourages people to interact with their surroundings is an act of care for one's community. In *The Bioregional Imagination* Lynch, Glotfelty, and Armbruster explain that "By reflecting and respecting the context – both cultural and natural – of specific places, bioregional literature and criticism make a powerful statement that where you are matters" (18). Munro's narratives evoke what critic Laurie Ricou calls a "regional allegiance" whose impetus "is not property rights, but imaginative rights, the need of a community, expressed in story, to take care of itself" (100). Environmentally attuned regional writing like Munro's inspires a community "to take care of itself" by supporting the well-being of the intertwined human and environmental relationships within given environmental regions. Bioregional literature and criticism does so by encouraging people to *dwell*, which for Lynch, Glotfelty, and Armbruster "means to live mindfully and deeply in place, to be fully engaged to the sensory richness of our immediate environment" (5) in a way that generates *sustainability* and works toward the restoration, or *reinhabitation*, of previously maltreated environments. To write one's region is a necessary pursuit that helps readers, myself included, who hope that by better understanding their surroundings they can contribute to their community through encouraging all local people and environments to thrive, now and in the future, in spite of past social and environmental ills.

But how exactly does Munro's use of wonder help awaken a community to a bioregional consciousness? Historian William Cronon explains the environmental potential of finding wonder in the ordinary. In contrast to the dominant perspective that locates wonder in the wilderness, Cronon argues that we can find wonder in daily life. He contends that "the tree in the garden is in reality no less other, no less worthy of our wonder and respect, than the tree in an ancient forest" (24). To find wonder in the mundane, not just in the wilderness, can help us dwell in, and care for, our bioregion as our home "where finally we make our living ... for which we take responsibility" (24).

Building on Cronon, ecocritic Louise Economides argues that finding wonder in the mundane is "an aesthetic response that celebrates difference, welcomes the unforeseen, and opens up a space for inquiry rather than valorizing already established meaning"; hence, "wonder is vital to emergent, postmodern ways of thinking ecologically" (23). Because wonder prompts open and attentive interaction, it can help people strengthen their relationship with their region. To attend to one's surroundings with wonder – amazement, curiosity, and an ability to celebrate the unexpected – encourages a bioregional perspective in which people are attuned to the land and to the other people and beings that share the same region.

Munro has a longstanding interest in approaching the mundane with a sense of wonder. In *Alice Munro: Writing Her Lives*, Munro's biographer Robert Thacker highlights her passionate commitment to her ordinary yet mysterious surroundings:

> This stretch along the [Meneseteung /] Maitland [River] by the Laidlaws' farm is a real place certainly, but more significantly it is the place that has fed Alice Munro's imagination since she began writing there during her teenage years, and she has drawn on it ever since – an "ordinary place," her own site for her imaginings, it "is sufficient, everything here touchable and mysterious." This place – Munro's own "home place" – is multifaceted, made up of a specific physical and cultural geography, the surrounding society populated by the people Munro knew, or knew of, and infused with the culture she herself came to own, embody, and understand. ... Her writing derives almost wholly from that "little stretch" along the Meneseteung / Maitland River, from the surrounding Lower Town, from Wingham and Huron County more generally. (46)

By making use of her ordinary surroundings as inspiration for her writing, Munro provides sophisticated representations of a place made worthy of attention not only because of her ability to capture the region's unique intertwined culture and environment, but because of her ability to render her surroundings as always full of wonder.

Despite Munro's interest in her region's mysteries, finding wonder in the ordinary was hard-earned for Munro because the Scots-Irish culture she was raised in discouraged her from inquiring about her environment. In *Alice Munro: A Double Life*, Catherine Sheldrick Ross explains that Huron County in the first half of the twentieth century was a place where being anything but ordinary was looked down upon. Wanting to be a "remarkable" individual was unacceptable and so was the desire "to celebrate" or to share the region's "secrets" (Ross 17, 21). In other words, the region and its people were ordinary – hard-working, practical, and reserved.

While this outlook may have spurred her obsession with the quotidian, it did not encourage Munro, or others, to dwell, or find wonder in their surroundings. Consequently, Munro experienced "a lifelong split between ordinary life and the secret life of the imagination" (Ross 17). One of Munro's many literary achievements is that in addition to representing the region in its complexity, her writing proposes an alternative to the social mores that dominated her childhood and her region. She does so by peeking through the façade of daily life to find that there is a mysterious and often wondrous hidden existence that must be seen if people are to live well. With imaginative agility Munro circles her ordinary surroundings and illuminates the wonders they hold.

One of the many rewards of reading *The View from Castle Rock* is that it considers the region's unique cultural and literary inheritance and offers new narratives that encourage community-oriented, environmentally-focussed ways of engaging with the region. For critic Katie Trumpener, Munro's writing "explores the ways a flat, uninflected, unrecorded, apparently inconsequential place not only produces but also necessitates literature" (53). Indeed, *The View from Castle Rock* is a necessary literary effort about a place in which Munro and by extension the reader lay claim to their right to participate fully in regional life, to be open to its peoples and environments, and to imagine what may be possible should we emphasize that our ordinary, yet unique, wondrous, and ever-changing surroundings deserve our care now and in the future.

Struggling To Dwell in Alice Munro Country

Munro's strength as a bioregionalist is evident in *The View from Castle Rock*'s ruminations on dwelling. In "Part One: No Advantages," Munro imagines her Scottish ancestors who settled in North America, yet struggled to dwell. These stories span several generations of Munro's semi-fictionalized family, many of whom were storytellers, thereby reaffirming critic Claire Omhovère's observation that "when Alice Munro is writing about place, she is also primarily *writing about* writing about place" (27). In the book's foreword, Munro writes about how her ancestors write place. Highlighting their interest in storytelling, she explains: "And I was lucky, in that every generation of our family seemed to produce somebody who went in for writing long, outspoken, sometimes outrageous letters, and detailed recollections" ([ix]).

While this extraordinary family trait serves as an invaluable primary resource for Munro's writing, her stories suggest that even those ancestors who are not writers still define their surroundings through particular and sometimes limiting stories – whether they are told by others or are ones people tell themselves based on highly personal perspectives involving issues such as age, gender, and nationality. In other words, even ordinary people story their world for better or for worse. Accordingly, the first half of the volume explores how stories define settlers' relationships with their environs. Specifically, Munro explores how narratives based on different philosophies such as Enlightenment rationalism and nineteenth-century romanticism influence Scottish settlers' perceptions of their surroundings in ways that discourage them from dwelling.

James Laidlaw, the early nineteenth-century patriarch of the title story, "The View from Castle Rock," will never be satisfied with his surroundings. At first, James is obsessive in his belief that America with its modern practices is the land of promise, whereas his downtrodden and superstitious home in Ettrick, Scotland is just the opposite. But although he tells everyone grand stories about America while in Scotland, once he and his family set sail for Canada West James becomes nostalgic for Ettrick. He states that North America "'cannot be my home'" (80) and tells stories that romanticize Ettrick as a marvellous place. Although James changes what side of the Atlantic he likes best, his stories signify an unwavering aversion to the location where he must live and curiosity and amazement about the location where he is not residing. His nostalgic view, in which wonder and care are always located elsewhere, limits his ability to dwell anywhere.

James's son Walter is also a storyteller, but unlike James's largely nostalgic oral tales Walter's narratives are largely objective journal entries. Walter believes journalling is a practical pursuit that will inform Scottish readers about his journey. He explains his process to a fellow passenger, Mr. Carbert: "'I only write what happens…. I am writing to keep track of every day so that at the end of the voyage I can send a letter home'" (60). For Walter, the act of writing is justifiable if it is reduced to work and if it can reflect his experiences in an impartial manner. However, his interlocutor undercuts Walter's beliefs by suggesting that writing is subjective: "'So you do not describe what you see? Only what – as you say – is happening?'" (60). Walter becomes confused, because he has just been thinking "if he writes that there is a rough wind, is that not describing?" (60).

Walter's struggle to differentiate between "describing" and "happening" suggests that despite his goal, he will never be able to produce purely mimetic accounts of his travels and that trying to be objective may limit his ability to represent his experiences. Although he is embedded in his environment and has a personal, sensory response to his surroundings, the philosophical underpinnings of his view require him to downplay any possible personal sense of amazement or curiosity. Consequently, he is unable to use writing as a means of helping him develop a deeper relationship with his environs.

Like Munro, Walter is prompted by his social context to separate writing from life, but the story's narrator, and by extension Munro, challenges these cultural norms by synthesizing Walter's and James's perspectives together within a single smooth description to show what is possible when narrative foregrounds the storyteller's relationship with her or his surroundings. On their own, Walter's rational journals and James's romantic oratory limit their ability to dwell in America, but when combined they may offer a way of responding to one's surroundings that encourages dwelling. The narrator brings together the best of each perspective in a passage joyfully depicting the first sight of Nova Scotia by rephrasing Walter's objective journals with simile- and metaphor-rich language that helps evoke a sense of amazement and curiosity:

> This is the day of *wonders*. The land is covered with trees like a head with hair and behind the ship the sun rises tipping the top trees with light. The sky is clear and shining as a china plate and the water just playfully ruffled with wind. Every wisp of fog has gone and the air is full of the resinous smell of the trees. Seabirds are flashing above the sails all golden like creatures of Heaven. (65; emphasis added)

The narrator takes James's romantic excitement about places and unites it with Walter's matter-of-fact interest in his surroundings, thereby using writing to emphasize both the emotional and the sensory impact of one's environs.

Unlike James and Walter who are antagonistic toward each other because each is committed to his own belief, the narrator is open to both perspectives. Through her broadmindedness, she generates a subjective and self-expressive style of writing that finds wonder in the immediate environment. Of course this is a calculated illusion, because the narrator is not literally present on the ship. Nevertheless, this type of narrative encourages a dwelling attitude that stresses the value of approaching one's surroundings with subjective and open engagement, rather than, in James's view, as something to be feared, or, in Walter's view, as something to be placed under rational domination.

The title story's preoccupations with the relationship between writing and life and with how narratives alter characters' relationships to their surroundings are reframed in the final story of the first section through a character's troubling turn to a particular sort of literary work popular at the time. Munro's father, as portrayed in "Working for a Living," turns to stories that shape the way he interacts with his region, promoting a "romantic" (132) environmentalism based on an individual's strength over the land. After reading "the myths or half-myths about wilderness" (131) found in James Fenimore Cooper's *Leatherstocking Tales*, Munro's father gives up farm work and takes to the woodlots and waterways alone where he works as a trapper until returning to a different kind of farming, breeding foxes for their pelts. Reading Cooper allows Munro's father an intimate connection to his region that stands in contrast to the attitude of prior generations whose farming practices disregarded and destroyed local flora, fauna, and landforms. And yet he still struggles to dwell because his work as a trapper and as a breeder continues the domination over the land practised by his ancestors.

As the narrator explains about early farming practices in the region,

> The farms had been cleared in the period between 1830 and 1860, when the Huron Tract was being opened up, and they were cleared thoroughly. Many creeks had been dredged – the progressive thing to do was to straighten them out and make them run like tame canals between the fields. The early farmers hated the very sight of a tree and admired the look of open land. And the masculine approach to the land was managerial, dictatorial. Only women were allowed to care about landscape and not to think always of its subjugation and productivity. (130)

For critic Caitlin Charman, this practical and organizational approach to land highlights a way "power is imposed" (269) by the men who settled the Huron Tract. Their obsession with controlling the landscape means they cannot approach their region with any sense of wonder. Trees, rivers, animals, and people who are different from the settlers, and their aims, are not met with wonder, but are "cleared" or "tame[d]" by a "managerial" and "dictatorial" settler masculinity (130) – as opposed to a feminine approach involving "care" for beings (130), regardless of their benefit to settler goals.

While Cooper's romances provide Munro's father with a deeper understanding of the region, his absorption with this material nevertheless results in his desire to control the environment in a way that is similar to dominant settler beliefs. Reading Cooper pushes her father to explore his surroundings, beyond the barns and fields, and to learn where and how the animals live. However, any bioregional potential is lost because instead of approaching a river, or foxes, with wonder, settler romances dictate that young resourceful men enter, understand, and master Indigenous land that is viewed as an unpeopled wilderness. Similarly, the medieval-like conditions of the local Foundry where he later works oppress both the environment and the people who inhabit it. The drudgery results in "yellow-faced, stoical men" (161) who are forced to endure a slow, undeserved, premature death from what the town recognizes as "*the foundry disease*, the dust in their lungs" (162).

Reflecting later in life on his years as a successful trapper and fox farmer with a combined sense of necessity and remorse, Munro's father states that "'You get into things, you know. You sort of don't realize what you're getting into'" (154). His response may be taken to suggest that the way people work for a living in Southwestern Ontario, including his later job as the caretaker at the Foundry, is not always as socially or environmentally responsible as might be hoped. It is also a testament to the bewitching influence of stories on his life. While his statement suggests a somewhat fatalistic approach, dwelling is possible: he made the choice to read Cooper and can, therefore, make the choice to read, and to live, a different narrative. And he may finally have discovered a different narrative. For in the conclusion to "The Wilds of Morris Township" the narrator describes her father's stance on two relatives who were ostracized: "He did not admire them, or blame them. He *wondered* at them" (126; emphasis added). If he did not find a story that allowed him to approach these outcasts with openness and non-judgment, he was surely creating one.

Learning To Dwell in Alice Munro Country

While "Part One: No Advantages" investigates how certain narratives discouraged settlers from deep engagement with their region, "Part Two: Home" follows an unnamed female character from childhood to adulthood as she works through this troublesome narrative inheritance and matures into a writer who creates her own stories that help her, and others, dwell. This group of stories continues Munro's literary exploration of how regional history affects contemporary life, an investigation which Katie Trumpener describes as involving Munro's attention to "colonial self-understanding and epistemology, as they shape contemporary life" (44). However, the semi-autobiographical stories in "Part Two" of *The View from Castle Rock* suggest that the protagonist, the narrator, and by extension Munro are more than a product of colonial knowledge. Rather, the narrator depicts her younger self as an inquisitive youngster repeatedly exploring the relationships among self, region, and story. Then in the section's final story, "What Do You Want To Know For?," after a lifetime of working at this complicated relationship, the narrator depicts herself in the present moment as an active participant in the region who writes herself and her surroundings in a way that exudes wonder and care for self, region, and story.

Like her father who turned to Cooper to help him make sense of his region, the young protagonist turns to fictional narratives with the hope that these stories will help her connect to her surroundings. In "Lying Under the Apple Tree," Munro depicts the protagonist as a child "secretly devoted to Nature" by way of reading L.M. Montgomery (198). Inspired by Montgomery's idealized rural scenes in which nature produces wonder, the thirteen-year-old protagonist lies under an apple tree in full bloom. Following these children's stories, the protagonist hopes to achieve a "state of mind, of worship," but the rotten apples and protruding tree roots make her experience less than she "had been hoping for" (200). Caitlin Charman argues persuasively that this is a moment when the protagonist's material reality intrudes upon her "romantic vision" (262) of her surroundings that is coloured by narrative. It is a moment when the protagonist learns that finding wonder in her region is no simple task, despite what romantic stories might suggest. Fortunately, she continues to develop her interest in narratives and her region, unlike her ancestor James who located his stories and his sense of wonder in far-off settings.

In the next story, "Hired Girl," the now seventeen-year-old protagonist displays an emergent bioregional identity in which she begins to understand the social and environmental nuances of her region. The protagonist, who is working as a maid at a cottage on an island in Georgian Bay, notices cultural and environmental differences between her home region, which lies just to the south, and the people and forests of her new Georgian Bay surroundings. Here,

> Nearly all of the trees were strict-looking, fragrant evergreens, with heavy boughs that didn't allow much growth underneath – no riot of grapevine and brambles and saplings such as I was used to in the hardwood forest. I had noticed that when I looked out from the train on the day before – how what we called the bush turned into the more authentic-looking *forest*.... It seemed to me that this real forest belonged to rich people.... (232)

The protagonist is sensitive to the class differences between these regions. She suggests that the natural border that splits deciduous and evergreen forests also splits those people who work the land from those who vacation on the land. With this realization, the protagonist displays her insecurity about the worth of her region, in comparison to the ostensible richness of cottage country.

Later in "Hired Girl," the anxiety that emerges alongside the protagonist's burgeoning bioregional awareness – where culture and environment are not distinct entities – changes into an appreciation of her own region's wonders. This occurs when a conversation between the protagonist and one of the young cottagers, Mary Anne, devolves into an altercation based on class differences. As the wealthy Mary Anne talks of leisure activities, the protagonist speaks of the struggles faced back home. Reflecting on her young self's bleak depiction of her home, the narrator observes: "as I talked to Mary Anne all the isolated incidents and bizarre stories I had heard spread out in my mind.... And this false impression I was giving seemed justified, as if my exaggerations or near lies were substitutes for something I could not make clear" (239). In this remarkable passage, the narrator highlights how she came to understand that her home region, with its working people and hardwood forests, contained amazing and curious stories that could captivate an audience, and yet she struggles to "make clear," or represent in narrative, the raw material provided for her by life in Huron County. At the young age of seventeen, representing her region in its complexities is beyond her abilities as a storyteller. However, this moment is significant in the protagonist's development, as she now understands that she can approach her region with a sense of wonder, albeit a more realistic and sometimes darker type than L.M. Montgomery offered.

While the young protagonist's inquisitive approach to narratives and to her environs continues to develop, there remains a disjuncture between story and life. The protagonist has yet to create her own narratives, or draw on other people's stories, in ways that allow her to live well in her bioregion. Even in the story "Home," the protagonist must continue to develop her ability to dwell. Travelling back into her home region, after splitting up with her husband Michael, the protagonist has the feeling when she looks out the bus window that "the countryside here is what I most want to see" (286). But despite her enthusiasm about "Such unremarkable scenes" (286), the protagonist sees herself as different from those townsfolk "who have to some extent flourished in this life" (312). Instead, she believes she is "more like one of those misfits, captives – nearly useless, celibate, rusting – who should have left but didn't, couldn't, and are now unfit for any place" (312). Although she is now an accomplished writer, the protagonist tells herself a disheartening story in which she, like certain others, is not fit for this place. At the same time, in the process of returning to and thinking about her childhood home, she is taking steps toward reconciling with her region.

Unlike the other stories in "Part Two" in which the protagonist struggles to dwell, the section's final story, "What Do You Want To Know For?," follows the protagonist as she enacts a dwelling practice in which narrative, regional life, and wonder are synthesized. In this story, the protagonist notices a raised grave when she travels around the region by car with her husband while waiting for the results of her biopsy. Through this exploratory process, the protagonist's "views eventually expand," states Christine Lorre-Johnston, "not because she is looking elsewhere, but because she is looking differently, in a more searching way, at what is around her" ("Remembering and Forgetting" 61). In doing so, the protagonist develops a comprehensive and personal relationship with her region.

Here the plot's focus on how the protagonist dwells is reinforced by the story's use of first-person narration. As distinct from the other stories in this section where the older narrator reflects on her younger self, this story is told at the same time as the protagonist's actions occur. Combining the storyteller and the story's main actor is symbolic of the synthesis of narrative and regional life that the protagonist/narrator finally achieves, after a lifetime of effort. That the protagonist/narrator unifies life and story is a moment of triumph, especially since Munro, according to Catherine Sheldrick Ross, was pushed to divide "ordinary life and the secret life of the imagination" (17). Consequently, both plot and form suggest that this story marks an important development in the protagonist/narrator's, and perhaps even Munro's, bioregional view.

In this story, the protagonist/narrator explores the region with her husband; however, they are not driving anywhere in particular. And instead of consulting a road map, she pores over a physiographical map that reveals the region's rock and soil formations in various colours. Here, the protagonist/narrator takes a publication made for a specialized reader and uses it as a guide for her personal non-specialist aims: by using the map to explore what is below the surface, the protagonist/narrator and her husband are finding wonder in the ordinary. They are developing their relationships to a place that holds unending possibilities.

For the protagonist/narrator, there is more to Souwesto than meets the eye. Indeed, the protagonist explains that her "favorite" geological features are those that promote a fondness for the unknown: the kame moraines that "are all wild and bumpy, unpredictable, with a look of chance and secrets" (321). That the protagonist/narrator, who is waiting on the biopsy of a potentially-cancerous lump, is enthusiastic about something "bumpy" and "unpredictable" is surprising, but she is encouraged by her belief in wonder. Wonder provides hope because, as Louise Economides explains, "it welcomes the strangeness of the new, in all of its unforeseen complexity" (21). In other words, the protagonist/narrator's open-minded approach to her region, and her body, allows her to dwell in both.

With the amazement and the curiosity of an open mind, she continues to explore the region with her husband, investigating a half-hidden burial mound located on the side of the road. Her curiosity leads her to a woman and her husband who know about the grave's history. They share stories about the Mannerow family crypt – an exchange that gratifies the protagonist/narrator. But she is not solely interested in the crypt; equally important to the curious protagonist/narrator are the ordinary yet important interactions that are a byproduct of her interest in the grave. For example, their conversation reveals that the woman's husband had worked with the protagonist/narrator's father. This connection evokes "a sense of *wonder* and refreshment" (331; emphasis added). They "explore the connection as far as it will go, and soon find that there is not much more to be got out of it. But we are both happy" (331). While the history of the crypt is of genuine interest, it is also an excuse: an excuse to situate oneself within the region's past and present. The result is happiness.

The welcoming attitude of the couple and the ensuing informal, yet valuable, sharing of local stories is contrasted with the protagonist/narrator's unwelcoming experience in a nearby city's college library. At the library, she suspects that the staff will likely ask her "what it is, exactly, that you want to know, and what do you want to know it for?" (326). Writing a research paper, or working on one's genealogy, is an acceptable reason for using archival material, whereas being "*just interested*" (326), like the protagonist/narrator, is not. However, the protagonist/narrator's story indicates that being "*just interested*" is a perfectly acceptable reason for using research material because this approach to research helps her dwell. So, what does she want to know for? Answering this question, at least prematurely, stands in the way of the protagonist/narrator's fulfilling her appreciation of the unknown.

For Tina Trigg, *The View from Castle Rock* embraces the unknown through "significant gaps in place, history, and self-knowledge" that remain unfilled and in doing so the volume "suggest[s] there is always another hidden story" (122). Consequently, the protagonist/narrator's concern with library procedure is that it would restrict the scope of inquiry so severely that the archive would not lead the protagonist/narrator toward "another hidden story." Instead, by approaching the archival material and the crypt with openness, curiosity, and amazement, or what I have been calling wonder, the protagonist/narrator explores the region, shares local stories, and builds friendships. There is no doubt that other unknown interactions among self, region, and story would emerge if her investigation of the crypt were to continue.

If finding wonder in one's region may seem too abstract for those who privilege practical concerns, "What Do You Want To Know For?" suggests that finding wonder in the mundane may in fact be an indispensable approach to life. In the final pages of the story, the fortunate protagonist/narrator learns that her potentially-cancerous lump is benign. The radiologist explains that she has now noticed the lump in scans from previous years and it has not changed in size. In response, the protagonist/narrator asks "why nobody had told me about the lump when it first appeared," to which the radiologist states that "they must not have seen it" (339). Luckily, their inability to notice the lump did not cause any harm, but in another case the difference between noticing and not noticing could be fatal. Of course, a potentially-cancerous lump is not a half-buried crypt, nor is it a kame moraine, but there are parallels among these bumpy features. For Linda M. Morra, the protagonist/narrator's curiosity about geological features "serves as a humbling reminder of the narrator's mortality – and ... it underscores the existential nature of human existence and, perhaps, the futility of knowing" (266).

While the protagonist/narrator's inquisitiveness leads to a sense of humility in relation to the environment, knowledge, and existence, the protagonist/narrator's intertwined curiosity about both the land and her body also serves the function of allowing her to maintain her mortal existence within her bioregion. The contrast between the medical personnel's potentially near-fatal mistakes and the protagonist/narrator's ability to notice all three bumps serves as a reminder of how to live well in the region. To notice the lump allows the protagonist/narrator to know her body, to care for it, making possible a longer and healthier life. Likewise, to notice the crypt and the moraine encourages the protagonist/narrator to live in a way that generates meaningful relationships that may help the region sustain itself. Her once nascent bioregional view has developed to the point that she can now dwell in a way that acknowledges the complexity of everything she sees.

Although the protagonist/narrator is confident that she can approach life with amazement and curiosity, she worries that many people in the region are not living sustainably. She explains that "As the notion of farming fades, unexpected enterprises spring up to replace it. It's hard to think that they will last.... Antiques and beauty treatments are offered. Brown eggs, maple syrup, bagpipe lessons, unisex haircuts" (327). Rather than using this economic transition as an opportunity to wonder about how they could alter their relationship with their surroundings in ways that would be socially and ecologically responsible, the proprietors of these "unexpected enterprises" are creating businesses that the protagonist/narrator suspects will not be sustainable.

In contrast to the local people who are weakened by the failure of colonial farming, the flora and fauna rebound: "The bush will never again take over completely, but it is making a good grab. The deer, the wolves, which had at one time almost completely disappeared, have reclaimed some of their territory" (327). Yet while the protagonist/narrator implies that nature will be fine, she is less certain that people will do their part to help themselves, their community, and nature thrive. Even the protagonist/narrator who has developed an acute bioregional view based on wonder ends her story with, I find, a disturbing though realistic admission that she herself is not unsusceptible to an uninspired outlook. In typically ironic Munro fashion, the protagonist/narrator's first thought on learning she is cancer-free is that "no great change seems to be promised beyond the change of seasons. Some raggedness, carelessness, even a casual possibility of boredom again in the reaches of earth and sky" (340).

Much of *The View from Castle Rock* explores how stories that influenced life in the region's colonial past generally discouraged people from finding wonder in their unique and valuable surroundings. And although the book's aptly titled Epilogue, "Messenger," signals to readers that early twenty-first-century Southwestern Ontario has reached a crossroads between a colonial past and a global future, that future looks as hostile to wonder and dwelling as did the past. Of the new globalized farming methods in "the region that I know" (345), the protagonist/narrator explains that "just in the recent decade the low barns as long as city blocks, as forbidding and secretive as penitentiaries, have appeared, with the livestock housed inside of them, never to be seen – chickens and turkeys and hogs raised in the efficient and profitable modern way" (344). There is no wonder to be found in these large, uniform, and closed-off barns. For the protagonist/narrator, these new structures encourage less amazement and curiosity than the irregular landscape of her youth that "made every fence corner or twist of a creek seem remarkable. // As if you could see more then, though now you can see farther" (344). To view these barns is to view any number of similar structures in locations around the world. Finding wonder in the mundane always involves effort, as the volume's many characters have demonstrated, but it is a lot harder to do when one is faced with overwhelming uniformity, when one's home region is no longer distinct from other regions.

Munro offers the people of Southwestern Ontario a story about the complicated, often troublesome, relationship that people of the region have had with each other and their surroundings. For Christine Lorre-Johnston, the collection is about remembering and forgetting the past in order to "define one's own home in the present," but it is also about considering the past to imagine the future ("Remembering and Forgetting" 49). Munro's story, therefore, is encouraging: through a conscientious effort to approach each other and our region with wonder, we may begin to live in a way that enacts an alternative to the threats posed by both colonialism and globalization in their attempts to impose external knowledge systems on regions which have developed their own unique and often ecologically mindful systems of knowing over many years.

We may resist efforts made to restrict local life in the name of profiteering that often benefits people living elsewhere who care little for a far-off region's future. We may begin to approach our unique region with openness. We may begin to care for each other and our environment, not in spite of our differences, but because of our differences. For as cultural critics Daniel Fischlin and Martha Nandorfy point out, it is through difference rather than "sameness at the expense of difference" that groups of people are able to negotiate changes and partake in the "co-creative potential out of which meaningful community grows" (15). In other words, we may learn to dwell – all of which starts, as Thomas King emphasizes, with the choice of a story. Munro's stories not only remind Souwesto readers that their region matters, but also provide readers with a deeper understanding of it. As William Butt phrases this sentiment in his essay "Killer OSPs and Style Munro in 'Open Secrets'," "We didn't need to watch American TV. Could have read Alice Munro instead. We still can" (100).

Munro's stories about people storying their region are so profoundly influential that they have served as a catalyst for Southwestern Ontario residents to pen their own narratives about the region. Consider *Alice Munro: A Souwesto Celebration*, a special issue of *The Windsor Review* edited by critic J.R. (Tim) Struthers and poet John B. Lee in honour of Alice Munro's being awarded the Nobel Prize in Literature in 2013. The outpouring of creative regional writing by budding and established writers, including William Butt's aforementioned essay and a moving bioregional tribute by Reg Thompson, is a testament to Munro's influence on the region. It is also a testament to the fact that people are eager to story their region, to wash Souwesto in wonder.

I am greatly encouraged by Munro's stories, and by the works of the many writers in *Alice Munro: A Souwesto Celebration*, which offer such personal and nuanced depictions of the region. Imaginative output of this nature helps us appreciate our surroundings and the optimist in me believes that it may even help us live better in relation to one another. Indeed, as I continue to reside in the region, I am increasingly aware of the impact of stories I tell, and the stories I turn to. As I continue to navigate daily life in the region, I will return to *The View from Castle Rock* because of the way in which Munro finds such wonder in the mundane here. And if I ever falter and become skeptical of Souwesto's possibilities, I will remind myself of Alice Munro's view: *everything here is touchable and mysterious.*

Works Consulted

Alexis, André. *Pastoral*. Toronto: Coach House, 2014.

Bigot, Corinne. "The Wonders of the Transatlantic Journey: Alice Munro's 'The View from Castle Rock'." *Crossings. Commonwealth Essays and Studies* 37.1 (2014): 25-34.

Brand, Dionne. "Islands Vanish." *Land To Light On*. Toronto: McClelland & Stewart, 1997. 71-77.

Butt, William. "Killer OSPs and Style Munro in 'Open Secrets'." *Alice Munro: A Souwesto Celebration.* Ed. J.R. (Tim) Struthers and John B. Lee. *The Windsor Review* 47.2 (2014): 94-100.

Chapman, L.J., and D.F. Putnam. *The Physiography of Southern Ontario.* 3rd ed. Toronto: Ontario Ministry of Natural Resources, 1984.

Charman, Caitlin. "'Secretly Devoted to Nature': Place Sense in Alice Munro's *The View from Castle Rock.*" *Critical Insights: Alice Munro.* Ed. Charles E. May. Ipswich, MA: Salem-EBSCO, 2013. 259-75.

Cooper, James Fenimore. *The Leatherstocking Tales: Volume I: The Pioneers, The Last of the Mohicans, The Prairie.* New York: The Library of America, 1985.

---. *The Leatherstocking Tales: Volume II: The Pathfinder, The Deerslayer.* New York: The Library of America, 1985.

Cronon, William. "The Trouble with Wilderness: Or, Getting Back to the Wrong Nature." *Environmental History* 1.1 (1996): 7-28.

Economides, Louise. *The Ecology of Wonder in Romantic and Postmodern Literature.* New York: Palgrave Macmillan, 2016. Literatures, Cultures, and the Environment.

Fischlin, Daniel, and Martha Nandorfy. *The Community of Rights, The Rights of Community.* Montreal, QC: Black Rose, 2012.

Heble, Ajay. *The Tumble of Reason: Alice Munro's Discourse of Absence.* Toronto: U of Toronto P, 1994.

King, Thomas. *The Truth about Stories: A Native Narrative.* Toronto: House of Anansi, 2003.

Lorre-Johnston, Christine. "Imagined Geographies and the Memory of Nature in Three Stories by Alice Munro." *The Memory of Nature in Aboriginal, Canadian and American Contexts.* Ed. Françoise Besson, Claire Omhovère, and Héllane Ventura. Newcastle upon Tyne, Eng.: Cambridge Scholars, 2014. 73-86.

---. "Remembering and Forgetting: Imagining Home in Alice Munro's *The View from Castle Rock.*" *Re/membering Place.* Ed. Catherine Delmas and André Dodeman. Bern: Peter Lang, 2013. 49-62.

Lynch, Tom, Cheryll Glotfelty, and Karla Armbruster. Introduction. *The Bioregional Imagination: Literature, Ecology, and Place.* Ed. Tom Lynch, Cheryll Glotfelty, and Karla Armbruster. Athens, GA: U of Georgia P, 2012. 1-29.

Montgomery, L.M. *Anne of Green Gables*. Illus. M.A. and W.A.J. Claus. Afterword by Margaret Atwood. Toronto: McClelland & Stewart, 1992. The New Canadian Library.

---. *Emily of New Moon*. Afterword by Alice Munro. Toronto: McClelland and Stewart, 1989. The New Canadian Library.

Morra, Linda M. "'Don't Take Her Word for It': Autobiographical Approximation and Shame in Munro's *The View from Castle Rock*." *Alice Munro's Miraculous Art: Critical Essays*. Ed. Janice Fiamengo and Gerald Lynch. Ottawa: U of Ottawa P, 2017. 255-69. Reappraisals: Canadian Writers 38.

Munro, Alice. "Everything Here Is Touchable and Mysterious." *Weekend Magazine* [*The Globe and Mail*] 11 May 1974: [33].

---. *The View from Castle Rock*. Toronto: McClelland & Stewart, 2006.

Omhovère, Claire. "'For There Is No Easy Way To Get to Jubilee from Anywhere on Earth': Places in Alice Munro's *Dance of the Happy Shades*." *The Inside of a Shell: Alice Munro's* Dance of the Happy Shades. Ed. Vanessa Guigery. Newcastle upon Tyne, Eng.: Cambridge Scholars, 2015. 26-45.

Parks Canada. "Point Pelee National Park: Park Management." 2019. <https://www.pc.gc.ca/en/pn-np/on/pelee/info>.

Rae, Ian. "Alice Munro and the Huron Tract as a Literary Project." *The Inside of a Shell: Alice Munro's* Dance of the Happy Shades. Ed. Vanessa Guigery. Newcastle upon Tyne, Eng.: Cambridge Scholars, 2015. 46-64.

Reaney, James. "Souwesto." *Performance Poems*. Goderich, ON: Moonstone, 1990. 36-37.

Ricou, Laurie. *The Arbutus/Madrone Files: Reading the Pacific Northwest*. Edmonton, AB: NeWest, 2002.

Ross, Catherine Sheldrick. *Alice Munro: A Double Life*. Toronto: ECW, 1992. Canadian Biography Ser. 1.

Simonds, Merilyn. "Where Do You Think You Are?: Place in the Short Stories of Alice Munro." *The Cambridge Companion to Alice Munro*. Ed. David Staines. Cambridge, Eng.: Cambridge UP, 2016. 26-44.

Struthers, J.R. (Tim). "Traveling with Munro: Reading 'To Reach Japan'." *Alice Munro:* Hateship, Friendship, Courtship, Loveship, Marriage; Runaway; Dear Life. Ed. Robert Thacker. London: Bloomsbury, 2016. 163-83, 231-44 passim.

Struthers, J.R. (Tim), and John B. Lee, eds. *Alice Munro: A Souwesto Celebration. The Windsor Review* 47.2 (2014). 1-137.

Thacker, Robert. "Alice Munro: Biographical." Nobel Media. 2014. <https://www.nobelprize.org/prizes/literature/2013/munro/biographical/>.

---. *Alice Munro: Writing Her Lives: A Biography*. 2005. Updated ed. Toronto: Emblem-McClelland & Stewart, 2011.

Thompson, Reg. "All Things Considered: Alice Munro First and Last." *Alice Munro: A Souwesto Celebration*. Ed. J.R. (Tim) Struthers and John B. Lee. *The Windsor Review* 47.2 (2014): 5-9.

Trigg, Tina. "Bridging the Gaps Through Story Cycle: *The View from Castle Rock*." *Alice Munro's Miraculous Art: Critical Essays*. Ed. Janice Fiamengo and Gerald Lynch. Ottawa: U of Ottawa P, 2017. 115-34. Reappraisals: Canadian Writers 38.

Trumpener, Katie. "Annals of Ice: Formations of Empire, Place and History in John Galt and Alice Munro." *Scottish Literature and Post-colonial Literature: Comparative Texts and Critical Perspectives*. Ed. Michael Gardiner, Graeme Macdonald, and Niall O'Gallagher. Edinburgh: Edinburgh UP, 2011. 43-56, 250-73 passim.

Intimate Dislocations:
Buried History and Geography
in Alice Munro's Souwesto Stories

Coral Ann Howells

Alice Munro's stories would seem to offer the most unpromising material for a contribution to a conference on "Dislocations,"[1] for her stories have none of the dazzling spatial and temporal disruptions that we associate with nomadic novels like Michael Ondaatje's *The English Patient* (1992) or Anne Michaels' *Fugitive Pieces* (1996), nor do they have the traumatized sense of exile that we find in much recent Quebec fiction. On the contrary, Munro's stories are based in home territory. As she said in an interview with Harold Horwood in 1984:

> I love the landscape. Love isn't the word really, because that sounds like I'm going out looking at sunsets and pretty views; it's not that. It's just that it's so basic like my own flesh or something that I can't be separated from. (Munro in Horwood 135)

That same sense of physical and psychic location persists in her subsequent work.[2] For decades Munro's fiction has carefully mapped the small-town communities and rural landscapes of Southwestern Ontario, where she was born and brought up in the 1930s and '40s and to which she returned in the early 1970s after twenty years away in British Columbia, and where she still lives in the small town of Clinton. Her own fascination with local history and geography has provided a realistic framework of small towns like Jubilee, Hanratty, Walley with its salt wells and its port on Lake Huron, Carstairs with its piano factory, and the network of farms and country roads in the surrounding region.

Souwesto is a settled place, where the wilderness of the Huron Tract was brought under control back in the mid-nineteenth century by pioneers of Scots, English, and Irish origin, among whom were Munro's own ancestors. Her great-grandfather Laidlaw came from the Vale of Ettrick via Illinois to Morris Township, where he and his brothers established farms in the early 1850s (Ross, *Alice Munro* 27-28). Yet there is a disturbance to this sense of place and history: how do we reconcile that feeling of settled community with her comment to Graeme Gibson: "the part of the country I come from is absolutely Gothic. You can't get it all down" (Munro in Gibson 248)?

Munro implies that there are scandals and secrets hidden in that place and that even the most careful documentation may fail to account for the complexities buried in local history. This sense of irreconcilable worlds is central to Munro's Souwesto fiction; her stories contain a representation of the familiar small-town everyday world as well as shadowy maps of other secret worlds laid over or hidden underneath the real one, so that in reading we slip from one world into the other. That storytelling programme with its dislocating double vision is the one outlined by Del Jordan back in 1971 in her unwritten but vividly imagined novel:

> All pictures. ... The main thing was that it seemed true to me, not real but true, as if I had discovered, not made up, such people and such a story, as if that town was lying close behind the one I walked through every day. (*Lives of Girls and Women* 248)

This paper is concerned with Munro's narrative mapping of alternative worlds in her version of spatial and historical discourses of region. Her stories are about both place and space, so it is perhaps worth clarifying my usage of these terms. "Place" is topographical, a mappable location, whereas "space" is rather more abstract and malleable as a concept. My critical reading here is indebted to Kathleen Kirby's fascinating analysis in her book *Indifferent Boundaries: Spatial Concepts of Human Subjectivity*. Her analysis offers particularly useful insights into Munro because her theory of subject construction highlights relationships between geographical place and individual psychic space in ways that help us to identify the locations and dislocations figured in Munro's narratives.

Kirby summarizes the interconnections between subjectivity and location in the following description of "the space of the subject" (17):

> Space can form a medium for reconnecting us with the material [world] while preserving a fluidity to subjective boundaries. It brings together the quantifiable and the qualifiable, the material and the abstract, the body and the mind, the outside and the inside. We locate our perceptions outside in it, and inside ourselves. It is our environment, it links us to our environment, and it also seems to fortify a distinction between self and environment, girding (and guarding) an interiority. (17-18)

Kirby's definition begins with the physical body located in a place, thereby providing a referential frame for shifting subjective positions and emotional responses to environment. Having established these co-ordinates for mapping subjectivity, it moves to the slipperiness of "space" in discourse, where spatial concepts may be used to represent location, positioning, and the boundaries of identity.

Munro's narratives are located geographically, and place is frequently a substantial support to her protagonists' senses of identity, and yet within that environmental shell she traces changes to landscape and character shifts in subjective positioning over time as her stories open out into the spaces of memory and imagination. These stories are full of hairline fractures and dark holes which draw attention to what has been hidden within familiar landscapes, so that as Munro says in "What Do You Want To Know For?," "the countryside that we think we know so well ... is always springing some sort of surprise on us" (318). So, how is a place known? It is known through maps and official historical accounts, but this is a partial knowledge which needs to be supplemented by the narrating subject's personal memories, family histories, and communal gossip, and that is where Munro's stories have their place as narratives which re-evaluate and revalidate what has been suppressed or forgotten.

Munro's stories provide the fictional equivalent of a Historical Atlas of Souwesto, tracing layers of its history and prehistory. She records the physical geography of the Great Lakes region with emphasis on the archaeology of place from an early story, "Walker Brothers Cowboy" (*Dance of the Happy Shades*), through to "Oranges and Apples" (*Friend of My Youth*) and "What Do You Want To Know For?" (*The View from Castle Rock*). Several stories are directly concerned with the history of nineteenth-century white settlement in the area, where Munro not only explores the Canadian trope of wilderness but also documents changing land use, patterns of industry, and urbanization, while gesturing towards landmarks that have disappeared ("Meneseteung" in *Friend of My Youth* and "A Wilderness Station" in *Open Secrets*).[3] Within this geographical and historical framework her stories also document family and community history, so that storytelling becomes a subjective mapping of private secret worlds. Again Kirby offers a helpful lens for analyzing Munro's techniques of fictional mapping, with her discussion of the boundaries of subjectivity and the positioning of the individual consciousness in psychic space: "I consider it necessary to view subjectivity as a place where we live," as "a space we are ... compelled to occupy" and "a space whose interiority affords a place for reaction and response" (35). Such spatial concepts point the way to a critical language which may respond appropriately to the shifting perspectives within Munro's stories.

Munro's stories follow a decentred patterning with their multiple narrative perspectives, their time shifts across decades from one episode to another, and their scrupulous notation of what people remember and what they forget. With all their overlapping complexity, her stories seem to conform to a depth model rather than to a flat map, so that it is not surprising to find the concept of "layering" being developed in Munro criticism of the 1990s, both in Canada and in Europe. Charles Forceville in the Netherlands has directed attention to Munro's imagery and narrative techniques in order to show how her representation of surfaces always hides something more which needs to be accommodated, while Canadian critics James Carscallen and Ajay Heble take different approaches to analyzing what Forceville calls her "layered structures" (310). For Carscallen, overlapping experiences and complex patterns of literary allusion figure an elaborate system of correspondences, while Heble proposes a model of reading instability – if not actual dislocation – through his analysis of Munro's narrative language with its potential for multiple meanings and constant deferrals.

Yet the concept of layers, exciting as it is, leaves out an important spatial dimension which we need for reading Munro and which we can most easily identify through the language of mapping.[4] As J.B. Harley and David Woodward point out: "Maps are graphic representations that facilitate a spatial understanding of things, concepts, conditions, processes, or events in the human world" (Harley and Woodward xvi, qtd. in Tyacke 573). Working on this paper, I realized with new force why cartography provides such attractive images and metaphors for Munro as well as for her critics: cartography is engaged with the representation of places and spatial (or temporal) relationships, just as Munro's stories are engaged with the representation of relationships between people as well as between people and place and time. In all her stories there is a crucial space from which the narrator is *shut out*; as with a blank space on a map, there is no possible relationship that the subject can establish with what may be in there. Not empty but inaccessible, this is the space of enigma which constitutes a boundary marker at the interface between fact and fiction.

Munro's stories are structured as narrative networks of relations with a hole in that network, which becomes the site of dislocation or deferral and which in turn generates the narrative. We could trace this pattern of geographical "place" giving out on to the subjective "space" of imagination and fictive artifice through most of Munro's stories, I suspect. However, I shall focus attention on two examples, "Chaddeleys and Flemings" (*The Moons of Jupiter*) with its account of local and family history stretching back over at least three generations and Munro's auto-biographical story "What Do You Want To Know For?" (*The View from Castle Rock*), while referring in passing to other works which provide fascinating glimpses of intimate dislocations.

To glance briefly at "Walker Brothers Cowboy," as Munro's earliest story about the shifting dimensions of subjective dislocation, we might see this as a child's conscious occupation of place and her first apprehension of imaginative space. Here a father begins to teach his young daughter to read landscape as both geography and history when he takes her for an evening walk through their familiar Tuppertown, down to the edge of Lake Huron, and explains to her "how the Great Lakes came to be" (3). By pressing his hand into the ground he manages to give her a graphic illustration of the advance and the retreat of the Ice Age fifteen thousand years ago:

And then the ice went back, shrank back towards the North Pole where it came from, and left its fingers of ice in the deep places it had gouged, and ice turned to lakes and there they were today. They were *new*, as time went. (3)

For the child, this story from prehistory destabilizes accustomed limits, just as her other visit with her father and younger brother to her father's former girlfriend opens up a new imaginative awareness of "all kinds of weathers, and distances you cannot imagine" (18). This sub-jectivized account of place has much in common with Roland Barthes' writing on landscapes of childhood memory: "reading a landscape is firstly perceiving according to one's body and one's memory, according to the memory of the body," Barthes asserts; for him, "the province is Bayonne, the countryside of my childhood" (Barthes, qtd. in Duncan and Duncan 34).

"Chaddeleys and Flemings" retraces the countryside of childhood from the viewpoint of a remembering adult narrator who has moved away. As the first story in *The Moons of Jupiter*, it is paired with the last story, the title story, as a framing narrative (both deal with Janet Fleming's family history) and is itself a mirror story in two parts: "Connection" and "The Stone in the Field," about Janet's double inheritance which is English on her mother's side and Scottish on her father's. (Indeed, both story titles are significant for Munro's analysis of geography, history, and identity.)

The story covers a long period of time for Janet's personal memories go back forty years, and behind that are her father's and mother's stories and the stories of their parents stretching back to nineteenth-century pioneer stories of settlement. As well as family history it is also the his-tory of a place, the small town of Dalgleish in Huron County. The story is told through Janet's memories of two childhood visits – a summer visit paid by her maternal aunts to Dalgleish, and a visit which her own family pays to her paternal aunts (who still live on the farm where they and Janet's father were brought up).

In "Connection," the visit of the four boisterous Chaddeley aunts, unmarried business women from the wider world of Philadelphia, DesMoines, Winnipeg, and Edmonton, is itself a dislocation, for they provide an outsider's view of the small town: "They didn't think Dalgleish was real" (4). Of course by the time Janet tells the story (long after the aunts and her parents are dead) the aunts have been proved right: that world has become unreal, for everything has changed. However, it is with the intimate dislocations in the companion piece, "The Stone in the Field," that I am most concerned here. Janet talks about a visit to her father's six unmarried sisters, who live fifteen miles away from Dalgleish in an old-fashioned farmhouse, where we have a glimpse of the dour Scottish pioneer work ethic and of these women's restricted lives. They live sealed-off lives in a sealed-off country, down twisting roads and over old covered wooden bridges.

Janet only learns a little bit about them thirty years later during her father's last illness, after the sisters are all dead, when he tells her the story of an Austrian immigrant called Mr. Black who lived in a shack on a corner of the grandfather's farmland and did subsistence farming himself. Her father remembers an old family joke that Mr. Black was in love with Susan, one of the sisters, though it was probably not true. Mr. Black died of cancer of the tongue and was buried on the farm under an unmarked boulder, "taking the mystery of his life with him" (33), according to a contemporary newspaper report.

After her father's death Janet goes back to try to find that burial stone in order to piece together this snippet of local and family history, but everything had changed. None of her relatives lives there anymore; the roads have been straightened; the farmhouse has been modernized; there are new owners and a new life style. Not surprisingly, just as times have changed so has the map of the landscape, and Janet and the young farmer cannot find the burial stone:

While carrying on this conversation we were walking up and down the corn rows looking for the stone. We looked in the corners of the field and it was not there. He said that of course the corner of a field then was not necessarily the corner of a field now. But the truth probably was that when the field got put in corn the stone was in the way, so they would have hauled it out. He said we could go over to the rock-pile near the road and see if we recognized it.

I said we wouldn't bother, I wasn't so sure I would know it, on a rock-pile. (35)

So the question is, how to tell the history of a place when that history is so full of gaps and mysteries and the evidence has vanished? How can Janet establish her identity as an inheritor when nothing is solid or plain anymore? This is perhaps the point where putting pressure on story titles may offer new insights. "The Stone in the Field" suggests location, solidity, specificity, where a field is a place whose boundaries have been redrawn as a consequence of new farming methods and a stone must still be there somewhere in the rock-pile, though it cannot be located because it is no longer identifiable. Yet throughout Janet's narrative, the ground has shifted into more subjective fields (like the social field of family relations which is comparable to Kirby's use of "field of cultural representation" [152]), and Janet's comment on herself as inheritor near the end merely makes explicit this progressively interiorizing movement: "However they behaved they are all dead. I carry something of them around in me" (35).

In this story about historical process, dislocations, and disappearances, "connections" are maintained as they are carried within the body through genetic inheritance across generations, however those connections have been modified by social factors and however much is lost or misremembered. Echoes or traces remain to be made into stories, which is where the role of the fiction writer assumes significance. Is Munro making an implicit comparison here between landscape as the spatial representation of history and the body as a place already inscribed by history? I believe she is, although she recognizes that analogy has its limits when the subjective dimension is added, for space becomes metaphorical when it is used to describe "layers" of consciousness or the "field" of interpersonal relationships.

How is Janet to locate herself in relation to the minds and the feelings of her vanished relatives who have been othered by time, though in their day they were living subjects, to quote Kirby, "endowed with the same interiority one supposes for the self" (152)? Some things are irretrievably lost, the dead do keep their secrets, "and the life buried here is one you have to think twice about regretting" (35). Change has inevitably occurred and the past is available for multiple interpretations where no version is definitive. As Munro told Stephen Smith in 1994 when her collection *Open Secrets* was published: "The older I get, the more I see ... the content of life as being many-layered. And in a way, nothing

that happens really takes precedence over anything else that happens"
(Munro in Smith 24). History, geography, memory, storytelling all mesh
together in Munro's subjective discourse of region.

Not all historical sites are blank, however, though they may be so
changed as to be indecipherable. The dislocations produced over time
are explored in "A Wilderness Station" where an old crime (if it was
ever committed) cannot be reconstructed. A hundred years later, the
log cabin which had been at the centre of the riddle has fallen down
and become an almost unrecognizable "mound pretty well covered with
wild grape, a few logs sticking out of it" (220). That same image of a
mound which contains secrets and hidden histories recurs in "What
Do You Want To Know For?" where the mound is a forgotten tomb in
a Souwesto cemetery which is no longer marked on the map. Munro
is offering a deep reading of landscape here, which takes into account
both place and time as she traces patterns that have already been laid
out thousands of years ago.

These patterns chart the historical geography of the region and
landscape changes since the Ice Age, so that the landscape itself "is a
record of ancient events" (318). Within that prehistoric record is situated
Munro's own comparatively modest project of retracing the history of
the landscape since its nineteenth-century European settlement – and
that is where the forgotten tomb finds its place in the story. Munro is
trying to read this indecipherable sign and the story buried inside it:

> I saw the crypt before my husband did. It was on the left-hand side, his
> side of the car, but he was busy driving. We were on a narrow, bumpy road.
>
> "What was that?" I said. "Something strange."
>
> A large, unnatural mound blanketed with grass.
>
> We turned around as soon as we could find a place, though we hadn't
> much time. We were on our way to have lunch with friends who live on
> Georgian Bay. But we are possessive about this country, and try not to
> let anything get by us.
>
> There it was, set in the middle of a little country cemetery. Like a big
> woolly animal – like some giant wombat, lolling around in a prehistoric
> landscape.
>
> We climbed a bank and unhooked a gate and went to look at the front
> end of this thing. A stone wall there, between an upper and a lower arch,

and a brick wall within the lower arch. No names or dates, nothing but a skinny cross carved roughly into the keystone of the upper arch, as with a stick or a finger. At the other, lower end of the mound, nothing but earth and grass and some big protruding stones, probably set there to hold the earth in place. No markings on them, either – no clues as to who or what might be hidden inside.

We returned to the car. (316)

(The first published version of this story, contained in *Writing Away: The PEN Canada Travel Anthology*, included a black-and-white photograph of the tomb, though that representation of surfaces gave no clue to what might be inside. It placed the reader in a similar position to the narrator, on the boundary line between seen and unseen / known and unknown.)

For Munro, the familiar landscape always invites further exploration; she wants to read the subtext. This is a kind of travel story through home territory as she and her husband – Gerald Fremlin, a cartographer – drive along the highways in the countryside around Lake Huron, seeing not only the familiar roads but what is off to the side, and gesturing toward what cannot be seen at all. This is a story about buried secrets and about death where the "unnatural mound" (316) in the landscape chimes uneasily with another unnatural mound, the "lump" (317) which has just been revealed in the narrator's left breast on her most recent mammogram.

In this densely layered story parallels are suggested between landscape and the female body, and the story moves freely between bodyspace and landscape as two kinds of physical geography. Having spotted the crypt, the narrator then turns to the secrets within landscape that she is able to decipher with the aid of "special maps" (319) in a book, *The Physiography of Southern Ontario* by Lyman Chapman and Donald Putnam,[5] where ancient features of the landscape with unfamiliar names like "moraines" and "eskers" are marked with vivid patches of colour over the map of roads and towns:

I get a naïve and particular pleasure from matching what I see on the map with what I can see through the car window. Also from trying to figure out what bit of landscape we're in, before I look at the map, and being right a good deal of the time. ...

But there is always more than just the keen pleasure of identification. There's the fact of these separate domains, each with its own history and reason, its favorite crops and trees and weeds – oaks and pines, for instance, growing on sand, and cedars and strayed lilacs on limestone – each with its special expression, its pull on the imagination. The fact of these little countries lying snug and unsuspected, like and unlike as siblings can be, in a landscape that's usually disregarded, or dismissed as drab agricultural counterpane. It's the fact you cherish. (321-22)[5]

These are the things she can know about, but in addition to the facts there is the mysterious crypt, like a black hole in the centre of this account. The crypt is the site of dislocation, and the story traces a double quest to find out the history of the crypt and the nature of the lump in her breast.

Munro manages to find out a lot of facts about this crypt, from local informants and from books in the college library in a nearby city; she learns that it was in a cemetery for German settlers who came to the district in the mid-nineteenth century, that it was built by a family called Mannerow in 1895, and indeed that there are two crypts, not one: a woman in Sullivan Township who represents the last Mrs. Mannerow there "brings out a book that I did not see in the Regional Reference Room. An old soft-covered history of the township. ... // ... In a short time she and I are reading together a section on the Mannerow Cemetery, 'famous for its two vaults'" (329). Munro also discovers that on the walls of the local Lutheran church there were texts in German from the Psalms which were whitewashed over in World War One, and only rediscovered when the paint peeled off after a more recent fire: since the War "nobody spoke of them, and so the memory that they were there had entirely died out" (334). The facts proliferate, but the enigma of what is in the crypt remains. As for the breast lump, that too remains unexplained. The radiologist announces that it was actually there on earlier mammograms but nobody had noticed it or thought it significant, and she advises against any further investigation: "you can be sure enough" that it "is safe" (339).

After all, Munro does hear from the last Mrs. Mannerow an eye-witness account of what was inside the crypt, for that woman had attended the very last funeral they had in it:

She did remember the last funeral they had when they put the last person in the big vault. The last time they had opened it up. It was for Mrs. Lempke, who had been born a Mannerow. There was just room for one more and she was the one. Then there was no room for anybody else.

They dug down at the end and opened up the bricks and then you could see some of the inside, before they got her coffin in. You could see there were coffins in there before her, along either side. Put in nobody knows how long a time ago.

"It gave me a strange feeling," she says. "It did so. Because you get used to seeing the coffins when they're new, but not so much when they're old."

And the one little table sitting straight ahead of the entranceway, a little table at the far end. A table with a Bible opened up on it.

And beside the Bible, a lamp.

It was just an ordinary old-fashioned lamp, the kind they used to burn coal oil in.

Sitting there the same today, all sealed up and nobody going to see it ever again.

"Nobody knows why they did it. They just did."

She smiles at me with a sociable sort of perplexity, her almost colorless eyes enlarged, made owlish, by her glasses. She gives a couple of tremulous nods. As if to say, it's beyond us, isn't it? A multitude of things, beyond us. Yes. (338-39)

This account would seem to solve the mystery, but of course it does not! Narrator and readers have come up against a black hole; but was it always black, or was it temporarily lit up?

One of the German texts was from Psalm 119.105: "*Thy word is a lamp unto my feet and a light unto my path*" (333). The Biblical allusion ought to shed light on the mystery of the lamp in the crypt, but all it does is to widen the imaginative space, so that the crypt comes to seem like a literalization of the secret life, where everything is hidden underground. In fact it is a brilliant example of the way in which documentary details split open to reveal what Catherine Sheldrick Ross, in the first critical essay collection on Munro in 1983, identified as the "powerful legendary shapes that lie behind the ordinary life presented in Munro's stories"

(113). Enlightenment is deferred indefinitely for some secrets remain secret, hidden within the earth – or inside the human body.

The story writes in these moments of dislocation and unknowing, but it ends with a return to ordinariness. The threat of breast cancer has been lifted and the mystery of the tomb has been assimilated "into a pattern of things we know about" (336). Munro and her husband are having a conversation in the car, driving home through familiar landscape with a sense of relief at the peacefulness of surfaces together with an awareness of what surfaces hide, which is the space of imagination where the story comes from:

> But for now, the corn in tassel, the height of summer passing, time opening out with room again for tiffs and trivialities. No more hard edges on the days, no sense of fate buzzing around in your veins like a swarm of tiny and relentless insects. Back to where no great change seems to be promised beyond the change of seasons. Some raggedness, carelessness, even a casual possibility of boredom again in the reaches of earth and sky. (339-40)

Munro's Souwesto landscapes seem ordinary and familiar as we look at them. Yet since her first collection her stories have followed an ongoing line of inquiry as her narrative art transforms those landscapes under our very eyes, in a manner eerily akin to the geological processes of dislocation which she describes: "as if a part of the landscape had managed, in a haphazard way, to turn itself inside out" (319).

Notes

1. The conference was hosted by the Department of American and Canadian Studies at the University of Birmingham on a Saturday in June 1998.
2. To give one example: though Munro's 1998 collection *The Love of a Good Woman* has three out of eight stories set in British Columbia, these are interestingly all stories about wanderers and unsettlement; it is only with the Souwesto stories that the subject feels grounded on home territory.

3. See Christopher E. Gittings, "Constructing a Scots-Canadian Ground: Family History and Cultural Translation in Alice Munro."
4. I prefer the map image as being more explicit in its representation of "blank spaces," though the layering model could accommodate the same narrative feature, i.e., "hidden spaces."
5. Warm thanks to David Ingram of the School of Geography, University of Birmingham, who produced his copy of Chapman and Putnam's book at the conference, together with their coloured map sheet of the Clinton area which would have been the one Munro used, and who took the trouble to explain to conference participants how to read this historical map.

Works Cited

Carscallen, James. *The Other Country: Patterns in the Writing of Alice Munro*. Toronto: ECW, 1993.

Chapman, L.J., and D.F. Putnam. *The Physiography of Southern Ontario*. 2nd ed. Toronto: U of Toronto P, 1966.

Duncan, James S., and Nancy G. Duncan. "Ideology and Bliss: Roland Barthes and the Secret Histories of Landscape." *Writing Worlds: Discourse, Text and Metaphor in the Representation of Landscape*. Ed. Trevor J. Barnes and James S. Duncan. London: Routledge, 1992. 18-37.

Forceville, Charles. "Alice Munro's Layered Structures." *Shades of Empire in Colonial and Post-Colonial Literatures*. Ed. C.C. Barfoot and Theo D'haen. Amsterdam-Atlanta: Rodopi, 1993. 301-10.

Gibson, Graeme. "Alice Munro." *Eleven Canadian Novelists*. Toronto: House of Anansi, 1973. 237-64.

Gittings, Christopher E. "Constructing a Scots-Canadian Ground: Family History and Cultural Translation in Alice Munro." *Studies in Short Fiction* 34 (1997): 27-37.

Heble, Ajay. *The Tumble of Reason: Alice Munro's Discourse of Absence*. Toronto: U of Toronto P, 1994.

Horwood, Harold. "Interview with Alice Munro." *The Art of Alice Munro: Saying the Unsayable*. Ed. Judith Miller. Waterloo, ON: U of Waterloo P, 1984. 123-35.

Kirby, Kathleen M. *Indifferent Boundaries: Spatial Concepts of Human Subjectivity*. New York: Guilford, 1996.

Michaels, Anne. *Fugitive Pieces*. 1996. London: Bloomsbury, 1997.

Munro, Alice. "Chaddeleys and Flemings." *The Moons of Jupiter*. Toronto: Macmillan of Canada, 1982. 1-35.

---. *Lives of Girls and Women*. Toronto: McGraw-Hill Ryerson, 1971.

---. *The Love of a Good Woman*. Toronto: McClelland & Stewart, 1998.

---. "Meneseteung." *Friend of My Youth*. Toronto: McClelland & Stewart, 1990. 50-73.

---. "The Moons of Jupiter." *The Moons of Jupiter*. Toronto: Macmillan of Canada, 1982. 217-33.

---. "Oranges and Apples." *Friend of My Youth*. Toronto: McClelland & Stewart, 1990. 106-36.

---. "Walker Brothers Cowboy." *Dance of the Happy Shades*. Fwd. Hugh Garner. Toronto: Ryerson, 1968. 1-18.

---. "What Do You Want To Know For?" *Writing Away: The PEN Canada Travel Anthology*. Ed. Constance Rooke. Toronto: McClelland & Stewart, 1994. 203-20. Rpt. (rev.) in *The View from Castle Rock*. Toronto: McClelland & Stewart, 2006. 316-40.

---. "A Wilderness Station." *Open Secrets*. Toronto: McClelland & Stewart, 1994. 190-225.

Ondaatje, Michael. *The English Patient*. London: Bloomsbury, 1992.

Ross, Catherine Sheldrick. *Alice Munro: A Double Life*. Toronto: ECW, 1992. Canadian Biography Ser. 1.

---. "'At Least Part Legend': The Fiction of Alice Munro." *Probable Fictions: Alice Munro's Narrative Acts*. Ed. Louis K. MacKendrick. Downsview, ON: ECW, 1983. 112-26.

Smith, Stephen. "Layers of Life: No More 'Single Paths' for Alice Munro." *Quill & Quire* Aug. 1994: 1, 24.

Tyacke, Sarah. "Intersections or Disputed Territory." Rev. of *The History of Cartography Volume 1: Cartography in Prehistoric, Ancient, and Medieval Europe and the Mediterranean*, ed. J.B. Harley and David Woodward. *Maps and Mapping*. Ed. Stephen Bann and John Dixon Hunt. *Word and Image* 4 (1988): 571-79.

Society and Culture in Rural and Small-Town Ontario: Alice Munro's Testimony on the Forty Years from 1945 to 1985

John Weaver

Anyone attempting to comprehend the culture and society of Ontario from 1945 to 1985 will find a valuable source in the writing of Alice Munro. Her stories possess settings, fantasies, genuine voices, and feelings for common and domestic life that create evocative chronicles of rural and small-town Ontario during these years. Munro offers not only a verifiable reality, but also what literary critics might call mythic insights. To ransack her works merely for the former would be crude labour, which would overlook her unique contribution, an account of feelings and emotions. The notion that common lives from the past ought to be subjects for reconstruction through statistical analysis and studies of men and women at work has been accepted only recently. To recommend now that common feelings resting on mythic insights should enter the repertoire of historical inquiry is bound to be thought of as a questionable proposal. Even granting that common emotions have a place in history, it is true that sources are rare, and seldom can they be expected to yield the same riches as the works of a sensitive writer long interested in the province's past. Thus there are solid grounds – as if any were needed – for accepting Alice Munro as a remarkable interpreter of Ontario's cultural history, in particular small-town social structure, community values, the migration to the cities, religious culture, sexuality, and the fantasies of adolescents.

No other important Ontario writer of fiction has so forthrightly discussed the writing of history and the limitations of traditional local history. Historians and the paraphernalia of research have figured in several of her stories, where adults read history books and school children memorize dates that they will recall as adults. A lover in "Hard Luck Stories" is in charge of acquisitions for the Provincial Archives (184). Patrick of *Who Do You Think You Are?* is interested in history; his "astonishingly belligerent" father is not ("The Beggar Maid" 84). More importantly, *Lives of Girls and Women* implies two poles of historical inquiry. At one pole, Munro places the historian as a collector who, at worst, reifies facts and artifacts without ordering their meaning. At the other, she places the creative soul who wants to record the concrete but also the passions. The first, represented by Uncle Craig, belongs to the tradition of the local amateur ("Heirs of the Living Body" 28-32). The same tradition receives passing treatment in the portrait of the father in "Walker Brothers Cowboy" (3) and of Blaikie Noble in "Something I've Been Meaning To Tell You" (1-3). For these enthusiasts, county histories open with dinosaurs and the origin of limestone, jump to discourses on Indians, and culminate with lists of the names of the settler families.

Though Uncle Craig of *Lives* impresses on young Del Jordan the importance of accuracy and of heritage, his conception of history is deficient. He sponsors Del's initial awareness of history and, in his desire to pour everything into his history, he even has a sense of common lives, but he cannot select and evaluate. Munro rejects the narrowness of a tradition that pursues certainty and precision in concrete matters but will not tackle the complex issues of community texture, of social and cultural attitudes, of the psychological compulsions that drive family and community. Even her non-amateurs seem deficient, perhaps lacking passion and the sensitivity to discern and communicate the intensity of ordinary lives. A budding professional historian, the student David in "Labor Day Dinner" cuts too solid a figure; "he is deliberate, low-voiced, never rash" (139).

Del eventually finds local reconstruction "crazy, heartbreaking" ("Epilogue: The Photographer" 253). Little wonder! What turns over in her mind are pieces of an independent artistic vision. When she tries to explain her own conceptions, they tumble out like fragments still mixed with the incidental and the concrete which made up Uncle Craig's form of history. Nevertheless, shapeless and confused though it is, Del's perception of what she needs to record includes sensations and emotions. "And no list could hold what I wanted, for what I wanted was every last thing, every layer of speech and thought, stroke of light on bark or walls, every smell, pothole, pain, crack, delusion, held still and held together – radiant, everlasting" ("Epilogue: The Photographer" 253). Hers is becoming an artist's vision, akin to an aspiration to total history. In 1971, the year *Lives of Girls and Women* was published, Uncle Craig's incomplete history of Wawanash County might well have been received more cordially by the historical academy than Del's wish.

Alice Munro shares the goals of social historians, and both have come to recognize certain themes as central to their inquiry and as frustratingly problematic: feelings, values, and motivation. The narrator of "The Stone in the Field" rediscovers a childhood mystery while reading a microfilmed newspaper at a Toronto library. Curiosity and the magnetism of the home region lure the narrator back into an on-site search and a questioning of local residents. Any hope of learning the truth evaporates:

> Now I no longer believe that people's secrets are defined and communicable, or their feelings full-blown and easy to recognize. I don't believe so. Now, I can only say, my father's sisters scrubbed the floor with lye. ("The Stone in the Field" 35)

Although warning that completeness must finally elude historians and other artists, Munro never abandons Del's quest. She presses boldly on to compile chronicles about common lives and, while these certainly go much further than Uncle Craig's notions about people's lives, she retains the material details of concrete history.

Munro's finely honed memory has certainly documented various drives and feelings among a number of small-town character types. Several of her very best stories (for example, "The Progress of Love" and "A Queer Streak") offer astonishingly compressed cradle-to-grave profiles of common folk. Moreover, these lives are shown to have been bewitched by unpredictable turns of fate or by incidents whose meanings have been incompletely grasped by the protagonists. Therefore, Alice Munro has left ample traces of her attempt to exhume and record the truth while appreciating both the material circumstances and the accidental influences on common lives in small communities.

Munro's own comments on her work are further reason to trust her material. About *Lives of Girls and Women* she states: "most of the incidents are changed versions of real incidents. *Some* are completely invented but the emotional reality ... is ... all solidly autobiographical" (Munro in Metcalf 58). Munro's remark concerning what townsfolk think about her work inspires confidence too. "[S]ometimes they feel cheated by not having the church on the right street [laughter]. Then you do, constantly, get the thing about 'But I grew up there, and life wasn't this bad'" (Munro in Struthers 33). Had they reacted enthusiastically, welcoming an Ontario *roman du pays*, the reader would have had cause for scepticism. Had she scathingly condemned her roots, there would have been a different basis for rejection or caution. In fact, her ambivalence – the occasional word of praise for rural and small-town Ontario's vanishing values – appears as a struggle to portray a particular culture as fairly as anyone can who has moved away. Tracks of honest effort wind through her tales as she moves from Southwestern Ontario to the cities and, in works such as "The Ottawa Valley" and "A Queer Streak," explores the Ottawa Valley.

Always the details ring true; it is worth noting how true by considering the similarity between her home town of Wingham and the fictitious town of Jubilee. *Lives of Girls and Women* presents a close mental mapping[1] of the region around Wingham, Ontario. Munro's disavowal of the importance of matching physical details in fiction with those in reality deflects the reader's attention from the remarkable similarities between her fictional world and a corner of Huron County. She may shuffle the furniture around, but her socio-demographic and religious portraits correspond to a census-based analysis with remarkable accuracy. Lesser touchstones of authenticity fill the stories: Silverwood's ice cream, a B.A. service station, the high dark-wood booth partitions in restaurants, linoleum, hands stamped with purple ink at the dance hall, the seals on the grade thirteen examination envelopes, the Legion Hall, the Kinsmen's fairs, the *Family Herald*.

Returning to the traits of the population, consider the census information for Wingham.[2] During the 1940s, the town barely broke the 2,000 mark, or about fifteen per cent below the turn-of-the-century enumeration. Wingham was a town in relative decline. Its high-water mark may have been attained in 1897, the year of the Jubilee. Ethnically, Wingham figures as a precise model for rural and small-town Ontario: sixty-five per cent English and Scottish; a quarter Irish; ten per cent "other." Ninety-five per cent had been born in Ontario. The distribution of religious denominations, however, varied markedly from the province as a whole, in that it was overwhelmingly United Church and Presbyterian. It is quite likely that the Presbyterian strain predominated, because the post-church union holdouts made up a quarter of the population, and half of the United Church may have consisted of unionist Presbyterians. Del's father's family, nominally United Church, had been Presbyterian at the time of union. A Presbyterian outlook, so much a part of Alice Munro's explanation of rural and small-town self-denial, probably influenced the mentality of half the town. If Munro's major characters stumble upon Roman Catholics with open-eyed disbelief – "a picture on the wall of Mary, Jesus' mother" ("Walker Brothers Cowboy" 14) is a clue to alien practices – it is because a mere six per cent of Wingham supposedly did "'what the Pope [told] them to do'" ("Baptizing" 225).

The most frequently cited level of education in Huron County in 1941 was grade seven; more girls than boys advanced to grades twelve and thirteen. Del of *Lives* goes on; her brother does not. This was the educational reality in the small-town schools of Ontario until the restructuring of secondary education in the mid-1960s. Alice Munro may have placed the church on the wrong street; yet she sensed the town's decline, depicted the influence of religious values, and remarked upon the modest formal education of its youth. *Lives of Girls and Women* and many of her stories point out the irony that English Canadians regarded French Canadians as suffering from a rural backwardness. Small-town Ontario values inhibited risk and non-conformity. In fact, one of Munro's major contributions to an understanding of the culture of rural and small-town Ontario has been her obsession with the values that have anchored people to a limited area, to conformity, and to a pride that is admirable, thwarting, and indolent.

The demographic and social traits are not the only ones that Munro depicts accurately, for she also has the geography correctly in place. For instance, the topography and man-made environment in and around fictional Jubilee resemble those of Wingham.[3] A road much like the Flats Road of fiction runs through Lower Wingham. To the north, the terrain becomes rugged in the vicinity of Alps Creek, and like the marginal region of Jericho Valley in *Lives*, it was mistakenly cleared by land-hungry settlers. "'They haven't progressed here much beyond the pioneer stage. Maybe they're too lazy. Or the land isn't worth it. Or a combination of both'" ("Baptizing" 221). The Maitland River becomes the Wawanash of fiction ("Heirs of the Living Body" 43); in "The Stone in the Field" there is less disguise, for the river is "'Old Father Maitland'" (23). Bluevale, south of Wingham, inspired the Blue River of *Lives*. The radio station in *Lives* sits on a rise outside the town on Highway 4. In later stories, the archetypal Ontario small town is brought up to date and, accordingly, has expanded at the margins. "A Canadian Tire store with a big parking lot" has been erected; "A Petro-Car [sic] gas station" has been built; senior citizens' housing has taken over the site of the old rink ("The Moon in the Orange Street Skating Rink" 133, 133, 159).

Munro not only has a way of evoking time and place with correct details, but she often refracts them convincingly through youthful eyes, establishing a hierarchy of places as seen by a young girl in the years before Ontario was shrunk by television and expressways. In the experimental exercises of mental mapping conducted by geographers, maps drawn from memory are dominated by frequently travelled corridors. Munro's recollections have the same minute detail along familiar routes and distortions on the outer fringes. Her observations made *en route*, in other words, have recorded authentically the sights and some of the feelings they have stirred among children; they also report on features that no longer characterize rural Ontario.

Usually the children of "The Progress of Love" go from Sunday school directly into church, but one morning the outsiders staying at their home whisk them away for a Sunday drive in a Chrysler car – not the farm pickup. They depart from the normally travelled paths:

> Today we spent this time driving through country I had never seen before. I had never seen it, though it was less than twenty miles from home. Our truck went to the cheese factory, to church, and to town on Saturday nights. The nearest thing to a drive was when it went to the dump. I had seen the near end of Bell's Lake, because that was where my father cut the ice in winter. ("The Progress of Love" 18)

Extensive mental mapping occurs early in *Lives of Girls and Women*. The Flats Road receives rich treatment. Later, when Del moves into town, she acquires a precise knowledge of the town's geography. "I had," says Del, "a sense of the whole town around me" ("Princess Ida" 70). The town she describes, like most of Ontario's small towns, had matured in the late nineteenth century: Victoria Street, Khartoum Street, the Orange Lodge, the absence of a bar. The second-hand images that Del receives about the United States, Windsor, and Toronto faithfully recreate a small-town youngster's attitudes about improper, dangerous, but exciting places.

On the margins of the youngster's mental map, there exists the commotion of the big cities. Uncle Benny's trip to Toronto in "The Flats Road" (23-25) is a wonderful anti-saga, repeated to some degree by Sam, Edgar, and Callie in "The Moon in the Orange Street Skating Rink" (153-57). Sam went to Toronto when he was ten, and he and his father used the wrong door on the streetcar. So now Sam feels he had "to anticipate the complexities ahead so they wouldn't take him by surprise" ("The Moon in the Orange Street Skating Rink" 153). Returning to *Lives*, Bobby Sherriff's breakdown occurs in the city. Nevertheless, Fern thrills Del with reports about the fast night life of Detroit. No television sets project city streets into front rooms. Urban ways are still thought of as mysterious and treacherous in a world where a drive to the next town is an adventure. "I hoped to travel as far as Porterfield or Blue River, towns which derived their magic simply from being places we did not know and were not known in, by not being Jubilee" ("Princess Ida" 68). The limited horizon and tentative spirit of exploration ring with an authoritative sense of how young eyes and minds perceive near and distant communities.

Munro is a trustworthy guide to the Jubilees of Ontario. From here onward, this supported claim must remain in mind as the discussion moves through ever more unverifiable insights: first, about the realms of work; second, about social rank; third, about religious identities or prejudices; fourth, about pride and denial; finally, about urges and inhibitions. No witness to history can hope to impart anything like completeness; that after all is one of Munro's major tenets. An absence of perspective too would be impossible. Alice Munro writes as a woman once steeped in the Presbyterianism of old Ontario, as someone exposed to "the scourging psalms" ("A Queer Streak" 216). It is from the feminine and Calvinist perspectives – tempered by later experiences – that she considers a host of fundamental social concerns, and this restricts her range.

Munro's female characters impart only rare glimpses of male work or of recreation. (See for example "The Moon in the Orange Street Skating Rink" 140). Occasionally men's work performs a plot function, for example, Garnet French's dead-end job at the lumber yard in "Baptizing" and the father's territory as a salesman in "Walker Brothers Cowboy." Often enough Munro conveys the drudgery of farm toil that held marginal operators and their families to a constricted routine interspersed with scheduled excursions to church and town. Her city women find creative though underpaid positions, but in the hinterlands women could exercise their enterprise only in a very few accepted roles, such as boarding-house keeper or music teacher. Her typical women in the visible workforce of the small town are school teachers, waitresses, cleaning women, casual workers in food-processing plants, bank tellers, and telephone operators. The narrator of "The Turkey Season" guts birds because she is "still too young to get a job working in a store or as a part-time waitress" (60).

A few noteworthy renegades, for so they are treated by townsfolk, stray from the norm. Del's mother sells encyclopedias, and Violet in "A Queer Streak" holds onto her wartime job with Bell Telephone. "There was some feeling that she should have stepped down when the war was over.... [I]t would have been the gracious thing to do" ("A Queer Streak" 235). The several descriptions of unappealing and gadget-free kitchens and floor scrubbing remind the reader of women's "invisible" labour. (See for example the references to the kitchen floor in "Royal Beatings" 14, 16; "Baptizing" 230; "The Stone in the Field" 26.) Uncle Craig's typing – his work – is oddly respected by his two sisters, who also regard it as frivolous. They respect the line between men's work and women's work – "the clearest line drawn":

The verandah was where they sat in the afternoons, having completed morning marathons of floor scrubbing, cucumber hoeing, potato digging, bean and tomato picking, canning, pickling, washing, starching, sprinkling, ironing, waxing, baking. They were not idle sitting there; their laps were full of work – cherries to be stoned, peas to be shelled, apples to be cored. Their hands, their old dark wooden handled paring knives, moved with marvellous, almost vindictive speed. ("Heirs of the Living Body" 32)

Workplaces – except in "The Turkey Season" – are not considered extensively. Neither really is social stratification, except that it intersects frequently with the religious denominations that engross Munro. In *Lives of Girls and Women* she describes the social standings without denominational adjuncts. At the apex of the town are "Mrs. Coutts, sometimes called Mrs. Lawyer Coutts, Mrs. Best whose husband was the manager of the Bank of Commerce" ("Princess Ida" 72). Del's mother, hoping to sustain independence by selling encyclopedias, tries to penetrate the charmed circle by aspiring to be an intellectual chatelaine. "My mother had hoped that her party would encourage other ladies to give parties of this sort, but it did not, or if it did we never heard of them; they continued giving bridge parties, which my mother said were silly and snobbish" ("Princess Ida" 73). Del's mother, in turn, had a negative reference group – the people on Flats Road. "She spoke to people here in a voice not so friendly as she used in town.... She was on the side of poor people everywhere ... but she could not bear drunkenness, no, and she could not bear sexual looseness, dirty language, haphazard lives, contented ignorance; and so she had to exclude the Flats Road people from the really oppressed and deprived people, the real poor whom she still loved" ("The Flats Road" 8).

All small towns probably have had a Flats Road – designated by equally evocative names – and residents whose poverty is attributed to "haphazard lives." On these urban fringes stand the houses where "half a wall would be painted and the job abandoned, the ladder left up; scars of a porch torn away were left uncovered" ("The Flats Road" 6). It is probable too that, in Jubilee as elsewhere, water and sewer lines have not extended into these areas with rural tax rates, just beyond the town's boundary. Neither the village bourgeoisie nor, usually, the terribly poor overwhelm Munro's accounts of social landscapes. Most often she writes of households where money has been very tight – poverty among people who never thought of themselves as poor. What are the consequences of this commonplace poverty?

It meant having those ugly tube lights and being proud of them. It meant continual talk of money and malicious talk about new things people had bought and whether they were paid for. It meant pride and jealousy flaring over something like the new pair of plastic curtains,

imitating lace, that Flo had bought for the front window. That as well
as hanging your clothes on nails behind the door and being able to hear
every sound from the bathroom. It meant decorating your walls with
a number of admonitions, pious and cheerful and mildly bawdy. ("The
Beggar Maid" 67-68)

The socio-economic divisions are usually reinforced by the religious
denominations, which announce social views in their architecture and
conceivably express the social drift of the congregation in rituals and
sermons. In fact, in Munro's work there is an almost inverse relationship
between social rank and the strength of evangelical faith. In Jubilee, as
in most southern Ontario towns, the United Church is "the largest, the
most prosperous" ("Age of Faith" 93). Inside it boasts glossy golden oak
pews, a splendid show of organ pipes, and stained glass windows. Owing
to some complex interaction of history and social dynamics, its members have come to avoid religious extremes and to sustain a bourgeois
liberalism in furnishings, liturgy, and sermons. Even seating expressed
the ethos, for amidst the subdued riches the pews "were placed in a
democratic fan-shaped sort of arrangement" ("Age of Faith" 95). All
other churches are relatively poor, but at the United Church "Doctors,
lawyers, merchants, passed the plate" ("Age of Faith" 95). In the title story
from *Who Do You Think You Are?* the Milton ladies, Miss Mattie and Miss
Hattie, epitomize an inherited prosperity allegedly found among established United Church families. "Their brick house, with its overstuffed
comfort, their coats with collars of snug dull fur, ... [e]verything about
them seemed to say that they had applied themselves to the world's work
for God's sake, and God had not let them down" ("Who Do You Think
You Are?" 197-98).

The United Church has been accorded a significant position in Alice
Munro's rendering of Ontario, and although her depictions betray a
critical bias, her commentary is authentic. The United Church, in her
accounts, plays down Christian orthodoxy. Thus it is the United Church
minister – thankfully – "who usually took up the slack [at funerals] in
the cases of no known affiliation" ("Fits" 122). Rather than for doctri-
nal rigour, the United Church is notable for its secular activities and
respectability, both of which are essential ingredients of the plot in
"A Queer Streak." Violet, who attends Ottawa normal school, switches

churches in the city. "She said that at the United Church there was a lot more going on. There was a badminton club ... and a drama club, as well as skating parties, tobogganing parties, hayrides, socials" ("A Queer Streak" 215). It is while bobbing for apples in a church basement that she meets Trevor, the assistant minister. "The ministry then, in that church, attracted vigorous young men intent on power, not too unlike the young men who went into politics" ("A Queer Streak" 216). The minister's role as a public figure and his standing as the quintessence of a bourgeois consensus guide Trevor's decision to break his engagement to Violet, who trustingly reveals the queer streak in her family. She cannot have anything in her background "that would ever give rise to gossip or cause a scandal" ("A Queer Streak" 230).

Except for the Loyalist lakefront towns, "where there was a remnant of the old Family Compact, or some sort of military or social estab-lishment to keep it going" ("Age of Faith" 94-95), the Anglicans have little prestige or money. Presbyterians "were leftovers, people who had refused to become United. They were mostly elderly" ("Age of Faith" 94). Nevertheless, the residual strength of the Calvinist sect persists in the mentalities of the "Scotch" and Irish stock.

Munro's account of Baptists presents an interesting counterpoint to the less socially fluid and less evangelical denominations that claim the bulk of the town. "No person of any importance or social standing went to the Baptist church, and so somebody like Pork Childs, who delivered coal and collected garbage for the town, could get to be a leading figure, an elder, in it" ("Age of Faith" 94; also see "Baptizing" 217). In "Baptizing" Del's boyfriend, Garnet French, introduces her to, among other things, Baptist rituals, and Garnet himself is shown to have gained a purpose through conversion. Yet Del is an adventurous young girl and the Baptists seem tedious. She cringes at the thought of becoming familiar with Pork Childs. It is the darker side of Garnet that interests her ("Baptizing" 217-21).

In a later short story, "Privilege," incorporated into *Who Do You Think You Are?*, Munro again equates evangelicalism or fundamentalism with poverty. "Many of the Protestants had been – or their families had been – Anglicans, Presbyterians. But they had got too poor to show up at those churches, so had veered off to the Salvation Army, the Pentecostals" ("Privilege" 24). The evangelical alternatives have been a part of Ontario

towns, but – here Munro's rendition seems plausible – they have had no
paramount influence on community values. That may help to explain
the understanding she reveals for them in *Lives of Girls and Women*, a
work that ever so tentatively dallies with the slight departures from the
norm that could be magnified into shocking deviation by contrast with
small-town order.

A "small but unintimidated tribe," the Roman Catholics worship
in modest churches, "bare and plain" ("Age of Faith" 94). Their unob-
trusiveness in southern Ontario towns helped define the cultural
boundaries that set most of Ontario apart from the cities or fringe
regions like the Ottawa Valley. Alice Munro does not explore the Roman
Catholic position from within the minority. She comes to it from a vantage point on one side of a traditional discord, a discord that tried to
banish inter-denominational intimacy. The father in "Walker Brothers
Cowboy" probably rejected an old sweetheart because she was Roman
Catholic. Relatives who marry Roman Catholics are lost oddities in the
family genealogy kept by Uncle Craig in "Heirs of the Living Body" (31).
House guests from outside the Ontario consensus who surface in "The
Progress of Love" cause muted consternation by driving their Anglican hosts' young lads over to the nearby McAllister farm to play: the
McAllister children whom the boys visit are Catholic girls (19). Munro
treats the expressions of bigotry like an outlandish but comfortable old
suit. Foolishness about "babies' skeletons and strangled nuns under
the convent floors, yes, fat priests and fancy women and the black old
popes" ("Age of Faith" 94) float about as chatter among innocuous old
folk. Munro's clearest exposition of outrageous anti-Catholic notions
and their common place in small-town talk of the 1940s, and beyond,
appears in "Accident."

> "Of course the O'Hares being Catholics, they've got four or five more.
> You know, the priest came and did the business on him, even if he was
> stone dead."
> "Oh, oh," said Frances' mother disapprovingly. There was not much
> hostility to Catholics in this disapproval, really; it was a courtesy Prot-
> estants were bound to pay to each other. ("Accident" 93)

In *Lives* Munro describes a seemingly benign Orange Lodge that does little more than organize card parties. Although "King Billy" has status as a commonly recognized cultural representation of something, that something has become a fuzzy concept now portrayed as a slightly foolish symbolic figure. In "A Queer Streak" he wears "a cardboard crown and a raggedy purple cloak" (209); the nickname is borne by Violet's poor bastard father and by a dapple-gray horse. Perhaps Munro revises history here, for this particular story could only have happened around 1900. From the vantage point of the 1980s, an innocent and spoofing characterization has a reason: why not help to douse the Orange embers with soft ridicule? However, in 1900 the lodge, which engaged seriously in exclusionary politics, was more than a farce. Indeed, one of the implications of the religious divide encouraged by Orangeism is hinted at in "The Progress of Love." The lawyer, Bob Marks, wants to start a practice in Euphemia's town, "But there already was one Catholic lawyer" ("The Progress of Love" 25). In the epilogue to his historical novel *The Orangeman*, Donald Akenson maintains that the Orange tradition may not have died out politically (315). If so, Alice Munro, no apologist, writes for those who recognize bigotry and hope to combat it by ridiculing it as a silly excess of the past.

Many church events inspire Alice Munro's satirical sketches and reflections on hypocrisy. On balance, her depiction of religion betrays no anti-clerical venom; she has too fine a touch and is too able a social chronicler for that, but she certainly runs close to witty caricature. Her capacity to see hypocrisy derives from an acute knowledge of several traditions of Ontario Protestantism. "The question of whether God existed or not never came up in Church. It was only a matter of what He approved of, or usually of what He did not approve of" ("Age of Faith" 96-97). Such were the sermons of the mainline denominations.

Morality and current affairs were frequently served to Protestants of mid-twentieth-century southern Ontario:

> My mother wanted to know what the sermon had been about.
> "Peace," said Fern. "And the United Nations. Et cetera, et cetera."
> "Peace," said my mother enjoyably. "Well, is he for it or against it?"
> "He's all in favour of the United Nations."

"I guess God is too then. What a relief. Only a short time ago He and
Mr. McLaughlin were all for the war. They are a changeable pair." ("Age
of Faith" 101)

Since Del's mother is an atheist, her conduct is described as eccentric.
Her daughter is more conventional.

As a young girl Del sought religious experience and a confirmation
of God. Later, as an adolescent, she attends an evangelical tent meeting
and understands, with slight amused detachment, the "balmy" comfort
("Baptizing" 213) that many derived from a fire-and-brimstone sermon.
The evangelical strain tended to be an embarrassing relative of mainline Protestantism in small-town Ontario. Mr. McLaughlin, the United
Church minister, is at the meeting. Consistent with her stereotype of
this denomination's ministers, he keeps "a suave downcast face; it was
not his kind of exhortation" ("Baptizing" 213).

Religion defines sub-communities within the town; that is to say, in
themselves the denominations divide but they also confirm the divisions of social rank. Concurrently, the images of the United States help
to reconstitute the community *qua* community and give it something
against which to exercise its pride. In truth, America was useful in defining what southern Ontario towns were not – not rich, not lively, not
chaotic, not "cultured," not even gauche. Godless and decadent, American civilization affronted, enticed, and informed. Defending the Lord's
Day meant opposing Sunday sports and newspapers, but American
Sunday editions from Detroit and New York were snapped up at local
drug stores, which were allowed to open on Sunday. Relatively poor and
self-consciously pious, the towns of southern Ontario concocted a sense
of identity that required American excesses.

For Munro, windfalls originate in the States and when they invade
poor Ontario homes, they incite ingratitude. In "The Progress of Love,"
Euphemia's mother burns her inheritance from Seattle, though not
necessarily because it comes from the States. Yet it is significant that
the source of the legacy, a disreputable father, ended his days in the
benighted republic ("The Progress of Love" 26). In *Lives of Girls and
Women*, Americans – Uncle Bill Morrison and his young wife Nile –
appear ludicrously affluent and generous, thus affronting local self-es-
teem. Their big car comes "nosing along between the snowbanks almost

silently, like an impudent fish" ("Princess Ida" 82). From this car, a vehicle of revelation, Del suddenly sees the town's shabbiness.

The saving grace in these confrontations between rich outsiders and local inadequacies is the former's alleged lack of taste and dignity. Nile's high heels are comic and her green fingernails are "perfect artificiality" ("Princess Ida" 87). Aunt Iris's gifts in "Connection" are extravagant (3). If asked for an appraisal of the United States, many small-town residents would agree with Del's mother: "Many bad, and crazy, as well as restless and ambitious people went there eventually" ("The Flats Road" 21). Nevertheless, the high culture of the great American cities reaches into small-town Ontario and Del becomes a culturally attuned and knowledge-hungry adolescent: what she "really wanted to do on Saturday afternoons was stay home and listen to the Metropolitan Opera" ("Baptizing" 182).

Although Munro shares the endeavours of cultural and social historians who want to understand common acts and attitudes, she does more than describe work and domestic situations, social ranking, denominational and community divisions, and such cultural phenomena as Ontario's two-faced glances across the border. Rather, she pushes boldly on to apply her insight to the psychological aspects of life in Ontario's small communities. For this ambitious enterprise she regularly makes special use of female characters, usually ones who have forsaken countryside or village – physically anyway. These deserters have advanced – or at least moved on – to Toronto, Vancouver, and Ottawa.

By focussing here on rural and small-town life, we do not need to follow these characters into their adult and urban lives. Although these women have gone out into a wider world and shaken off some of the small-town manners and mannerisms, Munro also deals extensively with the people who stayed behind. Outsiders and eccentrics, alien fortune seekers and seducers, perverts and fools walk and drive her streets, but they do not preoccupy her. She resists the temptation to dwell upon the colourful or outrageous, preferring instead the more universal characters who either accept the standards of the community or who, even though they move away, never quite overcome their early conditioning.

In *Lives of Girls and Women*, Del's mother urges her to leave. "Do you intend to live in Jubilee all your life? Do you want to be the wife of a lumber-yard worker? Do you want to join the Baptist Ladies Aid?"

("Baptizing" 220). Del's answer is an emphatic no, and soon her mother has no worries, as the university catalogues replace Del's romance with Garnet French: "he was fading in the clear light of my future" ("Baptizing" 231). In retrospect, "the clear light" registers irony, because Munro depicts the spiritual or emotional gains and losses of the great post-war migration from small towns to metropolitan centres ambiguously with occasional dollops of nostalgia. "We drove through country we did not know we loved.... Tall elm trees, separate, each plainly showing its shape, doomed but we did not know that either" ("Princess Ida" 68).

For every sentimental passage, one can find another of hard doubt somewhere in her stories. "The Stone in the Field" is unrelenting and concludes without a scrap of nostalgia: "Mount Hebron is cut down for gravel, and the life buried here is one you have to think twice about regretting" (35). It is one thing for the striver (deserter, traitor) to mull over these critical thoughts. It is another for the uninitiated to sneer at the hard lives. Richard, the affluent Vancouverite in "Connection," jeopardizes his marriage by treating his wife's roots as "a low-level obscenity" (12). "Richard always said the name of my native town as if it were a clot of something unpleasant, which he had to get out of his mouth in a hurry" ("Connection" 11).

Munro occasionally flays urban encroachment; she has excoriated the sprawl that consumes rural land and small towns in her two most overdrawn black-and-white short stories. In "The Shining Houses," new property-owners conspire to dispossess a long-time female resident, using the pretext of betterment for "'the community'" (29). Gordon, the transparently spoiled neurologist in "Prue," rattles about vacuously in a new house whose existence insults the efforts and values of old Ontario.

> His house is new, built on a hillside north of the city, where there used to be picturesque, unprofitable farms. Now there are one-of-a-kind, architect-designed, very expensive houses on half-acre lots. Prue, describing Gordon's house, will say, "Do you know there are four bathrooms? So that if four people want to have baths at the same time there's no problem." (130-31)

As a small-town product, Munro resents people without a sense of history who have no understanding of the community they either insult as a backwater or invade with outside ambitions and wealth. Nevertheless, as a renegade she herself cannot condemn them with an insider's passion.

Consequently, in "The Progress of Love" the narrator initially resents the hippie commune that occupies her parents' farm in the mid- or late 1960s. The members shun the electrical service that her family "finally" installed ("The Progress of Love" 24). "What makes you think you can come here and mock my father and mother and their life and their poverty?" ("The Progress of Love" 24). But she reconsiders, possibly because of the circumstances of her own development – as a divorcée she has even dated a Catholic separated from his wife:

> I knew they weren't trying to mock or imitate my parents' life. They had displaced that life, hardly knowing it existed. They had set up in its place these beliefs and customs of their own, which I hoped would fail them. ("The Progress of Love" 24)

The commune does collapse. The house sells for ten times its purchase price. Skylights and carriage lamps are among the improvements made by a young couple from Ottawa. "I've been told I'd never recognize it" ("The Progress of Love" 25). We know it is not just the house that has been changed several times, but the rural ways that introduced this story:

> My father was so polite, even in the family. He took time to ask me how I was. Country manners. Even if somebody phones up to tell you your house is burning down, they ask first how you are. ("The Progress of Love" 3)

Country manners are also mentioned in "The Flats Road" (8). Elsewhere, too, Munro writes of the allegedly vanishing values both critically and appreciatively. The manners and conduct – cleanliness, courtesy, and abstinence – taught by Aunt Ena to her children in "Jesse and Meribeth" made them feel superior "in spite of, or perhaps because of, relative poverty" (167). According to the narrator, "Nobody has a good word to say nowadays for such narrowness and proud caution and threadbare decency" ("Jesse and Meribeth" 168). The voice here is honest, for she continues by remarking on a very human dualism. She herself has circumvented the strict rules but generally "accept[s] that even a superiority based on such hard notions [is] better than no superiority at all" ("Jesse and Meribeth" 168).

Munro offers plausible insights into the mentality of local people who have stayed. She records practical decisions to adhere to the basic values of the community, for example to ensure against failing. She also recognizes cultural habits at work in the inertia of people's lives, habits that seem traceable to socio-economic and cultural sources. She lists "the hard-set traditions, proud poverty and monotony of farm life" ("The Flats Road" 8) that carried over in the farm service communities. In other words, the very material circumstances of life helped fashion a culture of moorings, but there is more – tradition. Del's father and brother in *Lives of Girls and Women* slide into a routine that brings regression. This pair is gripped by the apparent contentment with getting by. Did the failure of the fox farm trap them in a struggle to retain what was left? Described but not developed, these men have less revelatory significance than many other characters whom Munro marshals for depictions of the old Ontario values which nurtured roots.

Some of Munro's characters are more explicit about the practice of self-denial. "They liked people turning down things" ("Heirs of the Living Body" 38). Del's cousin turns down a scholarship. "Why was this such an admirable thing to have done?" ("Heirs of the Living Body" 38). There is, Munro plausibly suggests, a perverse pride in not being overtly prideful, in not being disrespectful of the community's ways. Family, community, and upbringing are understood to mean specific codes of self-denying but self-assured behaviour, absorbed at the family dinner table and in Sunday school. Pride sometimes meant outrageous insolence in order to maintain class distinctions, but its more likely and subtle expression in small-town Ontario included an egalitarian assault on haughtiness. One should not "'snivel'," "kowtow," or "high-hat" ("Connection" 9). This very spirit implies a sense of superiority and concurrently supports the local consensus; it may be thought of as parochial and self-deceptive and even as loyalty. Pride is a frequently mentioned quality in Alice Munro's stories. (See for example "Connection" 9). Throughout her stories, Alice Munro implies that there is a bond between hard lives and pride.

Moving on, flaunting personality, or innovating within the community insulted local pride. Leaving was an act that rebuked the grinding effort of honest folk and snubbed the wisdom of one's forebears. Del's father treats her politely but remotely at the time of her grade thirteen examinations, and she wonders why. "He approved of me and he was in some way offended by me. Did he think my ambitiousness showed a want of pride?" ("Baptizing" 230). Frances in "Accident" spent four years at the conservatory, enough time to shed her small-town instincts, and actually to believe her affair with Ted could remain a secret. The possibility is raised that she always was at odds with the community outlook. Too brazen! She did not fit in. "[S]he has the outsider's quick movements, preoccupied look, high-pitched, urgent voice, the outsider's innocent way of supposing herself unobserved" ("Accident" 81). "'Don't think you're any genius',' she has been told ("Accident" 81). Are Del and Frances victims of a resentment that girls can pursue education almost legitimately or of the small-town preference for self-denial? There is no one answer, but Munro is preoccupied with the mentality behind self-denial.

The narrator's father in "The Stone in the Field" arrives at certain insights about his own resemblance to a stone anchored in the field. He goes one step further by suggesting that self-knowledge and an understanding that one is tied down do not guarantee a means of escape. Because he used a wheelbarrow to feed the horses instead of honouring the tradition of carrying pails, the narrator's father was beaten for laziness. "Any change of any kind was a bad thing. Efficiency was just laziness, to them" ("The Stone in the Field" 30). The daughter observes, "'You ran away'" ("The Stone in the Field" 31). "'I didn't run far',' he retorts ("The Stone in the Field" 31). The father is perplexed by the lack of courage in the community – his own lack too. Their ancestors had the courage to emigrate, but somehow it "got burnt out of them'" ("The Stone in the Field" 30). It must be said that some descendants of Huron Tract settlers did move on; they migrated to western Canada. But Munro's obsession – a crucial contribution to understanding Ontario culture – is with the psychology of the persisters, not with that of the transients.

The father has identified the magnetism of static value systems and guessed at or reflected upon their roots. "'Their religion did them in, and their upbringing'" ("The Stone in the Field" 30). In the epilogue to *The Orangeman*, Donald Akenson contends that the patriotism and political culture of Ontario were coloured by Irish Protestantism (313-14). Conceivably, Scottish and Irish Protestantism engendered even deeper mental outlooks, which conditioned daily conduct at home, at work, and among neighbours. Self-denial could be one of those outlooks.

Munro's many references to religion, including canny details about church architecture and social hierarchy, bear witness to the imprint of Ontario Protestantism. How does she see this religious contribution to culture affecting people's lives? Older folks repress their impulses. The grandmother in "Winter Wind" may have wanted to run off with her old beau when they were both in their fifties. "Where could they have run to? Besides, they were Presbyterians. No one ever accused them of misbehavior" ("Winter Wind" 200). Instead, the grandmother prefers an enduring self-denying love. Commitments are made for a lifetime and alternatives not mentioned. "*We must never speak of this again*" ("Winter Wind" 200; emphasis in orig.).

It is conceivable that these attitudes, associated with a Presbyterian outlook, were what David the history student has in mind. "David says that everybody born in this country before the Second World War was to all intents and purposes brought up in the nineteenth century, and that their thinking is archaic" ("Labor Day Dinner" 157).

Slightly more adventurous characters depart, but it is not at all clear that they spring entirely free of old values. In "Accident" Frances journeys in several dimensions and the greatest possible distances from southern Ontario towns, short of living outside the province. She takes up with a "'foreign'" man ("Accident" 93) married with a family, never again plays the music for services in the United Church, and moves to Ottawa. However, she retains a moral sense that prevents her from thinking too much about the accident that changed (she cannot even say "improved") her life. It was "too ugly to think about" ("Accident" 109). The community had instilled a sense of natural right that shapes her in spite of her will. Perhaps, like Munro, she is properly confused.

Upbringing and the contradictory belief that "'We are more than products of our upbringing'" ("Accident" 157) struggle for ascendancy in Munro's central characters, although – and there is no occasion to dwell on it here – accidents or caprice have decisive functions in many stories. The influence of a religious element in upbringing can neither be extirpated nor starved out. "Purged from the rolls" may describe an official status for many Protestant Ontarians in the secularism of current times. Nevertheless, the moral precepts, scriptural literature, calendar, and ethnocentric Protestant sense of order remain part of the indelible upbringing that identifies Munro's generation.

Whereas Frances departs, Evangeline Steuer in "Jesse and Meribeth" returns and soon affronts community conventions. She buys the local paper for her husband to run and generally loses her function, getting things mixed up. "It was one thing to be a smoking, drinking, profane, and glamorous bachelor girl, and quite another thing to be a smoking, drinking, profane, and no longer glamorous expectant mother" ("Jesse and Meribeth" 171). The town can tolerate the doctor's affluent daughter only if she plays an accepted role or fits a stereotype, but she is too freewheeling. Consequently, Evangeline is an exemplar of wholly wrong values, those that mock self-denial. She illustrates "how money made you shameless, leisure made you useless, self-indulgence marked you out for some showy disaster" ("Jesse and Meribeth" 171).

The introspection and turmoil caused by flights from the rural and small-town ethos obviously have psychological dimensions resembling if not representing the archetypal conflicts between inner urges and social pressures. These are conflicts that Freudians assign to the ego. Indeed, the restraining ethos of self-denial has the function of the Freudian superego, of the inhibitions that society and conscience impose on the desires of the id. But Munro's stories also include drives, and the cravings and wishes, even the fantasies, of her characters should not be neglected as elements in a portrait of life in Ontario's small towns, regardless of how resistant these intangibles are to conventional historical inquiry. Adolescent urges, some powered as much by boredom and the will to excite envy as by sex, propel girls into encounters with worldly and threatening men; it cannot be readily confirmed that these "probable fictions" (to borrow Louis K. MacKendrick's term) were commonplace. Nevertheless, their presence in this body of fiction ought to provoke thought about sexuality and risk-taking in Ontario society.

A fascination with men who exemplify exciting possibilities and outside experiences, men who are attractive because they are different, is considered in the title story from *Lives of Girls and Women*, "Wild Swans" in *Who Do You Think You Are?*, "The Turkey Season," and "Jesse and Meribeth." These sordid encounters may be meant to be didactic, but besides exposing dangers and circulating warnings they really do emphasize that irrational risk-taking can counteract all that seems oppressive about small-town and rural life, especially to impressionable adolescents. The rural and small-town youths loitering around the theatre (today, the video shop and arcade), the café, and the poolroom or waving at passing cars, are trying to make something happen. Among the limited opportunities for amusement are the occasional organized events for a few males at the ball diamonds and arenas mentioned by Munro. Hampered by their size and codes of proper conduct, small towns have institutionalized monotony, challenging youths to fantasize, do the forbidden, and take risks – usually with cars, booze, and the opposite sex.

After taking their sexual education from a book that Del's friend Naomi discovered in a trunk, smothered with moth-balled blankets, Del and Naomi begin to tease the boyfriend of a boarder at Del's house. Art Chamberlain, the carnal radio announcer, takes advantage of the game, squeezing and jabbing Del, who places herself in hazardous and even provocative situations. Finally, he takes Del for an unromantic ride and a climactic walk in the country. An expression of raw common desire – "Evil would never be grand, with him" ("Lives of Girls and Women" 167) – his exploitative manner suggests guiltless possibilities. Del yields to these and to the adventure of taking a chance. Later, because "Curiosity could carry things quite a long way" ("Baptizing" 203), she takes off her clothes for Jerry Storey.

Rose in "Wild Swans" permits intimacies with a stranger on the train, even though she is offended by his repulsive advances. "Curiosity. More constant, more imperious, than any lust. A lust in itself, that will make you draw back and wait, wait too long, risk almost anything, just to see what will happen. *To see what will happen*" ("Wild Swans" 62; emphasis in orig.). The narrator in "The Turkey Season" likewise confesses to an irrational urge. "I can still feel the pull of a man like that, of his promising and refusing. I would still like to know things. Never mind facts. Never mind theories, either" ("The Turkey Season" 74). Jessie of "Jesse and Meribeth" – a girl with an active imagination – invents a fantasy to make her best friend envious and it almost becomes self-fulfilling, leading to her voluntary entrapment in the summerhouse by the experienced Mr. Cryderman. In this tense episode, the desires and rationalizations of the would-be seducer are played off against the desires and self-restraint of Jessie. Her pride wins out, but she nearly waits too long "to see what will happen." Pride and curiosity contend often and with different outcomes in common lives.

In postwar Ontario, the urban features of the province's culture and society have been dynamic, pronounced, and much celebrated. Besides overwhelming the old rural Ontario, they have threatened to obscure its brief and distinctive history by emphasizing urban workers, city building, and multiculturalism. The time has nearly passed when anthropological field-work investigations of traditional Ontario rural and village values and outlooks would be feasible. The neglect is understandable and, set beside a vision of earnest academic inquiry staffed with teams of social scientists descending upon Jubilee, not to be entirely lamented. Moreover, it is unlikely that conventional historical writing could convey the emotional richness found in Alice Munro's Ontario lives. For those reasons her work is a cultural resource for Ontario. Readers can enjoy the stories. Critics can praise their style. And all who have a regard for Ontario's past must celebrate the accomplishments of Alice Munro as a chronicler of deep feelings and changes. Del has supplanted Uncle Craig as the historian of Wawanash County.

Acknowledgements

I wish to thank Laurel Braswell-Means for initiating my interest in Alice Munro's small towns, Joan Weaver for widening my understanding of Munro's people, and Violet Croydon for preparing the manuscript – with toleration and humour. This article is dedicated to the memory of Bob Fazackerley, who returned to and worked for his part of rural Ontario.

Notes

1. Concerning mental mapping, see Roger M. Downs and David Stea, *Maps in Minds: Reflections on Cognitive Mapping.*
2. For statistical information on Wingham, see Canada, Dominion Bureau of Statistics, *Eighth Census of Canada, 1941*, Vol. 2, tables 10, 32, 38, 43, 58.
3. For a map of the Wingham area, see Canada, Department of Energy, Mines and Resources, Surveys and Mapping Branch, *Wingham 40 P/14 (1:50,000).*

Works Cited

Akenson, Don. *The Orangeman: The Life & Times of Ogle Gowan.* Toronto: James Lorimer, 1986.

Canada. Department of Energy, Mines and Resources. Surveys and Mapping Branch. *Wingham 40 P/14 (1:50,000).*

Canada. Dominion Bureau of Statistics. *Eighth Census of Canada, 1941.* Vol. 2, tables 10, 32, 38, 43, 58.

Downs, Roger M., and David Stea. *Maps in Minds: Reflections on Cognitive Mapping.* New York: Harper and Row, 1977.

MacKendrick, Louis K. "Probable Fictions: Alice Munro's Narrative Acts." *Probable Fictions: Alice Munro's Narrative Acts.* Ed. Louis K. MacKendrick. Downsview, ON: ECW, 1983. 1-4.

Metcalf, John. "A Conversation with Alice Munro." *Journal of Canadian Fiction* 1.4 (1972): 54-62.

Munro, Alice. "Accident." *The Moons of Jupiter.* Toronto: Macmillan of Canada, 1982. 77-109.

---. "Age of Faith." *Lives of Girls and Women.* Toronto: McGraw-Hill Ryerson, 1971. 92-116.

---. "Baptizing." *Lives of Girls and Women.* Toronto: McGraw-Hill Ryerson, 1971. 178-242.

---. "The Beggar Maid." *Who Do You Think You Are?* Toronto: Macmillan of Canada, 1978. 65-97.

---. "Connection." *The Moons of Jupiter.* Toronto: Macmillan of Canada, 1982. 1-18.

---. "Epilogue: The Photographer." *Lives of Girls and Women.* Toronto: McGraw-Hill Ryerson, 1971. 243-54.

---. "Fits." *The Progress of Love.* Toronto: McClelland and Stewart, 1986. 106-31.

---. "The Flats Road." *Lives of Girls and Women.* Toronto: McGraw-Hill Ryerson, 1971. 1-27.

---. "Hard-Luck Stories." *The Moons of Jupiter.* Toronto: Macmillan of Canada, 1982. 181-97.

---. "Heirs of the Living Body." *Lives of Girls and Women.* Toronto: McGraw-Hill Ryerson, 1971. 28-63.

---. "Jesse and Meribeth." *The Progress of Love.* Toronto: McClelland and Stewart, 1986. 162-88.

---. "Labor Day Dinner." *The Moons of Jupiter.* Toronto: Macmillan of Canada, 1982. 134-59.

---. "Lives of Girls and Women." *Lives of Girls and Women.* Toronto: McGraw-Hill Ryerson, 1971. 143-77.

---. "The Moon in the Orange Street Skating Rink." *The Progress of Love.* Toronto: McClelland and Stewart, 1986. 132-61.

---. "The Ottawa Valley." *Something I've Been Meaning To Tell You.* Toronto: McGraw-Hill Ryerson, 1974. 227-46.

---. "Princess Ida." *Lives of Girls and Women.* Toronto: McGraw-Hill Ryerson, 1971. 64-91.

---. "Privilege." *Who Do You Think You Are?* Toronto: Macmillan of Canada, 1978. 23-37.

---. "The Progress of Love." *The Progress of Love.* Toronto: McClelland and Stewart, 1986. 3-31.

---. "Prue." *The Moons of Jupiter.* Toronto: Macmillan of Canada, 1982. 129-33.

---. "A Queer Streak." *The Progress of Love.* Toronto: McClelland and Stewart, 1986. 208-53.

---. "Royal Beatings." *Who Do You Think You Are?* Toronto: Macmillan of Canada, 1978. 1-22.

---. "The Shining Houses." *Dance of the Happy Shades.* Toronto: Ryerson, 1968. 19-29.

---. "Something I've Been Meaning To Tell You." *Something I've Been Meaning To Tell You.* Toronto: McGraw-Hill Ryerson, 1974. 1-23.

---. "The Stone in the Field." *The Moons of Jupiter.* Toronto: Macmillan of Canada, 1982. 19-35.

---. "The Turkey Season." *The Moons of Jupiter.* Toronto: Macmillan of Canada, 1982. 60-76.

---. "Walker Brothers Cowboy." *Dance of the Happy Shades.* Toronto: Ryerson, 1968. 1-18.

---. "Who Do You Think You Are?" *Who Do You Think You Are?* Toronto: Macmillan of Canada, 1978. 189-206.

---. "Wild Swans." *Who Do You Think You Are?* Toronto: Macmillan of Canada, 1978. 55-64.

---. "Winter Wind." *Something I've Been Meaning To Tell You.* Toronto: McGraw-Hill Ryerson, 1974. 192-206.

Struthers, J.R. (Tim). "The Real Material: An Interview with Alice Munro." *Probable Fictions: Alice Munro's Narrative Acts.* Ed. Louis K. MacKendrick. Downsview, ON: ECW, 1983. 5-36.

Alice Munro and the Huron Tract
as a Literary Project

Ian Rae

Popular and academic criticism on Alice Munro often suffers from a glaring contradiction concerning the relation of Munro's writing to Huron County, where the majority of her fiction is set. Critics celebrate Munro's stories for their sensitivity to local histories, idioms, social mores, class tensions, and geography, but when it comes to demonstrating how these local factors combine to produce place-specific literary forms in Munro's writing, critics take flight for Russia or the American South or parts of Canada with very different histories and geographies. For example, Munro's citation for the 2013 Nobel Prize in Literature notes that "some critics consider her a Canadian Chekhov" because

> [h]er stories are often set in small town environments, where the struggle for a socially acceptable existence often results in strained relationships and moral conflicts – problems that stem from generational differences and colliding life ambitions. Her texts often feature depictions of everyday but decisive events, epiphanies of a kind, that illuminate the surrounding story and let existential questions appear in a flash of lightning. ("The Nobel Prize")

Other critics associate Munro's focus on small towns with the claustrophobic elements of the Southern Gothic tradition in the United States (Berndt 20; Thacker, *Alice Munro* 159). Canadian critics, in turn, produce a variation on this subgenre by emphasizing the regional "sense of entrapment in an antiquated, decaying social order" in what they call

Southern Ontario Gothic (Hurley 160) or Souwesto Gothic (Struthers, "Alice Munro" 101).

From a comparative perspective, all these critical strategies have their merits, but at the same time they avoid crucial questions about the literary history of the county at the heart of Munro's literary project. These questions are even more pressing when one considers that Munro's early writing is preoccupied with the function of literacy in Huron County, where writing is both esteemed for its association with administrative power and dismissed as non-productive labour (Munro, *Lives* 32).

This essay will examine how "Walker Brothers Cowboy," the opening short story in Munro's first collection, *Dance of the Happy Shades* (1968), relates to the literary legacy of John Galt and William Dunlop, the Canada Company "author-agents" (J.A. Scott iv) who were charged with opening the Huron Tract to British colonization. Galt and Dunlop blurred the boundaries between fiction and nonfiction and linked the local to the transnational in their emigrant guides and fictional portraits of Upper Canada, thereby establishing a literary legacy with which Munro's writing negotiates. Whereas Galt and Dunlop sought to map, survey, categorize, and illustrate Huron County in reports, articles, and books to facilitate emigration and resource exploitation, Munro employs these same techniques in "Walker Brothers Cowboy," as Ajay Heble observes, to highlight the "epistemological" limitations of these systems and the unknowable "ontological" qualities of the past, the landscape, and even the narrator's family members (24).

Annie Proulx's introduction to the Penguin Modern Classics edition of *Dance of the Happy Shades* exemplifies the contradiction in Munro criticism between place-specific content and place-independent form. Proulx begins by emphasizing the anomalous quality of Munro's literary genius by invoking the myth of the birth of Athena, the Greek goddess of wisdom:

> Alice Munro, like Athena, seems to have sprung full-grown from the head of Zeus. When *Dance of the Happy Shades* ... was published in 1968 it introduced a writer of astonishingly mature talent and a truly singular understanding of humankind's polarities of behaviour. (ix)

Proulx's purpose in invoking this myth is to suggest that Munro is not a literary product of her social milieu but rather a "singular" writer (ix).

For Proulx, it is easier to claim that "Munro's extraordinary visual and verbal sensitivity is truly rare, perhaps unique" (x), than it is to ground her culturally conditioned perceptions in space and time. Yet Proulx's argument eventually demands such localization because she demonstrates that Munro works creatively with local vernacular, folklore, and social conventions in a way that is culturally specific, not anomalous:

> Some people feel that Munro's stories can be easily overlaid on other cultures. I do not think this is entirely true, nor do I think that Munro's sensitivity to human behaviour makes these stories applicable to everyone. A kind of propriety, class structure, and social consciousness informs many of the stories in a way that is much more English Canadian than American, or Mexican, or Chinese. (xi)

While Proulx endorses the conventional comparison of Munro to Chekhov because of her sensitive depiction of the psychological lives of women (xv-xvi), Proulx nonetheless draws the conclusion that

> fiction writers are inescapably embedded in their own time and culture and cannot help but unconsciously reflect the period in which they live. At any rate, it is more accurate to say not that she is Canada's Chekhov, but that she is Canada's Alice Munro. (xv)

However, even a nationalist reading of "Canada's Alice Munro" avoids questions of local specificity in her writing because, at best, it situates her writing somewhere in the second largest country in the world — one where, as Jonathan Franzen observes, West Coast mores differ significantly from Huron County mores in ways that many of Munro's stories about a protagonist who returns to Huron County from British Columbia emphasize.

In 2006, Munro took control of the critical debate concerning her literary antecedents with the publication of her loosely autobiographical collection *The View from Castle Rock*, which itself blurs the boundaries between fiction and nonfiction in interesting ways. This collection fictionalizes the migration of her father's side of the family, the Laidlaws, from Scotland to Canada. This family story is also a literary genealogy that tracks the movement of a particular nineteenth-century ethos from Scotland to Canada, as Munro emphasizes in the first paragraph of her foreword:

> About ten or twelve years ago I began to take more than a random interest in the history of one side of my family, whose name was Laidlaw. There was a good deal of information lying around about them – really an unusual amount, considering that they were obscure and not prosperous, and living in the Ettrick Valley, which *The Statistical Account of Scotland* (1799) describes as having *no advantages.* I lived in Scotland for a few months, close to the Ettrick Valley, so I was able to find their names in the local histories in the Selkirk and Galashiels Public Libraries, and to find out what James Hogg had to say about them in *Blackwood's Magazine*. Hogg's mother was a Laidlaw, and he took Walter Scott to see her when Scott was collecting ballads for *The Minstrelsy of the Scottish Border*. (She supplied some, though she later took offense at their being printed.) And I was lucky, in that every generation of our family seemed to produce somebody who went in for writing long, outspoken, sometimes outrageous letters, and detailed recollections. Scotland was the country, remember, where John Knox had decided that every child should learn to read and write, in some sort of village school, so that everybody could read the Bible. (ix)

The ensuing stories in *The View from Castle Rock* trace the intergenerational migration of the Laidlaws from the Ettrick Valley to Edinburgh, then on to Nova Scotia, Illinois, and Ontario. Critics have also noted some of the literary traces of this migration in Munro's writing. For example, the comparison of Munro to Scott as a regionalist with an interest in the idiosyncratic speech and customs of rural regions has been established since early reviews of *Dance of the Happy Shades* (Claire Tomalin, qtd. in Thacker, *Alice Munro* 428-29; also see Duffy 208-12). And even before the publication of *The View from Castle Rock*, critics had begun to pay attention to echoes of Hogg in Munro's stories. For example, Magdalene Redekop argued in 1998 that "a Scottish oral tradition informs Munro's craft at the deepest level, particularly as it has come to her through the writings of her ancestor James Hogg" (23), the so-called "Ettrick Shepherd." However, Munro only learned of her family relation to Hogg in mid-life, so for the purposes of appreciating *Dance of the Happy Shades*, one must identify other ways in which this Scottish connection shadows her early writing. I propose that the connection can be found by investigating links between Hogg's contemporaries at *Blackwood's Magazine* and the opening of the Huron Tract.

By 1851, Munro's ancestors were heading west from Halton County into the Huron Tract, a 1.1 million acre territory that was ceded to the British crown by the Chippewa in 1827 and then sold to a private land corporation, the Canada Company, for settlement. The Huron Tract was a triangular wedge of land encompassing what are now Huron and Perth counties as well as parts of neighbouring counties. The Tract included extensive parts of the Lake Huron shoreline, including the port city of Goderich, which was to be the Tract's cultural and economic centre. Settlement of the Tract gradually branched out from Goderich into the swampy inland territory, from which emerged cities such as Wingham (where Munro was born and raised) and Clinton (where she settled in August 1975 [Thacker, *Alice Munro* 228]).

This territory required significant investment to enable settlers to get their products to market and the Crown sold the Tract to the Canada Company at a discounted price on the condition that they would undertake capital-intensive projects such as building The Huron Road from Guelph to Goderich. This road linked Canada Company holdings in the Guelph area to the Huron Tract and was "the first overland communication between the sweet water seas of Ontario and Huron" (Grant vi). The road enabled Munro's ancestors to travel west from the Halton region, near Guelph, to settle in Morris Township, near Blyth, in 1851 (Munro, *The View* 111-17).

The Canada Company's scheme differed from earlier waves of organized British emigration to Ontario, such as Lord Selkirk's 1804 resettlement of poor Scottish highlanders in Baldoon, near what became Wallaceburg (Campey 51-76), in that the Company was a for-profit venture which raised its capital through joint-stock issuances (J.A. Scott 36). The Company's Board of Directors entrusted the supervision of its Canadian operations to Hogg's friends John Galt and William Dunlop, part of a coterie of contributors who sustained *Blackwood's Magazine* in Edinburgh and, later, *Fraser's Magazine* in London. Thus, while Munro was reading through back issues of *Blackwood's* in search of commentary on the Laidlaws, she would also have been exploring the literary formation of the Huron Tract, since Galt and Dunlop used their periodical publications to promote emigration to Canada.

As Jennifer Anne Scott demonstrates in her 2013 dissertation, "The Business of Writing Home: Authorship and the Transatlantic Economies of John Galt's Literary Circle, 1807-1840," the publications of the Canada Company authors, particularly John Galt, "map multiple intersections between imperial politics, speculative capitalism, and authorship" (173). The Canada Company, incorporated in 1826, was conceived by Galt and supported by the London-based investors that he recruited. These investors appointed Galt Superintendent of their Canadian operations between 1826 and 1829, and Galt oversaw land sales in the Huron Tract and sundry other locations from his headquarters in the city of Guelph, which he co-founded with Dunlop. Critics might assume that Galt's North American writing was simply a by-product of his work for the Canada Company, but Scott argues that Galt's land speculation was an extension of his literary pursuits:

> Galt's initial entry into the British publication business speaks to a trend that would follow him throughout his literary career: the exploitation of the *idea* of North America as a vendible commodity for consumption in the British literary marketplace. His first such publication, "A Statistical Account of Upper Canada," appeared in *The Philosophical Magazine* (October 1807[-January 1808]), and like many others of its time, was an interpretation of North America based not on personal experience but on other already-published works. In his subsequent writing, wherever convenient, Galt takes advantage of the authority of print culture to use his publications as a venue to promote the Canada Company. At other times, he uses authorship to translate the lived reality of emigration to North America into an entertaining and palatable version of emigrant life. (18)

Galt thus capitalized on a market for writing about British North America to build his reputation as a writer; he then leveraged his print publications to make himself an authority on Upper Canada in governmental affairs. For example, Upper Canadian loyalists who had incurred damages by supporting British troops in the War of 1812 hired Galt to lobby parliament for reparations. Galt proposed that the government pay for reparations through the sale of Crown lands reserved for the support of the Anglican Church. Galt's proposal failed but it sparked the idea for a private venture that would purchase undeveloped land in Upper Canada from the Crown and resell it on a speculative basis (Hall and Whistler). The company that arose from this idea made unprecedented use of print advertising to promote land sales even as Galt exploited his connections to the periodical press to advance his business interests. For example, Jennifer Anne Scott calculates that "only four of Galt's eighteen contributions" to *Fraser's Magazine* between February 1830 and January 1833

> were not directly related to North America or the larger project of British colonial expansion. ... In spite of differing generic connections, the underlying purpose of each text is virtually the same: to promote emigration to North America to the readers of literary periodicals. (65)

In a slightly different vein, Gilbert A. Stelter argues that Galt's chief passion was for town building and that Galt subordinated his writing to that ambition: "Even in the book summing up his literary career [Galt] wrote that he had 'ever held literature to be a secondary pursuit ... but when my numerous books are forgotten, I should yet be remembered ... [for] I contrived the Canada Company, which will hereafter be spoken of among the eras of a nation destined to greatness'" (17).

After the Canada Company fired Galt in 1829 for poor accounting, he converted his Canadian experiences into a novel, *Bogle Corbet; or, The Emigrants* (1831), inspired by his time in Guelph. This novel blurs the boundaries between fiction and nonfiction by, in Scott's words, "conclud[ing] with an extended appendix offering practical advice for settlers" (25). The subtitle and appendix of *Bogle Corbet* thus make clear the connection between early Canadian fiction in English and the more established genre of emigrant guides. Galt was not alone in this multifaceted enterprise. Thelma Coleman has shown that the Canada Company made use of a range of writers to advertise its lands to a literate audience who were more likely to afford the higher cost per acre of land in the

Huron Tract (111; also see Lizars 139-40). Likewise, Scott demonstrates that Galt drew on the early-nineteenth-century logic of the new joint-stock companies to advance his business interests through the group efforts of a coterie of author-agents (170-71).

In the process, the Canada Company authors amassed an important body of early writing about Upper Canada as well as large collections of published texts on the Canadas in general. Consider, for example, the title of Andrew Picken's 1832 volume, *The Canadas, As They at Present Commend Themselves to the Enterprize of Emigrants, Colonists, and Capitalists. Comprehending a Variety of Topographical Reports Concerning the Quality of the Land, etc., in Different Districts; and the Fullest General Information: Compiled and Condensed from Original Documents Furnished by John Galt, Esq. Late of the Canada Company, and Now of the British American Land Association, and Other Authentic Sources.*

The underlying purpose of these Canada Company publications is to survey the lands available to the prospective emigrant and to argue for the superiority of the Canada Company lands and purchasing system. The reciprocal manner in which the authors also boosted their reputations through corporate-sponsored publication deserves further inquiry, but for the purposes of this essay it is enough to note that, a century before Alice Munro was born in 1931, the Canada Company lands had already been written and rewritten in English in a variety of fictional and nonfictional formats and distributed throughout a transatlantic literary market.

This literary legacy begs the question: might the Canada Company authors have influenced Munro, who is otherwise famous for her interest in regional history (Weaver) and her postcolonial "preoccupation with origins" (Ventura 93)? Galt's legacy is the most obvious starting point to begin such an inquiry, in part because he has the highest profile of the Canada Company authors and in part because critics such as Katie Trumpener have recently emphasized stylistic affinities between Galt's novels and Munro's fiction.

Broadly speaking, Galt's literary reputation is that of a man with innovative ideas and important connections who nonetheless did not succeed entirely in achieving lasting fame for his copious literary productions. In his day, Galt was known as the friend and biographer of the Romantic poet Lord Byron, but literary critics remember Galt's fiction for its regional content and for facilitating the transition from Romantic idealism to Victorian realism in the 1820s and 1830s. Galt preceded Walter Scott in trying to translate Scottish legends and dialect into prose for a larger English-speaking literary market and his Scottish novels documented a culture threatened by the strain of the industrial revolution and the highland clearances (J.A. Scott 1-2; Hall and Whistler).

Galt submitted a manuscript of his novel "The Pastor" to the Edinburgh publishing house Constable in 1813. Constable would seem to have been a good choice because this publisher would issue Sir Walter Scott's landmark Scottish novel *Waverley* in 1814. However, the previous year, Constable rejected Galt's novel because they felt that "there was no market for Scottish novels" (Gordon 2). Galt's "The Pastor" was eventually published in 1821 by Constable's rival Blackwood as the soon-to-be celebrated novel *Annals of the Parish*. Still, Galt felt cheated in his claims to posterity and forever envied Scott's fame (J.A. Scott 1-2). However, the eye for detail and the ear for dialect – what Galt called "local memory" (qtd. in O'Hagan 14) – in Galt's largely plotless novel anticipates Munro's work in the way that the minutely depicted "town becomes a simulacrum for the entire world at the same time as it embodies what is lost to the novelist himself" (O'Hagan 11). Galt's Ayrshire, as Andrew O'Hagan notes in a passage equally applicable to Munro's Huron County, is "both the centre of things and a backwater of the mind, irrigating everything" (12).

Galt's novels also responded to the empirical values of the Scottish Enlightenment, as Craig Lamont amply demonstrates, and hence philosophers celebrate Galt for coining the term "utilitarian" in *Annals of the Parish* (J.A. Scott 2), a term which John Stuart Mill subsequently elaborated into the quintessential Victorian philosophy of Utilitarianism. The empirical and didactic qualities of Galt's Scottish novels are so strong that Galt disliked categorizing them as novels, as Roger Hall and Nick Whistler observe:

> Although *Annals* was often taken for a novel, Galt referred to the group of works to which it belongs as "theoretical histories." Written in the fictional autobiographic form of which he is one of the earliest, most innovative, and prolific exponents, the book chronicles, through the eyes of a village priest, the social and industrial changes Galt observed sweeping across Ayrshire. His preservation of west country dialect was and remains relished by Scots....

It is this voice, regional focus, and the strong documentary com-
ponent of Galt's Scottish and North American novels that inspire
comparisons to Munro's works. For example, stories such as "Walker
Brothers Cowboy" make extensive use of autobiographical experience
(or at least autobiographical form); indeed, Isla Duncan notes that "[o]f
the 15 stories in Munro's prize-winning collection, *Dance of the Happy
Shades*, twelve are written from a first-person narrative perspective" (19).
Likewise, Katie Trumpener argues that

> Galt and Munro inhabit very different temporal, political and literary
> moments, yet describe the same area, in present-day Ontario, while
> sharing an interest in the local texture of historical experience, using
> annalistic accretion to ground new forms of historical fiction. (43)

The only problem with Trumpener's excellent comparison of Galt to
Munro is that the authors did not really inhabit the same area, even for
the three years that Galt lived in Canada. Guelph is more than a hundred
kilometres distant from Wingham; it was part of the Canada Company's
Halton Block and is closer to Lakes Erie and Ontario than it is to Lake
Huron. If one accepts the conventional argument that "Alice Munro
Country" is the triangular circuit taking in Wingham, Goderich, and
Clinton that shaped Munro's youth, then more critical attention should
be paid to the Canada Company authors who actually lived and wrote
in that area. In the interest of brevity, this essay will focus on William
Dunlop, the man charged with overseeing settlement in the Huron Tract
from Goderich, a city he co-founded with Galt.

As Carl F. Klinck describes in his pioneering scholarly study, *William
"Tiger" Dunlop, "Blackwoodian Backwoodsman"*, Dunlop was a British
military doctor who served in the War of 1812 and who established a
literary reputation as a learned man who enjoyed undertaking dangerous work in Britain's colonies and making light of the experience in
sprightly prose published in *Blackwood's*, *Fraser's*, and Montreal's *The
Literary Garland*, among other periodicals. Like Hogg, Dunlop built his
literary reputation on his status as a carouser whose witty, plaid-clad,
whisky-swilling Scots persona was as important to his contemporaries
as anything he wrote.

Recruited back to Upper Canada by Galt, Dunlop became "Warden of the Forests" for the Huron Tract in 1826 and his zeal for camping with the early settlers generated a *nom de plume*, "The Backwoodsman," that was very marketable to an imperial readership. For example, Samuel Strickland, Dunlop's assistant in the Huron Tract, devotes an entire chapter to reminiscences about Dunlop in *Twenty-Seven Years in Canada West* (1853), a work, Carole Gerson informs us, that was "[i]nstigated and edited" by his sister Agnes Strickland (61). Samuel famously encouraged his sisters Catharine Parr Traill and Susanna Moodie to emigrate to Upper Canada and the introductions to Traill's *The Backwoods of Canada* (1836) and Moodie's *Roughing It in the Bush* (the 1854 edition) frame their writing as feminist corrections to the bachelor's society depicted in Dunlop's writing. If Dunlop may not seem like a significant writer to contemporary critics, they nonetheless must recognize that he was a literary celebrity in his day.

Dunlop's most important book was his 1832 publication, *Statistical Sketches of Upper Canada, for the Use of Emigrants: By a Backwoodsman*. The dry-sounding title of Dunlop's book, like that of Galt's 1807-08 account in *The Philosophical Magazine*, signals its debt to *The Statistical Account of Scotland* (1791-99), as Kevin Halliwell explains:

> Guides to Upper Canada hardly existed in any form until the 1820s, when the number began to rise, and the first use of the word 'guide' as applied to North America hardly predates this. Another prototype that was in existence, however, which offered some detailed descriptions of a country, its inhabitants, their livelihoods and possibilities of improvement, was the 'Statistical Account,' which first appeared in Scotland in the 1790s. The 1791-99 *Statistical Account of Scotland* was an ambitious project that collected descriptions of the whole country provided by local parish ministers, but the word 'statistical' did not have its present meaning. It had been coined by Sir John Sinclair, editor of the accounts, from the German, and it meant for him: 'an inquiry into the state of a country, *for the purpose of ascertaining the* quantum *of happiness enjoyed by its inhabitants, and the means of its future improvement*.'

For Dunlop, a statistical account was a mixture of geology, botany, demography, political economy, economic speculation, pastoral description, and musings on local customs and idioms that would help prospective settlers to integrate into Upper Canadian society. Dunlop's *Statistical Sketches* instructed a target group of prospective emigrants but his alternation between helpful fact and amusing anecdote attracted a broad reading public and *Statistical Sketches* went through multiple editions. As Elizabeth Waterston notes, Dunlop's "pungent account does indeed include accurate information on everything under the Upper Canadian sun, but he also flips the facts around in deft, ironic, zestful style" (108). Dunlop's account also distinguished itself from the emigrant guides of his contemporaries by demonstrating an in-depth knowledge of the territories under discussion, as the ecologist John L. Riley notes:

> Dunlop managed to write a charming solicitation for the Company.... Unlike some of the other guides of the time, it reads not like an extended complaint by an inconvenienced tourist but, rather, like an engaging account by a long-time resident. (90)

It is possible that Munro uses the findings of these statistical accounts to ground her sketches of Huron County; indeed, Munro signals a connection to the statistical accounts in *The View from Castle Rock* by beginning her foreword with the dismissive portrait of the Ettrick Valley in *The Statistical Account of Scotland*, and then by titling the first story "No Advantages" and opening it with a long citation from *The Statistical Account*. At the same time, Munro reverses the colonial gaze of the imperial Scots and then re-enacts, in the reputedly barren Ettrick Valley, the literary process of investigation and reclamation through which the Huron Tract, originally perceived as undesirable land by colonists, was shown to be rich in material and literary resources.

***

Given these tantalizing connections between Munro and the Canada Company authors, the remainder of this essay will explore affinities between Munro's "Walker Brothers Cowboy" and the legacy of the Canada Company authors. Her story is set in the fictional town of Tuppertown, "an old grain port" (1) on Lake Huron loosely based on Goderich. Like Goderich, this port features a breakwater and swimming area along a shoreline that used to be occupied by "Indians" (3), in Goderich's case by the Chippewa who camped in the flats where the Maitland River – or as the Indigenous people originally called it, the "Meneseteung," a word that Munro's much-acclaimed story of this name plays on (see Struthers, "In Search" 180) – empties into Lake Huron. As Robina and Kathleen MacFarlane Lizars recall, about five hundred Chippewa still lived on the flats in the early years of the Goderich settlement, greatly outnumbering the Canada Company settlers (84). The young female narrator of "Walker Brothers Cowboy" has recently moved to Tuppertown from Dungannon, a real village in what is now the amalgamated township of Ashfield-Colborne-Wawanosh. These formerly distinct townships extending north of Goderich were once dominated by Dunlop and the group of highly literate landowners known as the Colborne Clique, who fought a war of words with the Toronto-based Family Compact for political control of the Huron Tract in the 1830s and 1840s, as the Lizars explain from the Clique perspective and Robert C. Lee explains from the Compact one.

Munro's short story is set during the Great Depression and the young narrator's family – her father, Ben Jordan, her unnamed mother, and her younger brother – have fallen on hard times:

> Up until last winter we had our own business, a fox farm. My father raised silver foxes and sold their pelts to the people who make them into capes and coats and muffs. Prices fell, my father hung on hoping they would get better next year, and they fell again, and he hung on one more year and one more and finally it was not possible to hang on any more.... (4)

The failure of this speculative venture is closely modelled on the failure of the "Laidlaw Fur Farm enterprise" (Ross 31) and hence critics hail "Walker Brothers Cowboy" as a strongly autobiographical fiction, particularly in its depiction of the parents' different reactions to the loss (Thacker, *Alice Munro* 52-53). The bankruptcy strikes the mother particularly hard in the short story because the loss represents a blow to her social status as a capitalist in a frontier society, where hard work and austerity are supposed to lead to fortune.

This class distinction is crucial to the mood of the story because it explains the mother's sense of superiority toward her poor neighbours in Tuppertown and her concept of poverty, which seems irrational to the narrator:

> my mother has no time for the national calamity, only ours. Fate has flung us onto a street of poor people (it does not matter that we were poor before, that was a different sort of poverty), and the only way to take this, as she sees it, is with dignity, with bitterness, with no reconciliation. No bathroom with a claw-footed tub and a flush toilet is going to comfort her, nor water on tap and sidewalks past the house and milk in bottles, not even the two movie theatres and the Venus Restaurant and Woolworths so marvellous it has live birds singing in its fan-cooled corners and fish as tiny as fingernails, as bright as moons, swimming in its green tanks. My mother does not care. (4)

This catalogue suggests that the material circumstances of the family's life have improved, from the daughter's perspective, and she must look to her father to understand better the familial tensions brought about by the loss of the farm.

Initially, the father appears to have adapted well to the family's change of fortune. Unlike many men during the Depression, he has a job that "'keeps the wolf from the door'" (13). He is a travelling salesman for the fictitiously named American firm of Walker Brothers:

> This is a firm that sells almost entirely in the country, the back country. Sunshine, Boylesbridge, Turnaround – that is all his territory. Not Dungannon where we used to live, Dungannon is too near town and my mother is grateful for that. (3)

The mother's shame hinges on the crucial distinction between owning a farm and working for a firm, of being a landowner and being "a pedlar knocking at backwoods kitchens" (4). Like the Canada Company before it, American corporations are carving up this backwoods territory and the father is a barely willing agent of this new wave of economic imperialism. Whereas the narrator's mother is resolutely British and considers herself "a lady" (5) and her husband "a gentleman" (9), their changing economic circumstances mean that Ben drives an American car that is British in name only, "an Essex, and long past its prime" (8). Like Moodie, the narrator's mother deplores the American influence on speech and dress in her society, but in a cultural crossroads such as Southwestern Ontario this sense of cultural crisis is perennial.

Ben Jordan employs a variety of coping strategies to deal with his changing circumstances. In his leisure hours, he takes the long view of historical change and his geologic sense of time echoes the statistical accounts. Munro introduces the father's scientific musings with a joking question that opens the short story: "After supper my father says, 'Want to go down and see if the Lake's still there?'" (1). The joke actually has some historical basis as early European accounts of the Great Lakes, by the likes of John Galt among others, speculated that "in time the lakes of Canada must also be exhausted, and lay open the bosom of the country" (Galt, "A Statistical Account" 3).

In Munro's story, the ensuing walk to the lake offers what Coral Ann Howells characterizes as "a scrupulously detailed map of the main street of Tuppertown" (17) as well as a sociological portrait of the narrator's neighbours. The narrative sensibility here is cartographic, mapping the city and its state of industrial decline, until father and daughter reach the lakeshore and he inadvertently shocks her by explaining "how the Great Lakes came to be" (3). Ben means to comfort his daughter with this geology lesson, underscoring how giant forces reshape particular landscapes. However, the father's scientific reasoning has the opposite effect on his daughter: "The tiny share we have of time appalls me, though my father seems to regard it with tranquillity" (3). Water represents "the uncontrollable" in this short story (Carrington 71-73) and the father's failed attempt to calm his daughter with an empirical explanation of the lake's mutations signals the beginning of an epistemological shift that is crucial to Munro's revision of the empirical sensibility that grounds the Canada Company narratives and statistical accounts.

The Jordans' vista of Lake Huron also suggests an intertextual connection to Dunlop's writing and a revision of his colonial perspective on the territory that early settlers called "the Huron." Dunlop established the original Canada Company headquarters in Goderich on a cliff with a view of Lake Huron and the Maitland River delta. Interestingly, J.R. (Tim) Struthers proposes that the meaning of the Indigenous name for the river, "Meneseteung," is "place of little islands" ("In Search" 180; "Imagining" 72-73). The site remained the office of the Canada Company Commissioner for decades and is now called Harbour Park, its view of the Maitland partly obscured by concrete silos servicing the docks below.

Part of the mystique of the Colborne Clique was the much-mythologized image of the local élite gathering on the bluffs of the Maitland River, where they drank and "laughed and danced and sang" and, as the Lizars describe,

> sat on the benches and sunned themselves of bright afternoons; where the seats along the bank were filled evening after evening with people who never wearied of that gorgeous pageant – not colour but conflagration – which the sunsets furnished. These sunsets were so famous that travellers hearing of them made the detour to that out-of-the-way corner of the world on purpose to enjoy them. (105)

Indeed, Dunlop concludes his *Statistical Sketches* with the envoi, "until we meet, as I hope we shall do next summer, on the banks of Lake Huron" (120).

Munro both invokes and revises this romantic portrait of colonial life when she depicts Ben taking his daughter to "a vacant lot, a kind of park really, for it is kept clear of junk and there is one bench with a slat missing on the back, a place to sit and look at the water" (2). In contrast to the brilliant sunsets that make this shoreline a tourist destination along the Bluewater Highway, Munro depicts a view of the water as "generally grey in the evening, under a lightly overcast sky, no sunsets, the horizon dim" (2). The clarity and command of Goderich's colonial vista have been clouded, in the short story, by the uncertain economic future of Depression-era Tuppertown and the collapse of the system of speculative capitalism championed by the Canada Company.

Ben's coping strategy during his work hours is an ironic stance toward his new job. Dressed in his "salesman's outfit" – light-coloured suit pants, a white shirt, with "pencils clipped in the shirt pocket" (6) – he composes a self-deprecating country and western song about himself as "'The Walker Brothers Cowboy'" (7) to entertain his two children who accompany him on his sales route. The song transforms the dire circumstances of the Depression into "a comic calamity" (7) that particularly involves the young boy. The father adopts an American vernacular for this song: "'Wisht I was back on the Rio Grande'," he sings, "'plungin' through the dusky sand'" (7).

Ben masters the Walker Brothers' pitch, which makes him sound like an American carney, and he also adjusts his mannerisms to suit his customers, which makes him a good salesman. However, Ben's light-hearted irony begins to dissipate when he knocks at a farm door and gets a bucket of urine dumped on his head, in full view of his children. The boy "laughs and laughs" (9) but the father is not amused and does not incorporate the event into his autobiographical song. Instead, he drives straight out of his Walker Brothers territory toward a destination even further into the back country, where his old girlfriend, Nora Cronin, lives. The drive represents a high-speed movement into an anachronistic space: toward the landscape of Ben's youth, toward his first love, and toward a woman who is poor but has not lost her farm.

Ben's social adaptability and his mastery of idiom have failed him on a grand scale in the case of Nora, who *"digs with the wrong foot,"* as the Jordans' Protestant relatives in Dungannon would say of Irish Catholics (14; see Cheape). Ben clearly pines for his lost love, who is a hardworking and sensuous woman with a talent for making Ben laugh. Although the daughter does not describe Nora's looks in flattering terms, Nora none-theless possesses an alluring vitality in comparison with Ben's wife, who oscillates between aggressive displays of propriety and withering inca-pacity. The daughter recognizes that Ben rejected Nora because of her religion, and the sense of mutual regret that colours the lovers' reunion is even more poignant if read in terms of the legacy of Galt and Dunlop.

Galt defended religious minorities in the Anglican-dominated era of the Family Compact. Indeed, the original idea for selling off the Anglican "clergy reserves" may have come from Galt's friend Alexan-der McDonell, the future Catholic Bishop of Upper Canada (Hall and Whistler). As Dunlop relates, McDonell, a veteran of the War of 1812 (99), subsequently became a friend of Dunlop (vi) and his influence helped to change Dunlop's view of Catholics:

> An elder of the [Presbyterian] Kirk, and bred in the most orthodox part of
> Scotland, I came to this country strongly prejudiced against Catholicism
> and its ministers; but experience has shown me that these prejudices

were unjust.... I look upon this public avowal and recantation as a penance for my sins of ignorance, and I hope it will be accepted as such. (100-01)

This recantation in *Statistical Sketches* comes in a section where Dunlop challenges the assumption, promoted by the Orange Order in the nineteenth century, that Irish Catholics were undesirable settlers and a threat to the stability of the British colony (72-73, 100). Ben Jordan, in yielding to the anti-Catholic prejudices of his family, fails to match Dunlop's liberality on this issue and he plainly regrets it.

In the terms of James Carscallen's book *The Other Country: Patterns in the Writing of Alice Munro*, the father's visit to Nora's farm is a typically Munrovian movement from Home to the Other Place and back again (123). The Other Place is embodied by Catholic Nora as the other woman in Ben's life (Dvořák 57) and highlighted by the question posed by Nora's aged mother: "'You haven't been to see us in the longest time. Have you been out of the country?'" (12). Yet the biblical resonances of Ben's last name complicate this Home / Other Place dynamic because, as Carscallen explains, the Jordan River connotes "the water of purification – the putting off of everything that belongs with Egypt or wilderness" (48).

Momentarily, at least, the father seems to have returned to the promised land from exile, and the daughter's exposure to this side of Ben's life precipitates an epistemological crisis even more appalling than the geology lesson:

> She and my father drink and I know what it is. Whisky. One of the things my mother has told me in our talks together is that my father never drinks whisky. But I see he does. He drinks whisky and he talks of people whose names I have never heard before. (15)

Here, water imagery initiates the narrator into adult mysteries whose significance she intuits but cannot articulate: the father's choice between whisky and "Walker Brothers Orange syrup" (13); Nora's perspiration from her aroused dancing (16); the grandmother's possible tear for her childless daughter when the narrator touches the blind woman's hand (12). The father does not explain any of these complexities to his daughter on the drive home, but there has been what Carscallen, echoing a term from the end of the final story of the collection, calls "a *communiqué*" (2; also see Munro, "Dance" 224) in the narrator's visit to the Cronins.

"Walker Brothers Cowboy" concludes by revising the introductory image of Lake Huron in light of the Jordans' visit to the Cronins' unpainted house, "dried to silver in the sun" (10). This revision underscores the daughter's new sense of epistemological uncertainty after the momentary *éclairage* of the visit:

> So my father drives and my brother watches the road for rabbits and I feel my father's life flowing back from our car in the last of the afternoon, darkening and turning strange, like a landscape that has an enchantment on it, making it kindly, ordinary and familiar while you are looking at it, but changing it, once your back is turned, into something you will never know, with all kinds of weathers, and distances you cannot imagine.
>
> When we get closer to Tuppertown the sky becomes gently overcast, as always, nearly always, on summer evenings by the Lake. (18)

Here, biographical time has become liquid, epistemological clarity has been replaced by a mostly overcast sky, and the landscape of "the Huron" mimics the changing qualities of the lake.

Munro's narrative also produces a sense of radical uncertainty in the reader when one considers Ben's status as a guide to the backwoods. Ben's impulsive visit to Nora's farm raises the question of whether Ben rashly exposes his daughter to a hidden side of himself or whether the visit is part of a lesson about love and/or religious tolerance. Munro leaves the former possibility open but weights the response in favour of the latter options, since Ben has not allowed the children out of the car at other stops on his circuit. As Coral Ann Howells observes, the father "shows his daughter how to read the landscape for what is hidden in it, though he is an ambiguous guide who sometimes interprets for her and sometimes deliberately leaves things unexplained" (17).

Ben guides the children through their various migrations within Huron County, but his perspective on the landscape is much less utilitarian than that of the emigrant guides. Ben seems to want his daughter to acquire a more nuanced perspective on the territory but he does not use his authority as guide to impose a singular interpretation of it. Hence, when the narrator asks her father why they are visiting the Cronins, he replies, "'You'll see'" (10), which could be a deferral of a response or could be an intimation of a perspective she must acquire herself or could be both. As E.D. Blodgett argues, "[w]hat Munro's early narrators endeavor to do is to find the meaning in a story that does not appear to have one" (17). In this instance, the narrator strives to discover the meaning of the visit to Nora's farm and her father's subsequent silence.

The short story's narrative also shifts from an empirical mode in its first half to a more mythopoeic mode in its second half. The daughter, who begins the story by aimlessly writing in the dirt "with a stick" (2), develops a new manner of describing Huron County after she has witnessed Nora touch the fender of her father's car, "making an unintelligible mark in the dust there" (17). Much as Del Jordan in *Lives of Girls and Women* must revise the legacy of the statistic-laden history of "Wawanash County" [sic] that she inherits from her Uncle Craig (60-63), the young narrator in "Walker Brothers Cowboy" develops a new way of perceiving the Tuppertown area by negotiating her father's intellectual and emotional legacy, which in itself seems to be a revision of the emigrant guides produced by the Canada Company authors.

Munro's short story both employs and exposes the limitations of the empirical modes of notation developed in these emigrant guides, even as it critiques the capitalist uses of writing implied by the pencils in Ben's salesman's outfit. In "Walker Brothers Cowboy," then, the multiple meanings of the word "tract" – as a parcel of land, a promotional pamphlet, or a political or religious treatise – are updated by Munro in her portrait of Huron County as a place with many historical and phenomenological layers. As Robert Thacker argues, "at the core of her art lies Munro's own experience of Huron County, Ontario: a place remembered, recovered, revised, and, at times, renounced" ("Connection" 214); and in the case of the anti-Catholic sentiments accepted by William Dunlop and Ben Jordan in their youth, one must add that renunciations can be recanted. "Walker Brothers Cowboy" is indeed, as W.R. Martin observes, a story about "the transmission and the inheritance of human tradition and spirit" (52), but here this literary and familial inheritance is negotiated and reinterpreted by both the father and the daughter and, in turn, by the reader.

Works Consulted

Berndt, Katrin. "The Ordinary Terrors of Survival: Alice Munro and the Canadian Gothic." *The Short Stories of Alice Munro*. Ed. Héliane Ventura. *Journal of the Short Story in English / Les cahiers de la nouvelle* 55 (2010): 19-35.

Blodgett, E.D. *Alice Munro*. Boston: Twayne-G.K. Hall, 1988. Twayne's World Authors Ser. 800.

Campey, Lucille H. *The Silver Chief: Lord Selkirk and the Scottish Pioneers of Belfast, Baldoon and Red River*. Toronto: Natural Heritage, 2003.

Carrington, Ildikó de Papp. *Controlling the Uncontrollable: The Fiction of Alice Munro*. DeKalb, IL: Northern Illinois UP, 1989.

Carscallen, James. *The Other Country: Patterns in the Writing of Alice Munro*. Toronto: ECW, 1993.

Cheape, Hugh. "Notes and Queries: Why Are Catholics Sometimes Called 'Left-Footers'?" *The Guardian* 12 June 2018. <https://www.theguardian.com/notesandqueries/query/0,5753,-1121,00.html?gusrc=gpd>.

Coleman, Thelma. *The Canada Company*. Stratford, ON: Corporation of the County of Perth, 1978.

Duffy, Dennis. "Too Little Geography; Too Much History: Writing the Balance in 'Meneseteung'." *National Plots: Historical Fiction and Changing Ideas of Canada*. Ed. Andrea Cabajsky and Brett Josef Grubisic. Waterloo, ON: Wilfrid Laurier UP, 2010. 197-213, 215-36 passim.

Duncan, Isla. *Alice Munro's Narrative Art*. New York: Palgrave Macmillan, 2011.

Dunlop, William. *Statistical Sketches of Upper Canada, for the Use of Emigrants: By a Backwoodsman*. 1832. 3rd ed. London: John Murray, 1833.

Dvořák, Marta. "Alice Munro's 'Lovely Tricks' from *Dance of the Happy Shades* to *Hateship, Friendship, Courtship, Loveship, Marriage*." *Alice Munro: Writing Secrets*. Ed. Héliane Ventura and Mary Condé. *Open Letter* 11th ser., no. 9 - 12th ser., no. 1 (2003-04): 55-77.

Franzen, Jonathan. "'Runaway': Alice's Wonderland." Rev. of *Runaway*, by Alice Munro. *The New York Times* 14 Nov. 2004. <http://www.nytimes.com/2004/11/14/books/review/14COVERFR.html?pagewanted=all&_r=0>.

Galt, John. *Annals of the Parish; or, The Chronicle of Dalmailing, During the Ministry of the Rev. Micah Balwhidder, Written by Himself*. Philadelphia: M. Carey & Sons, 1821.

---. *Bogle Corbet; or, The Emigrants*. 3 vols. London: Henry Colburn and Richard Bentley, 1831.

---. "A Statistical Account of Upper Canada." *The Philosophical Magazine* 29 (1807-08): 3-10.

Gerson, Carole. "Reframing National Literary History: Canadian Writers in the International Sphere, 1830-1910." *Global Realignments and the Canadian Nation in the Third Millennium*. Ed. Karin Ikas. Wiesbaden, Ger.: Harrassowitz, 2010. 57-68. Kultur- und sozialwissenschaftliche Studien / Studies in Cultural and Social Sciences 5.

Gordon, Ian A. *John Galt: The Life of a Writer*. Toronto: U of Toronto P, 1972.

Grant, G.M. Introduction. *In the Days of the Canada Company: The Story of the Settlement of the Huron Tract and a View of the Social Life of the Period. 1825-1850*. By Robina Lizars and Kathleen MacFarlane Lizars. Toronto: William Briggs, 1896. v-x. Toronto: Coles, 1972. Coles Canadiana Collection.

Hall, Roger, and Nick Whistler. "John Galt." *Dictionary of Canadian Biography*. <http://www.biographi.ca/en/bio/galt_john_7E.html>.

Halliwell, Kevin. "John Galt and the Paratext: The Discourse of Authentication in North American Emigration Literature." National Library of Scotland. 21 July 2014. <https://nanopdf.com/download /3-intratextual-and-intertextual-relations_pdf>.

Heble, Ajay. *The Tumble of Reason: Alice Munro's Discourse of Absence*. Toronto: U of Toronto P, 1994.

Howells, Coral Ann. *Alice Munro*. Manchester, Eng.: Manchester UP, 1998. Contemporary World Writers.

Hurley, Michael. *The Borders of Nightmare: The Fiction of John Richardson*. Toronto: U of Toronto P, 1992.

Klinck, Carl F., sel. and ed. *William "Tiger" Dunlop, "Blackwoodian Backwoodsman": Essays by and about Dunlop*. Toronto: Ryerson, 1958.

Lamont, Craig. "Finding Galt in Glasgow." *The International Companion to John Galt*. Ed. Gerard Carruthers and Colin Kidd. Glasgow, Scot.: Scottish Literature International, 2017. 34-43, 143-45. International Companions to Scottish Literature.

Lee, Robert C. *The Canada Company and the Huron Tract, 1826-1853: Personalities, Profits and Politics*. Toronto: Natural Heritage, 2004.

Lizars, Robina, and Kathleen MacFarlane Lizars. *In the Days of the Canada Company: The Story of the Settlement of the Huron Tract and a View of the Social Life of the Period. 1825-1850.* Introd. G.M. Grant. Toronto: William Briggs, 1896. Toronto: Coles, 1972. Coles Canadiana Collection.

Martin, W.R. *Alice Munro: Paradox and Parallel.* Edmonton, AB: U of Alberta P, 1987.

Moodie, Susanna. Introduction. *Roughing It in the Bush; or, Life in Canada.* 1852. 3rd ed., with additions. London: Richard Bentley, 1854. [vii]-xiii.

Munro, Alice. "Dance of the Happy Shades." *Dance of the Happy Shades.* Fwd. Hugh Garner. Toronto: Ryerson, 1968. 211-24.

---. *Lives of Girls and Women.* Toronto: McGraw-Hill Ryerson, 1971.

---. "Meneseteung." *Friend of My Youth.* Toronto: McClelland & Stewart, 1990. 50-73.

---. *The View from Castle Rock.* Toronto: McClelland & Stewart, 2006.

---. "Walker Brothers Cowboy." *Dance of the Happy Shades.* Fwd. Hugh Garner. Toronto: Ryerson, 1968. 1-18.

"The Nobel Prize in Literature 2013: Alice Munro: Biobibliographical Notes." *Nobelprize.org.* <https://www.nobelprize.org/prizes/literature/2013/bio-bibliography/>.

O'Hagan, Andrew. "John Galt's Ayrshire." *The International Companion to John Galt.* Ed. Gerard Carruthers and Colin Kidd. Glasgow, Scot.: Scottish Literature International, 2017. 8-14, 138-39. International Companions to Scottish Literature.

Picken, Andrew. *The Canadas, As They at Present Commend Themselves to the Enterprize of Emigrants, Colonists, and Capitalists. Comprehending a Variety of Topographical Reports Concerning the Quality of the Land, etc., in Different Districts; and the Fullest General Information: Compiled and Condensed from Original Documents Furnished by John Galt, Esq. Late of the Canada Company, and Now of the British American Land Association, and Other Authentic Sources.* London: Effingham Wilson, 1832.

Proulx, Annie. Introduction. *Dance of the Happy Shades.* By Alice Munro. Toronto: Penguin, 2005. ix-xvi.

Rasporich, Beverly J. *Dance of the Sexes: Art and Gender in the Fiction of Alice Munro.* Edmonton, AB: U of Alberta P, 1990.

Redekop, Magdalene. "Alice Munro and the Scottish Nostalgic Grotesque." *Alice Munro Writing On....* Ed. Robert Thacker. *Essays on Canadian*

Writing 66 (1998): 21-43. Rpt. in *The Rest of the Story: Critical Essays on Alice Munro*. Ed. Robert Thacker. Toronto: ECW, 1999. 21-43.

Riley, John L. *The Once and Future Great Lakes Country: An Ecological History*. Montreal, QC and Kingston, ON: McGill-Queen's UP, 2013.

Ross, Catherine Sheldrick. *Alice Munro: A Double Life*. Toronto: ECW, 1992. Canadian Biography Ser. 1.

Scott, Jennifer Anne. "The Business of Writing Home: Authorship and the Transatlantic Economies of John Galt's Literary Circle, 1807-1840." Diss. Simon Fraser U, 2013.

Scott, Sir Walter. *Waverley; or, 'Tis Sixty Years Since*. 1814. Rev. ed. Ed. Claire Lamont. Introd. Kathryn Sutherland. Oxford, Eng.: Oxford UP, 2015. Oxford World's Classics.

Sinclair, John, ed. *The Statistical Account of Scotland. Drawn Up from the Communications of the Ministers of the Different Parishes*. 21 vols. Edinburgh: William Creech, 1791-99.

Stelter, Gilbert A. "John Galt: The Writer as Town Booster and Builder." *John Galt: Reappraisals*. Ed. Elizabeth Waterston. Guelph, ON: U of Guelph, 1985. 17-43.

Strickland, Samuel. *Twenty-Seven Years in Canada West; or, The Experience of an Early Settler*. Ed. Agnes Strickland. 2 vols. London: Richard Bentley, 1853. Introd. Carl F. Klinck. Edmonton, AB: M.G. Hurtig, 1970.

Struthers, J.R. (Tim). "Alice Munro and the American South." *Short Story Criticism: Criticism of the Works of Short Fiction Writers*. Vol. 208. Ed. Lawrence J. Trudeau. Farmington Hills, MI: Gale, 2015. 99-117.

---. "Imagining Alice Munro's 'Meneseteung': The Dynamics of Co-Creation." *Alice Munro: A Souwesto Celebration*. Ed. J.R. (Tim) Struthers and John B. Lee. *The Windsor Review* 47.2 (2014): 68-91.

---. "In Search of the Perfect Metaphor: The Language of the Short Story and Alice Munro's 'Meneseteung'." *Critical Insights: Alice Munro*. Ed. Charles E. May. Ipswich, MA: Salem-EBSCO, 2013. 175-94.

Thacker, Robert. *Alice Munro: Writing Her Lives: A Biography*. Toronto: McClelland & Stewart, 2005.

---. "Connection: Alice Munro and Ontario." *Establishing Ontario: A Bicentennial Retrospective*. Ed. Viktor A. Konrad. *The American Review of Canadian Studies* 14.2 (1984): 213-26. Rpt. as "Connection: Alice Munro and Ontario (1984)" in *Reading Alice Munro 1973-2013*. By Robert Thacker. Calgary: U of Calgary P, 2016. 45-64, 272, 285-300 passim.

Traill, Catharine Parr. Introduction. *The Backwoods of Canada: Being Letters from the Wife of an Emigrant Officer, Illustrative of the Domestic Economy of British America.* London: Charles Knight, 1836. 1-6. The Library of Entertaining Knowledge. Toronto: Coles, 1971. 1-6. Coles Canadiana Collection.

Trumpener, Katie. "Annals of Ice: Formations of Empire, Place and History in John Galt and Alice Munro." *Scottish Literature and Postcolonial Literature: Comparative Texts and Critical Perspectives.* Ed. Michael Gardiner, Graeme Macdonald, and Niall O'Gallagher. Edinburgh: Edinburgh UP, 2011. 43-56, 250-73 passim.

Ventura, Héliane. "Genealogy and Geology: Of Metanarratives of Origins." *Commonwealth Essays and Studies* 34.1 (2011): 93-100.

Waterston, Elizabeth. *Rapt in Plaid: Canadian Literature and Scottish Tradition.* Toronto: U of Toronto P, 2001.

Weaver, John. "Society and Culture in Rural and Small-Town Ontario: Alice Munro's Testimony on the Last Forty Years." *Patterns of the Past: Interpreting Ontario's History.* Ed. Roger Hall, William Westfall, and Laurel Sefton MacDowell. Toronto: Dundurn, 1988. 381-402.

Alice Munro's Black Bottom; or Black Tints and Euro Hints in *Lives of Girls and Women*

George Elliott Clarke

It is sensible to read Alice Munro's *Lives of Girls and Women*, her break-through 1971 linked-story novel, as an Anglo-Canadian realist inter-vention in second-wave feminism. The very title and the narrative of the developing gynocentric and feminist consciousness of the primary protagonist, Del Jordan, stress notions of female physical, intellectual, and metaphysical empowerment. The publication of the book at the height of the Women's Liberation Movement demands the responsible teasing out of feminist thematics.

Less obvious is the 2013 Nobel Laureate's interest in the multicul-turalism that enters Del Jordan's world through radio broadcasts, mag-azines, books, and, crucially, travellers, and which enables her actual "baptism" unto mature, intellectual self-awareness as well as sexual experience. In Munro's fiction, multiculturalism is the subtle, 1970 Cana-dian "ism," the silent sister of feminism (so to speak), but whose presence – especially in its *black*, racialized guise – is the actual catalyst for Del Jordan's sudden advances in consciousness. With this frame in mind, enhanced is our appreciation of Jordan's acquisition of an education excellently exceeding the Victorian, Eurocentric, and parochial limits of her rural household, school, and community. However, that's not to say that Munro's vision is unhesitatingly progressive....

I

Doubtless, the climax of Alice Munro's set of sequential tales, *Lives of Girls and Women* (1971), is the moment when the principal protagonist, the now-late-teen heroine, Del (or Della [82]) Jordan, quits herself of her virginity. In the portentously titled story, "Baptizing," Del half-enjoys, half-endures, her spontaneous coitus with Garnet French, a lumberyard worker who has just had her over to visit his ramshackle country home and meet his backwater clan. As they return to her home in Jubilee, Desire overtakes Garnet, and soon he is thrusting lustily into Del as she heaves herself "up against the house wall trying to keep my balance" (227). While the nocturnal, *al fresco* fucking ensues, Del finds herself having to hold Garnet's pants up, for she's "afraid that the white gleam of his buttocks might give us away, to anybody passing on the street" (227). Once the "baptismal" hymen-smashing is done, Del puts her hand to her "wet leg and it [comes] away dark. Blood" (227).

Thus, in this ritualistic – if also (in pseudo-Aristotelian terms) "comic" – scene, Del passes from girlhood to young womanhood. She is relieved to make the passage; she is relieved also to break, ultimately, with Garnet, rejecting his effort, as a homespun Baptist preacher, to actually baptize her into his version of patriarchal, rough-hewn, backwoods Christianity (236-40). When Del fights off Garnet (both upright in the pond as they had formerly been upright in coitus [227]), she establishes her feminist ascension from dependent daughter and student to independent woman and intellectual.

So accomplished is this pilgrim's progress that Canadian scholar Neil K. Besner remarks, "*Lives of Girls and Women* is the most powerful and manifold exploration in contemporary Canadian writing of the development of a young girl's life, her imagination, and her imaginative life" (13). Besner also holds, "feminists ... see in Munro's depiction of Del Jordan's growing awareness of the complexities of her relationships within her family and with boys and men, and of her own developing consciousness, a strong and accurate representation of contemporary girls' and women's lives" (13-14). The book is "compelling ... because it renders such a full and frank depiction of Del's growth as she explores and defines her relationships within her family, her apprehensions of mortality and the nature of faith, her emerging sexuality, and always," asserts Besner, "the nature of her own imagination as she discovers how language means to her, how words shape her vision and lead to her vocation as a writer of fiction" (14-15). Crucially, *Lives* is, in Besner's terms, a gynocentric *Künstlerroman* (14). It is difficult to contest any of his considerations of the book as female-oriented, feminist (perhaps despite Munro), and successful.

But that passage of Del, from bobbysoxer to bluestocking, isn't as plain as it seems. For instance, we glimpse Garnet's humping white bottom and then Del's vaginal emission of blood running dark down her leg. It seems a (blasphemous) image of Communion: the female blood as wine; the pale, male buttocks as bread. Read such, it is a carnal, secular version (*not* inversion) of The Last Supper and even of The Crucifixion, given that Del yields her virginity, upright, as if on a cross, with her legs spread widely enough to allow Garnet his benediction (227). Of course, the religious (Christian) apparatus has been foreshadowed by the meeting of Garnet and Del at a church service, but also by her previous discussions of whether or not it is sensible to believe in God.[1] The symbolism here is pretty clear, with Del's conversion to heterosexual womanhood occurring on the road to Jubilee, if not to Damascus.

Less obvious perhaps is Munro's fealty to colour/racialized codes and multicultural references that enable us more fully to comprehend Ms. Jordan's gendered, biological segue from virgin to Venus, but also her progress from small-town, schoolgirl introvert to urbane, sophisticated-lady writer. In other words, Munro's subtle usage of black/white or dark/pale imagery, plus allusions to, especially, Italian and French culture, foreshadow and underscore Del's First Coitus, thus marking the moment as an awakening, jointly fleshy and philosophical.

To return, then, to the text's climactic passage, it is significant that Garnet's derrière, mooning the night, is as pallid as alabaster. This description serves to signal, already, his incipient loss of Del-as-his-Delilah.[2] In contrast, for her, that her "dark," hymeneal blood signs "the glory of the whole episode" (227) alerts us to her dawning sexual – and psychological – independence from one male in particular and from patriarchy in general.

This reading is germane because the implicit and gaudy symbolism of dark/black and light/white scores the text, almost as if we were regarding sheets of music. It acquires its crescendo just as Garnet penetrates Del; it then surges into her battle-over-baptism scene, where she resists the blandishments and rapacious force of Garnet to "come unto him" (given that she has already "*cum*," in the slang sense) and accept his would-be seminal Christianity. This image pattern is never innocent, for Del, in particular, senses continuously the attractive qualities of darkness and blackness, especially when these tints and tones are aligned with the wild, the free, the savage, the earthy, the sexual, the sensual.[3]

One may object that such connections are clichés, if not also conducive of stereotypes. Blogger Blue Telusma comments, "This idea that 'black equals erotic' is fetishism in its purest form" ("Kim"). In *Black Skin, White Masks* (1967), the Martiniquan-Algerian anti-imperialist Frantz Fanon insists: "The civilized white man retains an irrational longing for unusual eras of sexual license, of orgiastic scenes, of unpunished rapes, of unrepressed incest" (165); thus, says Fanon, "The Negro is taken as a terrifying penis" (177). Blackness is allied with aggressive sensuality, with licentious selfhood. Another scholar, Petrine Archer-Straw, holds: "For Europeans, Africa and the black man were framed in notions of high adventure, savagery, fear, peril and death" (13). According to Herbert Marcuse, thanks to the Black Arts and Black Power movements of the 1960s, the very idea of the *soul* "has been desublimated and in this transubstantiation, migrated to the Negro culture[,] [becoming, then,] black, violent, orgiastic" (42). "Similarly, the militant slogan 'black is beautiful' redefines another central concept of the traditional culture by ... associating [beauty] with the anti-colour of darkness, tabooed magic, the uncanny" (43).

There is, naturally, something sexual and fecund in black expressiveness. Sartre holds, "it is perhaps this nudity without color which best symbolizes Negritude" (62). Not only that, but "the black remains the great male of the earth, the sperm of the world" (45). It is not much of a leap from Sartre to Fanon, who understands that the semen-charged, black penis offers a potentially insurrectionist erection: "Whoever says *rape* says *Negro*" (166).

Read in unison, even if from opposing corners of our auditorium of black/white metaphors, Telusma, Sartre, Fanon, Marcuse, and Archer-Straw seem to agree that blackness – or darkness – is, for the European, Caucasian, and/or Occidental imagination, a cognate of the bestial, the illicit, the taboo and the tantalizing, the violent and the violating, the orgiastic and the anarchic. If their analyses are sound, we *should* expect Munro to traffic in these symbols.[4] In addition, therapeutic concepts of black-ness, derived from African American liberationist discourse, enjoyed cultural saliency in the later 1960s. Says William L. Van Deburg, "black self-actualization was accompanied by a corresponding questioning and rejection of many normative values forwarded by the majoritarian society" (52). Thus, *Black Is Beautiful* sloganeering could easily mutually reinforce feminist and/or sexual liberation discourse.[5]

For one thing, Munro tends to present attractive and/or likeable characters – if also flawed – as representing a shadowy whiteness, an albescent blackness, or a whiteness that is really an albino displacement of blackness. In this sense, then, Della Jordan becomes an honorary Negress, but she is not the only white character who is granted a spec-tral, black shadow, if not an actual, partial-African genealogy. Several of Munro's personages in *Lives of Girls and Women* could easily be con-nected, through imagery, to darkest Dixie or to exotic, Moorish-tinged Europe.[6] While Munro's direct narrative chronicles the sexual and intel-lectual liberation of a provincial, Ontarian adolescent at the close of the 1940s, her *shadow* narrative allows Del – in particular – access to racial markers (and European touchstones) that guide her transformation.

Notably, Munro's rural village – or town – Jubilee, situated in South-western Ontario, seems an extension of the Southern United States, employing descriptions of place that recall Erskine Caldwell's *Tobacco Road* (1932) and his novel's site of po' white trash as well as lyricists DuBose Heyward and Ira Gershwin's "Catfish Row," the demesne of mar-ginalized Negroes, in George Gershwin's opera *Porgy and Bess* (1935). Thus, the Jordan homestead on "The Flats Road" is situated in an area, the dead-end portion of Jubilee, which, in Dixie, would be dubbed The Bot-tom[7] or Bottoms. Whether we think of Del's neighbourhood as "Flats" or "Bottoms," there is an implication that we are among outcasts, the lowly, transients, and degenerates, or folks who entertain the forbidden, the illicit, the alluring, and the exciting, partly out of ignorance of anything better, and partly out of an effort to ameliorate desperate circumstances.

It is in this warren of the lower working-class (where Del's papa raises foxes), at the end of the Flats Road, where Del lives, that she encounters Uncle Benny, whose home, as if in Louisiana, is perched in a swamp, with "dark green blinds ... over all the windows" and "hot" black bush behind the dwelling (2). Here he presides over a welter of wreck and

ruin, cast-offs and junk, with his fixtures and furniture scavenged "from
the Jubilee dump" (4). If we imagine him as a bedraggled, albino version
of Uncle Ben's (the Negro mascot for the American rice company), we
might see him as resembling a resident of Africville, Nova Scotia, *circa*
1959, making a living by scavenging items from the city dump.[8]

Another Flats Road personage who resembles an albescent Negro
is "Pork Childs, who delivered coal and collected garbage for the
town" (94). His work is stereotypically the kinds of jobs that male
Canadian Negroes held in small-town Ontario and Nova Scotia in the
mid-twentieth century, partly because such employ was dirty and suited
the *de facto* caste system that was polite, unspoken, Canuck segregation.
But Pork's Christian name also conjures up, inevitably, Porgy,[9] the black
beggar and slum-dwelling protagonist in the black (or blackface) folk
opera *Porgy and Bess*.[10]

Like Porgy, Pork's circumstances are bleak. He dwells "down a poor
unnamed street" lacking sidewalks (159). Neither his barn nor his
house is painted (159). Too, Pork is a Baptist, a brand of Christianity
with particular appeal to African North Americans. Pork's most horrible
connection to archetypal, Black Dixie experience is that "All his toes had
been amputated ... after being frozen when he lay in a ditch long ago,
too drunk to get home" (159). One is reminded that partial amputation
of feet was one punishment meted out to runaway slaves in the ante-
bellum U.S. South: to hobble them so as to make future flight unlikely.[11]
I do submit that the portraits of Uncle Benny and Pork Childs configure
Jubilee as an extension of impoverished, retrograde, incestuous Dixie
and the Flats Road as an albino version of Catfish Row.

Later, when Del goes to Garnet's household and to what will be her
debut coitus, the rural setting of the French (and French-kissing) clan
is, again, reminiscent of the rickety shacks of the illiterate throwbacks
of *Tobacco Road*. So, Del sights an adolescent girl, "barefoot and brilliantly made up and swinging moodily around one of the verandah
posts" (222) – compare this description with low-brow, paperback cover
art of the era[12] – and a mother who carries "a package of tobacco and
some cigarette papers [in] her apron pockets" (223). Too, the French
household mirrors that of Uncle Benny: Del surveys strange furnishings, "walls ... covered with leafy floating shadows," and linoleum "black
and bumpy" (224).

When Garnet appears, he seems "dark against the glare of the back yard" (224). Though the French homestead is nothing like the French court at Versailles, it is invested with dark and lovely ("black, but comely" [Song Sol. 1.5, KJV]) references. Just before she accepts penetration from Garnet, Del sits to a Last-Supper-as-Virgin, which includes "a heavy molasses-flavoured cake, blackberry preserves,"[13] and a seating-plan for twelve that echoes the New Testament (226). The dark, sweet food; the dark-looking Garnet; and the shadowy, tobacco-smoky house, all prefigure Del's upright transfixing (if not orgasmic crucifixion) on Garnet's upright penis. Arguably, Del's assertion, "There is no denying I was happy in that house" (226) reveals that it was the portal for her midnight, outdoor, "joy-of-sex" experience.

The Flats Road (and like areas – Porterfield and Jenkin's Bend) is, then, the road-to-perdition, upon which one can be prodigal, for, in living here, in that whitewashed Black Bottom, one is actually beyond the pale. Thus, Uncle Benny's relative happiness is disrupted only when he moves from his dark swamps and accepts marriage, becoming "strange, pale, sacrificial" (13), while his bride is "thin, white, at first evasive" (17). Their whiteness is sickening, if slimming, and it is corrosive of their marriage. Similarly, the sight of Garnet's pasty fundament helps to spur Del's imminent rejection of her lover, the lumberyard pastor – a déclassé type of Christ the carpenter – and his white-bread Christianity.

Because Del spends her childhood on a road where "civilized, desirable things had come to an end" (6), it is also a place where whiteness comes into disrepute. Munro casts Irene, a bit character, as practically albino: she is "white-haired, not from age but because she was born that way, and her skin also [is] white as goosefeathers" (7). Too, Del imagines her grandmother, her "scalp unhealthily white. It was white as marble, white as soap" (75). Del also encounters "a very frail, weepy albino boy" (124). Such observations suggest that Del sees whiteness – at its most acute pitch – as defective or weak. No wonder, then, that Del dismisses her mother's story about how, as a girl in Porterfield, her brother, "a fat Indian,"[14] "tied [her] up in the barn" and "yelped and pranced about her" (77).[15] Eventually, her brother let her escape, "unscalped, unburnt," but "*tortured*," a memory that "darkened" her face, and a recollection that Del views as carrying her mother's typical "gloom ... in the vicinity of sex" (77).

The last phrase in the quotation alerts us that her brother – as a hollering, dancing "fat Indian" – has likely interfered sexually with his sister, whom he holds in bondage, tied upright to "a stake" (77), a position similar to that in which Del will have her first coitus. Arguably, the mother's tale of sibling cruelty carries the thrust – pun intended – of incestuous interference, either fondling or worse. Addie tells Del that, in her childhood environs, "'out there at the end of the world'," "'everybody [was] cross-eyed from inbreeding'" (78).[16] The rural sites in *Lives of Girls and Women*, whether the Flats Road or Addie Morrison's girlhood Porterfield, are locales of Vice, if not viciousness, and, again, seem to mimic Erskine Caldwell's imaginings of U.S. Southern towns and their licentious ways.

But Mrs. Addie Jordan's story of the tangentially incestuous "Indian" brother is not the only part of her biography to forward a Gothic racialism.[17] One other crucial narrative is her memory of her work in a dry goods store in Owen Sound (79), which was, though Munro doesn't tell us (which doesn't mean she doesn't know), the northern terminus of the Underground Railroad.[18] In other words, Owen Sound was then, and is still now, a site of blacks that may pass as white or, of whites whose genealogies are black at the root; it is, in brief, a site of tacit albinos. Yet, Miss Addie Morrison becomes "engaged to a young man who remained a shadow" (79), and then, "For mysterious reasons" is "compelled to break her engagement" (79).

I will speculate that the young man was mixed-race, a "black" that could pass for white. Thus, once his racial genealogy was revealed or discovered, he was no longer an eligible bachelor for Addie. Too, if Addie Morrison is herself part-black, her marriage to a part-black man could result in their bearing of an unmistakably black child. My suggestion here is not frivolous, for Del informs us that her mother's hair grows "in little wild grey-brown tufts and thickets; every permanent she got turned to frizz" (80). Her hair seems to owe a debt to Africa. Never mind her pedigree, however: Addie Morrison/Jordan is shown to be another albino – or white-masked black – in Munro's novel.

Given the argument advanced thus far, it is sensible that, following her premier fuck, Del, seeing her shadow, believes she resembles "a stately, unfamiliar African girl" (231). By now, she is a kind of White Negress, finding her sexual emancipation by appropriating blackness.

Similarly, the eponymous heroine of *Story of O* (1954) has her sex conveniently enlarged by – *naturally* – "an ebonite shaft" (42) and her body primped, pampered, and policed by a mulatto servant, Norah (91, 138, 178, 185), and by "a dark-complexioned little girl," Natalie (133). In other words, Munro has Del adopt the strategy of pornography, in presenting the "liberated" – or sexually available or amoral – white body as black-identified.

In the "Epilogue," the sad fate of Caroline, the protagonist of Del's novel, also depends on her being a girl who is white and in love with a photographer whose clothes are black, but who exhibits "pasty, flaky skin" (246). When Caroline becomes pregnant, by grace of the photographer, her womb swells *"like a hard yellow gourd"* (247), an image that connects the woman to an African fruit. When her lover abandons her, Caroline succeeds at suicide, her doom foretold by the fact that, in a school photograph that her brother reflects upon, *"Caroline's eyes were white"* (247).

The pattern of white failure and black fulfilment, or of whiteness that masks blackness (and vice versa, either positively or negatively), is also determinative in the story that Del's Aunts Elspeth and Grace tell her about how, as girls, they managed to deliver comeuppance to an Austrian labourer whose cursing they disliked. Elspeth recalls that Grace donned "'a pair of [men's] overalls and a shirt and stuffed yourself with pillows and put your hair up under a felt hat of Father's, and you blacked your hands and your face to look like a darky'" (33). In this guise, and holding a butcher-knife, Grace set out to *spook* (pun intended) "'the foreigner'" (33). She succeeds, and the man "'let[s] out a yell'" and skedaddles (33). Grace then changes and scours herself *fair* again, hoping to see the Austrian come to supper and "'mention there was some crazy darky loose in the county'" (34). Instead, the man returns, "'pale as a sheet and gloomy as Satan and sat down and never said a word'" (34). His blanching demeanour disappoints the tricksters, who had schemed that their minstrel masquerade as a dangerous Negro male would have frightened the Austrian enough to see him flee their home.

This incident accents again the tendency of Munro's white female characters to prefer risqué blackness/darkness to bland whiteness. Del herself indicates this preference in explicating her "crush" on a classmate, Frank Wales, whose "blue-grey sweater" (132) exoticizes his whiteness.

Del comments that "this smoky colour, so ordinary, reticent, and mysterious, seemed to me his colour, the colour of his self" (132). The male lead in the school operetta, *The Pied Piper* (see *The Pied Piper of Hamelin*), Frank is associated, in Del's mind, with attractive, seductive, darkening smoke, an accoutrement of the beloved boy that also conjures up the popular troupe of blackface musicians, The Smokey Mokes Minstrels, who were touring small-town Canada in the 1960s (Winks 294), as well as others who were touring rural Canada even earlier, playing scenes from *Uncle Tom's Cabin* (Beaton and Pedersen 2).

Most of Munro's references to darkness, blackface, and albinos (either "fake" blacks or too-white whites) are visual. But she also presents verbal cues that indicate a non-Caucasian speaker – or, rather, a Caucasian who wants to mask himself as Negro. An extended moment of such oral or tonal blackness or of deliberately agrammatical Standard English occurs in the context of the courtship between Jerry Storey – a high-school nerd and chum – and Del. Their conversations often take the form of what she describes as "*Pogo*" dialect, "based roughly on the comic strip" (204).[19] The playful language lets Jerry reference Del's attractiveness to him, her potential to provide him sexual pleasure, while her replies can be ironically comic, tacitly inviting, but not explicitly invitational. Hear this exchange that begins their closest attempt at coitus:

"Yo' is shore a handsome figger of a woman."
"Has I got all the appurtances on in the right places does yo' think?" (204)

Although this language is said to derive from a comic strip that did not feature black figures, the style and tone conjure up blackface minstrelsy.[20] For that matter, just as Jerry and Del engage in this comic, if tangentially racialized, repartee, so do adult male would-be seducers of Del and her friend, Naomi, resort to definitive, minstrel speech.[21]

The dialogue of Bert and Clive – an albino version of *Amos 'n' Andy*, to name the popular radio program of mid-century North America[22] (in which white actors put on "black" accents and mimicked black lingo for humorous intent) – also echoes the patter of school-auditorium operettas such as *Paints and Patches* (1932), scripted by Sarah Grames Clark with music by Arthur A. Penn, and also starring a black rascal named Rastus.[23] Keep in mind that the guys' repartee means to seduce Del and

Naomi (likewise, Jerry utilizes similar speech once he manages to get Del out of her clothes and on his bed[24]):

> "Hey Rastus," said Bert spookily.[25]
> "Yas?"
> "Is yo' fo' years old or is yo' five?"
> "Ah don' know. Ah don' know if Ah is fo' years old or five."
> "Hey Rastus? Yo' know 'bout women?"
> "No-o."
> "Yo' is *fo*." (191-92)

Munro's orthography (or typography), her use of "yo'" and "Ah" relates this black minstrel speech to the putative, *Pogo*-comic-strip-derived speech later voiced by Del and Jerry. Too, the lingo employed by Bert and Clive (whose names follow *Amos 'n' Andy* as "B" and "C" follow "A") is definitely black-influenced, for Naomi says, of the would-be seducers' routine, "'That was in the Kinsmen's Minstrel Show at Tupperton'" (192).[26]

The crucial point I underline here is that a black-inflected, black-nuanced scene is always, for Munro's backwoods, Ontario characters the preface to white ladies accepting to get sexual with white dudes. Yet, male whiteness is generally insufficient. This fact is borne out when Del slips away from Bert and Clive and, drunk, makes her way to Naomi's house, where her friend's father appears "in a nightshirt, with ... bare legs and white hair, [glowing] in the dark of the hall like a risen corpse" (193), representing dilapidated whiteness.

Pertinent here is Jerry's failed effort to shag Del. She does strip naked and lies down on his bed, feeling "absurd and dazzling" (204), and she encourages his inept, sexual touching by cartooning the moment via the *Pogo/Amos 'n' Andy* dialogue cited above. However, before Jerry can disrobe or do more than prod one of Del's nipples, his mother returns home early; he panics: "His face was white" (205). He manages to propel nude Del into a cellar and locks her in. Once her eyes become "used to the dark," she crawls out of a window and walks home through snow, all the while regretting bitterly that her hitherto closest scrape with coitus has been with a youth, "giggling and scared and talking dialect" (206).

Prior to her close encounters with Bert, Clive, and Jerry, but following her crush on Frank, Del allows the mature, World War Two veteran Art

Chamberlain, the lover of the boarder Fern, to touch her and ejaculate in front of (and accidentally upon) her, partly because he is black-identified. His voice is "welcome as dark chocolate" (149). Attracted to Art, Del dons her "mother's black rayon dressing gown" (152) and, excited by his voice, feels it acting upon her "like the touch of rayon silk on my skin, [surrounding] me, [making] me feel endangered and desired" (153). In this reverie, she envies girls – whores – having "Black Italian hair under their arms. Black down at the corners of their mouths" (153). Next, Del imagines Art ogling her, sexy in the "black flowered dressing gown" (154). She tells us, "His moral character was of no importance to me...; perhaps it was even necessary that it should be black" (168).

Eventually, on an outing with Art, Del feels "the whole of nature [become] debased, maddeningly erotic" (168). Once a relationship begins, Del discards "those ideas of love, consolation and tenderness, nourished by my feelings for Frank Wales; all that now seemed *pale* and extraordinarily childish" (162; emphasis added).[27] I emphasize *pale* because it is, throughout the text, a sign of sexual insufficiency as well as celibacy and/or sterility. In Munro's fiction, the pale phallus is often discouragingly flaccid.

Immediately following her debacle – or escapade – with Jerry, Del attends a Christian fundamentalist Revival Meeting in the Jubilee spring of her eighteenth year. Munro's unfolding of Del's psychology and sexuality torques, pitches, toward this moment, for it is Del's witnessing of the transcendent, Negro performance of spirituals and hymns that pushes her toward Garnet French, "French safes" – condoms (186), French kisses, and red-garnet-tinted, hymeneal blood. This final segment of Del's initiation into adult sexuality begins with her acceptance – out of contrariness – of a button that reads "*Come to Jesus*" (208). The slogan should not have any salacious intent, but it does, for Del will end up *coming*, climaxing, in a sexual position that is akin to crucifixion. True: when Del feels attracted to Garnet and wants to meet him, she reveals, "I desperately wished that he would come" (211). Garnet *becomes* her secular, sexual saviour.

Intriguingly, the Revival Meeting occurs in the Town Hall, which, we are told, is the site of "school operettas" and "the Kinsmen's Fair" (209); thus, it is a customary stage for blackface minstrelsy. In due course, then, "Four Negroes, two men and two women, walked on to the stage, and there was a craning of necks, a hush of appreciation. Many people in the hall, including me [says Del], had never seen a Negro before" (210). This sentence proves, supposedly, that my attempts to impute blackness to Pork Childs, Jerry Storey, Addie Morrison Jordan, Frank Wales, Art Chamberlain, and Garnet French, and others, must be in vain, for Del herself states that she has never seen a Negro prior to the Revival affair. Yet, I will hold, and believe I have shown, that many of the semi-positive white characters in Del's world, including Del herself, gain that positivity by being more dark than pale, more black than white, in style, speech, social background, and fashion. Even so, it is the appearance of the double-Adam, double-Eve, truly black singing troupe that foreshadows the rupture of virginity and Del's (growth) spurt in adult intelligence.

Del's description of the foursome requires repetition:

> One man was thin and prune-black, dried up, with a powerful, frightening voice; he was the bass. The tenor was fat and yellow-skinned, smiling, munificent. Both women were plump and well-girdled, coffee-coloured, splendidly dressed in emerald green, electric blue. (210)

Del's rendering of the singers clarifies that they are not to be confused with blackface minstrels (whose colour, artificial, would have been indistinguishable from one *comédien* to the next). She eyes authentic Negroes now. Still, the "frightening" singer (210) recalls Aunt Grace's identikit spook that scared the Austrian labourer decades ago (33); the black women in their "well-girdled," peacock-coloured dresses (210) remind one of Del's earlier donning of a "flowered, full-skirted" dress (186) and her need "to tighten" a plastic belt to hide "a little bulge" at her waist (186).

Prior to the materialization of real-deal, nitty-gritty Negroes before her eyes, Del has only witnessed whites "blackened" by shoe-polish, make-up, clothing, speech, and morals, and she has herself played at assuming a "blackness" that was imitative and unreal. Yet, it is her predilection for the real thing that allows her to realize the sexual attractiveness of Garnet French.

Thus, shortly after the Negro quartet appears on stage, Del realizes that "A young man, boy, on the other side of the hall was looking at me steadily" (211). Returning his gaze, she deems him "dark-skinned" (211).

This adjective, appearing so soon after the presentation of the black sing-ers, accords Garnet a degree of colour, of blackness, that renders him an honorary Negro. Too, his whiteness is suppressed for three paragraphs. First, the "dark-skinned" youth has to approach Del, and does, signifi-cantly, "At the end of the Negroes' singing" (211) *and* just as the assembly begins to sing a hymn about "*a gypsy boy*" (211), a phrase that the *Car-men*-loving Del (184) must subconsciously relate to Garnet. Too, her own desire to meet the "*gypsy boy*," the "dark-skinned" youth, is portrayed as a contrasting *whiteness*: "I concentrated my whole self into a kind of white prayer, willing him to show up beside me" (211). When Garnet does take up a space beside Del, he is mingled white and dark: he wears a "thin hot cotton shirt" (presumably white), but shows "sunburnt skin";[28] Del smells his "soap" (presumably white) and "machine oil" (presumably dark) (211).

Subsequently, as a sermon unfurls and then unfolds a hymn, the hands of Del and Garnet brush, touch, and, once fingers mingle, clasp, producing in Del an ecstatic "intimacy" (213). Crucially, at this moment, the last hymn begins, and, again the Negro quartet is front and centre:

> The Negroes led us, all of them except the little black man exhorting, drawing our voices upwards with their arms. ... A sharp green smell of sweat, like onions, smell of horse, pig manure, feeling of being caught, bound, borne away; tired, mournful happiness rising like a cloud. (213-14)

In this passage, the Negroes are declared a catalyst of rapture, and I will add, an aphrodisiac. But the olfactory imagery mirrors the blackened whiteness of Pork Childs, the town garbageman, as does the slavery imagery of "being caught, bound" (214), given that Pork loses his toes, while the bondage imagery echoes Addie's "dark captivity" (80). But Del's rapture forecasts her assumption of the "mournful happiness" (214) of adult coitus.[29] In any event, the black folks' singing proves consummate.[30]

Afterward, Del begins to lust for Garnet, to know him, to kiss "His dark, wary, stubborn face" (214) and to love "the dark side, the strange side, of him, which I did not know" (220). That he is a lumberyard worker assures her, doubtlessly, that he will be no effete intellectual like Jerry. Moreover, Garnet's metaphysical connotations combine the racialized epithet of the "nigger-in-the-woodpile" and the Christian notion of Christ the carpenter.

On their way to visit Garnet's family, Del is dismayed to know that Garnet is on "equal terms" with Pork Childs (217), for she believes that Garnet is superior to Pork. But another way to read this moment is to see that Del ranks the "dark" Garnet (214, 220) higher than she does the merely blackened Pork. Still, it is the "muddy road" (217) leading past Pork's home (and "Black rain on the closed [truck] windows" [217]) that conducts Del to her premiere, up-to-the-hilt conjunction with a penis.

First, however, she meets Garnet's young brothers, "savage, ... their bare backs as brown and smooth as bark is" (223), his sisters, his mother, and his father – a "big yellow man" (226), images that shade the family as not quite white.[31] Ensues the Last Supper-blaspheming scene of thirteen diners gorging on "molasses-flavoured cake" and "blackberry preserves," but, no matter, Del feels "happy in that house" (226). Then, Garnet trucks and walks Del back to her home, feels the urge to take and have her where she lives; and so, Del attains her climactic fucking, heaving herself "up against" her house's wall and also holding Garnet's "pants up, afraid that the white gleam of his buttocks might give us away" (227).

Thus, at the instant of their first upright, cruciform coitus, Garnet passes from "dark-skinned" (211) to "white gleam" (227). This chromatic shift prefaces both Garnet's dramatic failure to baptize Del *and* her decision to break with him, thus leaving behind "the dark not very heavy hairs on [his] forearms" (231), "his golden lover's skin" (238), and "His dark, amiable but secretive face" (238). Eventually, he will become part of the "black fable" – or novel – into which Del plans to project her memories of Jubilee (248).

One may speculate that Munro's alignment of blackness and darkness with sexuality, sensuality, seductiveness, soulfulness, and danger, risk, and peril represents her own absorption and recitation and application to femininity and/or feminism of the *Black Is Beautiful* aesthetic and ideology energizing the 1960s Black Freedom Struggle in the United States as well as in the decolonizing world. (Consult William L. Van Deburg [1992].) However, though *race* or *colour* serves to structure Del's thinking about class, gender, romance, and sex, her opening up to adult possibilities and consequences is also assisted by her access to literature and art, especially that of Europe, and, particularly, the cultures of Italy and France.

II

Being a female who will graduate from girlhood to womanhood and from the proletariat to the intelligentsia, Del reads widely, if only in English. Yet, her principal likes and allegiances, taken in tandem with her predilection for blackness/darkness, serve to afford her escape from the hypocritical, sexual Puritanism of her provincial town as well as from its petite-bourgeois politesse and small-minded Philistinism. Del's outward appropriation – at times – of blackness as signifying the sexual is supplemented by her interest in the foreign as a guarantor of non-conformist thought.

That Del is born to a cosmopolitan disposition is suggested by her name. She is actually Della (82), a German-derived name signifying *noble*. But Della may also allude to Blanche Dubois, the well-bred bluestocking and Southern-belle-reduced-to-streetwalking heroine of Tennessee Williams's play *A Streetcar Named Desire* (1947). In the dénouement of the play, when the mentally broken protagonist faces incarceration in an asylum, she is still able to identify a specific tint of blue as "Della Robbia blue. The blue of the robe in the old Madonna pictures" (2204). Blanche's learned reference to Florentine sculptor and painter, Luca della Robbia (1399/1400-82), alerts us that a person of refined taste is about to be locked up and – tragically – lobotomized. The connection between Del and Blanche is clear: neither can survive as independent, female intellects in *Tobacco Road*-style Jubilee or working-class New Orleans.[32]

Munro develops an alliance between black sensuality and Italian culture in Del's transition from her schoolgirl passion for "Pied Piper" Frank Wales (132) to her casual, private, sex-games with Art Chamberlain. Donning her mother's black nightgown, Del fancies herself a sultry – Shakespearean – Dark Lady, or perhaps, a provincial Juliet. Fascinated by Art's reports of pubescent *putains* in the Canuck-liberated portions of Italy (1943-45), Del pictures herself as similarly slinky, dark-in-tone, and available:

> Mr. Chamberlain's voice in my mind, saying [*girls*] *no older than Del here*, acted on me like the touch of rayon silk on my skin.... I thought of girls in Florence, girls in Rome, girls my age that a man could buy. Black Italian hair under their arms. Black down at the corners of their mouths. ... Roman Catholics. (153)

Previously, Del has considered Catholicism itself an exotic, peculiar faith, with its "black old popes" (94) and worshippers as "bizarre and secretive as Hindus, with their idols and confessions and black spots on Ash Wednesday" (94). Now, on the cusp of womanhood, Del conflates the Faith with Latin and blackness, racialized to hint at a lewd diabolism.

After fantasizing about the lives of prostitutes, including one Peggy, who had allegedly "been persuaded to serve a line-up [of men], standing up" (153), the stance itself premonitory of Del's position at her First Fucking, our junior protagonist sees herself as Italian, Catholic, nubile, and randy:

> I rubbed my hipbones through the cool [black] rayon. If I had been born in Italy my flesh would already be used, bruised, knowing. ... The thought of whoredom, not my fault, bore me outward for a moment.... (154)

Vital here, too, are the encyclopedia pages that present Italy as the place "where the old Popes were, and the Medici, and Leonardo. The Cenci. The cypresses. Dante Alighieri" (151). The references to the Cenci and Dante are also clandestine references to a female, teenage incest victim and parricide (Beatrice Cenci [1577-99]) and a pubescent, female Muse (Beatrice Portinari [1266-90]), respectively. Even her mother's encyclopedia encourages Del's accumulation of sexual knowledge.

The associations among Latin heritages, open sensuality, and blackness are sustained as well in Del's love of opera. Her mother owns "a book of operas" (145) and both she and her daughter listen regularly to radio-broadcast operas until Addie loses interest and Del becomes a solo fan (183):

> I preferred to be by myself, anyway, when I listened to *Lucia di Lammermoor, Carmen, La Traviata*. ... Yet I loved most of all *Carmen*, at the end.[33] ... I was shaken, imagining the other surrender, ... Carmen's surrender to the final importance of gesture, image, self-created self. (183-84)

Opera makes Del "hungry" enough to consume "a rich, secret, sickening mixture of cocoa, corn syrup, brown sugar, coconut and chopped walnuts" (184), thus anticipating her pre-coital supper of blackberries and molasses (226). "Greedy eating" reminds her also of "masturbating" (184). Thus, opera – Latinate – stimulates greed for food and lust for sex.

In grade school, Del remembers "the Italian girl who never spoke" and "a very frail, weepy albino boy" (124): both are outcasts; one represents a suspect ethnicity; the other a suspect racial identification.

Once Del's infatuation with Garnet French begins, Robert Browning's eponymous poem about the Italian Renaissance artist Andrea del Sarto (1486-1530) comes to mind (216-17). Through her high-school study, Del must know that del Sarto's shortcomings as an artist are related to his adulterous wife's money-hunger. Yet, Del will prove just as unfaithful to Garnet and to his Christianity as is del Sarto's wife disloyal to the painter.

Munro's novelized short stories in *Lives of Girls and Women* are rife with references to English literature and song, Italian opera, and American minstrelsy, comic strips, and pop culture, along with notice of the Russian novelists Tolstoy and Dostoevsky. However, another vital – if subtle – intertext is, I suggest, that premiere work of *l'écriture féminine*, namely, French novelist Violette Leduc's searing memoir, *La Bâtarde* (1964), issued in English first as *The Bastard* (1965) and then under the original French title, *La Bâtarde* (1966).

In her most successful book, Leduc (1907-72) presents, in effect, a prototype for *Lives of Girls and Women*. Leduc's work is both a *Künstlerroman*, detailing her progress from naïve waif to "A sort of bluestocking made up mainly of runs" (484), as well as a depiction of gynaecological, psychological realism. Leduc canvasses troubled mother-daughter bonding; precocious sexual fantasies and acts (including pubescent lesbianism); heterosexual coitus (dissatisfying); unrequited passions for male homosexuals; marriage and abortion and divorce; plastic surgery; "escape" from patriarchal oppression by finding relief in literature and fashion (and, to a lesser extent, theatre); plus profitable entrepreneurship, that is, black marketeering during the German Occupation of the Second World War.

If Munro is among the first second-wave-feminist Anglo-Canadian women writers to attempt to sketch the real – and inner – lives of girls and women, she had a model in Leduc. Certainly, there are multiple correspondences between the two books.

Simone de Beauvoir introduces *La Bâtarde* by proclaiming that, here, "A woman is descending into the most secret part of herself and telling us about all she finds there with an unflinching sincerity" (5). Surely this critique applies to Munro's linked-story novel. Too, if de Beauvoir is right that Leduc's memoir "demonstrates with exceptional clarity that a life is the reworking of a destiny by a freedom" (6), so does Munro provide a protagonist who performs the same intellectual odyssey in the transit from virgin to intellectual virago.

Again, what de Beauvoir says of Leduc, "Her broken relationships are reconquests of herself" (8), applies to Del's quittances from the lust of Chamberlain, her friendship with Storey, the erotic love of French, the maternal affection of her mother, the sisterly bonds with Naomi and others: by quitting them, one by one, she acquits herself well. At the conclusion of *Lives*, "carrying a small suitcase" (242), prepared to be a novelist, Del is not unlike Violette, earning her black market profits, "with my suitcases full of meat and butter" (503), and then becoming a writer, filling up "my exercise books with the blue tracery my pen lays on their pages with washable Parker ink" (496).

One notices other correspondences between Leduc and Munro. When Del writes, commencing a letter, "*Flats Road, Jubilee, August 22, 1942*" (11), one is reminded of Leduc's practice, throughout *La Bâtarde*, a memoir composed more than five decades after many events, of locating herself in specific time and place as she writes: "August 22, 1963. This August day, reader, is a rose window glowing with heat" (512).

When Leduc remembers her wartime, black market shunting of food-stuffs from Normandy to hungry Paris, and the lucre she gained, she also recalls, "There were days when the abundance around me affected my sight. I saw great vipers of black pudding coiled around on themselves ..." (472). Munro describes a similarly prosperous Ontario: "The war was still on then. Farmers were making money at last, making it out of pigs or sugar beets or corn" (65). Del learns about "Whisky and soda. Gin and tonic" (175); likewise, Leduc becomes *une parisienne*, taking Scotch, whisky and soda, and offered gin (283).

Preparing to accompany Naomi to a dance, Del "wore a crinoline, harsh and scratchy on the thighs, and a long-line brassiere that was supposed to compress my waist but which actually pinched my midriff and left a little bulge beneath that I had to tighten my plastic belt over" (186). Also dressing up for an evening out, Leduc bids her mirror, "say it's not a pretty sight, not really a pretty sight to see a thigh in the grip of a garter, squeezed by a stocking top" (217). In both cases, the heroines find themselves trussed – imprisoned – by their evening garb.

Another putative link between *La Bâtarde* and *Lives of Girls and Women* echoes Leduc's confession, "I suffered the pangs of love in churches" (443). Thus, when Del and Garnet mesh fingers – dextrous, sinister – at the Revival Meeting, the moment is prefigured in Leduc's recollection of a dalliance with a girl, Aline. So, Del finds her "attention ... taken up with our two hands on the back of the chair. He moved his hand slightly. I moved mine. Again. Until skin touched lightly, vividly, drew away, came back, stayed together, pressed together" (213).

Leduc narrates her love for Aline thus:

> Her arm slipped under mine, my hand was in hers, her fingers intertwined with mine. ... She squeezed my hand as hard as she could, I squeezed her hand as hard as I could.... Her fingers disengaged themselves from mine with all the delicacy of a flute separating itself from an oboe. ... With fingers intertwined once more we listened to the sermon. (75)

It is impossible that Munro does not respond to Leduc:

> Hesitation; my hand spreading out a bit, his little finger touching my fourth finger, the fourth finger captured, and so on, by stages so formal and inevitable, with such reticence and certainty, his hand covering mine. When this was achieved he lifted it from the chair and held it between us. I felt angelic with gratitude.... (213)

Recalling her erotic enthusiasm for Aline, Leduc registers:

> I had a secret, there was a driving force inside me: the image of her hand in mine. ... I lived my whole life for an arm, for a hand.... (76)

Likewise, Munro's Del is transfixed by the memory, the texture, of Garnet's hand: "I would try to recreate the exact texture of his skin, touching my own, try to remember accurately the varying pressure of his fingers" (214).

Although the church-borne seduction scenes – one heterosexual (Munro) and the other lesbian (Leduc) – offer points of comparison or likeness, other subtle links appear. For instance, Leduc tells us of Lady Abdy, an actress who appeared "in Antonin Artaud's version of *The Cenci*" (179). For her part, Del lists "The Cenci" as one of the works that, for her mother, constitutes Italy (151). Del also references the fashion designers, "Balenciaga, Schiaparelli" (175), and these names are crucial to Leduc as well. She admires her friend, Bernadette, wearing a striking black suit "'from Balenciaga'" as Bernadette explains (306), but Leduc is most besotted with Schiaparelli: "The great Schiaparelli had bewitched me, was obsessing me, dazzling me" (206). When Munro's Del reveals that Jerry Storey "called me *Eggplant*, in honour of a dreadful dress I had, a purply-wine coloured taffeta" (197), one might recall Leduc's mania for eel-coloured suits (227, 363) and eel-coloured shoes (238), garb boasting dark, purple shades related to Del's taffeta's tint.

Both *La Bâtarde* and *Lives of Girls and Women* affirm Leduc's proverb: "Literature leads to love, love leads to literature" (441). Both Leduc and Munro's Del become writers; both seek to present the "truth" about adult *amore*. De Beauvoir casts Leduc as "A schoolgirl of fifty-five ... writing down words in an exercise book" (12); Munro's Del, in high school, has "ink on my bare red hands" and a "schoolgirlish pile of books" (179). The signal alliance between Leduc and Munro is that the former's *Künstlerroman*, while celebrating Paris as a capital of sophistication, still sets the author's initial development – as sexual being, intellectual, and actual writer – in rural France, and Munro's own *Künstlerroman* adopts the Canadian countryside as the site for Del's first flowerings. (That blackness plays a lesser role in Leduc than in Munro underscores the contrast between a North America of once-Negro slaves and a French Empire of once-colonial – and still relatively alien – blacks.[34])

III

To conclude, Munro's charting of the arrival of Del Jordan as an ex-virgin, independent thinker, and a self-made – and self-(re)making – woman is shadowed, so to speak, by an acceptance of *blackness/darkness* as a sign of the sensual, the perilous, the daring, and the liberated, whether one is referencing "albinos" (such as black-haired Italians) or actual Negroes (such as the Gospel quartet). However, Del also advances toward an intellectualized womanhood by subscribing to cosmopolitan, European culture – literature and opera. But even European culture impinges on *blackness*: the Gypsy-related raciness of *Carmen* or the imagined jazz of *Porgy and Bess*. Del's liberation from the provincialism of "Deep South"-western Ontario is wrought by espousal of semi-stereotypical, *Black Is Beautiful* aesthetics ("sexthetics") and by the transplantation of the arc of the French feminist masterpiece, Leduc's *La Bâtarde*, to Del and her postcolonial environment. Indeed, it might be time to read Del as a type of Harper Lee's Scout, but one for whom sexual liberation displaces racial liberation.

Notes

1. See the chapter – or story – "Age of Faith," especially pp. 96-116.
2. The story of a girl who is assaulted and left lying naked in mud, "her prickly cold buttocks sticking out," thus exposing "the most shameful, helpless-looking part of anybody's body" (42), serves notice that Garnet's similar exposure cannot endear him to Del. But Munro likely also refers here to the rape and murder of twelve-year-old Lynne Harper, on the outskirts of Clinton, Ontario, only thirty-six kilometres (or twenty-two miles) from Munro's hometown of Wingham. The case became a *cause célèbre* because of the initial conviction and death sentence handed a fourteen-year-old youth (who was not cleared of the crime until fifty years later). Harper's body was found lying, partially nude, in a brush covered area of a farm woodlot. The True-Crime story of Lynne Harper might also inform Del's presentation of one of her novel characters as "the sacrifice, spread for sex on mouldy uncomfortable tombstones, pushed against the cruel bark of trees, her frail body squashed into the mud and hendirt of barnyards, supporting the killing weight of men" (246). This imagery reminds us that Del is "the sacrifice" in her initial coupling with Garnet. But Munro's (or Del-as-novelist's) imagery also mirrors the conclusion of *Story of O* (1954), the sado-masochistic novel by Pauline Réage (Anne Desclos). That novel ends with the heroine, at first sitting on "a stone bench covered with cushions" (202), being led "to the middle of the courtyard," made to recline "upon a table," and there be "possessed" by two men and a woman, "one after the other" (203). The "stone bench" and "table" and "courtyard" recall the setting of a graveyard as a *plein-air* fornication locale in Del's novel.

3. William L. Van Deburg repeats the Black American critique that "some 'soulful' whites" who consumed Soul music in the 1960s "simply wanted to learn 'how to shake their asses again' – an expertise supposedly lost when the Puritans escaped worldly corruption by leaving 'the terrors of the Body' to 'primitive' Africans" (205). By projecting earthy sexuality onto the bodies of Black Christians, Munro (and/or her protagonist) replicates a progressive, racial stereotype of 1960s pop culture, ascribing "Soul" to black people and its deplorable absence to whites.

4. Daniel Coleman's *White Civility: The Literary Project of English Canada* (2006) explores the literate ways in which White English-speaking Canadians, usually British and often Scottish, elevated the public stock of whiteness in North America by aligning it with Scottish Christian-capitalist virtues (thrift, invention, and toil) and with English (British) aristocratic chivalry and White-Man's-Burden imperialism. Munro may also be analyzed in regard to this project; however, I believe that her feminist inspirations motivate her to view *blackness* and *darkness* as affirming – or *shadowing* – potential resistance to *white*, patriarchal domination. Nobel Laureate Toni Morrison reads a Willa Cather character as fleshing out "the interdependent working of power, race, and sexuality in a white woman's battle for coherence" (20). Munro's study of Della Jordan executes a similar interest.

5. One example of the blending of black liberation, women's liberation, and sexual liberation discourses occurs in the 1979 film, *Good Luck, Miss Wyckoff,* starring Anne Heywood as a sexually repressed, liberal do-gooder, white high-school teacher, in 1954 Freedom, Kansas. As she begins to act on her sexual urges, Evelyn Wyckoff comes to the attention of a black student/janitor, Rafe, a generation younger, who rapes her on her school desk, and continues his assaults, daily, until she begins to imagine that he might love her. The affair ends badly, and the film was released nearly a decade after Munro's book. However, based on a 1970 novel by William Inge, the film sets teacher Wyckoff at the centre of a constellation of "isms": anti-racism, feminism, liberalism (free speech), and anti-puritanism. Indeed, by setting its liberation narrative in 1954, the year of the historic, anti-segregation decision of the U.S. Supreme Court (*Brown v. Board*

of Education of Topeka, [Kansas,] 347 U.S. 483), the film draws a subtle parallel between the U.S. Negro Civil Rights Movement and Miss Wyckoff's desire for personal liberation. (Intriguingly, Réage's *Histoire d'O* also appeared in 1954.) Yet, as Van Deburg notes, "the Age of Aquarius and ... Black Power" (66) were coexisting states of consciousness.

6.   Yes, these renderings can be cast as regressive romanticizations, but I believe that their intent is to join Del Jordan's everygirl strivings to the freedom struggles then underway in the postcolonial and "Coloured" worlds.

7.   Jonathon Green, in his *Dictionary of Slang*, defines "bottom" as "the Black area of a town," noting that "such areas were often on low-lying land, near a river" (138). Both the Wawanash River and the Grenoch Swamp separate Munro's Flats Road from "the rest of the township" (6). It mirrors, then, a Negro, Dixie locale.

8.   Intriguingly, Uncle Benny's "albino" condition runs in the family. His parents too are masked as putative, raggedy blacks, given their "dark layers of disintegrating clothes" (4).

9.   Historian Robin Winks reports, "Not until 1932 would a group of black actors tour Canada; Richard Huey of Louisiana produced *Porgy*, *Abraham's Bosom*, and *Harlem*" (294). Thus, "Porgy" – as an inspiration for "Pork" – may have entered rural Ontario and popular culture as early as The Great Depression.

10. Del is likely acquainted with *Porgy and Bess*, for we are told that her mother and their boarder, Miss Fern Dogherty, would listen, Saturday afternoons, "to the broadcasts of the Metropolitan Opera" (145; also see 182). Moreover, Mrs. Jordan owns "a book of operas" (145), and Del herself delights in opera, especially that most racialized and sexualized work, Bizet's *Carmen*, for its illustration of "Voluptuous surrender ... to darkness" (184).

11. See John Simkin, "Slave Punishments."

12. Check, for instance, the many James Avati covers for Erskine Caldwell's bestselling yarns about curvy farmgirls in shabby clothes and uneasy circumstances (Schreuders and Fulton).

13. As a girl, Del had enjoyed slathering her cereal with "black molasses" (45). Thus, she associates blackness/darkness with sweetness – at least some of the time.

14. When Art Chamberlain exposes himself to Del and masturbates before her, he seems "fantastically and predictably exaggerated, like an Indian dance" (170). The racialized imagery of "Indian," "dance," and "benighted" sexuality (170) hints that Addie Morrison, in her girlhood, endured molestation by her yelping, prancing, "fat Indian" brother (77). Similarly, in Réage's *Story of O*, Natalie, a girl described as O's "black little shadow" (201), performs "a kind of wild Indian dance around her" (194) to celebrate O's coupling with a new man. As in Réage, so it is in Munro: the "Indian dance" prefigures coitus.

15. Her story recalls also the racialized martyrdom of *Le père* Jean de Brébeuf (1593-1649), a Jesuit priest who is tortured and slain by Iroquois, in colonial Canada, and whose story is celebrated in E.J. Pratt's epic, *Brébeuf and His Brethren* (1940). Pratt imagines Brébeuf as dying upright, among "stakes" (2: 106, line 2012), and thus his death mirrors that of Christ on "two slabs of board, right-angled" (2: 108, line 2069). With deliberate blasphemy, then, Del's sexual initiation (as well as, perhaps, her mother's, incestuously) imitates the upright positions of the saint-making death accorded Brébeuf.

16. These observations are repeated in Del's playful repartee with her high-school almost-boyfriend Jerry Storey. They declare that the folk of Jericho Valley "'have cross-eyes, clubfeet'" (210). "'It's the inbreeding that does it'" (210). Recalling Fanon's claim that whites associate blackness with "unrepressed incest" (165), we should view this rural population as albino – or albescent – blacks.

17. In his biography of Munro, scholar Robert Thacker reports Munro's work on an "imitative Gothic novel" when she was a high-school girl alerted her to realize "'the twin choices' of her life, 'marriage and motherhood or the black life of the artist'" (213). Clearly, Munro perceives *blackness* as a Bohemian-oriented disruption of staid, bourgeois life.

18. The distance between Owen Sound and Munro's girlhood home of Wingham, Ontario, is 109 kilometres (or 68 miles), a two-hour trip by car, or train (perhaps).

19. The comic strip is situated in the southeastern United States; thus, its "swamp-speech" may echo "Negro" dialect.

20. William L. Van Deburg recognizes the widespread, North American presence of "a theatrical marketplace ... transfixed by comedic blackface imagery" (38).

21. The evening begins at the Gay-la Dance Hall, "a black and rumoured place" (186), composed of "chocolate-coloured imitation logs" (185). There, Del and chum Naomi (she of the suspect, "biscuit-pale" legs [186]) join "dim huddles" (187) in which glint only the prosthetic portals of frontal coitus: "cigarettes or belt buckles or bottles" (187).

22. *Amos 'n' Andy* ran as a *nightly* radio broadcast, 1928-43; then as a weekly sitcom, 1943-55; then as a nightly disc-jockey program, 1954-60; and as a television show, 1951-53, and in reruns, 1954-66 ("Amos 'n' Andy").

23. Rastus's speech is stereotypical, African American Vernacular English: "Ah does wish Roberta would take bettah care ob her war paint! De very idee persistin' on my huntin' dis heah powdah contract in a thundah storm!" (31).

24. Art Chamberlain prefaces his masturbation in front of Del with the possibly Negro dialect line, "'Sennamenal? I don't know what dose big words mean, little dirl'" (168).

25. The use of "spookily" (191) recalls Aunt Grace's blackface spooking of an Austrian workman (33-34), but also foresees the "frightening" – or awesome – spectacle of actual, Negro singers on the Jubilee Town Hall stage (210). Del is attracted by blackness/darkness, but also aligns the tint, the persons, with danger – alluring danger.

26. Her comment reminds us that blackface minstrelsy was popular entertainment in rural Ontario in Munro's girlhood. See Note [9].

27. After Chamberlain departs Jubilee, Del begins to apply makeup, "shading my face with dark and light powder" (180). Her ingress to adult sexuality will be as an albino Negress.

28. Munro presents a gender-inverted allusion to The Canticles: "I am black, but comely.... // Look not upon me, because I am black, because the sun hath looked upon me..." (Song Sol. 1.5-6, KJV).

29. After Del's frigging escapade with Art Chamberlain, the landscape seems "post-coital, distant and meaningless" (171). Coital bliss triggers post-coital blues.

30. Two points are salient here. First, as *de facto* exponents of Black Christianity, the Negroes embody a critique of "white religion" as

"Grounded in the inegalitarian beliefs of an idolatrous, slave-mongering people" and therefore is "most unsoulful" (Van Deburg 242). Moreover, the Negro women challenge "Protestant ideals of thin, beautiful bodies ... racialized as White" (Sharma 33). Secondly then, the Negro presence at the Revival Meeting works to help move Del from the conservative, social emphasis on "home-making" to the radical emphasis on "self-making" (Penny Marler; qtd. in Sharma 15).

31. Admittedly, the evidence is slight – or light, but the imagist association of the father with the "fat and yellow-skinned" Negro tenor at the Revival Meeting (210) suggests that he, too, may be racially mixed, and that, thus, Garnet is, actually, part-black himself (211). Of course, the "savage" epithet assigned the French lads (223) associates them with Addie Morrison's molestation by her "fat Indian" brother (77).

32. When Jerry teases Del about her dating a "'Neanderthal',", she retorts, regarding Garnet, "'He's Cro-Magnon'" (219). The exchange echoes Blanche DuBois's assignment of "Stone Age" status to Stanley Kowalski in Williams' *A Streetcar Named Desire* (2175). In contrast, though, while Stanley will rape Blanche to assert his brute authority (2202), Del – Della – will establish her independence by resisting Garnet's attempts to subjugate her. Thus, Del does represent "'a change ... in the lives of girls and women'" (176), as her mother, Addie, has foreseen.

33. From the opera's inception in 1875, the eponymous heroine has been viewed as erotic because she is exotic in "origins," even "'Judaic, Arab, Egyptian',", a "gypsy vamp" (Hutcheon and Hutcheon 188, 188, 185).

34. Yet, Leduc does include a blackface moment, where, to obscure her own tormenting features, she applies "the shelter of ... blackened skin" (66).

Works Cited

"Amos 'n' Andy." <https://en.wikipedia.org/wiki/Amos_%27n%_Andy>.

Archer-Straw, Petrine. *Negrophilia: Avant-Garde Paris and Black Culture in the 1920s*. New York: Thames & Hudson, 2000.

Artaud, Antonin. *Les Cenci*. 1935. Ed. Michel Corvin. Paris: Éditions Gallimard, 2011.

Beaton, Virginia, and Stephen Pedersen. *Maritime Music Greats: Fifty Years of Hits and Heartbreak*. Halifax: Nimbus, 1992.

Besner, Neil K. *Introducing Alice Munro's* Lives of Girls and Women: *A Reader's Guide*. Toronto: ECW, 1990. Canadian Fiction Studies 8.

Browning, Robert. "Andrea del Sarto." *Victorian Poetry*. 1942. Ed. E.K. Brown and J.O. Bailey. 2nd ed. New York: Ronald, 1962. 241-45.

Caldwell, Erskine. *Tobacco Road*. New York: Charles Scribner's Sons, 1932.

Clark, Sarah Grames. *Paints and Patches: A Musical Comedy in Two Acts for Junior High Schools or Upper Grades*. Book and lyrics by Sarah Grames Clark. Music by Arthur A. Penn. New York: Carl Fischer, [1932].

Coleman, Daniel. *White Civility: The Literary Project of English Canada*. Toronto: U of Toronto P, 2006.

De Beauvoir, Simone. Foreword. *La Bâtarde*. By Violette Leduc. 1965. Trans. Derek Coltman. New York: Dell, 1966. 5-18. Trans. of *La Bâtarde*. Paris: Éditions Gallimard, 1964.

Fanon, Frantz. *Black Skin, White Masks*. Trans. Charles Lam Markmann. New York: Grove, 1967. Trans. of *Peau noire, masques blancs*. Paris: Éditions de Seuil, 1952.

Good Luck, Miss Wyckoff. Screenplay by Polly Platt. Dir. Marvin J. Chomsky. Bel Air/Gradison Productions. 1979. Film.

Green, Jonathon. *The Cassell Dictionary of Slang*. London: Cassell, 1998.

Hutcheon, Linda, and Michael Hutcheon. *Opera: Desire, Disease, Death*. Lincoln: U of Nebraska P, 1996.

Inge, William. *Good Luck, Miss Wyckoff*. Boston: Atlantic-Little, Brown, 1970.

Leduc, Violette. *La Bâtarde*. 1965. Trans. Derek Coltman. New York: Dell, 1966. Trans. of *La Bâtarde*. Paris: Éditions Gallimard, 1964.

Marcuse, Herbert. *An Essay on Liberation*. 1969. Harmondsworth, Eng.: Pelican-Penguin, 1972.

Morrison, Toni. *Playing in the Dark: Whiteness and the Literary Imagination*. Cambridge, MA: Harvard UP, 1992. The William E. Massey Sr. Lectures in the History of American Civilization.

Munro, Alice. *Lives of Girls and Women*. Toronto: McGraw-Hill Ryerson, 1971.

The Pied Piper of Hamelin: Operetta for Treble Voices. Words by C.J. Brooks. Music by Walter H. Aiken. Cincinnati: Willis Music, [1917].

Pogo. By Walt Kelly. 4 Oct. 1948 - 20 July 1975. Daily (U.S.) Newspaper Comic Strip.

Porgy and Bess: An Opera in Three Acts. By George Gershwin. Libretto by DuBose Heyward. Lyrics by DuBose Heyward and Ira Gershwin. Production Directed by Rouben Mamoulian. New York: Random House, 1935.

Pratt, E.J. *Brébeuf and His Brethren.* 1940. *E.J. Pratt: Complete Poems: Part 2.* Ed. Sandra Djwa and R.G. Moyles. Toronto: U of Toronto P, 1989. 46-110. The Collected Works of E.J. Pratt.

Réage, Pauline. [Anne Desclos.] *Story of O.* Trans. Sabine d'Estrée. Pref. Jean Paulhan. 1973. New York: Ballantine, 1984. Trans. of *Histoire d'O.* Pref. Jean Paulhan. Paris: Jean-Jacques Pauvert, 1954.

Sartre, Jean-Paul. *Black Orpheus.* Trans. S.W. Allen. Paris: Présence Africaine, 1976. Trans. of *Orphée Noire.* By Jean-Paul Sartre. *Anthologie de la nouvelle poésie nègre et malgache de langue française.* By Léopold Sédar Senghor. Paris: Presses universitaires de France, 1948. ix-xliv. Colonies et Empires. Cinquième Série: Art et Littérature.

Schreuders, Piet, and Kenneth Fulton. *The Paperback Art of James Avati.* Pref. Stanley Meltzoff. Hampton Falls, NH: Donald M. Grant, 2005.

Sharma, Sonya. *Good Girls, Good Sex: Women Talk about Church and Sexuality.* Halifax: Fernwood, 2011.

Simkin, John. "Slave Punishments." 4 Jan. 2015. <http://spartacus-educational.com/USASpunishments.htm>.

The Song of Solomon. *The King James Bible.* <https://www.kingjames-bibleonline.org>.

Telusma, Blue. "Kim Kardashian Doesn't Realize She's the Butt of an Old Racial Joke." 12 Nov. 2014. *The Grio.* 5 Jan. 2015. <http://thegrio.com/2014/11/12/kim-kardashian-butt/>.

Thacker, Robert. *Alice Munro: Writing Her Lives: A Biography.* 2005. Updated ed. Toronto: Emblem-McClelland & Stewart, 2011.

Van Deburg, William L. *New Day in Babylon: The Black Power Movement and American Culture, 1965-1975.* Chicago, IL: U of Chicago P, 1992.

Williams, Tennessee. *A Streetcar Named Desire.* 1947. *The Norton Anthology of American Literature.* Third Edition: Shorter. Ed. Nina Baym et al. New York: W.W. Norton, 1989. 2148-2208.

Winks, Robin W. *The Blacks in Canada: A History.* 1971. Montreal, QC and Kingston, ON: McGill-Queen's UP, 1997.

Alice Munro as Small-Town Historian: "Spaceships Have Landed"

W.R. Martin and Warren U. Ober

In an interview with Eleanor Wachtel a few years before the appearance of *Open Secrets* (1994), Alice Munro said, "one of the things that interests me so much in writing, and in observing people, is that things keep changing. Cherished beliefs change. Ways of dealing with life change. The importance of certain things in life changes. All this seems to me endlessly interesting. I think that is the thing that doesn't change" ("Interview" 292). Her observation is worth pondering.

In "Society and Culture in Rural and Small-Town Ontario: Alice Munro's Testimony on the Last Forty Years," John Weaver shows how Munro's work has been a comprehensive record of the enduring conditions and details of the small town. At first glance, then, it might seem strange for Munro to put such emphasis on change, and indeed much of her work is a record of the seemingly unchanging life that she knew as a child and young adult. But the strangeness of her statement is only superficial. In *Lives of Girls and Women*, Del, the protagonist, tries to cram into what she writes the sorts of objective detail that Uncle Craig, the diligent amateur historian, has collected, but she comes to realize that "no list could hold what I wanted, for what I wanted was every last thing, every layer of speech and thought, stroke of light on bark or walls, every smell, pothole, pain, crack, delusion, held still and held together – radiant, everlasting" (210). In the end, Munro not only uses a much finer mesh than Uncle Craig but also, by capturing the "emotional" dimensions and intensities of that life through the magic of art, far transcends what he strives for.

As early as *Lives of Girls and Women*, then, as Weaver has shown, Munro identifies "two poles of historical inquiry" (381). At one pole is "the historian as a collector," who, like Uncle Craig, "reifies facts and artifacts without ordering their meaning"; at the other is "the creative soul," such as Del, who strives to "record the concrete but also the passions." The "artist's vision" possessed by this kind of historian involves "an aspiration to total history" (382). The passion and insight conveyed by what Weaver calls total history must go together with, and in part derive from, an awareness of the unique and delicate balance, as well as the transience, of the world of experience that the artist is driven to record and preserve, as it were, in amber. It is the artist-historian's way of arresting change, of preserving what is loved.

Hence, one can see why for Munro, as for many other artists, change is "endlessly interesting." Change is in fact Janus-faced: fascinating, in that the movement and the process involved in it transfix us; dreaded, in that it places at risk "cherished" beliefs and values. Munro's interest in change extends far back beyond individuals and society into the eons of prehistory. In "Walker Brothers Cowboy" (*Dance* 1-18), a father enthrals his young daughter with his graphic account of Lake Huron in the ice age; in an uncollected story, "Characters," the word *drumlin* becomes a point of fascination, and, more recently – in "What Do You Want To Know For?" – Munro gives an account of her fondness for driving through the countryside of western Ontario with her husband, a retired geographer and the editor of *The National Atlas of Canada* (Catherine Sheldrick Ross 78), and observing the "record of ancient events," the landscape "formed by the advancing, stationary, and retreating ice that has staged its conquests and retreats here several times, withdrawing for the last time about fifteen thousand years ago" ("What" 204). This alternating, backward and forward, movement might remind readers of "The Progress of Love" (*Progress* 3-31), in which "progress" is seen not as advance or betterment but – as in a tour or circuit – as change and recurrence on a microcosmic social scale, in contrast to macrocosmic geological processes.

The town of Carstairs, which resembles Wingham, Munro's home town, is the scene of most of the stories in *Open Secrets*; in "Spaceships Have Landed" (226-60), it assumes mythical and archetypal status. The Douds, the first family of Carstairs, with their piano factory, are classic exemplars of the small-town adage "Shirtsleeves to shirtsleeves in three generations." In the opening story of the collection, "Carried Away" (3-51), Louisa, the Carstairs librarian and the story's central consciousness, becomes the second wife of the widowed Arthur Doud, son of the founder of Douds Factory. The final two stories take the Doud narrative to its end. In the penultimate story, "Spaceships Have Landed," Billy Doud, Arthur and Louisa's son, sells the piano factory after his mother's death and converts the family mansion into "a home for old people and disabled people" after his half-sister Bea's death (260). In "Vandals" (261-94), the final story, Bea, Louisa's alcoholic stepdaughter, is involved in an obsessive relationship with a pedophile, the true vandal of the story. The Douds and their Carstairs factory also figure briefly in two other stories: Millicent, in "A Real Life" (52-80), readers are told, has "set her sights high" in the vain hope that "Mrs. Doud," Louisa, will become her "best friend" (56); in "Open Secrets" (129-60), Mary Johnstone, leader of the church hike in which one of the girls disappears and is presumably murdered, has "a job in the office at Douds Factory" (133), and in the same story the senile Mr. Siddicup, a suspect, "used to be the piano tuner at Douds" (146).

The Doud family, then, with its piano factory and its varying fortunes, serves as a sort of anchor for *Open Secrets*, a reminder that the stories have firm roots in the life of a small town, and its social and economic history, in "the country to the east of Lake Huron" ("Introduction to the Vintage Edition" xv). Even "The Albanian Virgin" (81-128), requiring a university in its setting, involves London, Ontario (110), which is the metropolis of so many of the small towns in Munro's stories, notably Jubilee (Wingham) in *Dance of the Happy Shades* – "Postcard" and "The Peace of Utrecht" (128-46, 190-210) – and throughout *Lives of Girls and Women*. Toronto, where Uncle Benny gets lost (*Lives* 20-22), is an almost legendary city and in "Wild Swans" the source of scary stories by Flo, Rose's stepmother, about white slavers and the police (*Who* 55), who'd "be the first ones to diddle you!" (56).

Munro, in her "evocative chronicles of rural and small-town Ontario," as Weaver observes, works tirelessly "to exhume and record the truth while appreciating both the material circumstances and the accidental influences on common lives in small communities" (381, 384). Her statement to Wachtel ends with "I think that [change] is the thing that doesn't change." Her interest in human affairs is not only with change but also with what is unchanging – or recurrent – within history. Although "Spaceships Have Landed" seems at first to be one more story about Carstairs, it is much more than a socio-economic study or history. Readers must keep in mind what Munro recently wrote in her "Introduction to the Vintage Edition" of *Selected Stories*: "I don't think I'm writing just *about* this life [in "the country to the east of Lake Huron"]. I hope to be writing about and *through* it" (xv). "Spaceships Have Landed" has firm roots in myth and allegory that make it rare and strange in her *oeuvre* – even "risky," to adopt the term that Munro used for some of the stories in *Open Secrets* when she was interviewed by Peter Gzowski on *Morningside* on 30 September 1994.

"Spaceships Have Landed" is unlike any other story that Munro has written, but intertextuality is nothing new in her work. In "Alice Munro and James Joyce," W.R. Martin points out similarities between Munro's *Dance of the Happy Shades* and Joyce's *Dubliners*, especially those between the last stories in the two volumes, both of which give their titles to their volumes. And in "Reality and Ordering: The Growth of a Young Artist in *Lives of Girls and Women*," J.R. (Tim) Struthers draws attention to parallels between Munro's book and Joyce's *A Portrait of the Artist as a Young Man*. The influence on Munro by Southern writers such as William Faulkner, Eudora Welty, Flannery O'Connor, and Carson McCullers has been acknowledged and widely discussed (for example, by Nora Robson in "Alice Munro and the White American South: The Quest").

In *Friend of My Youth*, there are several striking examples of Munro's use of allusion. In "Goodness and Mercy" (156-79), the twenty-third Psalm, quoted not only in the title but also at length in the text (169), and references to an aria from *Don Giovanni* (158, 168-69) help to elucidate and amplify the complex and ambivalent relationship between mother and daughter. "Oh, What Avails" (180-215) takes its title from Walter Savage Landor's poem "Rose Aylmer," which also provides a theme for the story (215). In "Hold Me Fast, Don't Let Me Pass" (74-105), the protagonist, an intelligent and observant woman from Huron County, visits the Scottish border country, and the story relates to a border ballad, "Tam Lin." In most of the earlier stories, interestingly, Munro uses writers such as Joyce indirectly, parallel to her texts, whereas later she deals with "Tam Lin" specifically and in detail. (For a discussion of the effects achieved by the way in which Munro turns the plot of "Tam Lin" upside down, see Martin and Ober, "Alice Munro's 'Hold Me Fast, Don't Let Me Pass' and 'Tam Lin'.")

Still later, in the title story of *Open Secrets* (129-60), Munro develops her own example of a "folk" ballad in stark counterpoint to the ambiguities and complexities of the story's plotline:

And maybe some man did meet her there
That was carrying a gun or a knife
He met her there and he didn't care
He took that young girl's life.
....
And nobody knows the end. (140)

In Munro's story "Jakarta," from *The Love of a Good Woman*, Kath and Sonje, in the midst of reading stories by D.H. Lawrence and Katherine Mansfield, discuss at some length the young woman, March, and the soldier in Lawrence's "The Fox" and Stanley Burnell in Mansfield in ways that bear on their own situations and problems (46, 48-49). Similarly, in Munro's story "Save the Reaper," also from *The Love of a Good Woman*, the title points to Alfred, Lord Tennyson's "The Lady of Shalott," imperfectly remembered by Eve, the story's significantly named protagonist. Munro's title perhaps becomes a prayer for a release from the exigent present and for a recovery of the past, simple and idyllic as Eve recalls it, in light of the awkwardness and disaffection in her family relationships and a life that now seems sordid and spoiled. "Save the Reaper" is a notable study of change and the futility of nostalgic longing.

Thus, Munro's stories gain in resonance and significance because they are written in the context of a wide range of literature in English and in the classical tradition. Her allusions show small-town Ontario to be part of the wider world. But, as Miriam Marty Clark argues in "Allegories of Reading in Alice Munro's 'Carried Away'," the word *allusion* "does not adequately describe" Munro's "lodgings at the intersection[s] of many texts" (50); recently, Munro's fiction "foregrounds and thematizes its own plurality, addressing itself directly to prior texts and other discourses" (53). "Spaceships Have Landed" provides a clear example of this intertextuality. Just how groundbreaking it is in Munro's work – assuming that her use of the ballad "Tam Lin" in "Hold Me Fast, Don't Let Me Pass" is a proleptic special case – is indicated by the fact that, only a short time before the story appeared, James Carscallen wrote, in his comprehensive study *The Other Country: Patterns in the Writing of Alice Munro*, that "Her work offers us the great human myths, but as half-concealed – both from the characters themselves and from the reader – behind a surface ordinariness that seems anything but mythical" (viii). In "Spaceships Have Landed," though ordinariness is maintained, the mythological analogue is hardly concealed from the reader.

"Spaceships Have Landed" is the most ambitious of Munro's stories about the history of small-town Huron County. It is ironic that but for editorial intervention it would be more difficult to see just how brilliant her conception and its execution are. The story first appeared in *The Paris Review* in 1994, but without the opening passage of six pages concluding with "A call of nature, then, all right, a call of nature" – the discussion in Monk's speakeasy – that occurs in *Open Secrets* (226-32). Munro, it seems, was persuaded by the editor of *The Paris Review* to cut the six pages; in their place, after the short paragraph "Wayne's sister's selfishness had made Lucille break out in hives" (*Open Secrets* 244), she substituted a passage of one page that doesn't appear until the twelfth page of the thirty-page *Paris Review* version. As Munro told Gzowski in the *Morningside* interview, the speakeasy passage is very significant, and she duly restored it in *Open Secrets*.

Nonetheless, with the caveat that it seems inferior to the book version because it discloses the scope of the story and Rhea's part in it too baldly, the passage that Munro substituted in *The Paris Review* and then omitted in *Open Secrets* is worth quoting at length:

> Something had changed in Rhea since she ... had been ... shown what respect was owing to her by becoming Billy Doud's girl. It was a matter of getting *inside*, of being entirely and gratefully normal, of living within the life of the town. Rhea used to see the town of Carstairs from outside, as if it had a mysterious personality hidden from all the other people who lived inside it. For instance, one day in winter, looking by chance out the back window of the library in the town hall, she saw a team of horses pulling a load of grain sacks on the municipal weigh scales. Snow was falling.... The big grain sacks, the heavy obedient animals, the snow,

made Rhea think suddenly that the town was muffled in great distances, in snow-choked air, and that the life in it was a timeless ritual.... These feelings or visions didn't come so much from what she could see before her as they did from books that she had got to read from that same library – Russian stories and *Winesburg, Ohio*. (276-77)

In this single passage, Munro took a shortcut to what is achieved in the opening six pages of the *Open Secrets* version, making two significant points while exploring Rhea's mind. The first point is that, for Rhea, becoming the girlfriend of Billy, who was with her at the bootlegger's, is "a matter of getting *inside*" Carstairs, from which she has felt "cut off" (277). But now the feelings and the visions that came first from literature come from her own apocalyptic insights. This is a turning point in her life: Rhea has realized her calling, which is to accept and live out within the community the physical-sexual life of the body that will propagate the race. It is on the same night that Eunie, Rhea's erstwhile closest friend, disappears and moves into her very different, indeed opposite, calling to the life of the spirit, in which the life of this world interacts with the life of the other world in sexless union. Thus, both Rhea and Eunie (as we will suggest in detail shortly) decisively abandon their old selves and embrace their new callings. In a small-town Ontario speakeasy and its immediate environs is to be found the whole range of human experience, and these two women, Rhea and Eunie, come to represent its opposite poles.

The other significant, and related, thought that Rhea "suddenly" has in the *Paris Review* meditation is that life in Carstairs is "a timeless ritual" and is thus *real* and meaningful (276). In her introduction to *Selected Stories*, Munro reveals that Rhea's epiphany involving the snowy day, the horses, the sleigh, the grain sacks, and the weigh scales was in fact her own, experienced at the age of fifteen. (She does not mention the parallel passage in "Spaceships Have Landed," which is not included in *Selected Stories*.) Munro says that she, *in propria persona*, saw the horses moving onto the scales, not as "framed and removed," but as "alive and potent, and it gave me something like a blow to the chest" (xvi). This experience is the archetype of what is at the centre of so many Munro stories: a turning point, an epiphany, a realization of something "for the first time" (*Progress* 103) – a change, whether tragic or triumphant, after

which everything is different and life begins anew. The moment is sometimes dramatized, or directly related, as in the *Paris Review* version of
"Spaceships Have Landed," but more often it is conveyed from a distance,
as in "Carried Away" when Louisa tells Jim Frarey about finding the
short note from Jack Agnew on her desk ("I was engaged before I went
overseas" [*Open Secrets* 18]), and sometimes it comes, just as effectively,
by implication, as it does in the speakeasy scenes in the book version of
"Spaceships Have Landed."

In "Walker Brothers Cowboy," the first story in Munro's first volume,
Dance of the Happy Shades, the girl narrator's life changes momentously
with her father's visit to Nora, and at the end of the story the narrator feels "my father's life flowing back from our car in the last of the
afternoon, darkening and turning strange, like a landscape that has
an enchantment on it" (18). In a similar manner, at the end of the last
story in that first volume, "Dance of the Happy Shades," the narrator
realizes that the handicapped girl's playing of the Gluck piece has been a
"communiqué from the other country where she lives" (224): everything
has changed, and a different life begins. In her introduction to *Selected
Stories*, Munro seems to suggest that this scene with horses, grain sacks,
and scales, viewed from a rural, small-town, Huron County library, was
a turning point in her own life, as it is in Rhea's.

These two points, Rhea's commitment to the physical-sexual aspect
of human experience and her epiphanic sense of life in Carstairs as a
timeless ritual, which are directly related in the *Paris Review* version
of "Spaceships Have Landed," are conveyed in the six speakeasy pages
in *Open Secrets* in an artistically suggestive rather than a baldly direct
manner. For instance, the reference in *The Paris Review* to Sherwood
Anderson's *Winesburg, Ohio*, the classic portrait in fiction of a North
American small town, is an obvious shortcut to the sort of effect that
Munro wants to achieve. Rhea, though still a girl, feels at home in the
heterogenous but representative group gossiping and arguing at Monk's,
and the reader senses that this aimless chatting is just what has been an
unchanging element of human cave dwellings, settlements, and villages
for millennia – one of the timeless rituals of Homo sapiens.

Carstairs, at the centre of "Spaceships Have Landed," is in Huron
County, but it is also an immemorial and universal human settlement.
It is, if not the eternal city, at least the abiding town; throughout its

history, despite all its changes, it has remained essentially the same. Although it is not really old, its present configuration has been through archetypal phases:

> On the river flats lay the old fairgrounds, some grandstands abandoned since before the war, when the fair here was taken over by the big fair at Walley. The racetrack oval was still marked out in the grass.
>
> This was where the town set out to be, over a hundred years ago. Mills and hostelries were here. But the river floods persuaded people to move to higher ground. House-plots remained on the map, and roads laid out, but only the one row of houses where people lived was still there, people who were too poor or in some way too stubborn to change. (234)

Fairgrounds, grandstands, racetrack oval, mills, hostelries, floods, house-plots – all are timeless features of human communal life; there are no garages, drive-ins, or strip malls to suggest organic discontinuity. When readers are told that Carstairs had its beginnings "over a hundred years ago," its roots are placed in the realm of "once upon a time"; with the loss of its fair to the county seat, it also becomes an image of human history in which, to compare the small and obscure with the large and famous, its eclipse by Walley is parallel to that of Babylon by Baghdad. At the end of the story, the eclipse seems complete: "The river houses all gone. The Morgans' house, the Monks' house – everything gone of that first mistaken settlement" (259). But Carstairs, though it undergoes changes, remains the archetypal town.

By holding a mirror up to unchanging aspects of human nature, the story's opening scene at the bootlegger's house effectively introduces the theme. Unlike the *Paris Review* passage, the restored narrative doesn't *tell* the reader about a timeless ritual; the ritual is enacted in the quotidian setting of the scene at the bootlegger's, a scene that is – to appropriate one of Munro's own phrases – both "touchable and mysterious" ("Everything"[33]).

Rhea, underage and the only female person in the scene apart from the bootlegger's wife, is present with her date, Billy, and his friend Wayne (whose surname is never mentioned). The group gathered in the speak-easy is representative of the community. Rhea knows many of them by sight: Mr. Monk, the bootlegger, who presides over the gathering; the enigmatic Mrs. Monk, whom Rhea rightly or wrongly imagines to be the local whore; a snow-shoveller; a salesman of pots and pans and former teacher; a dry cleaner; an undertaker; and two students – Billy, scion of one of the local first families (the Douds of the piano factory), and Wayne, the United Church minister's son. Class differences in this cross-section of society are conveyed not only by differing economic circumstances but also by changes in the behaviour of the young in the presence of their elders and in that of men in the presence of women.

One member of the group is known to readers only as the teller of a wonderful tale, purportedly true, about how a man, "Away up north in the Province of Quebec" (227), in answering "a call of nature" and looking for something "to come in handy" (226), finds "stuff" "Laying all over, in sheets"; "And on the spot they developed the biggest asbestos mine in the entire world. And from that mine came a fortune!" (227). (The true story of the discovery, though interesting, is more prosaic: in 1876, during "the building of the line of the Quebec Central Railway ... at Thetford and Coleraine, ... the accidental knocking off of a fragment of rock ... and the consequent exposure of a vein of chrysotile signalized the beginning of the asbestos industry in Canada" [Mendels 16-17].) Asbestos has been known and used since ancient times. The Romans are said to have used it for cremation cloths – "the funeral dress of kings" – and for lamp wicks (James Ross 3), and Marco Polo was shown asbestos cloth during his travels in what is now Siberia (3-4).

The asbestos story told at the bootlegger's is a tall tale, which indeed has a slender basis in fact, is "extravagant, outlandish or highly improbable," belongs to "the same family as fantasy and fairy tale" (Cuddon 684), and flourishes as lore "especially in rural areas" (685) or "on the ... frontier" (Brunvand 65). The story diverges from its point and is interrupted by misunderstandings, irrelevancies, non sequiturs, and even a discussion of which expressions are appropriate in the presence of women: for example, "a call of nature" is finally substituted for "something about a crap" in deference to Rhea and Mrs. Monk (226). Munro's handling of the episode suggests a community activity that has been repeated since the rise of Homo sapiens and the timeless ritual of storytelling around a campfire; it brings to mind David Helwig's inspired description of Munro's writing as "gossip informed by genius" (qtd. in

Turbide 47). Munro's story may be set in Southwestern Ontario, but its bearing is universal and timeless.

In this opening scene, Rhea begins to play the prominent role that her name boldly suggests. The Graeco-Roman goddess Rhea is an avatar of the Neolithic Great Mother goddess, "the earth mother and the corn mother, and the protector and multiplier of flocks and herds" (Mackenzie 172) – she has, in Robert Graves's poem "Rhea," a "mother-mind" (197). There also seems to have been an earlier pre-Hellenic and Cretan Rhea who "was at once Gaia, Demeter, Artemis, and ... Aphrodite" (Mackenzie 173-74).

Munro's Rhea is, like her namesake, passionately heterosexual and certainly philoprogenitive. She imagines Mrs. Monk going up to a bed and arranging herself "without the least hesitation or enthusiasm" for "a quick and driven and bought and paid-for encounter," "shamefully exciting" to Rhea, and she entertains the thought of being approached in the same manner, "To be so flattened and used and hardly to know who was doing it to you, to take it all in with that secret capability, over and over again" (232). Rhea possesses the mothering instinct; it would be unkind to describe her as promiscuous, but she embodies the kind of Shavian life force on which human continuity depends. She is conscious of her community and aware of the past, conceiving common processes as perpetually reenacted throughout the cycles of human life.

"Spaceships Have Landed" is in part an allegory on the nature of love, an allegory in which Rhea and Eunie are opposite yet complementary poles. If Rhea embodies a love that is sexual and fecund, then Eunie represents a love that is Platonic. If Rhea's love is existential, then Eunie's is mystical. If Rhea is *eros*, then Eunie is *agape*.

Eunie, as her name implies, is the embodiment of unique characteristics. Her given name may be Eunice, the name of the mother of St. Paul's beloved disciple, Timothy, whom Paul compliments on his "unfeigned faith," "which dwelt first in ... thy mother Eunice" (2 Tim. 1.5, KJV), a Jewish woman married to a Greek man (Acts 16.1). Readers are possibly intended to make such a connection, for within the allegory Eunie seems to represent the Judaeo-Christian mystical heritage, whereas Billy Doud, who becomes her husband, seems to embody the Greek, and especially the Platonic, tradition.

Although Eunie is not present at the bootlegger's, her importance in the story is suggested by the first sentence of the story: "On the night of Eunie Morgan's disappearance, Rhea was sitting in the bootlegger's house at Carstairs" (226). Despite their striking differences in temperament and symbolic significance, Eunie and Rhea converged in early girlhood to become the inseparable "Two Toms," playing games that were "the most serious part of their lives" (235) and in which there was an "intense and daily collaboration" (237). It is later, in maturity, that they become distinctively and consciously separate, though clearly complementary; this strange, almost symbiotic, relationship in youth between later opposites points to an archetypal structure in the story.

Whereas Rhea looks to the past and "is of the earth, earthy" (1 Cor. 15.47, KJV), Eunie seeks to transcend space and time. Unlike everyone else in Carstairs, she is imaginative, playful, and original; moreover, "Eunie never seemed subject to her parents, or even connected to them, in the way of other children. Rhea was struck by the way she ruled her own life ..." (237). It is Eunie who has the vision of the spaceship landing; she seems attuned to the supernatural and the ideal. The extraterrestrials from the spaceship, three children,

> took her to their tent. But it seemed to her that she never saw that tent once from the outside. She was just suddenly inside it, and she saw that it was white, very high and white, and shivering like the sails on a boat. Also it was lit up, and again she had no idea where the light was coming from. (255-56)

This play on the words *outside* and *inside* might remind readers of the significance of the same words in the passage quoted from *The Paris Review*.

Upon Eunie's return home the next morning, her father summons Billy, as the available representative of a first family of Carstairs: "Mr. Doud ... was always sent for in an emergency" (254). Before the episode at the Monks' house the night before, Billy was for some time Rhea's boyfriend, but, although he "brought her honor" and some importance (240), Rhea found little satisfaction in the affair. His necking always seemed like teasing and unimpassioned (242); "he himself might have been carved from soap," being "tall and pale, cool and clean" (240). In short, Billy comes across not as impotent but as somehow asexual.

However, he is "enchanted" by Eunie and the account of her adventure, and "His love – Billy's kind of love – could spring up to meet a need that Eunie wouldn't know she had" (257).

Readers are told in the windup of the story that Billy eventually turns the Doud-family mansion into "a home for old people and disabled people," "a place where they could get comfort and kindness," and then asks Eunie to marry him; "'I wouldn't want for there to be anything going on, or anything,' Eunie said" (260). Eunie, then, in her fulfilling if sexless marriage with Billy, exemplifies an emotional disposition certainly different from Rhea's, and she finds what she has been unaware of lacking. Their marriage seems to be founded on something like the love described by Plato, a love that transcends the world of concrete objects and becomes the selfless love of an ideal (201-09). When Billy devotes himself and his resources to serving humanity, Eunie brings to their partnership a visionary imagination that, in contrast to Rhea's, can fully respond to "Billy's kind of love" (257).

Munro further suggests the whole range of human diversity by placing between the socially conscious and philoprogenitive Rhea and the individualistic, imaginative, and promethean Eunie, distant opposite edges of the human psyche, a third girl, Lucille, who is colourless and unremarkable, fascinated by "the vagaries of her body," which she treats as though it were "a troublesome but valuable pet" (243). She is much concerned about "the conflict that was raging round her wedding, about whether the bridesmaids should wear picture hats or wreaths of rosebuds" (244).

After the memorable scene at the bootlegger's house, however, Wayne, Lucille's fiancé, leaves her virtually at the altar to elope to Calgary with Rhea. It is on the same night that, by a fine structural stroke, Munro brings the story to its climax: not only does Eunie walk out of her house in the middle of the night and have her vision, but also Rhea has the experience that changes her life and brings her to herself. Although her date is Billy, Wayne "caught Rhea's eye, and from then on ... watched her, with a slight, tight, persistent smile" (228); this flirting leads, after a few too many drinks, to the sudden coming together of Rhea and Wayne: "Up against the wall of the house, she and Wayne were pushing and grabbing and kissing each other" (248). But their passionate lovemaking is interrupted by the Monks' dog, Rhea's attack of vomiting, and Mrs. Monk herself – who imperturbably drives the very sick Rhea home.

The next morning, as Rhea's real life begins, she sees Eunie, at the beginning of *her* new life, returning from her encounter with the children from the spaceship. Wayne intends to marry Lucille, but Rhea persuades him to leave immediately for his job in Calgary and to drop her off on the way in Toronto or Winnipeg or wherever. For Wayne too, of course, this is a sudden breaking out into a different life.

> Soon after they got to Calgary, Rhea and Wayne were married. You had to be married then, to get an apartment together – at least in Calgary – and they had discovered that they did not want to live separately. That would continue to be the way they felt most of the time, though they would discuss it – living separately – and threaten it, and give it a couple of brief tries. (258)

This is as close as Rhea and Wayne – and Munro – come to saying that they love each other. But in the story's conclusion, readers are told that

> Rhea and Wayne have lived together for far more than half their lives. They have had three children, and between them, counting everything, five times as many lovers. And now abruptly, surprisingly, all this turbulence and fruitfulness and uncertain but lively expectation has receded and she [Rhea] knows they are beginning to be old. There in the cemetery she says out loud, "I can't get used to it." (259)

She belongs to *this* world, to *this* life.

In her introduction to *Selected Stories*, Munro says that she writes so often about "the country to the east of Lake Huron," with its "almost flat fields," "swamps," "hardwood bush lots," "brick houses," "falling-down barns," "burdensome old churches," et cetera, because she loves it. When she writes "about something happening in this setting," she says, "I don't think that I'm choosing to be confined. Quite the opposite." Munro is not simply writing "*about*" rural Ontario but also writing "*through*" it (xv).

Always concerned with change and its patterns of recurrence and permanence, Munro as the artist-historian of small-town Ontario, under a surface of ordinariness, repeatedly makes effective use of traditional genres and structures and of archetypal images, figures, and themes from the range of Western literature and myth, nowhere more

conspicuously than in "Spaceships Have Landed." It is extraordinary
in its daring and scope, a story in which are represented the span of
human history and myth and the range of the human psyche – and all
this neatly contained in and made compatible with the familiar realities
of a portrait of a small town in remote, rural Ontario. Alice Munro is not
confined to any view of history that ignores feelings and visions; she
transfigures daily life and gives her readers universal experience.

Works Cited

Anderson, Sherwood. *Winesburg, Ohio: Text and Criticism.* Ed. John H.
  Ferres. New York: Viking, 1966. The Viking Critical Library.
Brunvand, Jan Harold. *Folklore: A Study and Research Guide.* New York:
  St. Martin's, 1976.
Carscallen, James. *The Other Country: Patterns in the Writing of Alice
  Munro.* Toronto: ECW, 1993.
Clark, Miriam Marty. "Allegories of Reading in Alice Munro's 'Carried
  Away'." *Contemporary Literature* 37 (1996): 49-61.
Cuddon, J.A. "tall story." *A Dictionary of Literary Terms.* Rev. ed. Har-
  mondsworth, Eng.: Penguin, 1982. 684-85.
Gluck, Christoph Willibald. *Orfeo ed Eurydice.* 1762.
Graves, Robert. "Rhea." *Poems Selected by Himself.* Rev. and enl. ed. Har-
  mondsworth, Eng.: Penguin, 1961. 197.
Gzowski, Peter. Interview with Alice Munro. *Morningside.* CBC Radio.
  30 Sept. 1994.
The Holy Bible. Cambridge, Eng.: Cambridge UP, n.d. Authorized King
  James Vers.
Landor, Walter Savage. "Rose Aylmer." *The Oxford Book of English Verse
  1250-1918.* Ed. Sir Arthur Quiller-Couch. New ed. 1939. Oxford, Eng.:
  Clarendon, 1961. 680.
Lawrence, D.H. "The Fox." *The Short Novels.* Vol. 1. London: William
  Heinemann, 1956. 1-69. 2 vols. The Phoenix Ed. of D.H. Lawrence.
  26 vols.
Mackenzie, Donald A. *Myths of Crete & Pre-Hellenic Europe.* Illus. John
  Duncan. London: Gresham, n.d.
Mansfield, Katherine. "At the Bay." *Collected Stories of Katherine Mans-
  field.* London: Constable, 1945. 205-45.

Martin, W.R. "Alice Munro and James Joyce." *Journal of Canadian Fiction* 24 (1979): 120-26.

Martin, W.R., and Warren U. Ober. "Alice Munro's 'Hold Me Fast, Don't Let Me Pass' and 'Tam Lin'." *ANQ: A Quarterly Journal of Short Articles, Notes, and Reviews* 13.3 (2000): 44-48.

Mendels, M.M. *National Problems of Canada: The Asbestos Industry of Canada.* Orillia, ON: Packet-Times, 1930. McGill U Economic Studies 14.

Mozart, Wolfgang Amadeus. *Don Giovanni.* 1787.

Munro, Alice. "The Albanian Virgin." *Open Secrets.* Toronto: McClelland & Stewart, 1994. 81-128.

---. "Carried Away." *Open Secrets.* Toronto: McClelland & Stewart, 1994. 3-51.

---. "Characters." *Ploughshares* 4.3 (1978): 72-82.

---. "Everything Here Is Touchable and Mysterious." *Weekend Magazine* [*The Globe and Mail*] 11 May 1974: [33].

---. "Goodness and Mercy." *Friend of My Youth.* Toronto: McClelland & Stewart, 1990. 156-79.

---. "Hold Me Fast, Don't Let Me Pass." *Friend of My Youth.* Toronto: McClelland & Stewart, 1990. 74-105.

---. "Introduction to the Vintage Edition." *Selected Stories.* By Alice Munro. New York: Vintage, 1997. xiii-xxi. Vintage Contemporaries.

---. "Jakarta." *Saturday Night* Feb. 1998: 44-60. Rpt. (rev.) in *The Love of a Good Woman.* Toronto: McClelland & Stewart, 1998. 79-116.

---. *Lives of Girls and Women.* Toronto: McGraw-Hill Ryerson, 1971.

---. "Miles City, Montana." *The Progress of Love.* Toronto: McClelland and Stewart, 1986. 84-105.

---. "Oh, What Avails." *Friend of My Youth.* Toronto: McClelland & Stewart, 1990. 180-215.

---. "Open Secrets." *Open Secrets.* Toronto: McClelland & Stewart, 1994. 129-60.

---. "The Peace of Utrecht." *Dance of the Happy Shades.* Toronto: Ryerson, 1968. 190-210.

---. "Postcard." *Dance of the Happy Shades.* Toronto: Ryerson, 1968. 128-46.

---. "The Progress of Love." *The Progress of Love.* Toronto: McClelland and Stewart, 1986. 3-31.

---. "A Real Life." *Open Secrets.* Toronto: McClelland & Stewart, 1994. 52-80.

---. "Save the Reaper." *The New Yorker* 22 and 29 June 1998: 120-28, 130-32, 134-35. Rpt. (rev.) in *The Love of a Good Woman*. Toronto: McClelland & Stewart, 1998. 146-80.

---. "Spaceships Have Landed." *The Paris Review* 131 (1994): 265-94. Rpt. (rev.) in *Open Secrets*. Toronto: McClelland & Stewart, 1994. 226-60.

---. "Vandals." *Open Secrets*. Toronto: McClelland & Stewart, 1994. 261-94.

---. "Walker Brothers Cowboy." *Dance of the Happy Shades*. Toronto: Ryerson, 1968. 1-18.

---. "What Do You Want To Know For?" *Writing Away: The PEN Canada Travel Anthology*. Ed. Constance Rooke. Toronto: McClelland & Stewart, 1994. 203-20. Rpt. (rev.) in *The View from Castle Rock*. Toronto: McClelland & Stewart, 2006. 316-40.

---. "Wild Swans." *Who Do You Think You Are?* Toronto: Macmillan of Canada, 1978. 55-64.

Plato. "Symposium." *Lysis; Symposium; Gorgias*. Trans. W.R.M. Lamb. 1925. The Loeb Classical Library. Cambridge, MA: Harvard UP, 1961. 73-245. Plato V.

Robson, Nora. "Alice Munro and the White American South: The Quest." *The Art of Alice Munro: Saying the Unsayable*. Ed. Judith Miller. Waterloo, ON: U of Waterloo P, 1984. 73-84.

Ross, Catherine Sheldrick. *Alice Munro: A Double Life*. Toronto: ECW, 1992. Canadian Biography Ser.1.

Ross, James Gordon. *Chrysotile Asbestos in Canada*. Ottawa, ON: Mines Branch, Dept. of Mines, Canada, 1931. No. 707.

Struthers, J.R. (Tim). "Reality and Ordering: The Growth of a Young Artist in *Lives of Girls and Women*." *Essays on Canadian Writing* 3 (1975): 32-46.

"Tam Lin." *The English and Scottish Popular Ballads*. Ed. Francis James Child. Vol. 1. New York: Cooper Square, 1962. 335-58. 5 vols.

Tennyson, Alfred, Lord. "The Lady of Shalott." *The Oxford Book of English Verse 1250-1918*. Ed. Sir Arthur Quiller-Couch. New ed. 1939. Oxford, Eng.: Clarendon, 1961. 839-44.

Turbide, Diane. "The Incomparable Storyteller." Rev. of *Open Secrets*, by Alice Munro. *Maclean's* 17 Oct. 1994: 46-49.

Wachtel, Eleanor. "An Interview with Alice Munro." *The Brick Reader*. Ed. Linda Spalding and Michael Ondaatje. Illus. David Bolduc. Toronto: Coach House, 1991. 288-94.

Weaver, John. "Society and Culture in Rural and Small-Town Ontario: Alice Munro's Testimony on the Last Forty Years." *Patterns of the Past: Interpreting Ontario's History*. Ed. Roger Hall, William Westfall, and Laurel Sefton MacDowell. Toronto: Dundurn, 1988. 381-403.

Killer OSPs and Style Munro
in "Open Secrets"

William Butt

As in Poe's "The Fall of the House of Usher," where the mouldy ornate furnishings and eye-like windows of the house evoke its elegant but pathologically decadent owners, so in "Open Secrets" do architecture and interior design embody contending mental states. The house of Lawyer Stephens and his second wife, Maureen, is domestic with "peace of the kitchen" (157), yet the bedroom is a set for nasty sex. Amongst remnants from the era of the ghostly first wife, "front rooms ... full of valuable, heavy furniture ... and the curtains ... of green-and-mulberry brocade," Maureen struggles to express a modern, hospitable, informal self – "the breakfast table ... wedged into the old pantry," "new chintz in the sunroom" (132). Decor maps mental condition. The house of Theo Slater and his wife, Marian "the Corset Lady" (142), is a workshop for restraint and repression. Then too, at old Mr. Siddicup's home are women's tatty underwear "hanging from the backs of chairs ... or just in a heap on the table" (152); people are appalled and stop coming, things like that should be kept out of sight. Outer landscape likewise echoes these characters' psychology. The trees by the river are "A ragged sort of wall with hidden doorways, and hidden paths behind it where animals went, and lone humans sometimes, becoming different from what they were outside" (139-40).

All this in a Southwestern Ontario town called Carstairs, whose name suggests a vision of hoped-for upward mobility, to respectability, with its staid and proper institutions, ostensible bastions and instruments of an ordered society. Carstairs appears to brim with what Southwestern Ontario's John Kenneth Galbraith in *The Affluent Society* referred to as 'conventional wisdom' – here capitalized: United Church, Canadian Girls in Training, Post Office, Canadian Tire, Atomic Energy Station, Police Office, Town Hall, Preventive Custody, "Provincial Asylum, renamed the Mental Health Centre" (160). Above all, the capital-L Law, embodied in Lawyer Stephens with his unassailable credibility. "He knows the Law, they said.... Everyone believed he could have been a judge ..." (138). Unlike the story's garrulous inconstant narrators, "He never went in for much talk" (137), and "just a few words of his ... could cheer people up and lift a weight off them" (152). "He seemed to call upon a body of belief" (137), a social code that everyone implicitly, purportedly adheres to.

Yet in "Open Secrets" these rules and institutions are fossils, no-longer-believed-in bits from some myth of an orderly past. The Police don't appear, just one constable for one inconclusive sentence; we don't know if the Slaters ever go to the Police; we don't ever *see* the Police Office. Nor do we *see* the Atomic Energy Station or United Church, or the off-stage military college where Lawyer Stephens' son Gordon teaches, or any of this architecture that represents professed authority. In "Open Secrets" the institutions themselves are Open Secrets: supposedly acknowledged but in practice flimsily concealed. Like their polar opposites – aggression, defiance, cruelty, crime – hidden by nothing stouter than "soft skin ... on the back of a wooden spoon" till "memory will twitch" (160).

Munro in "Open Secrets" shows Southwestern Ontario WASPS as what we might instead rhymingly call OSPs. Open Secret People. OSPs need to conform, be socially useful; but they can't escape an opposite fundamental and anxiety-driven need to transgress. To rebel. "To be careless, dauntless, to create havoc – that was the lost hope of girls" (139); and not of girls only. Maureen who is childless supposes that having children "gave you the necessary stake in being grown-up" (132), made you responsible, domestic, civic-minded. But the story's core image is a hand pressed secretly by another hand onto a stove's hot burner. The dialectic of iniquities and punished hands will not be denied. They will come and come again. Complicitly, not forced: "In silence this is done, and by agreement – a brief and barbaric and necessary act" (158). Necessary: OSPs *need* the pain, need to both inflict and experience it, to punish others and themselves for everyone's chronic, serial transgressions. This is the OSP nature: the vision of Camille Paglia, out of Freud and de Sade.

"Open Secrets" starts with two stanzas of a ballad which the character Frances later says has been "typed out" (157). Then the prose of the story starts with Frances telling a second-hand version of the tale of Heather Bell: "Frances said that Mary Kaye said ..." (130). Another, subsequent tale told by Marian Hubbert/Slater comprises eight consecutive pages of the entire story: sometimes told within quotation marks, at other times without them, as if the overall unnamed narrator of "Open Secrets" perhaps has taken up the tale in some approximation of Marian's voice. Marian's tale itself includes an account of the tale which the non-verbal Mr. Siddicup tries to tell her. At the Post Office Maureen hears "two new reports" (140), fragmentary descriptions of (rumoured?) events after Heather's disappearance. On another occasion Maureen recalls two conflicting versions of how Marian and her husband Theo Slater met. Mary Johnstone tells the C.G.I.T. girls of meeting Jesus while she lay inert in an iron lung.

All this in the context of radio, newspaper, and oral narrations and speculations about Whatever Happened to Heather Bell. All this too in the context of recurrent narrative interstices in authorial voice – the unnamed narrator adopting the voice of a character narrator as described above, or writing in Style Munro, vocabulary and sound and rhythm which no mere character in this story would achieve. (Take for one of many adroit examples the phrase about Mr. Siddicup: "a morose and rather disgusting old urchin" [146]). All this, finally, in the context of a core narrative about a girl who disappeared in 1965, a mystery that no one since has solved, an episode which happens decades after the story's earliest events, and decades before the events at the story's end. It all adds up to an intricate organized blizzard of incomplete and mutually incompatible narrations.

Most of this narration is performance: sensational theatre for live audience. Frances snarkily to Maureen; crazed Mr. Siddicup to Marian; garrulous Marian to Lawyer Stephens; goody Mary to the C.G.I.T.; the delinquent girls to one another on a hot summer morning with a Freudian garden-hose prop, and at night in their tent playing Truth or Dare. Their dares when acted on become Artaud theatre of cruelty – "stick your head in the water pail and try to count to a hundred; go and pee in front of Miss Johnstone's tent" (139). Maureen in early puberty acts out with "a giddiness either genuine or faked or half-and-half" (139).

For her trip to the Lawyer's Marian "had put on a quantity of makeup" (143). She is "Dressed up" (141), sporting "a blue suit ... and her brown cloth gloves, and a brown hat made of feathers" (141-42); "Perhaps she saw herself transformed" (143). Her husband too is costumed as if for an occasion: in "a cheap cream-colored jacket with too much padding in the shoulders" (142). Lawyer Stephens "dressed every day just as he used to dress to go to his office – in a three-piece gray or brown suit" (137).

On their outing the girls wear costumes: theatrical C.G.I.T. uniforms, "navy-blue shorts and white blouses and red kerchiefs" (131). Marian acts out how Mr. Siddicup acted – "She got up and began to show them just what Mr. Siddicup had done" (148). Mr. Siddicup himself acts out, since he can't speak – "Back he went and pumped again, and stuck himself under again, and on like that, pumping and dousing" (148-49). Marian performs her husband's script for sex – "'Ta' dirty! Ta' dirty!'" (156). Frances reads out to Maureen the typewritten ballad of Heather Bell – "She read it through aloud" (157).

Mary calls Maureen "'Mrs. Stephens,' but she said it as if it was a play title" (133) – 'title' in the sense of designating royalty; 'play' in the sense of theatre or of something roguish, arch, facetiously performed. Sometimes a character is called by a sort of stage-name: to older people Alvin Stephens is Lawyer Stephens; Marian calls her husband "he" (144); Frances delights in naming Maureen "Missus" (132).

Yet normally the performances do not suffice, their audiences inattentive and/or uncomprehending. Though Maureen starts to listen to Frances' version of Heather's behaviour, she quickly dismisses it as "pretty farfetched" (130). She also ignores the ballad rendition by Frances near the story's end. During Marian's narration "Lawyer Stephens, as far as Maureen could see, had not glanced up at all" (148). While Mary Johnstone gives the girls her standard potted iron-lung-and-Jesus talk, they "make prepared faces at each other" (157). Marian can make nothing much of Mr. Siddicup's wordless, agitated contortions – "Now Mr. Siddicup, what's the matter? What are you trying to tell me?" (147). In Heather Bell's only public appearance after her disappearance, in the form of a posted missing-person photo, viewers perhaps perversely see only a "tight-lipped smile, bitten in at one corner as if suppressing a disrespectful laugh" (159).

To the reading audience of "Open Secrets," all the performances seem wobbly, distorted, like the Slaters glimpsed by Maureen through the wavy "pebbled glass in the front door" (141). Since his stroke Lawyer Stephens is nearly aphasic – "'Police. Who should gone to see'" (151). Since surgery on his throat Mr. Siddicup is entirely so, all frantic garbled gestures like something by the unhinged tramps in *Waiting for Godot*. Mary Johnstone's vision of Jesus as a doctor in a white coat is "crazy" (158) to everyone else, like the sugary, berserk dream of heaven at the end of Monty Python's *The Meaning of Life*. Marian's narration is erratic, digressive with irrelevant detail – "She wished now they'd bought a fan when the sale was on at Canadian Tire" (150). It feels hypnagogic, in the way it veers from straight-ahead plain tale to suddenly intruding, momentarily foregrounded images: the Atomic Energy Station, her boil, the doctor who whacks it.

Likewise the main narration: snippety as a dream. The story's last four paragraphs flash forward, skipping years, and are told in elliptical future tense – events that didn't and don't happen but hazily "will" (159-60 passim). We learn individuals' physical appearance in intense, hallucinatory detail – Maureen's hair "piled and sprayed like an upside-down mixing bowl" (132-33), Lawyer Stephens' "long, lumpy body" (137), Mary's ravaged "crooked shoulders, and a slightly twisted neck, which kept her big head a little tilted to one side" (133). We learn a fair bit about Lawyer Stephens' children, whom we zoom to inexplicably in close-up, via one long paragraph and one later scrap, though they've "grown up and lived away" (138). Yet at other times the unnamed main narrator doesn't tell what a baffled reader craves to know. We see only five stanzas of what must be a longer ballad of Heather Bell, and don't learn who wrote it, when or where or why or for whom. We get four perfunctory sentences on the actual search for Heather. We learn nothing directly of her mother – not even her name. "Open Secrets" reads like Kafka's *The Trial*, a mystery without a certifiable detective or crime.

Like Carroll's *Alice* books and Shakespeare's late romances and Conrad's *Heart of Darkness*, "Open Secrets" drops down through humans' consciousness to deep-bottom murk that words may try to depict but can only hint at slant-wise. Hence when Maureen looks out her sunroom window to the "old copper-beech trees" and "sunny lawn," we're told she's "seeing" the unruly trees along the river – "dense cedars and shiny-leaved oaks and glittery poplars" (139). *Seeing* in what sense? The front of the house is not far from the main street – the Slaters apparently have parked there and walked to the Lawyer's. How far then in another direction is the house from the river? Can Maureen *see* those trees in such sensory, hyper-acute detail? And when she peers in the other direction from the stairway landing toward the Slaters seated on the cemetery wall, how far are they away? Can she physically *see* the close-up detail of how Theo Slater "stroked that hat made of horrible brown feathers as if he were pacifying a little scared hen" (153)?

To what extent are imagination, intuition, attribution, or waking dream at work, as in the close-up "punished hand" (159) near the story's end? As in the "something" that Maureen sees or "has caught" – caught *how?*: "herself sitting on stone steps eating cherries and watching a man coming up the steps carrying a parcel" – a brief scene "so ordinary" (158) yet surreal because foreshortened, stripped of context enough to make sense of it. The narration of "Open Secrets" is hypnagogic Style Munro. A reader can barely spot places in certain paragraphs where a character's narration may dissolve into or reverse-dissolve out of that of the unnamed main narrator. A paragraph may begin in stylistically neutral third-person voice – "Frances worked for Maureen in the house, but she was not like a servant"; slip without quotation marks into the voice of Frances – "How much did you give for those chops, Missus?"; and then end in that Style Munro with its signature flourish of a cumulative triple-adjective thrust, Frances's "wild, uncharitable, confident speculations" (132-33).

Much in the way that the characters' narrations may start plain and straightforward but soon swivel or laterally skid, and self-subvert, so does each character reveal a double identity: demonic and innocent, transgressive and conventional, Hyde and Jekyll. Life in the world of Civilization and Its Discontents; the death drive Beyond the Pleasure Principle. The overtly Christian and uniformed 1965 C.G.I.T. girls mutter a bawdy parody of the pious old hymn "For the Beauty of the Earth" (131). In their tent the girls of Maureen's earlier C.G.I.T. generation goad one another to outrageous acts and accounts. "[T]ake off your pajama top and show your boobs ..." (139). "How many peckers have you seen and whose were they?" (139). Mary Johnstone, saintly polio survivor, devoted to girls' welfare, "wonderful" (133) – is also deformed and demented. Mr. Siddicup, once "a dignified, sarcastic little Englishman, with a pleasant wife. They read books from the library and were noted for their garden" (146), degenerates to "Dirty whiskers, dribbles on his clothes, a sour smoky smell, and a look in his eyes of constant suspicion, sometimes of loathing" (146).

Maureen is "A shrieker, a dare-taker," but shortly "a studious, shy girl" (139). As the all-competent adult employee of Lawyer Stephens, Maureen is "the Jewel" (138), and she's "in love when she married him," "how happy ... on her honeymoon" (154). But later she sits on a "chintz-covered hassock at her husband's side" (139), degraded and submissive as she is in their violent bouts of sex. She needs Frances to constantly subvert and undermine things, "someone around the house to have spats and jokes with" (133). Maureen, Marian, Mary, Mary Kaye: cognate names, one multiple, fragmented, self-conflicted identity.

OSPs would like to expurgate their double nature, lock it away like mad Mr. Siddicup, put it "buried underground" (152) like the daily contaminated irradiated rags at Douglas Point, remove it from public notice as the local newspaper editor stops covering the story of Heather Bell. And hardly ever will OSPs, as in this story's last words, even "think of trying to tell it" (160), though Alice Munro treasonously does tell it. Despite their editing super-egos, her OSPs go on telling and re-telling and re-enacting their dual natures vicariously and otherwise. The formidable decent Law may be "known to all decent people and maybe to all people" (137), but known only that it may be flouted.

Insecure and conflicted, OSPs urgently perform and narrate. They tell their demonic and their upright tales begging for approval, to be validated by others; like Marian, "to be taken account of" (143). Their performances and narrations are shrill, disjointed, neurotic. To buttress their narrations the OSPs perform them histrionically; they over-compensate. Likewise they devalue and deform those gaudy antic narrations of others: "eat a cigarette butt; swallow dirt" (139). A "shitty bastard" (156) Lawyer Stephens' daughter Helena calls her brother, in a short-lived excremental vision. "'Grow up'" (155) Lawyer Stephens tells his wife Maureen when she seems undignified, playful, ardent – though he himself lapses compulsively into lewd performance.

Where do little girls go to when they disappear? Into missing-person posters and then into OSP minds, undislodgeably, with their girlish wild "mockery" (159) of the decent, which prurient OSPs fix on and feast on while living out as well the opposite prim fiction, "the proper motherly kind of fit about rude language" (132). But Heather is a struck Bell which resounds for decades.

About the time that Alice Munro in Southwestern Ontario wrote "Open Secrets," David Lynch in Los Angeles was directing *Twin Peaks*. Small-town images surreally out of context. Fractured identities. Unexplained mystery and crime. Grotesque bodies and bodily acts. Suppression and repression. Stylized performances. We didn't need to watch American TV. Could have read Alice Munro instead. We still can.

Note

Page references are to *Open Secrets* (Toronto: McClelland & Stewart, 1994).

Not for Entertainment Purposes Only: Ethnicity and Alice Munro's "Powers"

Shelley Hulan

No Fault in Our Stars

In our twenties, a girlfriend and I went to a psychic who told futures from her shoreline bungalow on the outskirts of St. John's, Newfoundland. Afterwards, over lattes in one of the espresso bars just opening along the East Coast, we contemplated our golden stars in a caffeine-and-sugar-spiked euphoria. Those stars have mostly aligned for us ever since, as far as I can tell, though the years haven't always borne much resemblance to the psychic's predictions. Rereading the phrases I frantically scribbled as the cards were shuffled (travel over water ... trouble over money ... things fall into place), I see how much my twenty-something self read into what I heard. I told my own fortune, actually. I may have thought that I had many questions for the fortuneteller, but all I was really asking her was whether my future would be good, great, or fabulous. This question had just one answer, and I supplied that too.

"Powers," the final story in Alice Munro's 2004 collection *Runaway*, presents a psychic character who *does* supply answers that her visitors do not have. Her gift is genuine, whereas I have convinced myself that my Newfoundland seer's was probably fake. There are similarities, however. Like Munro's Tessa, my clairvoyant wore no turban and looked into no crystal ball. She had no beads, candles, incense, or anything else that other cottage dwellers wouldn't have in their homes. She wore fleece. She did not advertise. Tessa is an ordinary person living an ordinary life with an extraordinary ability, and her world corresponds in some respects to the real one I inhabit.

Set mainly in a small town on the Canadian side of Lake Huron, "Powers" unfolds in the heart of a Southwestern Ontario that Munro never entirely fictionalizes. As Coral Ann Howells remarks, Munro's narratives "represent negotiations between factual material and a textual construction where life is mediated and transformed by the writer's imagination and literary skill" (79); Munro's literary biographer, Robert Thacker, traces an artistic method that moves so regularly between fiction and memoir that "actual people, not characters" often show up in the stories (212). Repeated references by scholars and the author herself to the autobiographical details in the *oeuvre* draw attention to places where the real Munro and other real people dwell, places with a social order and ways of talking that naturalize that order.

In this context of a fictional world that refracts a real one, I want to examine another power operating in the story: the power to assign an ethnic minority identity to Tessa. This power circulates through Tessa's former schoolmate Nancy, the protagonist literally and symbolically at the heart of the society in which the two women grow up. Nancy equates ethnic difference with disadvantages that she sometimes deplores and never experiences. The ethnic minority status that she invents for Tessa via ethnicizing analogies and stereotypes allows her to ignore several possible reasons for Tessa's outsider status, in particular economic ones.

Critical discussions of difference, discrimination, and inequality in Munro's stories frequently focus on gender and class but rarely acknowledge matters of ethnicity and race except in passing (for instance, see McCaig 132; but for an important exception, see Clarke). Perhaps the setting of her Southwestern Ontario narratives in a region populated during the nineteenth century by high numbers of English, Scottish, Irish, and German emigrants makes the characters' largely homogeneous ethnicity seem inevitable. That homogeneousness has never truly existed either in the real Souwesto or in Munro's fictional accounts of it. Characters who do not belong to these settler groups recur throughout her stories, whether set in Southwestern Ontario or beyond; "Memorial," "Eskimo," "Five Points," "Save the Reaper," and "Home" provide a few of many examples. Sometimes these characters receive paternalistic and/ or unkind treatment of the sort that a gang of schoolgirls metes out to Myra Sayla and her brother in "Day of the Butterfly," a story from Munro's first collection, *Dance of the Happy Shades*. Sometimes they rebuff this treatment, as Myra's mother does. In "Day of the Butterfly," the school-girls' bullying demonstrates how the concept of ethnicity breaks down traits all human beings share (language, appearance, skin pigmentation, culture) into smaller subunits (specific accents and dialects, skin tones, religious practices) that may easily be incorporated into hierarchical social arrangements. In "Alice Munro Country," these arrangements often draw upon a myth of non-ethnicity, or the idea that the dominant group has no ethnicity whatsoever.

For much of the twentieth century in North America, White Anglo-Saxon Protestants have claimed this 'non-ethnic' status,[1] defining ethnicity as difference from the dominant race, geographical origins, and religion that they see themselves as embodying. Munro's characters almost never refer to persons' religion, skin colour, or culture unless to identify some quality they perceive as non-Whiteness, non-Anglo-Saxonness, or non-Protestantism; the schoolgirl narrator of "Day of the Butterfly" describes Myra's smell and accent, but no one else's. Not possessing one or more WASP traits makes one an outsider, as the attitude to Montene-grin clockmaker Danilo demonstrates in the *Runaway* story previous to "Powers," "Tricks." In that story, the mere smell of the Stroganoff Danilo prepares for Robin in Stratford is enough to raise the suspicions of Robin's sister Joanne in her town thirty miles away and to prompt numerous derogatory references to foreignness, the stigma and fear of which are very real to Joanne even when the "foreigner" (253) is nowhere near. As her keen sense of smell indicates, ethnic 'otherness' may register through any of the five senses. In "Powers," however, the eye – Nancy's WASP eye – is its major mediator.

The Kids Are All White

Being a WASP in North America, as I am, does not guarantee success or prosperity. However, membership in this category offers citizens the best odds of finding both, since the dominant population in any society exer-cises the greatest control over its resources. To belong is to be able seri-ously to believe that nothing except lack of effort impedes the movement from aspiration to the fulfilment of one's hopes. Poverty among those who belong to this group poses a problem for such a triumphalist trajectory because it undermines members' expectations of profit and improvement in their own lives, revealing these gains as random and shaped by forces beyond individual control. Ingrained WASP truisms such as the notion that personal industry brings tangible rewards, or that outer wealth and position signify inner virtue, transform economic precariousness into a taboo subject. When Nancy suppresses this social fact by attributing a minority ethnic identity to Tessa, she associates economic vulnerability exclusively with non-WASP ethnicities.

Nancy is a Souwesto WASP who is as close to the epicentre of privilege and influence as it is possible for a woman in her 1920s Southwestern Ontario town to be. Her family and social circles include the town's leading citizens. Her father owns a local factory. Her future husband, Wilf, is the town's new doctor. Nancy's father and Wilf employ full-time housekeepers. She and her friends have the education and leisure to plan an amateur theatrical production and, when a caved-in roof destroys their performance venue, to replace that project with a reading group that focusses on 'the classics.' In her diary she lists professions (doctor, optometrist) and pastimes (golf, driving excursions) that testify to the bourgeois affluence of this social set. By contrast, her diary description of Tessa after a chance encounter at the grocery store places the other young woman outside the group:

> She was all wrapped up in a big shawl and she looked like something out of a storybook. Top-heavy, actually, because she has that broad face with its black curly mop and her broad shoulders, though she can't be much over five feet tall. She just smiled, the same old Tessa. And I asked how she was – you always do that when you see her, seriously, because of her long siege of whatever it was that took her out of school when she was around fourteen. (270-71)

Nancy's use of first- and second-person plural pronouns to narrate a personal encounter suggests that she follows a protocol for interacting with Tessa, one observed by a group of people to which both she and her implied reader belong but Tessa does not.

Nancy's friendly greeting combines cordiality with social distance. Her diary description of the other woman affirms a longstanding acquaintanceship of some sort ("the same old Tessa") while revealing that the two are not close enough for Nancy to know what illness caused her to drop out of school. Tessa's childhood malady may have caused this protocol to evolve, but Nancy also regards it as the only appropriate response to Tessa owing to the separate life she leads:

> also you ask that [how Tessa is] because there isn't much else to think of to say, she is not in the world that the rest of us are in. She is not in any clubs and can't take part in any sports and she does not have any normal social life. She does have a sort of life involving people and there is nothing wrong with it, but I wouldn't know how to talk about it and maybe neither would she. (271)

Nancy will later explain that the people 'involved' in Tessa's life are the visitors who come to her for help finding their lost valuables. The oblique reference to Tessa's psychic ability introduces it into the story as a barrier to the "normal social life" that Nancy and her other friends enjoy.

Tessa's difference from her peers is most evident to Nancy in her physique, the childlike proportions of which she compares to "something out of a storybook." Aligning Tessa's adult body with childhood and storybooks situates her in a fairy tale, or the kind of storybook for children that, in European traditions, often inculcates "the Grand Narrative of the Judeo-Christian world" (Jędrzejko 69) that celebrates the able-bodied healers of the sick and the helpers of the poor. Heroes of the Grand Narrative save flawed humanity from its diseases and deformities, the visible signs of supposedly sinful natures, while their own internal goodness manifests in a combination of physical beauty, health, and mobility. Conceived as a character in a fairy tale, Tessa is an adult trapped in a sickly child's body, a person in need of rescue. The storybook analogy converts her history of illness into an enchanted passivity that prevents her from participating in the social life of the town.

As for the "life involving people," the storybook comparison assigns Tessa a position in Judeo-Christian fairy tales that is frequently portrayed as sinister: that of the 'gypsy'[2] fortuneteller. Historically, Wilhelm Solms explains, European fairy-tale depictions of the Roma peoples as predatory nomads who cheat and steal from settled populations perpetuated a medieval legend that "the Sinti and Roma, together with the Jews, were ... jointly responsible for the crucifixion of Christ" (92) and are therefore the villains of the Christ story. Some of the best-known tales, those gathered by the Brothers Grimm in the early nineteenth century, validate ideas of these groups as too different in body and behaviour to integrate into the larger society; thus they need surveillance, if not removal, by the Christian communities on the edges of which they live (Solms 105). Sometimes represented as black-skinned (Solms 102), fairy-tale 'gypsies' are also depicted as members of a different race hostile to Caucasians.

Still, while Nancy regards Tessa's curly hair and broad shoulders as sufficient markers of difference to identify the other woman as separate from the rest of the community, they seem a weak basis on which to explain the kind of social isolation with which Nancy associates her. No other body-difference markers for Tessa emerge in the story. Indeed, Nancy's storybook analogy aligns these minor visual differences with an ethnic minority identity that Tessa, in fact, shows no clear signs of having; if anything, her last name (Netterby) and blue eyes indicate that she is probably as White, Anglo-Saxon, and Protestant as Nancy herself.

Nancy, however, continues to 'other' Tessa in ethnic terms through a second analogy that appears when she brings Ollie, Wilf's visiting cousin, to Tessa's cottage because she is peeved that he doesn't "'think we have anything here [in the town] worth noticing'" (295). In this instance, she includes Tessa in the "we" for whom she speaks instead of excluding her as she did earlier. But when Tessa does not immediately oblige Nancy's request that she take a clairvoyant inventory of the items in Ollie's pockets, the cajolery with which Nancy pressures her reasserts the social and economic distance between the two women. Nancy's tone addresses Tessa as an inferior: "'Now it's time. Do me a favor. Please do.' // ... // 'Come on, Tessa, you know me. Remember we're old friends, we're friends since the first room of school. Just do it for me'" (291).

After the visit, Nancy confirms this social and economic distance for Ollie by offering a new analogy for Tessa: "'You think we're only worth making fun of. All of us around here. So I was going to show her to you. Like a freak'" (295). The idea that Nancy planned to "show" Tessa to an out-of-towner as if she were "a freak" evokes images of a carnival or circus act, the kind of "show" that puts people on display when their unusual appearances and/or talents assure the audience of its own normalcy. These are, of course, also the kinds of shows where fortunetellers ply their trade. Nancy offers this second analogy more tentatively than the first, her use of the continuous past tense ("I was going to show her" instead of the more accurate "I showed her") seeming to retract the image just as she introduces it. She does not withdraw it, however. *Freak* is precisely the term she deems most suitable for Tessa. Like the storybook comparison, the freak analogy emphasizes that there is something strange about Tessa that her special talent does not entirely explain, something that Nancy perceives as an absence (or violation) of the 'normal.'

The imagery through which Nancy describes what she sees in Tessa casts Tessa simultaneously as an afflicted body who needs help and a strange body who invites observation. The first requires protection; the second may require control. This double episteme of vulnerability and apparent threat is familiar to students of the postcolonial gothic in Canadian literature, especially with reference to its treatment of ethnic minorities. Gerry Turcotte points out that a dominant Euro-settler society has to contain and control whomever it oppresses, and it often achieves this aim by portraying oppression as protection. Canada's Euro-settler government, Turcotte notes, did so during World War Two when it imprisoned Japanese Canadians in internment camps on the pretext of protecting the rest of the population from the dangers that these incarcerated Canadians allegedly posed (82-88, 92-93). Nancy's representations of Tessa likewise imply that the 'ethnic' subject she represents as needing protection is simultaneously 'threatening' and 'threatened.'

On with the Show

Nancy's use of "freak" to characterize Tessa after Nancy wheedles a performance from her makes Tessa out to be a non-WASP in a second, subtler way, for events in the story – and elsewhere in *Runaway* – indicate that entertainers (even unwilling ones such as Tessa) cannot also be worthy Protestants. One of the insults the husband in *Runaway*'s sixth story, "Trespasses," hurls at his (formerly Catholic) wife when they argue is that she gives the neighbours "'a show'" on the lawn (229). Nancy's own adventures in acting confirm the disrepute in which Protestants hold the act of 'putting on a show' when she feigns illness as an April Fools' Day joke on Wilf. The scolding he gives her makes clear that, in his view, outer demeanour must never contradict inner reality: "'I happen to have [genuinely] sick people to see to, Nancy. Why don't you learn to act your age?'" (275). His response to her trick expresses a Protestant disapproval of performance as childish attention-seeking.

Nancy suspects that Wilf's disgust derives from his being a minister's son, an intuition that arises not so much from her familiarity with new-comer Wilf as from her familiarity with the prejudices customary in a small town on the Canadian side of Lake Huron in the 1920s. Historian John Weaver points out that in the early to mid-twentieth century, this was a region where the local circumstance of proximity to the much larger and ostentatiously wealthy United States created a peculiarly strong interdiction against the kind of self-advertisement that Protes-tantism also discouraged (392-93). Wilf did not grow up in Nancy's town, but Nancy did, and although she considers his disgust an overreaction, she defers to it by apologizing to him. Wilf's marriage proposal soon afterwards secures her position in the town's establishment.

By positioning Tessa as a performer, Nancy situates her outside this Protestant orthodoxy and outside the social hierarchy into which Nancy further embeds herself via her marriage. The freak analogy goes beyond representing Tessa as a performer, however. It makes her a spectacle. Nancy's purpose for taking Ollie to Tessa's cottage is to surprise him with the immediate shock of the encounter. She is not curious, as Ollie is, about the depths beneath the sensational surface. She directs his speculation about the scientific causes of Tessa's gift towards the only part of that gift that matters in her milieu, which is Tessa's exit from the town's social life: "'[Tessa] quit school and she never came back, and that's when she sort of fell out of things'" (294).

Notwithstanding the brief outburst of remorse Nancy has at having put Tessa on display "[l]ike a freak" (295), her lack of interest in Tessa's psychic ability demonstrates that she regards Tessa as a show that she can commodify in the interest of the town's reputation. As a freak, Tessa can be exploited by members of the very social order that excludes her. When Nancy attempts to parlay Tessa's divination of Ollie's pockets into an acknowledgement from Ollie that the town deserves respect, she self-servingly manipulates the difference she sees in Tessa.

The Show Must Go On

That Nancy considers Tessa a specifically non-WASP ethnic spectacle becomes clearest when Nancy, as an old woman ensconced in the same hometown, attempts to figure out how Tessa came to reside in the mental hospital where she turns up years later. Nancy pursues the attempt in a dream that begins with Tessa and Ollie's arrival at a small-town hotel, where Tessa dons a costume she wears for the performances the two give together:

> She is wearing the yellow satin ankle-length skirt, and the black bolero, with the black shawl patterned with roses, the fringe half a yard long. Her costumes are her own idea, and they are neither original nor becoming. Her skin is rouged now, but dull. Her hair is pinned and sprayed, its rough curls flattened into a black helmet. Her eyelids are purple and her eyebrows lifted and blackened. Crow's wings. The eyelids pressed down heavily, like punishment, over her faded eyes. In fact her whole self seems to be weighted down by the clothes and the hair and the makeup. (331)

Of course, the clothes, hair, and makeup reveal nothing whatsoever about Tessa since Nancy dreams her into all three, 'gypsifying' the other woman more overtly than she did through the storybook and freak analogies while imposing on her the same associations with vulnerability that those earlier comparisons introduced. The 'gypsified' Tessa is a spectacle and a performer, as Nancy has always made her out to be. For all its gaudy drama, the costume promises no new insight into Tessa's fate. Nancy's reverie is "defensive," as Lester E. Barber puts it (157), quite possibly a ruse by which her semi-conscious mind – after all, she "doesn't believe she is sleeping when she finds herself entering" Tessa and Ollie's hotel room (330) – conceals her complicity in Tessa's confinement by pretending to inquire into it.

Nor does the setting, a dream town discursively organized exactly as Nancy's hometown is, offer any new answers. Dream Ollie serves as Nancy's avatar, navigating a version of that town and its social order. When he refers to his and Tessa's potential sponsors in the town as "them," he divides town insiders from outsiders via the plural pronouns

Nancy uses to do the same. Like Nancy, dream Ollie locates normalcy in a dominant society that he can negotiate but that Tessa cannot because "she is not a normal person" (334). Combined with his charm and education, his movements around the towns they visit give him a means and perhaps a motive to get rid of Tessa when she can no longer put on a show. Regular engagement with members of town society puts him in touch with the doctor who supplies him with the commitment papers that will allow him to consign her to an institution.

The theatricality of this setting, with its costumed performer, its nefarious secret plot against Tessa, and its fourth wall opening onto Nancy's voyeuristic gaze calls to mind Anne McClintock's discussion of sadomasochism as a theatre of Western imperialism and domesticity, or the world and the home as regimented by a global commodification of labour, gender, and race in the service of European ambition. Like Victorian devotees of S/M, Nancy "borrows [the] decor, props and costumery ... and [the] scenes ... from the everyday cultures of power" (McClintock 143). Nancy reproduces her hometown in the town where she imagines Tessa and Ollie, as if to insist upon the universal propriety of its structure, and she adopts the role of a dominatrix who controls Tessa's and Ollie's movements.

Simultaneously, however, the "exaggerated emphasis on costumery ... and scene" exposes the arbitrariness of the rules governing economy, gender, and race (McClintock 143) in the social order of the hometown. Tessa's 'gypsy' costume is not simply exaggerated, but a caricature. The ethnic minority 'other' implicit in the freak and storybook analogies becomes explicit in Nancy's reduction of Tessa to this most hackneyed of clairvoyant stereotypes. Nancy even racializes the ethnicity she projects onto Tessa through the four instances of "black" in the description of dream Tessa's hair, makeup, and clothes. Dream Tessa is as Black as she can be without actually having black skin.

George Elliott Clarke finds in Munro's uses of such intricate black-white, dark-light imagery an escape route (at least for one of her more adventurous protagonists) from the mind-numbing "provincialism of 'Deep South'-western Ontario" (168) to the cosmopolitan, multicultural urban centres that many of Munro's Souwesto characters dislike and fear. However, no such escape presents itself in the 'gypsy' vision, for either Nancy or Tessa. Associating Tessa for a second time with a racist stereotype of the 'sinister' fairy-tale Roma, the blackness that Nancy projects upon the other woman helps Nancy reassert her control over Tessa, this figure she imagines as "weighted down by the clothes and the hair and the makeup." Meanwhile, Nancy goes on dreaming in her airy sunroom, a "bright room" on "a bright afternoon" (330).

Nancy's dream of 'gypsy' Tessa indicates that she is unable to relinquish her lifelong invention of Tessa as a non-WASP ethnic subject, an invention to which she is so devoted that, in her dream, she changes the facts of Tessa's story rather than probe the reasons why Tessa winds up in the mental hospital. While Nancy believes she embarks on her visit to Tessa and Ollie's past to "get one good look at it" (330), her dream merely displaces that past with an alternative scenario in which no one is ever seen to be accountable for making the decision to have Tessa committed. This scenario permits Nancy to avoid contemplating what that decision has meant for the life Tessa really lived, and may still be living, in an institution. The 'gypsy' costume, then, obscures the possible causes of Tessa's confinement. It suggests, too, that Nancy ethnicizes what she does not comprehend.

Showstopper

Perhaps because Nancy always appears dimly aware of the social structures that shape her life and Tessa's, her ethnic stereotyping of Tessa serves purposes too important for her to abandon. The real Ollie gestures towards these purposes early in "Powers" when he pointedly asks Nancy about Tessa's diet, her means of earning a living, and her pastimes. His questions recognize that Tessa's marginality in the town may have less to do with her psychic powers than her economic circumstances. Nancy has no answers for him and no interest in finding any. Her later dream of the 'gypsy'-costumed Tessa confirms the same lack of interest many years later, depicting her former acquaintance as an exotic spectacle even as the hotel room's threadbare curtains, creaky bed, and cramped dimensions make poverty part of the scene. When the dreaming Nancy turns quickly away from a description of these dilapidated quarters to a description of Tessa's outfit, she substitutes the costumery for the economic and class divisions that she tries to ignore. While the tawdriness of the costume corresponds to the tawdriness of the room, it also creates a distraction.

'Gypsifying' Tessa allows Nancy to continue to camouflage the economic precariousness of Tessa's life that Nancy never explicitly acknowledges. She relies upon this vulnerability to affirm her own social position, nowhere more clearly than when she declines to remove Tessa from the mental hospital where she has resided for many years. Nancy's immediate reason for refusing is that Wilf, now suffering from mental illness, has rights to her care and attention that trump Tessa's. The terms in which she puts this reason to Tessa – "'He's been a good husband to me, just as good as he could be. I made a vow to myself that he wouldn't have to go into an institution'" (311) – baldly clarify that Tessa, as a woman with no immediate family and no financial resources (as opposed to a man with a wife and considerable means), must remain in the institution where Nancy finds her. Wilf is entitled to his wife's protection and the respect due his profession. Thus he too remains where *he* is, at the centre of town and in his lifelong home.

This is not the first time in the story that illness operates as a fault line that divides Tessa in economic and class terms from the others in Nancy's peer group, as a comparison of young Tessa's and young Ollie's differing recoveries from early illnesses demonstrates. Both characters survive a serious affliction in young adulthood, but after recovery the orphaned Tessa is expected to support herself unaided while Ollie convalesces in a sanitarium. Released shortly before he arrives in town for Nancy and Wilf's wedding, he is jobless and, though cultured, does not appear to be qualified for any profession. Notwithstanding this lack of credentials (and enthusiasm), Nancy's father immediately envisions Ollie taking over his factory one day, and Nancy introduces him to her friend Ginny as a marriage prospect. A stranger to the town, his connection to Wilf and his sophisticated air generate this determined effort to integrate him into town society.

By contrast, Nancy knows far less about Tessa's childhood ailment than she does about Ollie's despite Tessa's having grown up in the town; moreover, in the aftermath of Tessa's illness, neither Nancy nor her friends attempt to restore whatever social relations they once had with her through school. While a place promptly opens for Ollie in the economy of the town as well as in its social life, Tessa becomes a person forever associated with sickliness, romanticized as a mysterious childlike creature who is shut out of the hierarchy which Ollie may ascend without delay if he wishes.

When the young Nancy thinks of Tessa prior to the latter's surprise elopement with Ollie, she thinks of someone whose illness makes her fragile and limits her social sphere. Ostensibly, the risks she sees in the elopement lie in Tessa's going to places where no one knows her, as Nancy warns in a letter imploring Tessa not to leave town with Ollie: "I just feel in my heart it is not a good thing for you to leave here ... and go where nobody knows you or thinks of you as a friend or normal person" (301). Coming from a character who repeatedly attributes abnormality to Tessa, the intimation that townspeople think of her as a "normal person" suggests that Nancy is confusing safe space for Tessa with the space Tessa occupies on the edge of a town whose inhabitants either use her to aggrandize themselves and their community or forget about her altogether. Nancy's fear that Tessa endangers herself by eloping with Ollie sublimates another, less admirable fear: that Tessa possesses a power of self-determination Nancy has never believed possible.

Rivalling the strength of Nancy's conviction that only the hometown can keep Tessa safe is her anxiety that Tessa is slipping beyond, and undermining, its social dynamic. She conveys this anxiety by inviting Tessa to see her new house shortly after she weds Wilf, when Tessa has become a celebrity thanks to Ollie's *Saturday Night* piece about her. Before his marriage, Wilf's renovated and enlarged house is the envy of Nancy's social set. After they marry, it stands for the couple's social importance. The increased traffic to Tessa's cottage at the very moment when Nancy becomes the chatelaine of this impressive home prompts Nancy's perturbed realization that Tessa attracts people away from the town towards its periphery. Years later, Nancy's leaving Tessa in the mental hospital ensures that she cannot return to upset the centre-periphery balance of the social order on which Nancy depends for her identity.

I Can Check Out Any Time I Like, But She Can Never Leave

Ethnicizing Tessa camouflages the economic and class dimensions of her marginalization. The analogies Nancy draws among Tessa, the storybook girl, and the freak portray her as both in danger and dangerous, in need of protection and in need of surveillance. When Nancy ethnicizes the mystery of Tessa's psychic gifts once again through the stereotype of the 'gypsy' fortuneteller, she diverts attention from Tessa's economic vulnerability – her scant resources, her isolation, and later her cohabitation with Ollie, whose charm, education, and movements around the towns they tour give him a means and possibly a motive to get rid of her when she can no longer perform. While any of these factors poses a greater threat to Tessa's liberty than does the minoritized ethnicity that Nancy projects onto her, Nancy depicts Tessa's putative ethnic difference as the menace that incorporates and conveys all other threats that Tessa's psychic powers and economic circumstances make to Nancy's understanding of her world.

It's worth pausing on this point to consider its implications for Munro scholarship. This scholarship rightly credits Munro's stories with bringing into vivid focus the ordinary lives of girls and women, following them through twentieth-century changes to the roles they take on outside the home and their simultaneous struggles for respect from lovers, neighbours, and family. The same subject matter permeates the stories of *Runaway*. Yet in "Powers," readers cannot readily interpret Tessa's class or economic status independently of the ethnicizing terms through which Nancy ignores them. When she chooses to assign a minority ethnicity to Tessa while trying to avoid acknowledging the role that economic hardship may play in her marginalization, Nancy emphasizes rather than minimizes the intersection of poverty and ethnicity at the borders of the WASP society to which she belongs.

If the WASP imaginary as iterated in Nancy configures disadvantage as non-WASP ethnicity, then social concerns that Munro critics have historically treated as discrete, such as class and gender, may in fact require them to investigate an ethnic bias woven into the social fabric of the Souwesto that Munro offers. Nancy's 'gypsification' of Tessa hints at what being considered ethnically different from a dominant population means in mid-twentieth-century Southwestern Ontario: the denial of ethnic minorities' right to, and even their capacity for, self-definition.

What does it mean to regard ethnic minority identity as inseparable from the idea of disadvantage, and what does it mean when the person who fuses the two invents an ethnic minority identity in order to ignore the very disadvantage with which she associates it? The answer I might supply from my own experience is that WASP entitlement is least visible to those who benefit the most from it, and those who benefit most from it have a measure of financial security. That security produces the confident expectation that life always gets better. What I never once questioned in visiting the psychic in Newfoundland was the inevitability of my moving past her. While I was curious to hear what she would have to say about my stars, I took for granted that I would overcome any obstacles she might see on the path to my glorious tomorrows. She might illuminate that path, but I would travel it. She, by contrast, would remain frozen in the time and space of our encounter.

Sitting in that coastal cottage, I did not realize how exceptional I thought I was, nor just how many young hopefuls like me unconsciously chart the same bourgeois course to the same luminous future. If that realization has come, it has come much later. Yet some things have not changed. As I see them in hindsight, the powers of the psychic I visited are doubtworthy, but like Nancy's my own as an affluent white Euro-settler subject never have been. I don't believe I have ever striated this confidence concerning my powers into a hierarchy of ethnicities. Then again, Nancy doesn't think she does so either.

Notes

1. See Ronald H. Bayor's "Introduction: The Making of America" in *The Oxford Handbook of American Immigration and Ethnicity*, especially page 5, for a discussion of the WASP as the dominant American ethnicity.
2. The term 'gypsy' is often used pejoratively to refer to Roma peoples. While strongly opposing this negative representation, I have chosen to employ this term and variations on it to refer to the prejudicial ethnic imagery that Nancy uses to characterize Tessa. I argue that this imagery betrays Nancy's marginalization and derogation of non-WASP ethnic groups.

Works Consulted

Barber, Lester E. "'Old Confusions or Obligations': Comic Vision in *Runaway*." *Alice Munro: Hateship, Friendship, Courtship, Loveship, Marriage; Runaway; Dear Life*. Ed. Robert Thacker. London: Blooms-bury, 2016. 137-58, 227-29.

Bayor, Ronald H. "Introduction: The Making of America." *The Oxford Handbook of American Immigration and Ethnicity*. New York: Oxford UP, 2016. 1-13.

Clarke, George Elliott. "Alice Munro's Black Bottom; or Black Tints and Euro Hints in *Lives of Girls and Women*." *Alice Munro: Reminiscence, Interpretation, Adaptation and Comparison*. Ed. Mirosława Buchholtz and Eugenia Sojka. Frankfurt am Main, Ger.: Peter Lang, 2015. 147-71. Dis/Continuities: Toruń Studies in Language, Literature and Culture 8.

Howells, Coral Ann. "Alice Munro and Her Life Writing." *The Cambridge Companion to Alice Munro*. Ed. David Staines. Cambridge, Eng.: Cambridge UP, 2016. 79-95.

Jędrzejko, Pawel. "Fat, Green and *Schrecklich*: Mistaken Identities, Trans-humanity and Fairy-Tale Excuses." *Open Letter* 13th ser., no. 3 (2007): 69-88.

Martin, W.R., and Warren U. Ober. "Alice Munro as Small-Town Histo-rian: 'Spaceships Have Landed'." *Alice Munro Writing On...*. Ed. Robert Thacker. *Essays on Canadian Writing* 66 (1998): 128-46. Rpt. in *The Rest of the Story: Critical Essays on Alice Munro*. Ed Robert Thacker. Toronto: ECW, 1999. 128-46.

McCaig, JoAnn. *Reading In: Alice Munro's Archives*. Waterloo, ON: Wilfrid Laurier UP, 2002.

McClintock, Anne. *Imperial Leather: Race, Gender and Sexuality in the Colonial Contest*. New York: Routledge, 1995.

Munro, Alice. "Day of the Butterfly." *Dance of the Happy Shades*. Toronto: Ryerson, 1968. 100-10.

---. "Eskimo." *The Progress of Love*. Toronto: McClelland and Stewart, 1986. 189-207.

---. "Five Points." *Friend of My Youth*. Toronto: McClelland & Stewart, 1990. 27-49.

---. "Home." *The View from Castle Rock*. Toronto: McClelland & Stewart, 2006. 285-315.

---. "Memorial." *Something I've Been Meaning To Tell You*. Toronto: McGraw-Hill Ryerson, 1974. 207-26.

---. "Powers." *Runaway*. Toronto: McClelland & Stewart, 2004. 270-335.

---. "Save the Reaper." *The Love of a Good Woman*. Toronto: McClelland & Stewart, 1998. 146-80.

---. "Trespasses." *Runaway*. Toronto: McClelland & Stewart, 2004. 197-235.

---. "Tricks." *Runaway*. Toronto: McClelland & Stewart, 2004. 236-69.

Redekop, Magdalene. *Mothers and Other Clowns: The Stories of Alice Munro*. London: Routledge, 1992.

Solms, Wilhelm. "On the Demonising of Jews and Gypsies in Fairy Tales." Trans. Susan Tebbutt. *Sinti and Roma: Gypsies in German-Speaking Society and Literature*. Ed. Susan Tebbutt. New York: Berghahn, 1998. 91-106. Culture and Society in Germany 2.

Thacker, Robert. "Alice Munro's Ontario (2007)." *Reading Alice Munro: 1973-2013*. Calgary: U of Calgary P, 2016. 201-16, 282.

Turcotte, Gerry. "'Horror Written on Their Skin': Joy Kogawa's Gothic Uncanny." *Unsettled Remains: Canadian Literature and the Postcolonial Gothic*. Ed. Cynthia Sugars and Gerry Turcotte. Waterloo, ON: Wilfrid Laurier UP, 2009. 75-96.

Weaver, John. "Society and Culture in Rural and Small-Town Ontario: Alice Munro's Testimony on the Last Forty Years." *Patterns of the Past: Interpreting Ontario's History*. Ed. Roger Hall, William Westfall, and Laurel Sefton MacDowell. Toronto: Dundurn, 1988. 381-402.

Thoughts from England:
On Reading, Teaching, and Writing Back
to Alice Munro's "Meneseteung"

Ailsa Cox

Setting the Scene: Small Towns and Rural Landscapes

October is a lovely month in England, the trees in their final flush of gold and ochre, the dying light so bright it can sometimes scorch your eyes. West Lancashire is one of those landscapes, like Norfolk or the Shetland Islands, that seem to be almost entirely sky. The flat fields stretch towards the Irish Sea, north of Liverpool – the region's farmlands doll-sized in comparison with even the smallest slice of Huron County. Until the late seventeenth century, much of this area was submerged beneath the largest lake in England, with a circumference of about twenty miles (Hale and Coney 2). In Alice Munro's "Walker Brothers Cowboy" (*Dance of the Happy Shades*, 1968), the narrator's father talks about the time when Lake Huron was a great plain, a conversation that alerts her to the microscopic scale of human existence. The lost lake of Martin Mere is mere indeed, compared to Lake Huron, but both of them large or small droplets within the unimaginable darkness of time and space. In October 2015, at Edge Hill University, we are reading "Meneseteung" (*Friend of My Youth*, 1990) in West Lancashire.

When I first encountered Alice Munro, I was barely aware that she was Canadian. I read Katherine Mansfield in exactly the same way, scarcely registering her New Zealand origins or the precise settings of "At the Bay" or "The Doll's House." Now, whenever I introduce Alice Munro to a new set of students I begin with Southwestern Ontario and the cultural heritage as she describes it, usually adding something about British Columbia as the setting for more of the stories than is usually acknowledged. Yet

281

fictional territories are always landscapes of the mind, visited primarily through the imagination, and overlaid by analogies from the reader's experience. When the teenage Alice Munro was spellbound by *Wuthering Heights*, she was inhabiting her own private Yorkshire;[1] and when her narrator, Hazel, visits the Scottish borders in "Hold Me Fast, Don't Let Me Pass" (*Friend of My Youth*, 1990), the ground beneath her feet is haunted by the memories, true or false, passed on by her late husband.

The small town where "Meneseteung" is set remains nameless, though its streets are mapped with some precision. It is cut from the same template as Walley in "Hold Me Fast, Don't Let Me Pass," or the many other versions of Alice Munro's hometown, Wingham, and the nearby town of Goderich.[2] It is distinctly Canadian, but also archetypal, like small towns everywhere, with its local dignitaries and eccentrics, its church and its school and the local newspaper. Like Ormskirk, perhaps, the West Lancashire town where my university, Edge Hill, is based. The campus is situated a mile or so from the statue of Benjamin Disraeli in the town centre; the classroom where I'm teaching "Meneseteung" overlooks that wide horizon to the west.

In his discussion of the literary configuration of space and time that he calls the chronotope, the Russian critic M.M. Bakhtin identifies a chronotope of the provincial town, where "A day is just a day, a year is just a year – a life is just a life. Day in, day out the same round of activities are repeated, the same topics of conversation, the same words and so forth" (Bakhtin 248). In "Meneseteung," the *Vidette*'s coyly insinuating "*May we surmise?*" is the type of petty gossip that "pops up in the *Vidette* all the time" (58); the tiresome goings-on of the married women, smugly "creating their husbands" (60), are equally predictable. Provincial time, according to Bakhtin, is circular and repetitious, "viscous and sticky time that drags itself slowly through space" (Bakhtin 248) – like Almeda's grape jelly dripping into the basin which it eventually overflows.

Bakhtin observes that the potential for the novel within this chronotope is limited, because of the shortage of dramatic events. In a short story this is not such a problem. "Meneseteung" turns on a series of non-events. A violent death turns out to be nothing of the sort and a budding courtship withers before it has properly begun; in fact the closing lines, "I don't know if she ever took laudanum. [...] I don't know if she ever made grape jelly" (73), could be said to turn the whole story into a non-event.

For Bakhtin, the sterile repetitions of small town life are altogether different from the productive recurrence of the seasons within the natural cycle. In "Meneseteung," the intolerable heat of summer disrupts the usual patterns, provoking a kind of delirium in which misdemeanours abound, accidents increase, and sleep is almost impossible. The central events – or non-events – of the narrative take place one weekend in August 1879, a time when Almeda takes laudanum to counter this sleeplessness. Despite what Bakhtin says, I wonder if these seasonal disruptions are not themselves incorporated into the recurrences of the provincial chronotope; is there really such an opposition between the deadening effects of routine and the turning of the seasons?

A university in some ways resembles a small town, and university life is also cyclical, the yearly progression through recruitment, teaching, assessment, graduation seeming to roll along at greater speed with every fresh intake. In October 2015, at Edge Hill in West Lancashire, teaching of this year's MA Creative Writing course has just begun. We're talking about "Meneseteung" as the Bewick's swans begin their annual migration from Siberia. There are ten more light evenings left before the clocks go back an hour for winter. According to my diary, the hairdresser has told me that curly perms are in for men this season, a prediction that, thankfully, will turn out false. The diary records other things too – portentous dreams, missing objects, disks mysteriously wiped; and an image of the grandchildren, perching in the branches of a tree like fairies, shaking the red apples to the ground.

This year's crop of MA students is smaller than usual, no more than ten at tonight's session, their ages ranging from early twenties to mid-sixties. They all come from Northern England, mostly Lancashire and Merseyside. The core of the course consists of practical workshops, where the students can get feedback about their work in progress, but we also study published texts from a writerly perspective and encourage the students to develop their own philosophy of writing by exploring the concept of poetics.

In his influential pamphlet, *The Necessity of Poetics* (2000), the course leader, Professor Robert Sheppard, defines poetics as, amongst other things, "products of the process of reflection upon writings, and upon the act of writing, gathering from the past and from others, speculatively casting into the future." He points out that poetics can often be manifested within the creative work itself, and that is certainly true of the many stories by Munro that figure a creative artist as protagonist or reflect on the transmission of fact into fiction. And of course "Meneseteung" does both.

In the next section, I'll talk about the experience of rereading the story for the MA course, before turning to the students' creative responses to her work. I'll then end this essay with some thoughts on imaginary poets, followed by a personal postscript concerning truth and fiction.

A Session on Alice Munro

After my general introduction to Alice Munro and to *Friend of My Youth*, I turn to "Meneseteung" itself, drawing attention to the story's forensic opening passages – the book, *Offerings*, with its photograph of the author and the literary dissection of its contents; Almeda Joynt Roth's house, still standing "at the corner of Pearl and Dufferin streets" (53); copies of the local newspaper, the *Vidette*. These pages are packed with solid objects. When Munro describes the blue cover and gold lettering on Almeda's book, you can feel the rough texture of the cover and the stale scent of old paper. We are entering a virtual museum, with the glass cases removed, the narrator assuming the role of tour guide.

Gradually, historical reconstruction shades into subjective experience. The bridge between the outer world and the inner is the one-sentence paragraph: "I read about that life in the *Vidette*" (54). The act of reading animates the pages of this rather stuffy newspaper, bringing the past back to life, and populating it with townsfolk – in the first instance, the children, who do not write for the *Vidette*, whose voices are rarely heard in the history books. Here, they are a collective, boys who "rove through the streets in gangs" (54), and they supply the stuff of fiction, which is mood and atmosphere:

> they keep an eye out for any strangers coming into town. They follow them, offer to carry their bags, and direct them (for a five-cent piece) to a hotel. Strangers who don't look so prosperous are taunted and tormented. Speculation surrounds all of them – it's like a cloud of flies. (54-55)

The abstract noun "Speculation" is "like a cloud of flies," but so, we might imagine, is the persistent gang of boys. And "Speculation," of course, is exactly the process in which the narrator is engaged, a process in which we, the story's readers, are invited to participate. The trail leads, inevitably, from the "real" evidence of the outer world to that which is more insubstantial; and a simple figure of speech, "like a cloud of flies," marks the turning-point between the cataloguing of the traces of the past and its fictive resurrection.

Some commentators, even several who admire Munro's work, claim that her stories aren't "really" short stories at all, but condensed novels. I couldn't disagree more. Any one of her stories is a master class in the art of short fiction, in that she fully exploits its formal specificity, especially its engagement with time as a continuum, interweaving past and present, fusing memories, impressions, and the imaginary within the passing moment. Her work teaches new writers how a story can be assembled like a collage, rather than as a linear chain of cause and effect. There is no need to join the dots or fill the gaps, and this gives the writer almost limitless freedom to experiment with what Frank O'Connor regards as the purest form of storytelling (O'Connor 27).

The short story is also a notably dense and allusive genre, and with every rereading of Alice Munro, there's always some little detail that has previously escaped your notice. There is, for example, "the young girl Annie, who helps her with her housecleaning" (56), Annie who lives in the row houses, backing on to Almeda's respectable street, Annie who is a decent girl, and would never stray too far from home. This is all we know of Annie, before she vanishes from the scene. Perhaps she is given the weekends off; or, most likely, she comes round only occasionally to take on the heavier tasks, such as cleaning windows and scrubbing floors. A single lady will not generate much housework, except, of course, for those stubborn purple stains on the staircase. She might have been let go altogether, as a consequence of the doctor's recommendation of vigorous housework as a cure for feminine nerves and insomnia. Almeda is not only cleaning her own house, but the church as well, and giving a hand to any friends in need of extra help. When Jarvis Poulter opines that "'A lady oughtn't to be living alone so close to a bad neighbourhood'" (67), is he asking himself what has happened to the hired help?

A changed Annie surfaces towards the end of the story when a 1903 issue of the *Vidette* reports the death of Almeda, "*attended at the last by a former neighbour, Mrs. Bert (Annie) Friels*" (72). Annie has moved up in the world, and would evidently choose to consider her relationship with Almeda in this way; it is also technically accurate, topographically speaking. For in my reading of the text, it's Annie who lays the stone marked "Meda" (73). Who else could it be, with the family dead? Not Jarvis Poulter – on those Sunday strolls, the only topic that interests him is his business projects. Unmoved by Almeda's fanciful allusions to "'The salt of the earth'" and a primeval sea (58), he seems unlikely to have read Almeda's poetry. This Annie is rather like "Old Annie" in "A Wilderness Station" (*Open Secrets*, 1994), most likely Scots-Irish, and invisible to those above her station, the generic nineteenth-century Annie whose story you must dig even deeper to find than Almeda's.

An Exercise

Although I often bring creative writing exercises into the undergraduate classroom, there is an expectation, at the MA level, that the students shouldn't need that kind of prop. They should be able to generate their own work without being prompted by a teacher; and indeed, in *The Necessity of Poetics* (2000), Sheppard warns against creating "workshop junkies." That night in October 2015 we departed from our usual practice, in an experiment that combined a critical discussion of Munro with a creative response that I hoped would help the students to reflect on the process of writing and how it might be represented in fiction itself. I also hoped that by inventing fictional writers of their own they might think about the cultural context in which writing takes place and how that might shape their own practice.

Before moving on to the writing exercise, I divided the students into two groups, for a close reading of sections towards the end of the story. The first half looked at the last few paragraphs of section V, exploring how creativity is represented in those passages where Almeda is composing her poem:

the name of the poem will be – it *is* – "The Meneseteung." The name of
the poem is the name of the river. No, in fact it is the river, the Meneseteung, that is the poem – with its deep holes and rapids and blissful
pools under the summer trees and its grinding blocks of ice thrown up
at the end of winter and its desolating spring floods. (70)

That transition from future tense to present exemplifies the heightened
sense of the present moment in Munro's work. With that sudden break-
through the poem begins to take shape, in a form that Almeda intuits
but cannot fully grasp any more than any of us can fully explain a work
in progress.

William Butt's essay "Southwestern Ontario, the Narrator, and 'Words
with Power' in Alice Munro's 'Meneseteung'" invokes both Coleridge and
the Gospel of St. John to describe the magical potency of naming, an act
which releases an unstoppable creative surge. Externally, as I have suggested, the narrative is punctuated by a series of non-events. Internally,
this epiphanic moment signals a transformation far more profound
than anything that takes place on the surface of the real world. When
Munro describes Almeda's mind concentrating on the poem, and her
gaze focussing on the roses on the tablecloth, which swim before her
eyes, these things paradoxically represent a fracturing of logic and a
temporary dissolution of the self-identity. Many critics have discussed
the effects of laudanum and menstruation on Almeda's mental condition; but, important as these vectors are, the heightened states that they
induce are ultimately analogous to the creative consciousness rather
than its cause. The philosopher Henri Bergson contrasts our everyday
consciousness, apprehending time as a successive and homogeneous
medium, with a deeper understanding of time as flux: "the deep-seated
self which ponders and decides, which heats and blazes up, is a self
whose states and changes permeate one another" (125). Almeda's "deep-
seated self" forgets the grape jelly, engaging at a deeper level with the
seasonal continuum and, through sense impressions, with an essential
reality. As Bergson suggests, this is the state of consciousness attained
in a creative frame of mind.

I asked the other half of the students to read the sixth and final section of the story, so that we could discuss the effect of the ending. Robert Thacker's introduction to the Winter 1998 Alice Munro issue of *Essays on Canadian Writing* (reissued by ECW Press as *The Rest of the Story*, 1999) details the revisions made to this ending, with its additional note of caution in the final published version: "I may have got it wrong" (73). He sees the *New Yorker* version as more hopeful, ending with the promise that the past is not entirely irrecoverable, that something may be salvaged, a "trickle in time" (73). The *Friend of My Youth* version asserts that even history must be reinvention. But this provisional status is, I think, implicit already in the story, with its emphasis on subjective perceptions and the ambiguities of historical record. I am not convinced that the difference in mood between these versions is so clearly marked. Yet whatever we may feel about the need for that final paragraph, and however we choose to interpret its effect, Munro's constant revisions provide another invaluable lesson about the writing process, that – as she says in "What Is Real?" – "Every final draft, every published draft, is still only an attempt, an approach, to the story" (225).

Now to the exercise. I began with a made-up writer version of that game where you find your "porn star name" (there are various versions, for instance combining the name of your first pet with your mother's maiden name, making my alias "Rex Mountford"). For my, of course, much more serious enterprise, I asked the students to choose a first name from their family, as far back as they could go. This was then combined with the surname of their favourite teacher from school. (Thacker's biography tells us that "Joynt" was the name of a schoolteacher in Wingham in the 1930s [434].) This made my character "Ethel Webb," quite a satisfying result, though I didn't take part in the fiction-making on that night.

After we'd all been amused by the names, I asked the students to describe that person's daily routine, using a similar narrative perspective to Munro's, that is a seemingly dispassionate narrator who witnesses or reconstructs. And part of that daily life would be, as it was for Almeda, their own writing practice. I encouraged them to write up the exercise in any way they wanted after the session, and to send me the results. Charlotte, Brian, and Adam sent me completed first drafts of stories and poems, and I'm very grateful to each of them for sharing their work and helping me to reflect on the characters they have created in the afterglow of "Meneseteung." I'll now discuss each writer's work in turn.

I

Charlotte Booth comes from a small town in North Yorkshire. Charlotte's creation, the "Ada-May Morley" of her story's title, fuses the figure of the spinster poet with the idea of a local paper such as the *Vidette*, in that Ada-May is a journalist who has been fired from her local paper for her lack of creativity. Now, with time on her hands, she turns her attention to writing poetry. The "click-clickety-click of the typewriters" in the newspaper office is implicitly contrasted with the silence of the fountain pen (both these antiquated writing devices signalling a time some decades past).

Ada-May's efforts are conventional in form, and even more senti-mental than Almeda's; the first letters in every line of her poem "Family" spell out its title. Ada-May's life is devoid of sexual passion: "Only one man had ever been near her, and he had soon fled for The Dales." Yet her senses are finely tuned, and she is vividly aware of everyday pleasures on this summer's day as she makes her first attempt at putting pen to paper.

Despite an optimistic start, Ada-May becomes demoralized, beset by financial worries and haunted by the contempt of the editor who fired her. A doctor is called when a neighbour spots her sitting on the door-step, rocking herself and weeping, but she refuses all help. Ada-May's only consolation is through words, and yet the words refuse to come. The final paragraph of Charlotte's story describes Ada-May sitting at her desk, the inkwell dried up and her fountain pen dropped to the floor:

> She hasn't left the house in days. She wants to, tries to make herself, but is too afraid of the looks people on the street will give her. She shifts uncomfortably in her seat, trying to block out the words which echo through her mind.

Charlotte arranges these words on the page in a pattern that suggests an unwritten, and perhaps unwritable, poem arising from these blocked words:

Failure

Bankruptcy

Selfish

Insane

Useless ...

The final word reminds her of the day of her dismissal. She has promised herself she will not let him destroy her.

He already has ...

Stripped bare, she admits defeat.

Like Almeda, Ada-May is without a family, her mother having died some time ago; and in some way as yet unexplored by the writer, the loss of the mother and the inability to grieve seem linked with the creative blockage and her social vulnerability.

II

Brian O'Reilly's roots reach back to County Cork, a place he regularly visits from his home on the Lancashire coast. When he brought "Drafting Alone" to a workshop, some weeks later, I didn't initially realize, despite the use of italics, that the opening of his story was to be read as the creation of his fictional protagonist:

> *Gerry started to feel weak and light-headed immediately after handling the new batch of cattle feed. As usual, he hadn't worn any gloves when he scooped the feed into the trough. The cows rose and hulked slowly towards him as he tipped the last of their food from the bucket. By the time he returned to the farmhouse he was already sweating. He wanted to lie down, but couldn't face climbing the stairs to his bed. So he stretched out on the*

*cold ceramic tiles of the kitchen floor and closed his eyes. When he heard
Sheila's car on the drive he hauled himself up to sit at the dining table,
facing the door.*

*Sheila shouldered the door open and heaved in the bags of shopping.
She stopped in the doorway. "Jesus, Gerry. You look like a ghost."*

As Sheila unpacks the shopping, chatting about their plans for a trip to
County Wicklow, Gerry experiences hallucinatory effects, possibly attrib-
utable to smelling the cattle feed, yet not wholly explicable. Then the lid
of the laptop is slammed, and Gerry is revealed as the construction of the
author-figure, Brendan. We are indeed on a farm in the west of Ireland,
territory that might belong in a story by John McGahern. But Brendan is
a London-based novelist visiting his parents, a visit that is also a kind of
time-travel. Brendan pokes the coal fire and looks out over fields that are
pitch black at night: "He couldn't live here full time, obviously. How could
anyone? But he'd make the most of it for now and get on with his writing."

The narrative describes his attempt to do exactly that, while also
considering the options for taking care of his parents in their declin-
ing years, and reflecting on his life as a call-centre worker in London.
He remembers ordering Guinness at the village pub, in an attempt to
conform to an outdated concept of Irish identity, and he contemplates
a black-and-white photograph:

> His parents together at a dance hall before they were married. His Dad
> gawping at the camera, his Mum trying out an early version of her cam-
> era smile. They weren't his parents back then, of course. They were just
> normal people.

Brian's story shows that time and distance alienate us from our own
beginnings, and that our insights into the lives of even those closest to
us are by necessity fictive reconstructions.

Like Charlotte, Brian suggests that it's easier to start writing a piece
than to continue; and like Charlotte's story his ends mid-composition,
with the writer at an impasse:

> It needs something more. What happened to the feed to give it this power?
> Not lightning, definitely not lightning. And if Gerry's affected by the feed,

then surely others will be too. So are there dozens of farmers, hundreds even, all walking around looking out for red glows? No, that wouldn't work. What about the character in Stephen King's *The Dead Zone*? How did he start out? That wasn't lightning. A car crash, maybe. And then a coma. Brendan lifted the lid of his laptop and pressed the power button.

Brendan has not quite managed to synthesize his fertile observations of the reality around him with the mode he wants to write in, a mode seemingly closer to American popular fiction than the Irish literary heritage. Yet the story ends in a spirit of hope and endeavour, as the laptop springs to life.

III

Adam Hampton's protagonist, in the short sketch "Elsie Barnes," is, like Adam himself, a poet "from Liverpool, a Scouser." An ex-nurse, she has retired to a small village at the foot of Pendle Hill, much further east in Lancashire (Pendle is still best-known for its infamous witch trials in the seventeenth century). Adam pictures Elsie in her Lancashire setting:

> When she writes it's lamenting. She sits at a large, wooden desk beneath a lead-lined window in an alcove. On the desk are measurements, scribbled on in pencil: for the putting up of a curtain pole or picture frame by Ted some time ago.

Ted is Elsie's late husband, and his name might recall that other northern poet, Ted Hughes. Elsie's writing is closer to Hughes's work or that of his Irish contemporary, Seamus Heaney, than to the concrete poetry that is her creator's speciality.[3]
This is one of the two "Elsie" poems:

Flint Napping

In the garden we dug test pits.
A metre square, or thereabouts,
Measured with a yardstick,
Away from the roots of the plum tree.

Is this a worked edge? Is this a tool?
Have the dead shaped this for cutting?
We piled the finds in a seed tray, to grow
Narratives of huntsman and old stone.

Sitting inside, clenching my two clean hands,
From the window the half-cut turf in a metre
Squared, his shovel dropped at the back's snap
And inside to see him in a frame.

A chip of flint napped at the sink,
Copper and tin, lichen wetted
At morning's lips, a fog of ghosts
From postholes and thighbones and bed linen.

Flint knapping (with a k) is the ancient process whereby pieces of flint
or other stone are knocked into shape by striking with another object –
the technique used to produce Stone Age weaponry. Adam's "napping"
suggests Elsie's afternoon doze and a dreaminess that may remind us
of Almeda. It also chimes with "bed linen," one of several references to
self-contained domestic spaces that are brought into harmony with the
external, timeless zone of the landscape by the workings of memory.

In his sketch, Adam tells us that Elsie Barnes "scales the hill each
Sunday as she did with her late husband, to touch the trig point, measure the seasons by the wind on her face, finger the stones of the cairns,"
concepts of measurement and assessment in full accordance with both
of the poems, and with poetry itself as the measurement of line and
the metaphorical weighing-up of words. Like the other two fictional
writers, Elsie leads a solitary life, with only her dog for company; and
yet she is no hermit, volunteering in the local schools and meeting
"half-friends" for lunch. Solitude, for her, seems to have its compensa-
tions, in laying the groundwork for her "lamenting," which seems to be
a form of homage to the land and to the dead. Furthermore, Elsie is the
only one of the three fictional authors whose writing is not blocked by
psychological factors.

Real and Invented Writers

Invented poets are not uncommon in fiction, the figures of the poet serving as proxies for their creators, enabling them to reflect on the relationship between authors and their texts; or to celebrate, in some instances, their unsung predecessors. As a form that is even more elliptical and fragmentary than the short story, and that also tends to foreground the musical aspects of language, poetry could be said to distill literary writing to an Orphic essence. For many authors, poetry represents their first attempts at writing, and perhaps that contributes to the sense that poetry is a point of origin for creative writing as a whole. Speaking more pragmatically, the fictional poet's output need only be quoted in snatches and epigrams – the long sections of Victorian pastiche in A.S. Byatt's *Possession* (1990) being the exception to the rule. Both Byatt's novel and Carol Shields's *Swann* (1987) focus, like "Meneseteung," on the efforts of contemporary characters to reconstruct the truth about a poet, proving that a definitive reading of a life is as elusive as a definitive reading of a literary text.

One of the books that students read for the MA at Edge Hill is Peter Carey's *My Life as a Fake* (2003), inspired by the Ern Malley hoax.[4] Their tutor Robert Sheppard's poetry collection *A Translated Man* (2013), partially inspired by Carey's novel, is the work of the fictional Belgian poet, René Van Valckenborch, allegedly translated from Flemish and Walloon. The figure of Van Valckenborch presides over the European Union of Imaginary Authors (http://euoia.weebly.com), in which several real-life poets collaborate with their fictitious counterparts. One MA student (not Adam) is even attempting to replicate Malley by submitting the work of various fictitious alter egos to literary magazines, complete with fake biographies and separate e-mail accounts.

This fascination with invented authors comes as a liberation from romantic concepts of authorship as self-expression. As Mark McGurl points out in his book *The Program Era* (2009), the need to "'find your voice' has become one of the controlling imperatives of writing instruction of all kinds" (235). But what if you can't find that unique, personal style, or don't want to be defined by how you speak? Spoof writers such as Ern Malley and Van Valckenborch provide a clearer illustration of the disjunction between the live individual who produces a text and what Foucault calls the "author function" shaping its reception (211).

Almeda Joynt Roth may seem very far removed from the Ern Malley hoax; and yet, Munro's mimicry of both historical and autobiographical forms of discourse might easily fool the reader into believing she really existed, like Margaret Atwood's Susanna Moodie. Magdalene Redekop claims that she "got several librarians sleuthing for me in order to prove to myself that Almeda Joynt Roth is a fiction" (216). Munro's essay "What Is Real?" draws attention to the blurring of the categories in fiction of all kinds; the whole enterprise of fiction is designed to fool the reader.

Returning to "Meneseteung" years after my first reading, I'm reminded of the closing passages in the autobiographically based title story in Munro's 2012 collection, *Dear Life*. The story – or memoir – is a re-evaluation of an incident from infancy, now passed into family legend, "The visitation of old Mrs. Netterfield" (315). The narrator's mother is fond of telling how she panicked at the sight of the local eccentric close to the house, snatched her child from its pram, and hid inside until the woman went away. Many years later, when the narrator is living in Vancouver, British Columbia, she comes across a letter in the weekly paper from back home. Its author is a woman in Portland, Oregon, who turns out to be the daughter of this Mrs. Netterfield. The house the narrator grew up in had once been the old woman's family home.

This correspondent from Portland has also supplied a selection of her poetry, verses commemorating the landscape of her youth – including the Maitland River, reimagined in the earlier story as the eponymous "Meneseteung":

> *The sun upon the river*
> *With ceaseless sparkles play*
> *And over on the other bank*
> *Are blossoms wild and gay*[....] (317)

The Portland poet shares a taste for conventional forms with Almeda Joynt Roth. But while there are some similarities between the two, Almeda would appear to be the greater talent. We never read the masterwork, "The Meneseteung," and there is no evidence that it was ever completed, but the fragments of verse in the text show more originality than the offerings of the Portland amateur.

The narrator of "Meneseteung" comments that "The countryside that she has written about in her poems actually takes diligence and determination to see" (61), necessitating a sanitization of the natural world and the removal of the signs of a working landscape. Yet, despite the limitations of Almeda's verse, the extracts suggest a writer striving, in her own way, to convey what she sees:

> Here where the river meets the inland sea,
> Spreading her blue skirts from the solemn wood,
> I think of birds and beasts and vanished men,
> Whose pointed dwellings on these pale sands stood. (56)[5]

Speaking of the Portland poet's verse, the "Dear Life" narrator confesses: "[...] I had once made up some poems myself, of a very similar nature, though they were lost now, and maybe had never been written down" (317). The life of this poet clearly parallels her own, in that she too has moved away from her hometown and her mother, and is now writing about them from a distance. But the Portland poet is much older – born in 1876, which puts her mother, Mrs. Netterfield, in the same generation as Almeda Joynt Roth.

Is the Portland poet "real"? The "Finale" texts, amongst them this one, that conclude *Dear Life* are, we are told, "*autobiographical in feeling, though not, sometimes, entirely so in fact*" (255). Or is she a composite, based on several real-life models, as was Almeda Joynt Roth in "Meneseteung"?[6] The degrees of difference are so fine, they scarcely matter. What is important is that the urge to write poetry stands for the primacy of the creative impulse, even when it is channelled into forms that may not appeal to, let's say, the average *New Yorker* reader.

Mrs. Netterfield herself is not a poet – so far as we can tell – but in her later years she becomes, like Almeda, "*a familiar eccentric, or even, sadly, a figure of fun*" ("Meneseteung" 71). To be an artist is to be an outsider, figuratively and sometimes literally, to risk being that figure of fun, and to fail. As I have already suggested, Munro's poetics of the short story accepts the inevitability of failure; all writers must face the fact that language can never fully represent or encapsulate the flux of time and lived experience. It is also almost impossible to represent the compositional process, with its combination of intention and happenstance. Like many others before them, my students Charlotte and Brian chose to write about writing by describing being blocked. One of the most striking aspects of "Meneseteung" is its evocation of the opposite process.

Postscript 2010: Sifting Through the Rubbish

I was spending one last day in Toronto before flying home from a conference, escaping the heat by staying inside various museums and galleries. I'd seen everything I really wanted to see; the Art Gallery of Ontario was not at the top of my list. The Grange, a nineteenth-century house that was the old gallery, was approached through the bright new building, and somehow contained within it. I signed up for a tour, thinking I'd see some antique furniture and gloomy portraits. Why not? It didn't cost me anything.

During the tour, the young guide told us about some exciting excavations at The Grange. Some papers have been acquired from a butler who served there in the old days, including some maps marked with crosses. The butler had observed an Irish maid, Mary O'Shea, stashing something at these points within the house. Sure enough, the archaeologists had discovered little balls of wax hidden in these secret places, containing a tiny doll or a milk tooth or a sprig of hibiscus. At the back of a kitchen, a deer bone, a hank of hair – all these things buried and preserved. As a special treat, we were taken behind the scenes, to see these objects as they were being catalogued and scrutinized. They included letters written in Gaelic, on both sides of the paper, sent back and forth to Ireland and coated now in wax.

The group speculated: Why did Mary do this? The museum leaflet spoke of her as an artist, the wax balls as an artistic project, but did she ever think of these objects in that way? Some of the tourists put it down to OCD. But it seemed obvious to me that Mary was working some kind of sympathetic magic, keeping safe those back home.

Suddenly we were interrupted. Someone was shouting: "You must not go into Dr. Lee's office!" A German voice – an angry voice storming at us. There was important scientific evidence here. It must not be contaminated.

The scene was so dramatic, and so embarrassing, it felt like a show. All we could do was watch, and then politely leave. In fact, this was the last day on which we could have seen those objects, we'd been told. They were going back tomorrow, to where they'd been found.

I was haunted by the image of the wax balls, and wanted to hoard it for myself. It was perfect material for a fiction writer, so perfect I was afraid that someone else was already spinning it into a postmodern novel. But I didn't know what to do with it, until I was thinking about "Meneseteung" and this essay, and the idea of a story that opens almost as a virtual museum.

Somewhere in my extremely messy office there is a very informative leaflet I took away from the exhibition; but not knowing where to start looking I searched for the museum on the Internet, and was surprised there was little about her on the website for The Grange. A few searches later, the truth began to dawn on me as I happened on the archive of visitor e-mails. Most expressed gratitude for the profound impact the artifacts had made on them, but one of the subject lines mentioned being "taken on this ride" (Patton).

I had indeed been hoaxed and eventually tracked down May Chew's book chapter "Archaeological Detritus and the Bulging Archive: The Staging of *He Named Her Amber* at the Art Gallery of Ontario," which discusses Iris Häussler's installation. According to Chew, there is a disclaimer at the end of the leaflet given out to visitors; but she implies that, such is the detailed pseudo-scientific information, few readers ever get that far. Chew is worried that the installation's subversive value is undermined by the fact that most visitors take it at face value. In her view, this lies mainly in exposing the mechanisms by which the archive as an institution "unintentionally produces the phantasmagorias or hallucinations that expose the hauntedness of the settler-colonial imaginary" (Chew 285).

I was disappointed to discover that Mary O'Shea's story was a fiction. I felt like a fool. As I've said, it crossed my mind when I witnessed the argument between the tour guide and the German woman (possibly Häussler herself?); but I processed the flare-up as "like" a performance, rather than a staged event, because it was disturbing and therefore in some way unreal. Did I not read the leaflet as carefully as I thought or was I so entranced by the story that I didn't absorb the disclaimer? If I had fictionalized Mary O'Shea, as Alice Munro has fictionalized the various models for Almeda Joynt Roth, would I have been a plagiarist? (Häussler has published a book based on the installation.)

What interests me now is the potency of those "phantasmagorias or hallucinations" so distrusted by Chew. Mary's story felt authentic to all of us in the museum on that day because it spoke to some deep need within every one of us. We wanted to believe. Coleridge's phrase the "willing suspension of disbelief" has become a cliché, but this willingness, even eagerness, to embrace the fictional world as reality seems to me fundamental to the reading of art and literature, and even to its making. We all know that the best fiction is hypnotic, persuading the reader of another reality; Magdalene Redekop set out to prove to herself that Almeda Joynt Roth did not actually exist. Of course Almeda is "real," as real as "Alice Munro" or "Mary O'Shea" or "Ethel Webb." As real as you or me. If we want to make her so.

Acknowledgements

With thanks to all the MA Creative Writing students at Edge Hill University.

Notes

1. Interviewed by Thomas E. Tausky, Alice Munro has spoken about the importance of *Wuthering Heights* to her as a young reader, and its influence upon her own writing (Munro in Tausky x).
2. William Butt's essay "Southwestern Ontario, the Narrator, and 'Words with Power' in Alice Munro's 'Meneseteung'" draws specific parallels between the topography of Munro's fictional town and Goderich (Butt 25).
3. See <http://www.m58.co.uk/post/138345034299/two-pieces-by-adam-hampton-the-interrogation> for examples of Adam's published poetry.
4. See Heyward, *The Ern Malley Affair* for details of the hoax.
5. "Pale sands" is an odd phrase, reminding this writer both of the stereotypical term "paleface" used by "Red Indians" in Hollywood Westerns and of that Edwardian parlour song "Pale Hands I Loved by the Shalimar" ("Kashmiri Song," <https://www.poetryfoundation.org/poems/53821/kashmiri-song>). The poem "Kashmiri Song" was

written by a largely forgotten female poet, Adela Florence Cory, under the pen name Laurence Hope. Cory committed suicide at the age of thirty-nine (<https://www.poetryfoundation.org/poets/laurence-hope>).

6. See Thacker, *Alice Munro: Writing Her Lives: A Biography* (434); and J.R. (Tim) Struthers, "Imagining Alice Munro's 'Meneseteung': The Dynamics of Co-Creation" (78).

Works Consulted

Art Gallery of Ontario. "The Grange: Overview." <http://www.ago.net/the-grange-national-historic-site>.

Atwood, Margaret. *The Journals of Susanna Moodie.* Toronto: Oxford UP, 1970.

Bakhtin, M.M. "Forms of Time and of the Chronotope in the Novel: Notes Toward a Historical Poetics." *The Dialogic Imagination: Four Essays.* Ed. Michael Holquist. Trans. Caryl Emerson and Michael Holquist. Austin: U of Texas P, 1992. 84-258.

Bergson, Henri. *Time and Free Will: An Essay on the Immediate Data of Consciousness.* Trans. F.L. Pogson. London: Swan Sonnenschein, 1910.

Booth, Charlotte. "Ada-May Morley." Unpublished.

Brontë, Emily. *Wuthering Heights: The 1847 Text; Backgrounds and Contexts; Criticism.* 4th ed. Ed. Richard J. Dunn. New York: W.W. Norton, 2003. A Norton Critical Edition.

Butt, William. "Southwestern Ontario, the Narrator, and 'Words with Power' in Alice Munro's 'Meneseteung'." *Alice Munro and the Souwesto Story.* Ed. J.R. (Tim) Struthers. *Short Story* ns 21.1 (2013 [2015]): 13-43.

Byatt, A.S. *Possession: A Romance.* London: Chatto & Windus, 1990.

Carey, Peter. *My Life as a Fake.* London: Faber and Faber, 2003.

Chew, May. "Archaeological Detritus and the Bulging Archive: The Staging of *He Named Her Amber* at the Art Gallery of Ontario." *Material Cultures in Canada.* Ed. Thomas Allen and Jennifer Blair. Waterloo, ON: Wilfrid Laurier UP, 2015. 283-99.

Coleridge, Samuel Taylor. *Biographia Literaria.* 1817. <http://www.english.upenn.edu/~mgamer/Etexts/biographia.html>.

European Union of Imaginary Authors (EUOIA). <https://euoia.weebly.com>.

Foucault, Michel. "What Is an Author?" *Aesthetics, Method, and Epistemology*. Ed. James D. Faubion. Trans. Robert Hurley and others. New York: New, 1998. 205-22. Vol. 2 of *Essential Works of Foucault*.

Hale, W.G., and Audrey Coney. *Martin Mere: Lancashire's Lost Lake*. Liverpool, Eng.: Liverpool UP, 2005.

Hampton, Adam. "Elsie Barnes." Unpublished.

---. "Two Pieces by Adam Hampton." 2016. <http://www.m58.co.uk/post/138345034299/two-pieces-by-adam-hampton-the-interrogation>.

Häussler, Iris. *He Named Her Amber*. Toronto: Art Gallery of Ontario, 2011.

Heaney, Seamus. "Digging." *Death of a Naturalist*. London: Faber and Faber, 1966. 13-14.

Heyward, Michael. *The Ern Malley Affair*. Introd. Robert Hughes. London: Faber and Faber, 1993.

Hope, Laurence. "Kashmiri Song." 1906. <https://www.poetryfoundation.org/poems/53821/kashmiri-song>.

Hughes, Ted. "Lumb Chimneys." *Remains of Elmet: A Pennine Sequence*. Poems by Ted Hughes. Photographs by Fay Godwin. London: Faber and Faber, 1979. 14.

"Laurence Hope." <https://www.poetryfoundation.org/poets/laurence-hope>.

Mansfield, Katherine. "At the Bay." *The Collected Stories of Katherine Mansfield*. 1945. Introd. Ali Smith. London: Penguin, 2007. 205-45.

---. "The Doll's House." *The Collected Stories of Katherine Mansfield*. 1945. Introd. Ali Smith. London: Penguin, 2007. 383-91.

McGahern, John. "The Country Funeral." *The Collected Stories*. London: Faber and Faber, 1992. 374-408.

McGurl, Mark. *The Program Era: Postwar Fiction and the Rise of Creative Writing*. Cambridge, MA: Harvard UP, 2009.

Munro, Alice. "Dear Life." *Dear Life*. London: Chatto & Windus, 2012. 299-319.

---. *Dear Life*. London: Chatto & Windus, 2012.

---. "Hold Me Fast, Don't Let Me Pass." *Friend of My Youth*. London: Chatto & Windus, 1990. 74-105.

---. "Meneseteung." *Friend of My Youth*. London: Chatto & Windus, 1990. 50-73.

---. "Walker Brothers Cowboy." *Dance of the Happy Shades*. 1968. London: Allen Lane, 1974. 1-18.

---. "What Is Real?" *Making It New: Contemporary Canadian Short Stories*. Ed. John Metcalf. Toronto: Methuen, 1982. 223-26.

---. "A Wilderness Station." *Open Secrets*. London: Chatto & Windus, 1994. 190-225.

O'Connor, Frank. *The Lonely Voice: A Study of the Short Story*. London: Macmillan, 1963.

O'Reilly, Brian. "Drafting Alone." Unpublished.

Patton, Andrew. "Wow – I so enjoyed being taken on this ride – thank you!" <http://www.ago.net/wow-i-so-enjoyed-being-taken-on-this-ride-thank-you>.

Redekop, Magdalene. *Mother and Other Clowns: The Stories of Alice Munro*. London: Routledge, 1992.

Sheppard, Robert. *The Necessity of Poetics*. 2000. <http://www.pores.bbk.ac.uk/1/Robert%20Sheppard,%20'The%20Necessity%20of%20Poetics'.htm>.

---. *A Translated Man*. Bristol, Eng.: Shearsman, 2013.

Shields, Carol. *Swann: A Mystery*. Toronto: Stoddart, 1987.

Struthers, J.R. (Tim). "Imagining Alice Munro's 'Meneseteung': The Dynamics of Co-Creation." *Alice Munro: A Souwesto Celebration*. Ed. J.R. (Tim) Struthers and John B. Lee. *The Windsor Review* 47.2 (2014): 68-91.

Tausky, Thomas E. "Biocritical Essay." *The Alice Munro Papers First Accession: An Inventory of the Archive at The University of Calgary Libraries*. Comp. Jean M. Moore and Jean F. Tener. Ed. Apollonia Steele and Jean F. Tener. Calgary: U of Calgary P, 1986. ix-xxiv.

Thacker, Robert. *Alice Munro: Writing Her Lives: A Biography*. Toronto: McClelland & Stewart, 2005.

---. "Introduction: Alice Munro, Writing 'Home': 'Seeing This Trickle in Time'." *Alice Munro Writing On....* Ed. Robert Thacker. *Essays on Canadian Writing* 66 (1998): 1-20. Rpt. in *The Rest of the Story: Critical Essays on Alice Munro*. Ed. Robert Thacker. Toronto: ECW, 1999. 1-20.

Giving Tongue: Scorings of Voice, Verse, and Flesh in Alice Munro's "Meneseteung"

Louis K. MacKendrick

I

Here are some instances of "giving tongue," normally a term with canine or animal pack associations, present in Alice Munro's "Meneseteung," a story which is a compound of voices, and voicings:

> The sound they make becomes very confused – gagging, vomiting, grunting, pounding. Then a long, vibrating, choking sound of pain and self-abasement, self-abandonment, which could come from either or both of them. ... As she bangs her head, she finds her voice and lets out an openmouthed yowl, full of strength and what sounds like an anguished pleasure. (64, 66)

These noisy climaxes are sounds which the story's heroine, Almeda Joynt Roth, first overhears, imperfectly seeing their sources, and later both hears and witnesses in person. The word "climaxes" is intentional: the yowl sounds orgasmic, and the clamour in the first participle-rich sentence, which Almeda has thought to be murder, has been interpreted by two of Munro's commentators as "violent copulation" (Carrington 11) or apparent rape (Wall 85, 89). As well as manners of articulation, then, there is a related degree of carnal undercurrent in the narrative.

"Giving tongue" is a contemporary vulgarity for cunnilingus, an activity not present in this text. More orthodox sexual imaginings do exist in the story, and even as these have no documentary guarantee, they are proposed by a narrative voice which is rarely disinterested. Indeed, perhaps the least unsure or ambivalent element in "Meneseteung" is the guiding voice of its narrator, who imposes a series of literary patterns on some re-created small-town (Ontario) life. Munro's critics have examined this pseudo-historian and fictioneer, and some further selective attentions to the character confirm her crafted literary awareness – in essence, her creative freedoms with the historical imagination.

"Meneseteung" is a studied and often amusing fiction whose enactment has little of the accidental about it. Granted, the story is a congeries of rampant misrule, accidents, and disruptions, even as it is largely presented under a pretense of historical re-creation. However, the accidents in point are not those mortal and grotesque occurrences about which the narrator reads in a local newspaper, the *Vidette*. In proper complement, animals do make unbridled appearances on the streets of Miss Roth's town, one light-hearted aspect of the uncontrollable elements in this fiction. However, a rigorous control is exercised in the telling of what the narrator would like Almeda's story to have been – not unlike the married women who "have to go about creating their husbands" (60), town mythology as fiction.

The devisings of Munro's nameless narrating voice are multiple: see, for example, Mark Nunes's discussion of the narrator's use of "construction and artifice" (23) to tie together her un-factual history of Almeda Roth in discernible patterns. Ajay Heble's look at the narrative persona, her "interpretative and inferential strategies," and her "speculative reconstruction" of Almeda Roth (171), is equally instructive. The narrator has invested a wealth of inventions, impositions, and honest tricks in her creation. Over much of this splendidly Munrovian fiction, therefore, hovers a modestly reflexive, ironic, and at times reductive or cheeky comic spirit. "Meneseteung" is the narrator's own calculated artistic performance that, in effect, equals or supersedes the climactic one devised for Almeda.

Who do you think you are? the story asks in so many ways, as so many of Munro's stories do. It is a great irony: in this story all the potential sureties of romance are reduced, and Almeda's genuine poetic inspiration will remain unvoiced, its wide-ranging materials unassembled. The story also manages to patronize stereotypical small-town mores and characters, traditional butts. Altogether we allow ourselves to be entertained – and instructed – by a self-directed host who broadcasts her small fund of modest jokes, whimsies, several impolite raw interpolations, or guesses, and some purely literary layerings.

It is consistently evident that the narrator of "Meneseteung" has employed some clearly literary figurations of theme and motif. The point becomes acute when a concluding paragraph added to the collected version in Munro's *Friend of My Youth*, as distinguished from the original version in *The New Yorker* of January 11, 1988, radically alters the story's perspective (Thacker 3) – an almost O. Henry manner of ending with a reversal or surprise. By offhandedly foregrounding the seemingly shallow matters of laudanum and grape jelly, the narrator can minimize her invention and inversely, cleverly, imply that she has gotten all the rest of this story exactly right.

In and at the end, the narrator concludes as she began, by drawing attention to herself. It is her flow of words alone which has been her story. Heble has argued for "the gradual effacement of the first-person narrator" (173); I instead believe her structural and stylistic gestures are particularly first-person, and even blatant. As Almeda's familiar domestic surroundings begin to unsettle in the throes of her vision, or laudanum – "For every one of these patterns, decorations seems charged with life, ready to move and flow and alter" (69) – it is the narrator's associational style, or habit, not Almeda's new awareness, which is the true ascendant.

Munro's work has often dealt with the relations of Art and Life, and this is not the first of her disingenuous and artful narrators – a character who employs "interpretive and inferential strategies" (Heble 171), whose literary fashionings are self-conscious (Redekop 221). A number of carefully allocated patterns are this stylist's concern; any anachronisms or ahistorical impositions are sacrificed to self-conscious technique. For example, it hardly bears noticing that the narrator's final image of researchers trying to put things together *post facto*, "in the hope of seeing this trickle in time" (73) is a broad allusion to the Meneseteung (later called the Maitland River), to Almeda's menses, to her "flow of words" (69), and even to the "stream of abuse" (63) in Pearl Street which has begun this final post-mortem dance – among other such unblushing, deliberate, even forced appearances of the motif.

Of the origins of "Meneseteung" Munro has said, "I knew for years that I wanted to write a story about one of the Victorian lady writers, one of the authoresses of this area [Clinton, Ontario]. Only I couldn't find quite the verse I wanted; all of it was so bad that it was ludicrous. I wanted to have it a little better than that. So *I* wrote it" (McCulloch and Simpson 245). In the contributor's note to the reprint of "Meneseteung" in *The Best American Short Stories 1989* Munro wrote of these South-western Ontario small-town poetesses, "They prattled in quatrains and couplets about an innocence, an idyllic world, quite at variance with the one before their eyes, and they were despised and quaintly exalted for this blinkered exercise" (322).

Like the unnamed writer whom Munro identified as the so-called "'Sweet Songstress of La Mer Douce'," these women "indulge in constant raptures about flowers," among other topics, and "are fussily virginal, conventional, silly" (322). Yet they are "paying attention"; Munro created one with "some talent..., just enough to give her glimpses, stir her up" in relation to such matters as "poetry, sex, and living, in that town, that time, when so many sturdy notions were pushing up together" (322).

The proximate model for Almeda Roth was Eloise Ann Skimings of Goderich, Ontario, author of *Golden Leaves* (139 pp., Star Book and Job Print, 1890; a second greatly expanded edition, xii + 346 pp., The Signal Press, 1904). She was at best only a type for Munro. Miss Skimings, born in Ontario, was a small-town spinster who kept her father's, then her brother's house, undoubtedly performed some of the social and church-related functions attributed to Almeda Roth, and wrote minor verse that was largely commemorative, memorial, or floral. The family was Irish in origin, and Catholic.

In the 1861 Census of Canada, it was recorded that "Eliza Ann," a school teacher, would be 18 on her next birthday: she was born, then, in 1843 (or possibly very early in 1844, since the official date of recordings for this census was the night of Sunday, January the 13th, 1861). In 1871, she was "Elizabeth"; in 1881, she was listed as a music teacher. Like Almeda, she had a younger brother, William (d. 1924). She died on either the 7th or the 8th of April, 1921, according to the Goderich newspaper *The Signal* or *The Clinton New Era*, respectively; as reported by the latter, she was 81 ("Local News" 6), a statement that either undermines or is undermined by the supposition about her year of birth, leaving many such details suspect.

Ironically, Skimings (in several censuses spelled "Skimming" or "Skimmings") died in Clinton, Alice Munro's later, long-time home. She is buried in the Maitland Cemetery (Lot 199, Section 6, Range F), but no stone exists to locate her. On April 14, 1921 *The Signal* promised that a held-over "more extended reference to the life and work of Miss Skimings" ("Obituary" 4) would be printed in its next issue, a week later; however, this piece never appeared, perhaps bumped by a sensational case of strychnine poisoning or the extensive obituary of a well-connected local woman.

The language of the notice in *The Signal* is colourless, noting of "the mortal remains" that at the undertaker's "a number of citizens had gathered to pay the last tribute of respect to the departed" ("Obituary" 4). The only incidental information about Skimings is found in brief notes which surface in *The Signal*. The paper would record those activities which the poetess wished publicized: among undoubted others, a copy of a song to the Secretary of the provincial Boy Scout movement, her picture to the Duchess of Connaught, and acknowledgement of a birthday gift of *Golden Leaves* (second edition) to Queen Alexandra.

Skimings' note to the first edition of *Golden Leaves* had nothing like the generous family information and personal work ethic found in the lengthy preface to *Offerings*. Almeda also concluded with a sly reflection on stereotypical embroidery figures – women's work – and a modest, conventional dismissal of her efforts at poetry. Skimings' narrower range was implicit in her idealism: "Like whisperings from soul to soul, may these GOLDEN LEAVES inspire my readers, as I have been inspired, to acts of benevolence, to a study of our beautiful English language, to keep it pure and unsullied, and to acts of kindness, no matter in what sphere of life we are placed" (*Golden Leaves* [1890] iii).

The undistinguished poems of Skimings' collection contain many standard religious tropes and figures, conventional sentiments, high or fervent spirits, and an acute level of sentimentality. There are many brief elegies for the deceased (most often infants and children), consolations, and multitudes of acknowledgements for gifts of flowers and fruit. Quaint, unselfconscious lines are addressed to royalty, to the seasons, to distinguished visitors to Goderich, to the indisputably glorious afterlife and heavenly translation, to friends, and to local politicians and citizens. Most have a dedicatory explanation after the title, as in "Lines respectfully (affectionately, lovingly) inscribed (presented, dedicated) to -----," often naming the event prompting the lines: this is genuinely occasional verse. Hackneyed biblical forms like thee, thy, thou, wast, didst, and canst appear frequently, as do such overworked contractions as flow'ry, e'en, roam'd, thro', and 'tis.

Like her subjects, Skimings' verse forms have a narrow compass of manners. In "Meneseteung," the description of Almeda's rhyme schemes, with the implicit, oblique irony about "'masculine'" forms (53), applies equally here: these rhymes are ever predictable, facile, and exact; the rhythms are unerring; most of the poems are very short. For example, from "Honor to Whom Honor is Due," celebrating a bouquet,

> Thy gift was quite regal as well as thy manner,
>> When you gave me the asters with petals so white,
> Yet no purer are they than thy own heart, Lindsay,
>> In the prime of thy boyhood, so buoyant and bright.
>> (*Golden Leaves* [1904] 10)

And the opening verse from "Water Lilies" declares,

> Flowers of the deep, how grand in thy beauty,
>> Ever floating with pride o'er Huron's pure breast
> Like cups of pure gold, luring man from his duty
>> And filling his mind with a Heavenly rest!
>> (*Golden Leaves* [1904] 294)

"Elise Tye" contains many of Skimings' themes:

> Beauteous flow'r queen, didst thou know
> That poesy from my pen doth flow?
> 'Mong roses thou shouldst alway dwell,
> For they thy charms alone can tell;
> They look so happy ev'ry day,
> E'en when the wanton wind doth play
> Among their leaves – and seem to know
> That to their fragrant charms we owe
> The wreath that decks a bride's fair head
> Or adorns the casket of our dead.
> (*Golden Leaves* [1904] 60)

The Signal of February 15, 1906 reprinted under "Local Topics," with the heading "Her Fame Spreads Abroad," a flattering and irresistible notice of *Golden Leaves* from *The Minneapolis Journal*. The piece celebrated Skimings' "graceful imagery and nervous diction," admiring without irony the "blank verse thrown off by the ever-active poetess in the pauses of her daily toil and moil at Goderich" (4). The uncritical review also noted, "In her 'appreciations' many of the quiet and even ordinary citizens of Goderich are embalmed like flies in the clear amber of her verse" (4). Self-evidently, Skimings' work does not stand up to much scrutiny.

Almeda's poems are very much more accomplished, a careful selection from which serves as epigraph to each of the story's six sections. The narrator gives brief digests of seven of these, only once losing her objectivity for a cleverly ambiguous remark about "A Visit to My Family": "A visit to the cemetery, a one-sided conversation" (52). However, two descriptions – of "Children at Their Games" and "The Gypsy Fair" – are sombre if not terrible: the latter is about a child's stolen family – Almeda is living alone when *Offerings* is published – while the former has a playing child, growing darkness, and a summons by her now ghostly companions.

"Angels in the Snow" features her brother's "angel with a crippled wing" (52), which may be appreciated as another troubling disappearance. These several notes are unsettling, not at all like the other innocent summaries. The poet herself is removed in the poetic epigraph to Section V – "*I sit at the bottom of sleep, / As on the floor of the sea. / And fanciful Citizens of the Deep / Are graciously greeting me*" (68) – in which her menstrual and poetic flows begin. Each epigraph has a clear metaphorical relationship to the part of the story which immediately follows it, another demonstration of the narrator's overt and thoroughly modern literary ends, of her distance from Almeda's actual, because largely unknown, history. Compared to Skimings' verse, what Munro has invented for Almeda's work is altogether darker, metaphorical, less cloistered, and with a significantly greater imaginative and formal variety.

The portrait of Eloise A. Skimings by Reuben R. Sallows in *Golden Leaves* (and included in the 1977 sesquicentennial volume *Memories of Goderich* as a specimen of his work) shows a slender woman, thin of feature and wrist, holding a bouquet, with a peaked headdress surmounting and concealing ringletted dark hair, and an elegant dress, with generous cuffs, whose central panel and arms are in a plaid pattern. She is perched at a sharp angle on the front of a standard photographer's high-backed chair; a lean hand rests in her lap; she wears a medal, or brooch, high about her neck; her shoulders are covered by a fichu. Her unsmiling face is calm, perhaps weary, passive; she looks resigned, and her features are not animated.

The name "Meneseteung" continues to pervade the Goderich region of Huron County, and appears in promotional materials for the town. In the 1820s and early 1830s there were two short-lived ships named *Minnesetung*; and the Menesetung Canoe Club has existed for more than a hundred years. In 1992 the portion of the then recently discontinued CPR line extending over the Maitland River was named the Menesetung Bridge. The Chippewa or Ojibway name, originally "*Minnesetung*," is taken to mean "laughing waters" ("Heritage Walking Tour 3"); "healing waters" is another regional interpretation (*The Goderich Harbour*). Munro's additional "e" in the name seems to mark the story, and the region, as completely fiction: it is an implicit disclaimer. Though the village of the story is never named, Munro has said of her research into old newspapers that "I got very strong images of the town, which I call Walley" (McCulloch and Simpson 245) – a name also found in "Wigtime" and "Oranges and Apples," other stories from *Friend of My Youth*.

An important voice in "Meneseteung" is that of the local newspaper, the *Vidette*, which the narrator at first summarizes and thereafter cites. Information from *Memories of Goderich* confirms the accuracy of Munro's research: "Successive editors [of the Goderich newspaper *The Signal*] waged war on the cows, pigs, geese and horses that roamed the streets and at night, in the poor light, presented a real hazard. They did not approve of the use of Courthouse Park as a cow pasture, either. The streets were only clean, they said, on the rare occasions when the cows were in the pound. In spite of all their caustic remarks the town cow was to be around for a while yet" (74).

The narrator's digest of the nature of the town is lively and not completely objective. For her other municipal data, her selections from the paper, presumably a weekly, reveal a style of journalism that is founded on implication, gossip, and social middle-of-the-roadism. The name is not exotic: a weekly *Vidette* existed in the Ontario towns of St. Marys

(1870-72), Munro's home town of Wingham (1883-85), the nearby town of Gorrie (1885-1924), Drayton (c. 1887), and Grand Valley (1899?-1900?) (Gilchrist sec. 2, p. 49; sec. 1, pp. 142, 199, 37, 51; North Huron Museum, "Facades of Wingham"; "District Matters: Gorrie" 8).

Over the cited material hangs an air of a sincere irony that is, at base, chiding: occasionally, these tones also seem to characterize the narrator. Heble has rightly noted a shared manner of "speculatory procedures" (172) between the two. The paper's characteristic note of elaborate euphemism archly remarks any falling-away from what is implied as accepted behaviour. Social conformism is offered through a self-delighting and obliquely censorious vehicle which never becomes caustic. After the narrator's first citation of substance, about Jarvis Poulter's economical closeness, she comments that the *Vidette*'s style is "full of shy jokes, innuendo, plain accusation that no newspaper would get away with today" (57) – again, somewhat of a self-description. Though Jarvis is reportedly written of "with great respect" (57), the voice is gently derogatory; greater objectivity will not appear until his and Almeda's obituaries – the real inspiration for this narrator's freehand inventive reconstruction of the poet.

The paper's prying surmise about a possible Poulter-Roth alliance is greeted in a dismissive aside: "This kind of thing pops up in the *Vidette* all the time" (58). Its smirking treatment of the fallen woman – again, a literal and broadly metaphorical figure, like so many physical elements in this fiction – receives no comment from the narrator: the paper's laboured wordplay is archly self-evident. The conclusion to the notice, "*Incidents of this sort, unseemly, troublesome, and disgraceful to our town have of late become all too common*" (68), is serious and at odds with the light and superior tone of the scandalous report.

Later, Almeda's obituary is respectful, fair, perhaps sincere, as never before. Some of the notice is phrased in conventional terms – especially her faithful adherence and contribution to the town's (and the *Vidette*'s) social requirements. Jarvis's death is recorded in relatively unspecific phrases, obituary boilerplate. The narrator's last comments on these testimonials are "So the *Vidette* runs on, copious and assured. Hardly a death goes undescribed, or a life unevaluated" (72). In her words and often ironic perspective she has, in effect, incorporated the spirit of the paper into her own narrative inventions.

II

The sexual level of "Meneseteung" is everywhere implicit. Canitz and Seamon point out that "The narrator makes up a very modern tale of repressed desire, of symptoms and symbols that have resonance for the sexually liberated" (78). Not all of this is projected by Munro's persona; some of it is documentary, from the *Vidette*, and as such is reasonably trustworthy. The narrator begins by commenting on Almeda's photographic frontispiece to *Offerings*: "From the waist up, she looks like a young nobleman of another century" (51) – not impossibly a contemporary notation on gender ambivalence. Before long the image is made ridiculous when balanced against dogs napping "in a lordly way on the boardwalks" (54) – an almost characteristic reduction: nothing fine may remain unstained. Who do you think you are?

When the *Vidette* itself is first invoked it is rich in matchmaking suggestion, snidely ageist, never quite leering though eager to assume and publish, affected in manner about Jarvis and Almeda's homeward stroll after church: "*May we surmise?*" (58). Facing such innocent socializing, in a town rampant with human disorder, accident, and animal uncontrol, the paper's jest on "*salty*" (58), in the immediate sexual context, may well be knowing, and in line with the couple's putative fertility. In Walley, no social discrepancies will be overlooked, nor any decency unpunished.

There is a related joke, here: according to *Webster's Third New International Dictionary*, a "poulter" is a person who deals in poultry, and Jarvis, "*not perhaps in [his] first youth but by no means blighted by the frosts of age*" (58), is clearly no spring chicken. By no means does the narrator let this comic potential rest; among other features, the unbruised skin of the beaten harridan "is grayish, like a plucked raw drumstick" (65). Not coincidentally, "raw" has already been used, not euphemistically, to describe the new place of the town (54) as well as the countryside (61). The "plucked-chicken haunch" recurs as Almeda contemplates her "one very great poem" (70).

Jarvis, then, is impolitely but appropriately named, and perhaps this metaphorical witticism is allied to Almeda's middle name, Joynt, primarily defined as a piece of meat with a bone in it. This range of serendipitous association is often to be found in a Munro story. Here, "joint" also suggests Pearl Street and a possible origin of the night's giving tongue

– the indecent world of inspiration and alleged derangement into which Almeda will be released. The surname did belong to residents of the Goderich area; *The Signal* of April 28, 1921 noted county visits by Miss Fanny Joynt ("St. Helens" 4), perhaps unaware, then, of the grotesque picture suggested by the unhappy conjunction of her names.

"Everyone" greedily presumes a potential Poulter/Roth romance, though Almeda would "like a signal" (59). The narrator begins to invent, or, more properly, fabricate their connection, extrapolating from her reading of the *Vidette*. After she has proposed typical courtship figures and activities, she turns strict ironist when she considers Almeda's not inviting Jarvis in after their walk – for "a woman living alone could never do such a thing" (59):

> As soon as a man and woman of almost any age are alone together within four walls, it is assumed that anything may happen. Spontaneous combustion, instant fornication, an attack of passion. Brute instinct, triumph of the senses. What possibilities men and women must see in each other to infer such dangers. Or, believing in the dangers, how often they must think about the possibilities. (59-60)

Simultaneously suggestive and sophisticated, this comic reflection again removes the narrator from any consideration as historian. The image of sexual encounter as "combustion" (59) anticipates Almeda's imaging of the nighttime altercation as "a ball of fire rolling up Pearl Street, shooting off sparks" (63) – and that has already been interpreted as some form of sexual encounter. These amusing observations are about the sexual world of social disarray in that Pearl Street world – a name richly and pointedly ironic. It is important to note, however, that this is a contemporary extrapolation of the *Vidette*'s politer inferences, a rawer version of unrestrained human nature, almost as impolite for its as for our time. And the narrator has now, irremediably, made the suggestion, despite her condescending attitude of the preposterous and her ironic tone, which borders on ridicule.

Characteristic of this inventive storyteller, any undocumented, undeclared feature created for Almeda's environment assumes very nearly the force of fact. The reference to "decent" females not venturing to the last block of Pearl Street (56) ironically anticipates Almeda's eventual escape from the social orbit and her *"ramble"* (72) in the swamp. Her indecorous behaviour is estimated by the *Vidette* as that of an *"eccentric"* (71) – an unsubtle reminder of her mother, "who lost her reason" (59), and an unhappy link with the disgraceful alcoholic Queen Aggie. (It is, of course no coincidence that the narrator, who is not always subtle, notes that in her time the manager of the liquor store lives in Almeda's house.)

Further to the oblique sexual suggestions in the notion of Jarvis's clothes reminding Almeda of her father, the narrator does not resort, after a protracted estimate of Almeda's marriageability, to easy, contemporary insinuations of impropriety. Almeda's supposed image of Jarvis coming into the bedroom in long underwear and hat, prepared to embrace her, is wonderfully ludicrous. However "at this point a fit of welcome and submission overtakes her, a buried gasp. He would be her husband" (60). This passage shows the narrator in full constructive career: the wedding night is not pursued further, but the loaded, anticipatory "fit" which, echoed, leads to Almeda's pneumonia, is reinforced as a motif, and the shameless adjective "buried" looks to the narrator's final scrabbling in the Roth family plot. The intimate tableau is a catalogue of Almeda's romantic imaginings into which no real body, and no real romance, trespasses.

Almeda's bromides and nerve medicine, which may generate illusions, prompt another sexually-related joke, as the daring narrator gets increasingly high-handed about the world she is creating. The doctor's response to Almeda's physical complaints is purely ironic, a delightful one-liner: "He believes that her troubles would clear up if she got married. He believes this in spite of the fact that most of his nerve medicine is prescribed for married women" (62). The passage is rich with the real sociology of marriage. Sexual intimacy, it is implied, settles nervy married women down, relieves the problems brought on by study, reading, a lack of exercise, and an inattention to housework – well-meant Victorian bromides all. But Munro's narrator is no churlish feminist: her poet is being saved for a better self-actualizing experience. She does not comment seriously on this strait and narrow conjugal repression; it is allowed to generate its own wry recognitions.

Almeda's first Pearl Street adventure follows. It is violent, if not explicitly sexual: the narrator's language and the terms of her descriptions are suggestively ambiguous – after all, at first Almeda hears but does not see the actual events. When she goes out to investigate the body, she is led down a symbolic path. "Spiders have draped their webs over the doorway in the night, and the hollyhocks are drooping, heavy with dew. By the fence, she parts the sticky hollyhocks and looks down and she can see" (65). The careful details have a near-Lawrentian air of sexuality, while the heaped stinking body is bare-breasted and bare-haunched, an appearance which confirms at least its beating and possibly its carnal violation. Shortly thereafter, bloated and disarranged, all unaware, Almeda attracts Jarvis's erotic attentions as a possible wife: "He is sufficiently stirred by her loosened hair – prematurely gray but thick and soft – her flushed face, her light clothing, which nobody but a husband should see" (67). He is after all, an entrepreneurial opportunist by nature, though here he has of course been stirred by the stripped, abandoned woman.

To qualify what might be mistaken for cheap sensationalism, the narrator amplifies the situation as a scene of vulnerable innocence: "And by her indiscretion, her agitation, her foolishness, her need?" (67). We have been prepared for this: as he is now not married, Jarvis is not protected from "the extremities of his own nature" (57). His lust is sheer unashamed projection, but it stops short of a modern, possibly off-stage consummation, or pornography. In short, and again, the narrative voice is managing the literary effects of an artful story; it is a self-referential fiction with many of the hallmarks of a story by Alice Munro.

When Jarvis gives tongue, his voice, like many other of the story's elements, has its own range of associations, and it, too, is subject to a degree of narrative whimsy. When he supposedly speaks to Almeda of his salt wells, he is said to frown at what he may perceive as her sally, "'The salt of the earth'" (58). This was Jesus's metaphorical identification of the persecuted, in the Sermon on the Mount, the Beatitudes (Matt. 5.13). Here is another deliberate structural figuration which looks backward and forward to the persecuted figures of Queen Aggie and the woman in Pearl Street. Both females suffer what Jarvis calls "'the consequences of drink'" (67), and Almeda, too, will make free with her dizzying bromides. In another context, of course, the grape juice for her prospective jellies, a form of non-poetic "offerings" (62), is the base for wine, a potentially consequential drink. In such an unforced manner may "Meneseteung"'s internal relations, whether involuntary or deliberated, be suggested.

Jarvis's other speaking role is as rescuer, when, barely awake but not yet aroused, he responds to Almeda's mistaken identification of a dead body. He addresses the heaped woman with a practical roughness, in abrupt words and phrases (as well as with a foot and holding of her hair) and with the repeated elision, "'Gwan'" (67), at odds with his otherwise informative, proper, humourless, and business-like manner of speech. In this scene he sounds, and acts, suspiciously gutter-familiar. Earlier, the narrator had speculated about his appearance, including the one incongruous detail of "a large pale wart among the bushy hairs of one eyebrow" (57). This is a nice anticipation of his being awakened by the frantic Almeda with dank breath, creased face, and bloodshot eyes – details inimical to romance.

Now Jarvis's unusual "tone of harsh joviality" after he escorts her home, and his arousal at her disarray, have been prefaced by his unwittingly symbolic joke at her naïve expense, "'There goes your dead body!'" (67). Though his is a man's world, Almeda's imagination will free her from all forms of control: as Deborah Heller has detailed, Almeda will get loose from "her fenced-in world" (73) and stereotypical "plotlines" (71, 78). As for Jarvis in this story, he passes over in the *Vidette*'s merely functional notice.

There are other instances of the narrator's literary inclinations. The story, as story, has a goodly number of imagistic patterns, or motifs – Munro's customary and accomplished practice – a few of which are particularly useful, or apt, even if not patently foregrounded. For example, illuminations, literal and figurative, appear as a not inconsiderable set; most if not all examples invite a metaphorical reading. When Almeda wakes to the Pearl Street brouhaha, she sees that "Pegasus hangs straight ahead, over the swamp" (63) – as her gravestone will be said to be "staring at the sky" (73). The winged horse – unlike those running loose in Walley – is a symbol for the poetic imagination; before Almeda is overrun by her transcendent, teeming imagination, the inclusion of this figure is another remembrance of her father, as her zodiacal instructor, and a relatively heavy-handed preface to her moment of vision. The stars above, the street below: the contrast is elementary and, in "Meneseteung," it recurs in many obvious forms as a structural feature.

We remember, too, from the narrator's reading of the *Vidette*, that the town's horses become wild in hot weather – and Almeda is aware of, and subject to, many forms of heat: the night, the ball of fire, hot tea, the roads

hot as ashes, her house getting hot. Later, after her unwilling but life-al-
tering encounter, and in the throes of her re-vision, she is said to reflect,
"The changes of climate are often violent, and if you think about it there is
no peace even in the stars" (70). This is perhaps another example of what
has been identified by Pam Houston as "metonymic meaning" (83) in the
story. It is not difficult to nominate light as a surrounding, complementary
narrative environment, as an imagistic complex with both literal and figurative meaning, in another of the story's potential "unlimited contextual
configurations" (Houston 83). And this surely exemplifies Alice Munro's
characteristic deftness with the potentials of structural and associative
arrangements. Here as elsewhere the narrator has interpreted, has created
literary patterns, echoes, and repetitions, making figurations which draw
attention to themselves and to her as guiding intelligence. In "Meneseteung" contingency may be a subject, but never a technical practice.

Pegasus as constellation has been linked to the swamp: despite its
inelegant associations with the indecent Pearl Street, the bog has its own
transcendent or visionary aspect, a natural world superior to the nasty,
brutish, and ruffianly lives adjacent to it. "From her window she can see
the sun rising, the swamp mist filling with light, the bulky, nearest trees
floating against that mist and the trees behind turning transparent"
(56). The notion of elevation, of rising above, of visionary flight, enters
Almeda's second waking. Another flying creature is the sibylline and
symbolic talking crow with its cryptic scolding message: the oracle is
from the Queen Aggie world of public disgrace and human heaps to
be moved in a wheelbarrow, "something foul and sorrowful" (64). The
beaten woman's condition of "*heavenly – or otherwise – stupor*" (68), the
Vidette here observing in its characteristically genteel-snide manner, has
been a nice preparatory comment on any aspirations of rising above in
this society, this story.

Almeda's "*somewhat clouded*" mental condition in her later life (71)
is raised in her obituary, which is ostensibly positive and sympathetic,
but is also disingenuously sensational in its details. The narrator has
clearly used this source, working back in time to construct a profound
creative derangement in her version of the poet: effect has suggested
cause. This is followed by Almeda's walking upstairs now redolent of
blood, sweat, and grape juice – in elementary terms, another smelly,
abandoned woman:

No need for alarm.

For she hasn't thought that crocheted roses could float away or that tombstones could hurry down the street. She doesn't mistake that for reality, and neither does she mistake anything else for reality, and that is how she knows that she is sane. (71)

This is completely gratuitous, like everything the narrator includes about Almeda's imagined creative outbreak, and it only leads, in time, to the swamp. The *Vidette*'s memorial notice of this now "*familiar eccentric*" (71) follows immediately.

There is a good deal of "foul and sorrowful" (64) matter in "Menese-teung," apart from the human and animal misrule, noise, and noisomeness. Here, too, the narrator demonstrates her commitment to patterns of imagery. Most directly, in this town of human busyness the loose animals "leave horse buns, cow pats, dog turds that ladies have to hitch up their skirts for" (54) – not unlike the Pearl Street residents who "would just as soon go in the bushes" (56). It is no accident that the stinking woman who gives tongue so appallingly is moved by Jarvis's boot "just as you'd nudge a dog or a sow" (66). Is it the merest coincidence that some of Almeda's verse is called "doggerel" (52)? The town's other fecal streets are also trod by the gang of sensation-seeking youths who follow strangers: "Speculation surrounds all of them – it's like a cloud of flies" (55). The comedy is ripe: the simile means to evoke the excrements of the preceding paragraph in a direct fly-blown association with dung.

Clearly, this is not an isolated instance of play in this story; for example, the "swollen" and draining cheesecloth bag (68) blatantly suggests the menstruating and inspired Almeda, while her surname linked to her jelly-making affords an excruciating pun, the grapes of Roth. Even in such small matters a controlling literary intelligence may be identified, even as the genteel subject is earning an authentic self.

Piles of manure occur in the countryside as well, the region Almeda knows and uses in her verse. Here her active imagination, her somewhat ironic sense of classification, her self-awareness, come to the fore: "The countryside that she has written about in her poems actually takes diligence and determination to see" (61). Her vision of this provisional, raw, untidy, and swarming place is prim and selective, but undeluded: "Some things must be disregarded" (61). This is the rural equivalent of

Pearl Street, the epitome of indecency, a place of "refuse and debris" (55). In town as well, the foul anonymous woman with the bouquet of "Urine, drink, vomit" (65) has emerged from the nighttime fireworks, some of which have been vocal – "a rising and falling howling cry and a steady throbbing, low-pitched stream of abuse that contains all those words which Almeda associates with danger and depravity and foul smells and disgusting sights" (63).

This stream, hardly a trickle, belongs to the fundamental world which is both shameful and now, in Almeda's first-hand experience, undeniable. It is an aspect of the inevitable, inescapable stain that will never come out – the old thrill and the old despair – which has its own equally positive side in her creative process: inspiration "channelled into a poem," in the Meneseteung "that is the poem," emerging from the depths of "the river of her mind" (70). Though the narrator seems to credit Almeda with a solid grasp of metaphor, we recognize her constructive hand again, aggressive in self-conscious motif and forward in thematic consistency. Magdalene Redekop has correctly noted "the self-consciously purple prose passages in this story" (221): this entire sequence alone is confirmation.

When at the end the narrator speaks in her own voice, deprecating researchers who seek a connection, "rescuing one thing from the rubbish" (73), another link with the "foul and sorrowful" (64) is forged, and authenticated. The word "connection" reappears from Almeda's reaction to the human frenzy in Pearl Street: "she has noticed that before – it is always partly a charade with these people; there is a clumsy sort of parody, an exaggeration, a missed connection" (63-64). These people – not our sort at all, but merely low comic mechanisms – surrender to passion, to the moment; their behaviour is not civil. Yet eventually Almeda is to be connected with this gross, teeming world. Even in the prefatory photograph to *Offerings* her hat is described as "untrimmed, shapeless" (51) – a harbinger of her fate in miniature, the outlines blurred.

To make an end of it, what may be appreciated as the recurrent and literary aspects of "Meneseteung" are not merely incidental and matter of chance. They are employed by a self-serving narrator who, under the guise of historical re-creation, is conscious of her effects. Her intentional humour works toward a serious end, high and low amusements become as it were the life-affirming release of hallucination, inspiration, derangement – in a word, the freedom of Almeda Joynt Roth.

One final example is Almeda's alleged audition of Jarvis's retreating footsteps, disappointed of a walk to church, and so – it is implied – of their eventual situation as a couple. She is beginning her new, unconventional, inspired living: "An image comes to her of tombstones – it makes her laugh. Tombstones are marching down the street on their little booted feet, their long bodies inclined forward, their expressions preoccupied and severe" (69).

The grossly symbolic image emerges during a careful sequence which includes a passage from Almeda's poem "A Visit to My Family," the *Vidette*'s reports of mortal accidents to rash youth and heat-stricken babies in Walley, all the crude negatives of her environment, and beyond all this fiddle, the narrator's graveyard search. Almeda's metaphorically appropriate vision, which may precipitate her awareness of explosive patterns and potential changes in her father's house, of shifting and breaking free, could be a John Tenniel illustration from *Through the Looking-Glass*.

At the conclusion of her inspired afternoon, Almeda's attitude toward her mother's decorative roses – "their effort, their floating independence, their pleasure in their silly selves do seem to her so admirable. A hopeful sign" (70) – is light and wistful, even restorative. The narrator carefully points out, almost predictably, that there is no rosebush in the Roth plot – "perhaps it was taken out" (72) – as a bathetic conclusion to her sometime immodest floral imagery. However, Almeda's generous and positive personification makes a more suitable epitaph for her than anything the ungenerous *Vidette* could produce as copy, or the narrator uncover and improve upon. *Requiescat in pace.*

Works Consulted

Canitz, A.E. Christa, and Roger Seamon. "The Rhetoric of Fictional Realism in the Stories of Alice Munro." *Canadian Literature* 150 (1996): 67-80.

Carrington, Ildikó de Papp. *Controlling the Uncontrollable: The Fiction of Alice Munro*. DeKalb, IL: Northern Illinois UP, 1989.

Carroll, Lewis. *The Annotated Alice:* Alice's Adventures in Wonderland *and* Through the Looking-Glass. Introd. and notes by Martin Gardner. Illus. John Tenniel. Rev. ed. Harmondsworth, Eng.: Penguin, 1970.

"District Matters: Gorrie." *The Huron Expositor* [Seaforth, ON] 28 Aug. 1885: 8. *Google News.*

Gilchrist, J. Brian, comp. and ed. *Inventory of Ontario Newspapers 1793-1986.* Toronto: Micromedia, 1987.

The Goderich Harbour: Walking Tour. Goderich, ON: Local Architectural Conservation Advisory Committee, 1989. Rpt. (rev.) as *The Goderich Harbour: Past & Present.* Goderich, ON: Town of Goderich and Local Architectural Conservation Advisory Committee and Goderich Tourism Committee, 1994.

Heble, Ajay. *The Tumble of Reason: Alice Munro's Discourse of Absence.* Toronto: U of Toronto P, 1994.

Heller, Deborah. "Getting Loose: Women and Narration in Alice Munro's *Friend of My Youth.*" *Alice Munro Writing On....* Ed. Robert Thacker. *Essays on Canadian Writing* 66 (1998): 60-80. Rpt. in *The Rest of the Story: Critical Essays on Alice Munro.* Ed. Robert Thacker. Toronto: ECW, 1999. 60-80.

"Heritage Walking Tour 3: North to the Maitland." *4 Heritage Walking Tours: Port of Goderich.* Goderich, ON: Heritage Goderich, 2009. <https://www.goderich.ca/en/my-goderich/resources/Walk_3_2015.pdf>.

Houston, Pam. "A Hopeful Sign: The Making of Metonymic Meaning in Munro's 'Meneseteung'." *The Kenyon Review* ns 14.4 (1992): 79-92.

"Local News: Passed Away Friday." *The Clinton New Era* 14 Apr. 1921: 6.

"Local Topics: Her Fame Spreads Abroad." *The Signal* [Goderich, ON] 15 Feb. 1906: 4.

McCarthy, Dermot. "The Woman Out Back: Alice Munro's 'Meneseteung'." *Studies in Canadian Literature / Études en littérature canadienne* 19.1 (1994): 1-19.

McCullough, Jeanne, and Mona Simpson. "Alice Munro: The Art of Fiction CXXXVII." *The Paris Review* 131 (1994): 227-64.

Munro, Alice. "Contributors' Notes." *The Best American Short Stories 1989.* Ed. Margaret Atwood with Shannon Ravenel. Introd. Margaret Atwood. Boston: Houghton Mifflin, 1989. 322-23.

---. "Meneseteung." *The New Yorker* 11 Jan. 1988: 28-38. Rpt. (rev.) in *Friend of My Youth.* Toronto: McClelland & Stewart, 1990. 50-73.

---. "Oranges and Apples." *Friend of My Youth.* Toronto: McClelland & Stewart, 1990. 106-36.

---. "Wigtime." *Friend of My Youth.* Toronto: McClelland & Stewart, 1990. 244-73.

North Huron Museum, Wingham, Ontario. "Facades of Wingham – Past and Present." "Community Memories." *Virtual Museum of Canada (VMC).* <http://www.virtualmuseum.ca/sgc-cms/histoires_de_chez_nous-community_stories/pm_v2.php?id=exhibit_home&fl=0&lg=English&ex=00000544>.

Nunes, Mark. "Postmodern 'Piecing': Alice Munro's Contingent Ontologies." *Studies in Short Fiction* 34 (1997): 11-26.

"Obituary: Skimings." *The Signal* [Goderich, ON] 14 Apr. 1921: 4.

Redekop, Magdalene. *Mothers and Other Clowns: The Stories of Alice Munro.* London: Routledge, 1992.

Skimings, Eloise A. *Golden Leaves.* Goderich, ON: Star Book and Job Print, 1890. Enlarged ed. Goderich, ON: Signal, 1904.

"St. Helens." *The Signal* [Goderich, ON] 28 Apr. 1921: 4.

Thacker, Robert. "Introduction: Alice Munro, Writing 'Home': 'Seeing This Trickle in Time'." *Alice Munro Writing On....* Ed. Robert Thacker. *Essays on Canadian Writing* 66 (1998): 1-20. Rpt. in *The Rest of the Story: Critical Essays on Alice Munro.* Toronto: ECW, 1999. 1-20.

Wall, Kathleen. "Representing the Other Body: Frame Narratives in Margaret Atwood's 'Giving Birth' and Alice Munro's 'Meneseteung'." *Canadian Literature* 154 (1997): 74-90.

Wallace, Dorothy, gen. ed. *Memories of Goderich: The Romance of the Prettiest Town in Canada.* Goderich, ON: Jubilee 3 / Intercollegiate, 1977.

"Pearl Street ... is another story": Poetry and Reality in Alice Munro's "Meneseteung"

Marianne Micros

Within Alice Munro's "Meneseteung" are many stories: the story of the fictional poet Almeda Joynt Roth; the story of the narrator, who invents the story of Almeda Joynt Roth; the story of Alice Munro, who created all these stories; and each reader's story, including my own, as we consider this work from our individual perspectives. Underlying "Meneseteung" are stories of the history of this region of Southwestern Ontario, of women, of female poets, of poetry itself. Pearl Street is "another story" (55) – one of many yet one that combines them all.

The *Oxford English Dictionary* lists a number of definitions of "story": (1) "An account of imaginary or real people and events told for entertainment," including "A plot or storyline," "A report of an item of news in a newspaper, magazine, or broadcast," and "A piece of gossip; (2) a rumour"; (3) "An account of past events in someone's life or in the development of something," including "A particular person's representation of the facts of a matter" ("story"). All of these types of story are found in "Meneseteung."

The phrase "but that's another story" is said to be "[u]sed after raising a matter to indicate that one does not want to expand on it for now" ("story"). The narrator's reference to Pearl Street as "another story" indicates that Pearl Street's story is long and complicated[1] and that it is very different from the story of the respectable Dufferin Street that adjoins it. Pearl Street, in fact, is a story in itself.

Pearl Street should be a beautiful gem hidden in a shell: William Butt, in his essay on "Meneseteung," writes, "In Revelation 21.21 the twelve gates of Heaven are each a pearl, and in the great medieval poem of that name the Pearl is the human soul" (38). Pearl Street should be similar to the "pearl of great price" that Jesus likened to heaven: "Again, the kingdom of heaven is like unto a merchant man, seeking goodly pearls: / Who, when he had found one pearl of great price, went and sold all that he had, and bought it" (Matt. 13.45-46). In the Sermon on the Mount, Jesus said that one should not throw pearls before swine: "Give not that which is holy unto the dogs, neither cast ye your pearls before swine, lest they trample them under their feet, and turn again and rend you" (Matt. 7.6). Perhaps Almeda is the pearl who should not be given to Jarvis Poulter, or her poems are the pearls that will not be appreciated by the public. Pearls, then, because they are connected to the kingdom of heaven,[2] should not be maligned by those who cannot understand their worth.

A pearl is formed as a defense against a threat or attack ("Pearl"). Dufferin Street and Pearl Street were built in an attempt to control the uncontrollable, as Ildikó de Papp Carrington would say. However, what should be pure becomes adulterated as Pearl Street becomes a boghole with "piles of refuse and debris and crowds of runty children" (55-56). Pearl Street is a cleaned-up, man-made façade at one end; at the other, a place of uncontrolled nature, a swamp where crime and filth abound, where "[n]o decent woman" would ever go (56). In-between are workmen's houses, including the one occupied by Annie, the girl "who helps [Almeda] with her housecleaning" (56), and who witnesses Almeda's *"calm and faithful end"* (72; emphasis in orig.). In that middle area workers tried to clean up the dirt before it became visible to those considered respectable – but could not entirely succeed.

Nor are the two ends of Pearl Street entirely opposite. Within the civilized section, hypocrisy and inhumanity exist. Within the unruly, there is beauty. Almeda can see beyond the wildness and recognizes that the "same swamp ... presents a fine sight at dawn" (56). The dangerous side of Pearl Street may well be the place where one's imagination arises, where one finds the depths of creativity, where one gains experience and maturity. When a woman's drunken cries awaken Almeda one night, she sees the constellation of Pegasus, named for the flying horse that represents poetic imagination (as discussed also by MacKendrick 82), hanging "straight ahead, over the swamp" (63). The teeming bog and the heavenly vision co-exist and intersect; poetic inspiration emerges from the depths as well as from the heights.[3]

Pearl Street, Dufferin Street, entire towns and cities, were all imposed on nature, creating cultural conditions that often dictated human behaviour and controlled women. Almeda's house, situated at a boundary line between the civilized and the unruly, represents an attempt to keep out the dirt and the chaos. It symbolizes an escape from the outside world; yet it brings not only order but also confinement. The front windows face Dufferin Street, "a street of considerable respectability" (55), probably named for Lord Dufferin, who was the Governor General of Canada from 1872 to 1878 (see Butt 23). The back windows look out on Pearl Street – with its "decent row houses" (55) closest to Almeda's house; however, "[t]hings deteriorate toward the end of the block, and the next, last one becomes dismal" (55). Significantly, Almeda chooses to sleep "at the back of the house" (56), despite the availability of the front bedroom that had belonged to her parents. From her childhood bedroom at the back, Almeda can safely observe what is dangerous and possibly adventurous while still remaining within her comfortable cocoon.[4]

The fact that Almeda Joynt Roth lives on Pearl Street resonates for me since I once lived on Pearl Street in the town of Wellsville, New York. A young widow with a two-year-old daughter, I was teaching high-school English and Spanish and struggling with the aftermath of rheumatic fever, probably caused by the shock of my husband Stelios's recent death in a car accident. Near the end of the school year, incredible humidity was followed by torrential rains – and a flood that badly damaged the high-school gymnasium, as well as many houses, and demolished one wing of the hospital. The hospital was also located on Pearl Street, but at the lower end of it – West Pearl Street.

My house, on East Pearl Street, was safe. Without electricity for three days, and hearing reports that our drinking water could be contaminated, I boiled water for myself and for my neighbours, since I was lucky enough to have a gas stove. Helicopters clattered overhead, dropping bundles of food. The main street had become a river which people negotiated in rowboats. I heard that two men died when trying to cross the Pearl Street Bridge after it had collapsed. I huddled in the dark with my daughter Eleni, listening to the transistor radio to find out who was missing, who had been found, who was offering rooms in their houses to those displaced by the turbulent waters.

The dangerous part of Pearl Street, where a whole section of a hospital meant to heal people had collapsed into the river, was a place to avoid. Pearl Street up the hill, where I lived, was something of a comfort, though not so much for a young widow – a poet like Almeda – who could not yet write of her grief. While we did not have a Pearl Street Swamp, part of our Pearl Street almost became that during the flood. Coincidentally, the flood was caused by Hurricane Agnes, and in Munro's story the drunken old woman whom a gang of boys haul around in a wheelbarrow is called Queen Aggie.

At Almeda's house, the two doors seem to lead to different worlds, the front to apparent respectability, the back to possible danger. Almeda makes use of both doors, but, like Alice in Lewis Carroll's *Through the Looking-Glass*, who learns that the front door and the back door are the same at the house where she is to reign as Queen Alice, Almeda realizes that the two doors of her house lead to the same world. Upon hearing one night in her back yard the cries of a woman who was beaten and possibly raped, she exits through the back door and fetches Jarvis, who sends the drunk woman away after poking her with his boot and saying "'Gwan home!'" (67).[5] When he walks Almeda home, they must enter by the back door, since the front door is locked.

Almeda has now experienced that other side of town – the Pearl Street side and even the lower part of Pearl Street – and Jarvis Poulter has entered her house through that back door and come into the back hall. For her, he is now a part of that seamy underworld and has polluted her house with it. After he leaves, she locks the back door and places a note for Jarvis on her front door, stating that she is not well enough to accompany him to church that morning; then she locks that door as well. Almeda has imprisoned herself in her house – neither door providing escape or comfort.[6] Though the house may protect her in some ways, it is also exposed, a bit shabby looking, and surrounded by stray animals and noise. The house straddles the boundary but connects realities in an in-between place where Almeda shuts herself away rather than joining society as a conventional married woman.

The house that I lived in on Pearl Street had been divided into three apartments, with a shared basement. The back yard had more dirt than grass, and the driveway had specific parking areas for each tenant. I almost always used my back door, since I parked my car next to it. I rarely used the front door at all. But whichever door I used, I could not escape the reality of my husband's death, my illness, and, for a time, the raging flood only a short distance away.

Just as the views from the front and back windows of Almeda's house give very different impressions of the world outside, so does Munro's story present us with different attitudes to poetry and the realities, or truths, that it reflects. Kim Jernigan has discussed the "complex layering of competing narratives" in "Meneseteung" (45) – for example, the narratives of Almeda Joynt Roth, Jarvis Poulter, the first-person narrator of the story, and Munro herself, as well as those conveyed through poems, newspapers, and underlying "cultural narratives" (46).[7] And just as the story includes different narratives, so does it present different theories of poetry – what poetry is and what it can be.

Almeda's view of life is altered by experience, leading to a change in her style of poetry, at least in her mind and at least according to the narrator. Munro provides us with conflicting types of poetry, beginning with the romantic poems first written by Roth, who initially avoided much direct experience of the world outside her home, who wrote about the countryside while remaining within her house most of the time. However, once Almeda seeks meaning in her life, her poetry moves from romanticism to realism and perhaps even to surrealism – or so the narrator proposes, and perhaps wishes.

The narrator, whether she or he, as William Butt stresses (35-36),[8] seems to find Almeda's poetry old-fashioned with its regular rhythm and simple rhyme schemes, declaring rather disapprovingly, "No poem is unrhymed" (53). She/he describes the content of some of the poems, reducing them to the simplest explanations, but still sensing the loss and loneliness within them. Arguably, the narrator too is something of a poet in her/his descriptions, embellishments, imaginings.

We also have another point of view, that of the journalist who writes for the *Vidette*, the local newspaper, where "[h]ardly a death goes undescribed, or a life unevaluated" (72). The narrator reads articles in this paper and is influenced by them. Though they provide a contrast to Almeda's own poetry, they are at times poetic themselves: the journalist embellishes and dramatizes the events of the town in a "copious and assured" manner (72).

The story's author, Alice Munro, juxtaposes all these attitudes and styles and writes startlingly original poetry or poetic prose herself. Her writing, J.R. (Tim) Struthers has observed, is in the tradition of what Eileen Baldeshwiler calls "The Lyric Short Story" (Struthers, "Learning To Read" 335-36). In "Meneseteung," Munro writes the real poem, its nuances, metaphors, and layers evoking the layers within a single woman, a single poet.

The topic of poetry is complicated by the setting of the story in a period when women were not expected to have careers – but could perhaps "play" at writing poetry. The plight of a female poet in the nineteenth century (and indeed earlier than that, as evidenced by the lives of the seventeenth-century poets Aemilia Lanyer, whose first name sounds similar to Almeda's, and Mary Wroth, whose surname sounds identical to Almeda's), is reflected in the responses to Almeda and her writing.

We are reminded of particular women poets of the nineteenth century: Emily Dickinson, for example, who lived from 1830 to 1886. (The fictional Roth lived from 1840 to 1903.) Like Roth, Dickinson lived in isolation for many years and was rumoured to have suitors. She did, however, have family around her and therefore intellectual stimulation. Munro even mentions Dickinson in the "Contributors' Notes" to *The Best American Short Stories 1989*, where she writes of her idea for the story "Meneseteung": "So I thought, What about imagining one of these women and giving her some talent – not enough to make her any sort of Emily Dickinson, just enough to give her glimpses, stir her up?" (322).

Another prominent nineteenth-century female poet was Christina Rossetti, who lived from 1830 to 1894. Like Roth, Rossetti suffered from depression and a mental breakdown; she also refused offers of marriage, in her case possibly three times.[9] And, importantly, there were the Brontë sisters, who published a book of poems in 1846 under male pseudonyms.[10] Most especially, as J.R. (Tim) Struthers has argued, Emily Brontë, "author of the magnificent lyric novel *Wuthering Heights* (1847)" that Munro, starting at age fourteen, read and reread with "enormous admiration..., indeed intoxication" (Struthers, "In Search" 185, 191).

Well-known Canadian female writers during this time included Anna Brownell Jameson, Catherine Parr Traill, Susanna Moodie, Isabella Valancy Crawford, E. Pauline Johnson, and Sara Jeannette Duncan. A likely Canadian model for Almeda Joynt Roth, as proposed by Coral Ann Howells (107-08), Robert Thacker (434), and Louis K. MacKendrick (73-76), is Goderich, Ontario poet Eloise A. Skimings (1843-1921; sources vary on her year of birth), who published a book called *Golden Leaves* in 1890, with a much longer edition in 1904 (see MacKendrick 73). Munro acknowledges this connection: "... Goderich, on Lake Huron, had someone known as 'the Sweet Songstress of La Mer Douce'" ("Contributors' Notes" 322). Robert Thacker has also found a prototype for Roth in Clinton, Ontario painter and poet Clara Mountcastle (1837-1908), who published books in the 1880s and 1890s (see Thacker 434).[11] As Munro again acknowledges, "The town where I live had a Miss Mountcastle, who sometimes signed her poems 'Carissima'" ("Contributors' Notes" 322).

We can see that success in the field of literature and other arts was difficult for women to achieve. Roth's evolution as a poet is incomplete, in large part because the time is not yet ready for a new style of poetry, especially one created by a woman, that will include disturbing details about life. We do, however, see exceptions to this statement – for instance, Christina Rossetti's "Goblin Market." As a result, questions arise. Is poetry-writing a trap for idealistic women who cannot face their realities? Does it offer consolation or even escape? Should poetry be regarded as a mere exercise, not meant to be a profession or a way of life – at least for women? Must the gender of the writer be a factor? And how does one judge the quality of a poem? The narrator of the story wants to find solutions, wants to find some meaning to Almeda's life story.

Like Almeda, I was once called a "poetess" in an article in my hometown newspaper. I took offense at this. I did not write about flowers and sunshine. The term branded me as a mere female, not really a poet at all. It was the same for Almeda; the narrator says of the *Vidette*'s description of her, "There seems to be a mixture of respect and contempt, both for her calling and for her sex – or for their predictable conjuncture" (50). Yes, I experienced that attitude in the description of me. The narrator even says of Almeda, in reference to "all that reading and poetry," "Anyway, it's five years since her book was published, so perhaps she has got over that" (59).

Almeda's progression as a poet is similar to that of Emily in L.M. Montgomery's *Emily of New Moon*, a novel that Munro has loved since her childhood, as she has remarked in interviews with J.R. (Tim) Struthers

(18-19) and Catherine Sheldrick Ross (15-16) and in her afterword to the New Canadian Library edition of the book published in 1989. Munro states in the afterword that she sees *Emily of New Moon* as describing "the development of a child – and a girl child, at that – into a writer" (359). In the final chapter of the book, Emily's poetry is assessed by her teacher, the alcoholic failed poet Mr. Carpenter. He criticizes her romanticism, her clichés, the sentiments expressed that she has never experienced and does not understand, as well as her borrowings from other poets, her repetitions, and her exaggerations. But he praises her "'[t]en good lines'" (352) – and when she accidentally hands him her book of prose, with her depictions of him, he recognizes her real talent: "'By gad, it's literature – *literature* – and you're only thirteen'" (354). He encourages her to write what is real, to describe what she sees and knows.

Munro identifies the important difference between Emily's poetry and Emily's prose: poetry being her response to moments of joy, prose "her way of dealing with people, and often with situations in which she is in fact powerless" (359). We see such variations in writing style and genre in "Meneseteung" as well: the prose of the journalist as a way of sensationalizing; the prose of the narrator as a way of explaining and suggesting; the poetry of Almeda as a way of enduring while somewhat romanticizing the sadness of her life; the writing of Alice Munro as a combination of prose and poetry. For Munro, the boundary between prose and poetry is fluid; her prose is filled with the sounds, rhythms, and images of poetry (see MacKendrick 82-85 for discussions of the patterns of images in this story). Language such as "Spontaneous combustion, instant fornication, an attack of passion. Brute instinct, triumph of the senses" (59-60). "The grape pulp and juice has stained the swollen cloth a dark purple. *Plop, plup,* into the basin beneath" (68). "No, in fact it is the river, the Meneseteung, that is the poem – with its deep holes and rapids and blissful pools under the summer trees and its grinding blocks of ice thrown up at the end of winter and its desolating spring floods" (70). This is poetry.

The six verses by Almeda used as epigraphs for the story's six sections are reminiscent of Robert Louis Stevenson's *A Child's Garden of Verses* (1885). Stevenson's poems are rhymed and simple, seemingly playful and delightful, yet possess undercurrents of fear, sadness, illness, a desire for escape from that sickbed where the child lies. The shadow waits;

however, the swing brings temporary pleasure and a view of the outside world from a distance; and the lamplighter brings comfort in the dark night. Like the child in Stevenson's poems, Almeda longs for the exotic – but the gypsies she longs to bargain with have gone (62) and she is bound closely to her household and to her dead family members.

Magdalene Redekop suggests that "[a]n exaggerated focus on rhyme for its own sake is, of course, a feature of bad poetry" but continues that "... Munro here displays a talent ... for writing excellent bad poetry" (225).[12] Redekop also suggests that "art itself ends up acting as a kind of feminine escape from the brutality enacted on Pearl Street" (227). To the contrary, I do not see Almeda's poems as "bad poetry" or as helping the poet escape from the disturbing realities around her. Nor do I see Almeda's poems as transformative in the way that Kim Jernigan proposes (50) – though they are a controlled means for Almeda to deal with the difficulties of her life, albeit by the use of romantic imagery and playful rhymes. Rather, Almeda's verses share with Stevenson's the use of simple rhymes, regular rhythms, and a tone which, though childlike, is laced with an undercurrent of sadness and an awareness of death.

Those short verses with simple vocabulary provide a contrast with Munro's prose, prose that illustrates the simultaneous deterioration and emancipation of a confined woman – a theme similar to that of Charlotte Perkins Gilman's short story "The Yellow Wallpaper." In both Munro's and Gilman's stories, inanimate objects in enclosed rooms come to life in threatening ways that reveal the states of mind of the protagonists. For example, in Almeda's dining room, "every one of these patterns, decorations seems charged with life, ready to move and flow and alter. Or possibly to explode. Almeda Roth's occupation throughout the day is to keep an eye on them" (69). This is similar to Gilman's narrator Jane's description of the wallpaper in her bedroom: "The color is hideous enough, and unreliable enough, and infuriating enough, but the pattern is torturing. // You think you have mastered it, but just as you get well underway in following, it turns a back-somersault and there you are. It slaps you in the face, knocks you down, and tramples upon you. It is like a bad dream" (25). Nevertheless, Jane and Almeda continue to resist society's expectations – in Almeda's case by refusing to marry, to clean house, to do charitable work. "The Yellow Wallpaper" has been interpreted as a feminist statement. Is "Meneseteung" also that?

Roth has written poetry that may be conventional but that provides her with a means of expression, of voicing both her joy and her sadness. She addresses her deceased family members in her verses: *"Father, Mother, / Sister, Brother, / Have you no word to say?"* (71; emphasis in orig.). They have indeed lost their voices, but Roth speaks out in a way that is possible for her. The narrator suggests that Almeda wishes to go beyond that, to take her poetry in a new direction, toward a new style,[13] one precipitated by the loss of her idealism and her subsequent wish to include in her poems "the obscene racket on Pearl Street and the polished toe of Jarvis Poulter's boot and the plucked-chicken haunch with its blue-black flower" (70). The narrator imagines that Almeda wants to include concrete details, notably those that point to the ugliness, violence, and tragedy in the world around her. According to the narrator, Almeda now wishes to write "one very great poem that will contain everything" (70), a poem that will be named "The Meneseteung": "The name of the poem is the name of the river. No, in fact it is the river, the Meneseteung, that is the poem" (70).[14] Or perhaps the poem can become the river, just as the river can become the poem.

Almeda, according to the narrator, sees the difference between the name of something and the thing itself.[15] This view may be connected to the philosophy of the thing itself proposed in the early twentieth century. Wallace Stevens wrote, in "Not Ideas about the Thing but the Thing Itself," the poem chosen to conclude his *Collected Poems*, "... It was like / A new knowledge of reality" (534). William Carlos Williams, too, in his long poem *Paterson*, declared: "no ideas but in things" (6). How fitting that Munro's story twice mentions a wheelbarrow (54, 64), reminding us, as Redekop also observes (226), of Williams' poem "The Red Wheelbarrow." Things, concrete images, were all important to Williams and other poets, such as T.E. Hulme and Ezra Pound, pioneers in the Imagist movement, along with H.D. (Hilda Doolittle), a poet who, like Almeda, struggled with her craft, her reputation, and her relationships with men (see Guest).

The Imagist poem has been defined by M.H. Abrams and Geoffrey Galt Harpham as a poem in free verse which "undertakes to render as precisely, vividly, and tersely as possible, and without comment or generalization, the writer's impression of a visual object or scene; often the impression is rendered by means of metaphor, or by juxtaposing, without indicating a relationship, the description of one object with that of a second and diverse object" ("Imagism" 174). This technique resembles Munro's use of images in her stories. However, like Munro's prose, Almeda's new style will go beyond Imagism to include details that are much more realistic, as well as providing readers with the narrator's thoughts and explanations. The wheelbarrow in "Meneseteung" is not simply sitting, as Williams wrote, "beside the white / chickens" but is transported around town, with the drunken Queen Aggie inside it, by a gang of boys who "then dump her into a ditch to sober her up" (54).

Later, when Almeda thinks a crow is telling her to move the wheelbarrow, she "understands that it means something else" (64) – "'wheelbarrow'" means "something foul and sorrowful" (64). In fact, what the imagined and itself symbolic crow[16] calls a wheelbarrow is a "woman's body heaped up there, turned on her side with her face squashed down into the earth" (65). Munro's use of similes in her description of the woman is an example of the concrete and unromanticized details of her images: "But there is a bare breast let loose, brown nipple pulled long like a cow's teat, and a bare haunch and leg, the haunch showing a bruise as big as a sunflower. The unbruised skin is grayish, like a plucked, raw drumstick" (65). Munro, or her narrator, focusses on the raw details, not on abstractions or idealizations of reality.

Therefore, it is presumably not Almeda who is evolving away from romanticism toward writing more realistic poetry, poetry in free verse rather than in regular rhythm and rhyme. It is the story's narrator who seems to want Almeda to write something closer to realism or even naturalism, a term used to describe a movement by fiction writers to include "bodily functions" and "strong animal drives" in their works ("Realism and Naturalism" 334). It is the narrator who wants Almeda to write of the ugliness around her and to let the world know about her position in society and the plight of women at that time – yet she/he also wants Almeda to include the joys and beauties of life with those harsher realities. The narrator describes the Meneseteung's "deep holes and rapids and blissful pools under the summer trees and its grinding blocks of ice thrown up at the end of winter and its desolating spring floods" (70). For the narrator, life's small everyday objects – the grape jelly, the menstrual blood, the crocheted roses – and life's disturbing events – the tormented Queen Aggie and the drunken woman who was possibly raped and apparently beaten almost to death – are the poem.

It is, arguably, the narrator who wants to be a poet, who wants to learn something from the story of this unknown local poet.

One of Alice Munro's most important influences, Eudora Welty, stated that "I think we write stories in the ultimate hope of communication, but so do we make jelly in that hope" (160). Almeda writes poems, and the narrator tells a story, to communicate. Almeda's grape jelly, like her poems, represents an attempt to express her emotions and a way of giving something of herself to others. She is making jelly to give as "fine Christmas presents, or offerings to the sick" (62) – and her book of poems is titled *Offerings*. However, now that she has been suddenly confronted with the harshness of the outside world, the jelly and the type of poem she previously wrote are no longer possibilities: "The basin of grape juice has overflowed and is running over her kitchen floor, staining the boards of the floor, and the stain will never come out" (70).[17] Those simple poems that showed glimpses of her childlike hopes and innocence, that intimated yet controlled her deep sorrow, will no longer suffice. This is what the narrator concludes, or wishes to believe, in the hope that Almeda can evolve into a more modern poet dealing with the thing itself, but also with the realities of life, the beautiful and the menacing: "It's true that you can gather wildflowers in spring in the woodlots, but you'd have to walk through herds of horned cows to get to them" (61).

In "Meneseteung," however, the meaning of reality is questionable, and questioned. As Ajay Heble suggests, Munro's writing "reveals itself to be maintaining and undoing reality at one and the same time" (4). Almeda, we are told, has "[a]n image ... of tombstones ... marching down the street on their little booted feet" (69); yet, according to the narrator, "She doesn't mistake that for reality, and neither does she mistake anything else for reality, and that is how she knows that she is sane" (71). If Almeda mistakes nothing for reality, one wonders if she is living in any kind of reality at all – or if there is such a thing.

Gregory Cowles, in his review of Mary Karr's *The Art of Memoir*, writes, "... Munro is constantly interrogating the past to get at the real" (20-21). Speaking of "the deeper truth," he goes on to say that Munro's "fiction works hard to reveal it, to show us how memory actually operates" (21). However, the narrator of "Meneseteung" is obviously making things up, imagining the specifics behind the sparse facts of someone's life. The narrator even admits to inventing aspects of Almeda's reality:

"I may have got it wrong. I don't know if she ever took laudanum. Many ladies did. I don't know if she ever made grape jelly" (73).[18] Clearly, then, Munro is questioning the whole notion of "reality" and the possibility of knowing it.

My Pearl Street home was respectable and comfortable; but in the dark, with the helicopters whirring overhead and the radio telling us of missing family members and dangerous roads, the façade meant nothing. The river that threatened my home was the Genesee – a name connecting, as does Meneseteung, to wilderness, aboriginal inhabitants, and uncontrolled yet beautiful nature[19] – to times and realities disappearing, as current inhabitants regularly ignore and disrespect the beauty of nature, lose the awe we should feel in the presence of its power.

The peaceful appearance of Pearl Street belied the hidden turmoil underneath, spring flooding bringing fear to the surface and leaving the playground in our back yard sunk in the mud. When my daughter Eleni grew up, she wrote a story about an overturned swing set in a back yard ravaged by flood waters – about an out-of-control river that tried to demolish society's impositions. The Genesee and the Meneseteung, ancient waterways with aboriginal names, connect past and present, symbolizing the power that lies under and around all the forms and structures that society devises, the power that forces images into our minds and into our writing, that can be creative as well as destructive.

When I visited Pearl Street many years later, mature trees still towered over the road and sheltered the houses. I was shocked, though, when I saw the house, its shabbiness, its flaking exterior and rundown appearance, its need of paint and repairs. Roth's house, too, became "shabby, in need of paint," as seen in a photograph from the 1880s (53). Later, the liquor store manager would live there and it would be covered with aluminum siding, its open porch closed in. I had thought my house quite impressive at the time, and perhaps it was. I tried to ignore the hardships of my life, as I struggled to teach school while suffering from rheumatic pain, as I took my daughter for ice cream in the evening, as I lay in bed unable to sleep, hearing the rain beating down on the roof. I would perhaps have been attracted to someone like Jarvis Poulter, someone to rescue me from loneliness. I did not write poems during that time in my life, but resumed writing a few years later. It was not a time for poetry.

The story of Almeda Joynt Roth is the narrator's creation, the narrator's own poem, the thing itself. But the narrator leaves many questions unanswered. Did Jarvis Poulter have a wart on one eyebrow? How did his wife die? Did Almeda start to menstruate on the same day that she discovered the drunk woman behind her house? The narrator does not know, nor do we. If Pearl Street is "another story," as the narrator claims (55), what is the first story and what are the other stories?

Munro's story, "Meneseteung," is the story of poetry, with words, images, small everyday objects leading us to deeper consideration of the significance of our lives while challenging us to question the nature of reality. The story changes every time one reads it. I have mingled my own story, and my own poem, with Almeda's, the narrator's, Alice Munro's, yours – all blended into "another story," where poetry and prose engage with each other in a complicated but rewarding relationship, where a street named Pearl is both a pathway and a dwelling place as it attempts to control the forces that could undermine it. Pearl Street attempts to impose order on chaos, but it leads both away from and toward a swampy bog. Pearl Street is a story. It is also a poem.

Pearl Street

look out the back window
the bog
gangs of rough boys
the drunks
screaming swearing
murder

the front door
is locked
open the back gate
see the piles of manure
hear the noise
of things that are not
respectable

the bog beckons
the wheelbarrow is ready
to cart you away

the pearl
once safe in its shell
has opened itself
to sun
to storms

someone has cut down
trees
someone has straightened
roads
put up fences

the ancient river
your poet's mind
flows
through
everything

erasing boundaries
flooding
freeing

the river is the poem
the poem is the river
carrying you to death
awakening you to life

just as you named the poem
the poem names you

your name cut short
Almeda to Meda
to suit the intimacy
of the grave

look again
out the back window
see the sun rising

once more
in its shell
the pearl rests
safely

Notes

1. As Dermot McCarthy observes, "Pearl Street, the narrator remarks,
    is 'another story' (['Meneseteung'] 55). But that other story *is* the
    story that is told, the story of the other that Almeda represents for
    the narrator, the 'Meda' submerged in Almeda, and that the swamp-
    woman represents in the story for Almeda herself" (4).
2. The name of the Southwestern Ontario town, Goderich, on which
    Almeda's hometown is based, has an equivalent, J.R. (Tim) Struthers
    points out, in the Old English *Godes rice*, meaning "the kingdom of
    God" (Struthers, "Imagining" [69]). Also see William Butt (15, 25-26,
    32) and Louis K. MacKendrick (76-77) on Goderich as a model for
    Almeda's town and Struthers on Munro as allegorist in "Traveling
    with Munro" (179-82).
3. Catherine Sheldrick Ross writes that Munro "wants to present ordi-
    nary experience with such intensity that it stands revealed as some-
    thing extraordinary," to "find the legendary shapes that lie behind
    ... everyday experience" in order to show the value of "the ordinary
    world" ("'At Least'" 112, 125).
4. Ildikó de Papp Carrington suggests that the location of Almeda's
    house "symbolizes her social position as an outsider and her psy-
    chological position as a borderline case" (214). She also comments
    that Munro herself, like Almeda, "dives underwater" (215) or into
    a "'peculiar limbo'" in her creative process, as Munro noted in an
    interview with Geoff Hancock cited by Carrington (215-16).

5. Klaus P. Stich speculates that in the mind of Almeda, "Poulter has become ... the drunk woman's likely Saturday-night consort" (114). I do not find enough evidence in the story to prove or disprove this theory.

6. Kim Jernigan writes that Almeda seems "to sense as much danger from respectable Dufferin Street as from poor and dissolute Pearl Street" (56).

7. As Kim Jernigan emphasizes, "It is only through a complex layering of competing narratives – of deceptions, revisions, and alternate versions – that [Munro] begins to achieve a sort of emotional truth, one which acknowledges that disparate people experience, understand, and explain a shared reality in disparate and revealing ways" (45).

8. William Butt argues that the narrator could be either male or female, that the gender is meant to be indeterminate (35-36), and that the narrator "combines factual research with a willingness to indulge her own imaginative inner self" (14). I agree with both of these ideas.

9. See Georgina Battiscombe, *Christina Rossetti: A Divided Life*.

10. J.R. (Tim) Struthers suggests that the name Almeda may have been borrowed from "the Brontës' imaginary history of Gondal" whose queen "is named Augusta Geraldine Almeda" (Struthers, "Imagining" 78). Elsewhere he writes, "Among a few different pseudonyms that Emily selected for herself in the [Brontës'] richly developed childhood fantasy about ... Gondal ... was the name Almeda" (Struthers, "In Search" 185, 191).

11. See Barbara Godard, "Mountcastle, Clara H."

12. Munro describes the poetry by women in the nineteenth century who lived in small Canadian towns as "poetry that was sometimes mediocre and sometimes very bad, about Nature, Love, Childhood, Christianity, the British Empire. They prattled in quatrains and couplets about an innocence, an idyllic world, quite at variance with the one before their eyes, and they were despised and quaintly exalted for this blinkered exercise.... // Just the same, they're paying attention, they're making something" ("Contributors' Notes" 322).

13. Dermot McCarthy suggests that the poem the narrator imagines Almeda "wanting to write is a modern, if not even modernist, poem of encyclopedic scope, of contraries and contradictions held in equilibrium, in the meaningful but fictive order of a constellation" (8).

14. For a discussion of possible meanings of the word "Meneseteung," see
J.R. (Tim) Struthers, "In Search" (180-81). Also see Sabrina Francesconi
(114-17), Kim Jernigan (56, 57), and Louis K. MacKendrick (76).
15. This notion is reminiscent of one in Lewis Carroll's *Through the
Looking-Glass*, where the White Knight distinguishes among things,
the names of things, and the names of names of things.
16. Traditionally, the crow represents death or prophesies something
dark or evil to come. The symbolic import of the crow is described in
T.H. White's *The Bestiary: A Book of Beasts* in this way: "Soothsayers
declare that it has to do with the troubles of men by omens, that
it discloses the paths of treachery, and that it predicts the future"
(142). In some cultures crows signify wisdom and are considered
messengers that give warnings. The crow in Munro's story represents
Almeda's conscience, her feeling of guilt at not responding sooner
to the cries outside her window, and also her unconscious understanding of her dismal future if she were to marry Jarvis Poulter. The
imagined crow is a forewarning to Almeda to beware of anyone who
would treat her inhumanely, as if she were an object.
17. Kim Jernigan (55-56), J.R. (Tim) Struthers ("In Search" 180), and others have identified the grape juice as signifying Almeda's menstrual
blood, which, as Jernigan writes, "will be wasted" since Almeda has
decided to refuse Jarvis Poulter's offer and therefore any hope of
marriage (56). I do not disagree with this reading but suggest that the
juice may also signify her creativity as a poet. Jernigan, in fact, does
see the dripping juice as symbolizing Almeda's creativity in relation
to her poetry (55-56), and Struthers proposes that the grape juice is
a metaphor for "an imaginative process or flow" apparent on four
levels: Almeda's, the narrator's, Munro's, and our own as readers ("In
Search" 181). While Ildikó de Papp Carrington interprets this menstruation as "the absence of conception" (215), Dermot McCarthy
proposes that it is "a sign of her continuing fertility, her potential to
create future presence, rather than ... a sign of past failure" (8).
18. Several critics have noted the fact that this ending was not in the
original publication of the story in *The New Yorker* but restored later.
See Robert Thacker (434-35); Coral Ann Howells (111-13); William
Butt (37). Butt writes, "Munro's revised ending brings her readers
back to what Yeats calls the rag and bone shop, to the world where

imagination starts: poised between object and subject, fact and fiction; where both are material for whoever has the strength to conceive and shape; where each depends for its creation on the other. The altered ending reminds us that the world we imagine is one which we must neither entirely believe in nor entirely disbelieve" (37).

19. J.R. (Tim) Struthers has proposed that in Ojibway "Meneseteung" means "place of little islands" (Struthers, "In Search" 180 and "Imagining" 72).

Works Consulted

Baldeshwiler, Eileen. "The Lyric Short Story: The Sketch of a History." *Short Story Theories*. Ed. Charles E. May. Athens, OH: Ohio UP, 1976. 202-13. Rpt. in *The New Short Story Theories*. Ed. Charles E. May. Athens, OH: Ohio UP, 1994. 231-41.

Battiscombe, Georgina. *Christina Rossetti: A Divided Life*. London: Constable, 1981.

Bell, Currer, Ellis, and Acton. *Poems*. London: Smith, Elder, 1846.

Butt, William. "Southwestern Ontario, the Narrator, and 'Words with Power' in Alice Munro's 'Meneseteung'." *Alice Munro and the Souwesto Story*. Ed. J.R. (Tim) Struthers. *Short Story* ns 21.1 (2013 [2015]): 13-43.

Carrington, Ildikó de Papp. *Controlling the Uncontrollable: The Fiction of Alice Munro*. DeKalb, IL: Northern Illinois UP, 1989.

Carroll, Lewis. *Through the Looking-Glass and What Alice Found There*. *Alice in Wonderland*. Ed. Donald J. Gray. 3rd ed. New York: W.W. Norton, 2013. 99-208. A Norton Critical Edition.

Cowles, Gregory. "The Liars' Club: Is There Such a Thing as a Reliable Memoir?" Rev. of *The Art of Memoir*, by Mary Karr. *The New York Times Book Review* 25 Oct. 2015: 20-21.

Dickinson, Emily. *Final Harvest: Emily Dickinson's Poems*. Ed. Thomas H. Johnson. Boston: Little, Brown, [1961].

Francesconi, Sabrina. "Negotiation of Naming in Alice Munro's 'Meneseteung'." *The Short Stories of Alice Munro*. Ed. Héliane Ventura. *Journal of the Short Story in English / Les cahiers de la nouvelle* 55 (2010): 109-22.

Gilman, Charlotte Perkins. *The Yellow Wallpaper*. Afterword by Elaine R. Hedges. Old Westbury, NY: Feminist, 1973.

Godard, Barbara. "Mountcastle, Clara H." *Dictionary of Canadian Biography*. Vol. 13. <http://www.biographi.ca/en/bio/mountcastle_clara_h_13E.html>.

Guest, Barbara. *Herself Defined: The Poet H.D. and Her World*. Garden City, NY: Doubleday, 1984.

Hannay, Margaret P. *Mary Sidney, Lady Wroth*. Farnham, Eng.: Ashgate, 2010.

Heble, Ajay. *The Tumble of Reason: Alice Munro's Discourse of Absence*. Toronto: U of Toronto, P, 1994.

The Holy Bible. Grand Rapids, MI: Zondervan, 1962. Authorized King James Vers.

Howells, Coral Ann. *Alice Munro*. Manchester, Eng.: Manchester UP, 1998. Contemporary World Writers.

"Imagism." *A Glossary of Literary Terms*. By M.H. Abrams and Geoffrey Galt Harpham. 11th ed. Stamford, CT: Cengage Learning, 2015. 173-74.

Jernigan, Kim. "Narrative Hauntings in Alice Munro's 'Meneseteung'." *Alice Munro and the Souwesto Story*. Ed. J.R. (Tim) Struthers. *Short Story* ns 21.1 (2013 [2015]): 44-69.

Lanyer, Aemilia. *The Poems of Aemilia Lanyer:* Salve Deus Rex Judaeorum. Ed. Susanne Woods. New York: Oxford UP, 1993. Women Writers in English 1350-1850.

MacKendrick, Louis K. "Giving Tongue: Scorings of Voice, Verse, and Flesh in Alice Munro's 'Meneseteung'." *Alice Munro and the Souwesto Story*. Ed. J.R. (Tim) Struthers. *Short Story* ns 21.1 (2013 [2015]): 70-87.

McCarthy, Dermot. "The Woman Out Back: Alice Munro's 'Meneseteung'." *Studies in Canadian Literature / Études en littérature canadienne* 19.1 (1994): 1-19.

Montgomery, L.M. *Emily of New Moon*. 1923. Afterword by Alice Munro. Toronto: McClelland and Stewart, 1989. The New Canadian Library.

Munro, Alice. Afterword. *Emily of New Moon*. By L.M. Montgomery. Toronto: McClelland and Stewart, 1989. 357-61. The New Canadian Library.

---. "Contributors' Notes." *The Best American Short Stories 1989*. Ed. Margaret Atwood with Shannon Ravenel. Introd. Margaret Atwood. Boston: Houghton Mifflin, 1989. 322-23.

---. "Meneseteung." *Friend of My Youth*. Toronto: McClelland & Stewart, 1990. 50-73. [Originally published in *The New Yorker* 11 Jan. 1988: 28-38 without its final paragraph. Subsequently published in *Friend of My Youth* with the final paragraph restored, after Munro expanded the beginning of it by two sentences (see Thacker 434-45). Rpt. from *The New Yorker* in *The Best American Short Stories 1989*. Ed. Margaret Atwood with Shannon Ravenel. Introd. Margaret Atwood. Boston: Houghton Mifflin, 1989. 247-68. Rpt. in *The Best American Short Stories of the Century*. Ed. John Updike and Katrina Kenison. Introd. John Updike. Boston: Houghton Mifflin, 1999. 633-51.]

"Pearl." <https://en.wikipedia.org/wiki/Pearl>.

"Realism and Naturalism." *A Glossary of Literary Terms*. By M.H. Abrams and Geoffrey Galt Harpham. 11th ed. Stamford, CT: Cengage Learning, 2015. 333-35.

Redekop, Magdalene. *Mothers and Other Clowns: The Stories of Alice Munro*. London: Routledge, 1992.

Ross, Catherine Sheldrick. "'At Least Part Legend': The Fiction of Alice Munro." *Probable Fictions: Alice Munro's Narrative Acts*. Ed. Louis K. MacKendrick. Downsview, ON: ECW, 1983. 112-26.

---. "An Interview with Alice Munro." *Canadian Children's Literature / Littérature canadienne pour la jeunesse* 53 (1989): 14-24.

Rossetti, Christina. "Goblin Market." *Poems and Prose*. Ed. and introd. Simon Humphries. Oxford, Eng.: Oxford UP, 2008. 103-19. Oxford World's Classics.

Skimings, Eloise A. *Golden Leaves*. Goderich, ON: Star Book and Job Print, 1890. Enlarged ed. Goderich, ON: Signal, 1904.

Stevens, Wallace. "Not Ideas about the Thing but the Thing Itself." *The Collected Poems of Wallace Stevens*. New York: Alfred A. Knopf, 1954. 534.

Stevenson, Robert Louis. *A Child's Garden of Verses*. 1885. New ed. 1952. Decorations by Eve Garnett. London: Puffin-Penguin, 1994.

Stich, Klaus P. "Letting Go with the Mind: Dionysus and Medusa in Alice Munro's 'Meneseteung'." *Canadian Literature* 169 (2001): 106-25.

"story." <https://en.oxforddictionaries.com/definition/story>.

Struthers, J.R. (Tim). "Imagining Alice Munro's 'Meneseteung': The Dynamics of Co-Creation." *Alice Munro: A Souwesto Celebration*. Ed. J.R. (Tim) Struthers and John B. Lee. *The Windsor Review* 47.2 (2014): 68-91.

---. "In Search of the Perfect Metaphor: The Language of the Short Story and Alice Munro's 'Meneseteung'." *Critical Insights: Alice Munro*. Ed. Charles E. May. Ipswich, MA: Salem-EBSCO, 2013. 175-94.

---. "The Real Material: An Interview with Alice Munro." *Probable Fictions: Alice Munro's Narrative Acts*. Ed. Louis K. MacKendrick. Downsview, ON: ECW, 1983. 5-36.

---. "Traveling with Munro: Reading 'To Reach Japan'." *Alice Munro:* Hateship, Friendship, Courtship, Loveship, Marriage; Runaway; Dear Life. Ed. Robert Thacker. London: Bloomsbury, 2016. 163-83, 231-44 passim.

Thacker, Robert. *Alice Munro: Writing Her Lives: A Biography*. Toronto: McClelland & Stewart, 2005. Updated ed. Toronto: Emblem-McClelland & Stewart, 2011.

Ware, Tracy. "'And They May Get It Wrong, After All': Reading Alice Munro's 'Meneseteung'." *National Plots: Historical Fiction and Changing Ideas of Canada*. Ed. Andrea Cabajsky and Brett Josef Grubisic. Waterloo, ON: Wilfrid Laurier UP, 2010. 67-79, 215-36 passim.

Welty, Eudora. "The Reading and Writing of Short Stories." *Short Story Theories*. Ed. Charles E. May. Athens, OH: Ohio UP, 1976. 159-77.

White, T.H. *The Bestiary: A Book of Beasts; Being a Translation from a Latin Bestiary of the Twelfth Century Made and Edited by T.H White*. 1954. New York: Capricorn-G.P. Putnam's Sons, 1960.

Williams, William Carlos. *Paterson*. Rev. ed. Ed. Christopher MacGowan. 1992. New York: New Directions, 1995.

---. "The Red Wheelbarrow." *Selected Poems of William Carlos Williams*. Introd. Randall Jarrell. 1949. Enlarged ed. New York: New Directions, 1968. 30.

Wolff, Cynthia Griffin. *Emily Dickinson*. New York: Alfred A. Knopf, 1986.

Woods, Susanne. *Lanyer: A Renaissance Woman Poet*. New York: Oxford UP, 1999.

Wroth, Lady Mary. *The Poems of Lady Mary Wroth*. Ed. Josephine A. Roberts. Baton Rouge: Louisiana State UP, 1983.

A Bibliographical Tour
of Alice Munro Country

J.R. (Tim) Struthers

A Preface to A Bibliographical Tour of Alice Munro Country

Choices in this bibliography represent forty-five years of personal study of Alice Munro's writing and of works pertinent to understanding it, while also reflecting idiosyncrasies which characterize my own particular (some might say "peculiar") forms of curiosity and humour. At the same time, I am very happy to be able here to express my debt to, and my gratitude for, the notable research found in the monumental *Alice Munro: An Annotated Bibliography of Works and Criticism* compiled by Carol Mazur and edited by Cathy Moulder, in Corinne Bigot's "Alice Munro: A Bibliography" published in the *Journal of the Short Story in English / Les cahiers de la nouvelle*, and in the decades of work by the always cordial and helpful Alice Munro authority Robert Thacker. For just as literary critics are indebted to and need to acknowledge other literary critics – including Munro enthusiasts in Europe such as Corinne Bigot, Mirosława Buchholtz, Ailsa Cox, Isla Duncan, Sabrina Francesconi, Coral Ann Howells, Catherine Lanone, Christine Lorre-Johnston, Claire Omhovère, Oriana Palusci, Eleonora Rao, Ulrica Skagert, Michael Toolan, and the ever-prolific, ever-insightful Héliane Ventura, along with Gianfranca Balestra, Giuseppina Botta, Mary Condé, Amelia DeFalco, Thomas Dutoit, Marta Dvořák, Charles Forceville, Adrian Grafe, Vanessa Guignery, Adrian Hunter, Jean-Jacques Lecercle, Maria Löschnigg, Reingard M. Nischik, Pilar Somacarrera, Simone Vauthier, and Per Winther – so bibliographers are indebted to and need to acknowledge the work of other bibliographers. On my own part, it has for a number of years amused me to imagine compiling a bibliography of exactly 401 items focussing on Alice Munro and the culture of the region where I was born and still live that is known as "Souwesto" – the decision to include precisely 401 items representing a tip of the hat to work by two old London, Ontario-born boys like me: to the celebrated painting *401 Towards London, No. 1* by the late artist Jack Chambers and to the book *God's Big Acre: Life in 401 Country* by the late writer George Elliott, first editions of whose second, third, and fourth story collections, successors to his immortal *The Kissing Man*, I had the honour to publish with my small press here in Guelph, Red Kite Press.

Items that on initial inspection it may seem surprising to see cited here include the following. First, a group of foundational books of short story theory and criticism: H.E. Bates's *The Modern Short Story: A Critical Survey* (1941), Sean O'Faolain's *The Short Story* (1951), Frank O'Connor's *The Lonely Voice: A Study of the Short Story* (1963), F.C. Driessen's *Gogol as a Short-Story Writer: A Study of His Technique of Composition* (1965), Mary Rohrberger's *Hawthorne and the Modern Short Story: A Study in Genre* (1966), T.O. Beachcroft's *The Modest Art: A Survey of the Short Story in English* (1968), Ian Reid's *The Short Story* (1977), Walter Allen's *The Short Story in English* (1981), Helmut Bonheim's *The Narrative Modes: Techniques of the Short Story* (1982), Peter M. Bitsilli's *Chekhov's Art: A Stylistic Analysis* (1983), Susan Lohafer's *Coming to Terms with the Short Story* (1983), Clare Hanson's *Short Stories and Short Fictions, 1880-1980* (1985), W.H. New's *Dreams of Speech and Violence: The Art of the Short Story in Canada and New Zealand* (1987), Charles E. May's *Edgar Allan Poe: A Study of the Short Fiction* (1991), Charles E. May's *The Short Story: The Reality of Artifice* (1995), W.H. New's *Reading Mansfield and Metaphors of Form* (1999), Susan Lohafer's *Reading for Storyness: Preclosure Theory, Empirical Poetics, and Culture in the Short Story* (2003), Margot Norris's *Suspicious Readings of Joyce's Dubliners* (2003), Adrian Hunter's *The Cambridge Introduction to the Short Story in English* (2007), Paul March-Russell's *The Short Story: An Introduction* (2009), Michael Toolan's *Narrative Progression in the Short Story: A Corpus Stylistic Approach* (2009), Charles E. May's *"I Am Your Brother": Short Story Studies* (2013), Maria Löschnigg's *The Contemporary Canadian Short Story in English:*

Continuity and Change (2014), and, most recently, John Metcalf's critical masterpiece, his anatomy of criticism, *The Canadian Short Story* (2018).

Then, to broaden the scope of this list and to emphasize ways in which we are able to think more creatively even when preparing bibliographies, various illuminating texts on writing and reading such as Jack Hodgins' *A Passion for Narrative* (1993; rev. ed. 2001), Ursula K. Le Guin's *Steering the Craft* (1998; rev. ed. 2015), Francine Prose's *Reading Like a Writer* (2006), and Ailsa Cox's *Writing Short Stories* (2005; 2nd ed., 2016). Beyond these, if space permitted – it doesn't, but at least I can take a moment here to call your attention to these next titles – I would definitely enjoy adding the following uniquely imaginative and therefore profoundly delightful books: *Curiosity* (2015) by Alberto Manguel; *The Pleasures of Reading: A Booklover's Alphabet* (2014) by the distinguished Munro critic Catherine Sheldrick Ross; *The Topological Imagination: Spheres, Edges, and Islands* (2016) by Angus Fletcher, in part because I suspect that Alice Munro thinks of short stories as islands; *The Enamoured Knight* (2004), a study of Cervantes' *Don Quixote* and the nature of fiction by Souwesto-born fiction writer Douglas Glover; the eternally fresh essay cycle *Intentions* (1891), including both "The Decay of Lying" and "The Critic as Artist," by the writer whom Harold Bloom has called "the divine Oscar"; and, for pure fun, at the suggestion of my good-humoured friend Alec Follett, Umberto Eco's *The Infinity of Lists* (2009).

In the same spirit, I was tempted to add to the present selection another item of my own composition, or perhaps I should say of my own invention, "The Bibliographer as Artist," the lead piece in the new issue of *The Oscar Wilde Revue*, but I thought doing so might be pushing my luck. So here for your edification and I trust your enjoyment are the promised 401 items. You'll have to trust me about the number, I guess or else count them and maybe recount them for yourself.

***

Agee, James, and Walker Evans. *Let Us Now Praise Famous Men*. 1941.
    2nd ed. Boston: Houghton Mifflin, 1960.
Akenson, Donald Harman. *The Irish in Ontario: A Study in Rural History*.
    1984. 2nd ed. Montreal, QC and Kingston, ON: McGill-Queen's UP, 1999.

Allen, Walter. *The Short Story in English*. Oxford, Eng.: Clarendon, 1981.

Arbus, Diane. *Diane Arbus: An Aperture Monograph*. Ed. Doon Arbus and Marvin Israel. New York: Aperture, 1972. Fortieth-anniversary ed. New York: Aperture, 2011.

Atwood, Margaret. Introduction. *Carried Away: A Selection of Stories*. By Alice Munro. New York: Alfred A. Knopf, 2006. ix-xxi. Everyman's Library 302. Rpt. in *Alice Munro's Best: Selected Stories*. By Alice Munro. Toronto: McClelland & Stewart, 2008. vii-xviii.

---. "*Lives of Girls and Women*: A Portrait of the Artist as a Young Woman." *The Cambridge Companion to Alice Munro*. Ed. David Staines. Cambridge, Eng.: Cambridge UP, 2016. 96-115.

Avison, Margaret. *History of Ontario*. Illus. Selwyn Dewdney. Toronto: W.J. Gage, 1951.

Balestra, Gianfranca. "Alice Munro as Historian and Geographer: A Reading of 'Meneseteung'." *Intersections: la narrativa canadese tra storia e geografia*. Ed. Liana Nissim and Carlo Pagetti. Bologna, It.: Cisalpino, 1999. 119-36. Quaderni di Acme 38.

---. "Goat, Heifers, Wolves and Other Animals in Alice Munro's *Runaway*." La question animale dans les nouvelles d'Alice Munro / *The Animal Question in Alice Munro's Stories*. Ed. Héliane Ventura. *Caliban: French Journal of English Studies* 57 (2017): 123-38.

Balestra, Gianfranca, Laura Ferri, and Caterina Ricciardi, eds. *Reading Alice Munro in Italy*. Toronto: The Frank Iacobucci Centre for Italian Canadian Studies, 2008. Monograph Ser. 3.

Barlow, William. *Goderich: Link to the Past: An Illustrated Local History*. Ed. Barry J. Page. 2001. Goderich, ON: n.p., 2019.

Baskerville, Peter A. *Sites of Power: A Concise History of Ontario*. Don Mills, ON: Oxford UP, 2005.

Bates, H.E. *The Modern Short Story: A Critical Survey*. London: Thomas Nelson and Sons, 1941. Rpt. (rev.) as *The Modern Short Story: A Critical Survey*. London: Michael Joseph, 1972. Rpt. as *The Modern Short Story: From 1809 to 1953*. London: Robert Hale, 1988.

Beachcroft, T.O. *The Modest Art: A Survey of the Short Story in English*. London: Oxford UP, 1968.

Beecroft, Margaret S. *Windings: A History of the Lower Maitland River*. Wroxeter, ON: Maitland Valley Conservation Foundation, 1984.

Bentley, D.M.R. "The Short Stories of Alice Laidlaw, 1950-51." *Alice Munro's Miraculous Art: Critical Essays.* Ed. Janice Fiamengo and Gerald Lynch. Ottawa: U of Ottawa P, 2017. 137-57. Reappraisals: Canadian Writers 38.

Besner, Neil K. "The Bodies of the Texts in *Lives of Girls and Women*: Del Jordan's Reading." *Multiple Voices: Recent Canadian Fiction.* Ed. Jeanne Delbaere. Sydney, Austral.: Dangaroo, 1990. 131-44.

---. *Introducing Alice Munro's* Lives of Girls and Women: *A Reader's Guide.* Toronto: ECW, 1990. Canadian Fiction Studies 8. Rpt. (excerpted) as "Remembering 'Every Last Thing': Alice Munro's Epilogue to *Lives of Girls and Women*" in *Alice Munro Everlasting: Essays on Her Works II.* Ed. J.R. (Tim) Struthers. Toronto: Guernica Editions, 2020. Essential Writers Ser. 52.

Bigot, Corinne. "Alice Munro: A Bibliography." *The Short Stories of Alice Munro.* Ed. Héliane Ventura. *Journal of the Short Story in English / Les cahiers de la nouvelle* 55 (2010): 189-214.

---. *Alice Munro: Les silences de la nouvelle.* Rennes, Fr.: Presses Universitaires de Rennes, 2014. Collection ‹‹Interférences››.

---. "Alice Munro's 'Silence': From the Politics of Silence to the Rhetoric of Silence." *The Short Stories of Alice Munro.* Ed. Héliane Ventura. *Journal of the Short Story in English / Les cahiers de la nouvelle* 55 (2010): 123-38.

---. "'And Now Another Story Surfaced': Re-Emerging Voices, Stories and Secrets in Alice Munro's 'Family Furnishings'." *Resurgence.* Ed. Christine Lorre. *Commonwealth Essays and Studies* 31.1 (2008): 28-35.

---. "Discontinuity, Disjointedness: Parenthetical Structures and Dashes in Alice Munro's Stories from *Dance of the Happy Shades*." *Stylistic Perspectives on Alice Munro's* Dance of the Happy Shades. Ed. Manuel Jobert and Michael Toolan. *Études de Stylistique Anglais* 8 (2015): 17-35.

---. "Forsaken Objects, Haunted Houses, Female Bodies, and 'the squalor of tragedy in ordinary life': Reading *Dance of the Happy Shades* with Later Stories." *Alice Munro: Writing for Dear Life.* Ed. Corinne Bigot. *Commonwealth Essays and Studies* 37.2 (2015): 15-25.

---. "Fur and Sublime: Becoming Animal, Becoming Child in 'Face' and 'Child's Play' by Alice Munro." La question animale dans les nouvelles d'Alice Munro / *The Animal Question in Alice Munro's Stories.* Ed. Héliane Ventura. *Caliban: French Journal of English Studies* 57 (2017): 21-35.

---. "Ghost Texts, Patterns of Entrapment, and Lines of Flight: Reading Stories from *Too Much Happiness* and *Dear Life* in Connection with Earlier Stories." *Alice Munro: Reminiscence, Interpretation, Adaptation and Comparison.* Ed. Mirosława Buchholtz and Eugenia Sojka. Frankfurt am Main, Ger.: Peter Lang, 2015. 59-73. Dis/Continuities: Toruń Studies in Language, Literature and Culture 8.

---. "'Locking the Door': Self-Deception, Silence and Survival in Alice Munro's 'Vandals'." *Trauma Narratives and Herstory.* Ed. Sonya Andermahr and Silvia Pellicer-Ortín. New York: Palgrave Macmillan, 2013. 113-26.

---. "Mapping the Vernacular Landscape in Alice Munro's 'What Do You Want To Know For?' and Other Stories." *Space and Place in Alice Munro's Fiction: "A Book with Maps in It".* Ed. Christine Lorre-Johnston and Eleonora Rao. Rochester, NY: Camden House, 2018. 63-81.

---. "Patterns of Entrapment and Lines of Flight in Alice Munro's 'Thanks for the Ride' and 'The Shining Houses'." *The Inside of a Shell: Alice Munro's* Dance of the Happy Shades. Ed. Vanessa Guignery. Newcastle upon Tyne, Eng.: Cambridge Scholars, 2015. 130-43.

---. "The Wonders of the Transatlantic Journey: Alice Munro's 'The View from Castle Rock'." *Crossings.* Ed. Françoise Karal. *Commonwealth Essays and Studies* 37.1 (2014): 25-34.

Bigot, Corinne, ed. *Alice Munro: Writing for Dear Life. Commonwealth Essays and Studies* 37.2 (2015): 1-104.

Bigot, Corinne, and Catherine Lanone. *Sunlight and Shadows, Past and Present: Alice Munro's* Dance of the Happy Shades. Paris: Presses Universitaires de France – Cned, 2014. Série Anglais.

Bigot, Corinne, and Catherine Lanone, eds. *"With a Roar from Underground": Alice Munro's* Dance of the Happy Shades. Paris: Presses Universitaires de Paris Ouest, 2015.

Bitsilli, Peter M. *Chekhov's Art: A Stylistic Analysis.* Trans. Toby W. Clyman and Edwina Jannie Cruise. Ann Arbor, MI: Ardis, 1983.

Blodgett, E.D. *Alice Munro.* Boston: Twayne-G.K. Hall, 1988. Twayne's World Authors Ser. 800.

---. "Once Upon a Time: Temporality in the Narration of Alice Munro." *Alice Munro's Miraculous Art: Critical Essays.* Ed. Janice Fiamengo and Gerald Lynch. Ottawa: U of Ottawa P, 2017. 271-85. Reappraisals: Canadian Writers 38.

Bloom, Harold, ed. and introd. *Alice Munro*. New York: Bloom's Literary Criticism-Infobase, 2009. Bloom's Modern Critical Views.

Blumenson, John. *Ontario Architecture: A Guide to Styles and Building Terms 1784 to the Present*. Toronto: Fitzhenry & Whiteside, 1990.

Bonheim, Helmut. *The Narrative Modes: Techniques of the Short Story*. Cambridge, Eng.: D.S. Brewer, 1982.

Bothwell, Robert. *A Short History of Ontario*. Edmonton, AB: Hurtig, 1986.

Botta, Giuseppina. "Searching for Lake Huron: Songs, Journeys and Secrets in 'Walker Brothers Cowboy'." *Stylistic Perspectives on Alice Munro's* Dance of the Happy Shades. Ed. Manuel Jobert and Michael Toolan. *Études de Stylistique Anglais* 8 (2015): 57-69.

Boyanoski, Christine. *Sympathetic Realism: George A. Reid and the Academic Tradition*. Toronto: Art Gallery of Ontario, 1986.

Boyle, Harry J. *Memories of a Catholic Boyhood*. Toronto: Doubleday Canada, 1973.

Brand, Dionne. *No Burden To Carry: Narratives of Black Working Women in Ontario 1920s-1950s*. Toronto: Women's, 1991.

Brown, Vanessa, and Jason Dickson. *London: 150 Cultural Moments*. Windsor, ON: Biblioasis, 2017.

Buchholtz, Mirosława. "Alice Munro's Legacy: The 'Finale' of *Dear Life*." *Alice Munro: Writing for Dear Life*. Ed. Corinne Bigot. *Commonwealth Essays and Studies* 37.2 (2015): 69-77.

---. "Pseudo-Longinus and the Affective Theory in Alice Munro's Stories about Childhood." *Alice Munro: Writing Secrets*. Ed. Héliane Ventura and Mary Condé. *Open Letter* 11th ser., no. 9 - 12th ser., no. 1 (2003-04): 89-102.

Buchholtz, Mirosława, ed. *Alice Munro: Understanding, Adapting and Teaching*. Basel, Switz.: Springer International, 2016. Issues in Literature and Culture.

Buchholtz, Mirosława, and Eugenia Sojka, eds. *Alice Munro: Reminiscence, Interpretation, Adaptation and Comparison*. Frankfurt am Main, Ger.: Peter Lang, 2015. Dis/Continuities: Toruń Studies in Language, Literature and Culture 8.

Butt, William. "Killer OSPs and Style Munro in 'Open Secrets'." *Alice Munro: A Souwesto Celebration*. Ed. J.R. (Tim) Struthers and John B. Lee. *The Windsor Review* 47.2 (2014): 94-100. Rpt. (rev.) in *Alice Munro Country: Essays on Her Works I*. Ed. J.R. (Tim) Struthers. Toronto: Guernica Editions, 2020. Essential Writers Ser. 51.

---. "Messengers and Messaging in Alice Munro's *The View from Castle Rock*." *Alice Munro Everlasting: Essays on Her Works II*. Ed. J.R. (Tim) Struthers. Toronto: Guernica Editions, 2020. Essential Writers Ser. 52.

---. "Southwestern Ontario, the Narrator, and 'Words with Power' in Alice Munro's 'Meneseteung'." *Alice Munro and the Souwesto Story*. Ed. J.R. (Tim) Struthers. *Short Story* ns 21.1 (2013 [2015]): 13-43.

Byers, Mary, and Margaret McBurney. *The Governor's Road: Early Buildings and Families from Mississauga to London*. Photographs by Hugh Robertson. Toronto: U of Toronto P, 1982.

Cameron, Mary Lou, et al. *One Hundred Years of Memories: A Commemorative Book for Wingham Centennial 1879-1979*. Wingham, ON: The Centennial Book Committee, 1979.

Carrington, Ildikó de Papp. *Controlling the Uncontrollable: The Fiction of Alice Munro*. DeKalb, IL: Northern Illinois UP, 1989.

---. "'Don't Tell (on) Daddy': Narrative Complexity in Alice Munro's 'The Love of a Good Woman'." *Studies in Short Fiction* 34 (1997): 159-70.

---. "Double-Talking Devils: Alice Munro's 'A Wilderness Station'." *Essays on Canadian Writing* 58 (1996): 71-92.

---. "Other Rooms, Other Texts, Other Selves: Alice Munro's 'Sunday Afternoon' and 'Hired Girl'." *Journal of the Short Story in English / Les cahiers de la nouvelle* 30 (1998): 33-43.

---. "What's in a Title?: Alice Munro's 'Carried Away'." *Studies in Short Fiction* 30 (1993): 555-64.

---. "Where Are You, Mother?: Alice Munro's 'Save the Reaper'." *Canadian Literature* 173 (2002): 34-51.

Carroll, Jock. *The Farm*. Photographs by Reuben Sallows and John de Visser. Toronto: Methuen, 1984.

Carscallen, James. *The Other Country: Patterns in the Writing of Alice Munro*. Toronto: ECW, 1993.

Chapman, L.J., and D.F. Putnam. *The Physiography of Southern Ontario*. 1951. 3rd ed. Toronto: Ontario Ministry of Natural Resources, 1984.

Charman, Caitlin. "'Secretly Devoted to Nature': Place Sense in Alice Munro's *The View from Castle Rock*." *Critical Insights: Alice Munro*. Ed. Charles E. May. Ipswich, MA: Salem-EBSCO, 2013. 259-75.

Clarke, George Elliott. "Alice Munro's Black Bottom; or Black Tints and Euro Hints in *Lives of Girls and Women*." *Alice Munro: Reminiscence, Interpretation, Adaptation and Comparison*. Ed. Mirosława Buchholtz and Eugenia Sojka. Frankfurt am Main, Ger.: Peter Lang, 2015. 147-71. Dis/Continuities: Toruń Studies in Language, Literature and Culture 8. Rpt. in *Alice Munro Country: Essays on Her Works I*. Ed. J.R. (Tim) Struthers. Toronto: Guernica Editions, 2020. Essential Writers Ser. 51.

Condé, Mary. "Clothes in *Dance of the Happy Shades*." *"With a Roar from Underground": Alice Munro's* Dance of the Happy Shades. Ed. Corinne Bigot and Catherine Lanone. Paris: Presses Universitaires de Paris Ouest, 2015. 109-16.

---. "Coded Language in 'Runaway'." *Alice Munro: Writing Secrets*. Ed. Héliane Ventura and Mary Condé. *Open Letter* 11th ser., no. 9 - 12th ser., no. 1 (2003-04): 177-83.

---. "'True Lies': Photographs in the Short Stories of Alice Munro." *Études Canadiennes / Canadian Studies* 32 (1992): 97-110.

Cox, Ailsa. "'Age Could Be Her Ally': Late Style in Alice Munro's *Too Much Happiness*." *Critical Insights: Alice Munro*. Ed. Charles E. May. Ipswich, MA: Salem-EBSCO, 2013. 276-90.

---. *Alice Munro*. Tavistock, Eng.: Northcote, 2004. Writers and Their Work.

---. "'Almost Like a Ghost': Spectral Figures in Alice Munro's Short Fiction." *Liminality and the Short Story: Boundary Crossings in American, Canadian, and British Writing*. Ed. Jochen Achilles and Ina Bergmann. New York: Routledge, 2015. 238-50. Routledge Interdisciplinary Perspectives on Literature 34.

---. "'Bizarre but Somehow Never Quite Satisfactory': Storytelling in 'The Office'." *Stylistic Perspectives on Alice Munro's* Dance of the Happy Shades. Ed. Manuel Jobert and Michael Toolan. *Études de Stylistique Anglais* 8 (2015): 135-48. Rpt. (rev.) as "'The Office'" in "Chapter Seven: The Artist and Society" in *The Mind's Eye: Alice Munro's* Dance of the Happy Shades. By Ailsa Cox and Christine Lorre-Johnston. Paris: Éditions Fahrenheit, 2015. 177-89.

---. "'The Emptiness in Place of Her': Space, Absence, and Memory in Alice Munro's *Dear Life*." *Space and Place in Alice Munro's Fiction: "A Book with Maps in It"*. Ed. Christine Lorre-Johnston and Eleonora Rao. Rochester, NY: Camden House, 2018. 119-32.

---. "'First and Last': The Figure of the Infant in 'Dear Life' and 'My Mother's Dream'." *Alice Munro's Miraculous Art: Critical Essays*. Ed. Janice Fiamengo and Gerald Lynch. Ottawa: U of Ottawa P, 2017. 177-90. Reappraisals: Canadian Writers 38.

---. "Looking Back with Alice Munro." *"With a Roar from Underground":
Alice Munro's* Dance of the Happy Shades. Ed. Corinne Bigot and Catherine Lanone. Paris: Presses Universitaires de Paris Ouest, 2015. 55-64.

---. "'Rage and Admiration': Grotesque Humor in *Dear Life*." *Alice Munro:
Hateship, Friendship, Courtship, Loveship, Marriage; Runaway; Dear
Life*. Ed. Robert Thacker. London: Bloomsbury, 2016. 184-202, 229,
231-44 passim.

---. "Thoughts from England: On Reading, Teaching, and Writing Back
to Alice Munro's 'Meneseteung'." *Alice Munro Country: Essays on Her
Works I*. Ed. J.R. (Tim) Struthers. Toronto: Guernica Editions, 2020.
Essential Writers Ser. 51.

---. *Writing Short Stories: A Routledge Writer's Guide*. 2005. 2nd ed. London: Routledge, 2016.

Cox, Ailsa, ed. *Teaching the Short Story*. New York: Palgrave Macmillan, 2011.

Cox, Ailsa, and Christine Lorre-Johnston. *The Mind's Eye: Alice Munro's*
Dance of the Happy Shades. Paris: Éditions Fahrenheit, 2015.

Creighton, David. "In Search of Alice Munro: Finding Out Where Fact
and Fiction Combine To Create 'Munrovia'." *Books in Canada* May
1994: 19-25.

Dahms, Fred. *Wandering the West Coast of Ontario: Towns, Ports and
Beaches Along the Huron Shore: Southampton, Pt. Elgin, Kincardine,
Goderich, Bayfield, Grand Bend*. Guelph, ON: n.p., 2018.

DeFalco, Amelia, and Lorraine York, eds. *Ethics and Affects in the Fiction
of Alice Munro*. Cham, Switz.: Palgrave Macmillan, 2018. Palgrave
Studies in Affect Theory and Literary Criticism.

Driessen, F.C. *Gogol as a Short-Story Writer: A Study of His Technique of
Composition*. Trans. Ian F. Finlay. The Hague, Neth.: Mouton, 1965.
Slavistic Printings and Reprintings 57.

Duffy, Dennis. "Alice Munro's Narrative Historicism: 'Too Much Hap-
piness'." *The Genius of Alice Munro*. Ed. Robert Thacker. *American
Review of Canadian Studies* 45 (2015): 196-207. Rpt. in *Alice Munro
Everlasting: Essays on Her Works II*. Ed. J.R. (Tim) Struthers. Toronto:
Guernica Editions, 2020. Essential Writers Ser. 52.

---. "'A Dark Sort of Mirror': 'The Love of a Good Woman' as Pauline Poetic."
Alice Munro Writing On.... Ed. Robert Thacker. *Essays on Canadian
Writing* 66 (1998): 169-90. Rpt. in *The Rest of the Story: Critical Essays
on Alice Munro*. Ed. Robert Thacker. Toronto: ECW, 1999. 169-90.

---. "Too Little Geography; Too Much History: Writing the Balance in 'Meneseteung'." *National Plots: Historical Fiction and Changing Ideas of Canada*. Ed. Andrea Cabajsky and Brett Josef Grubisic. Waterloo, ON: Wilfrid Laurier UP, 2010. 197-213, 215-36 passim. Rpt. as "Too Little Geography; Too Much History: Writing the Balance in Alice Munro" in *Alice Munro Country: Essays on Her Works I*. Ed. J.R. (Tim) Struthers. Toronto: Guernica Editions, 2020. Essential Writers Ser. 51.

Duncan, Isla. *Alice Munro's Narrative Art*. New York: Palgrave Macmillan, 2011.

---. "'A Cavity Everywhere': The Postponement of Knowing in 'Corrie'." *Alice Munro: Writing for Dear Life*. Ed. Corinne Bigot. *Commonwealth Essays and Studies* 37.2 (2015): 57-67.

Dutoit, Thomas. "Boring Gravel: Literary Earth, Alice Munro's Ontario Geolithic." [*Alice Munro's Short Fiction Writing*.] Ed. Françoise Le Jeune. *Études Canadiennes / Canadian Studies* 77 (2014): 77-109.

---. "'In Lovely Blue': Seeing Outside 'The Shining Houses'." *"With a Roar from Underground": Alice Munro's* Dance of the Happy Shades. Ed. Corinne Bigot and Catherine Lanone. Paris: Presses Universitaires de Paris Ouest, 2015. 145-64.

Duval, Paul. *High Realism in Canada*. Toronto: Clarke, Irwin, 1974.

Dvořák, Marta. "Alice Munro's 'Lovely Tricks' from *Dance of the Happy Shades* to *Hateship, Friendship, Courtship, Loveship, Marriage*." *Alice Munro: Writing Secrets*. Ed. Héliane Ventura and Mary Condé. *Open Letter* 11th ser., no. 9 - 12th ser., no. 1 (2003-04): 55-77.

---. "The Other Side of Dailiness: Alice Munro's Melding of Realism and Romance in *Dance of the Happy Shades*." *Études anglaises* 67 (2014): 302-17.

Elliott, George. *God's Big Acre: Life in 401 Country*. Photographs by John Reeves. Toronto: Methuen, 1986.

English, John, and Kenneth McLaughlin. *Kitchener: An Illustrated History*. Waterloo, ON: Wilfrid Laurier UP, 1983.

Faflak, Joel, and Sky Glabush, eds. *(Re)imagining Regionalism*. London, ON: McIntosh Gallery Curatorial Study Centre, 2014.

Fiamengo, Janice. "Encountering 'Blocks of Solid Darkness' in Alice Munro's 'Vandals'." *Alice Munro Everlasting: Essays on Her Works II*. Ed. J.R. (Tim) Struthers. Toronto: Guernica Editions, 2020. Essential Writers Ser. 52.

Fiamengo, Janice, and Gerald Lynch, eds. *Alice Munro's Miraculous Art: Critical Essays*. Ottawa: U of Ottawa P, 2017. Reappraisals: Canadian Writers 38.

Follett, Alec. "'The Region That I Know': The Bioregional View in Alice Munro's *The View from Castle Rock*." *Alice Munro Country: Essays on Her Works I*. Ed. J.R. (Tim) Struthers. Toronto: Guernica Editions, 2020. Essential Writers Ser. 51.

Foran, Charles. "Alice in Borderland: A Trip through Munro Country, Where the Writer Became Herself, and History and Memory Often Blur." Photographs by Christopher Wahl. *The Walrus* 6.7 (2009): 40-46.

Forceville, Charles. "Alice Munro's Layered Structures." *Shades of Empire in Colonial and Post-Colonial Literatures*. Ed. C.C. Barfoot and Theo D'haen. Amsterdam-Atlanta: Rodopi, 1993. 301-10.

---. "Language, Time and Reality: The Stories of Alice Munro." *External and Detached: Dutch Essays on Contemporary Canadian Literature*. Ed. Charles Forceville, August J. Fry, and Peter J. de Voogd. Amsterdam: Free UP, 1988. 37-44. Canada Cahiers 4.

Fowke, Edith. *Traditional Singers and Songs from Ontario*. Collected and ed. Edith Fowke. Musical Transcriptions by Peggy Seeger. Illus. Katherine Boykowycz. Don Mills, ON: Burns & MacEachern, 1965.

Francesconi, Sabrina. "Alice Munro and the Poetics of the Linoleum." *The Inside of a Shell: Alice Munro's* Dance of the Happy Shades. Ed. Vanessa Guignery. Newcastle upon Tyne, Eng.: Cambridge Scholars, 2015. 86-97.

---. "Alice Munro as the Master of Storytelling." *Alice Munro and the Anatomy of the Short Story*. Ed. Oriana Palusci. Newcastle upon Tyne, Eng.: Cambridge Scholars, 2017. 45-57.

---. *Alice Munro, il piacere di raccontare*. Rome: Carocci, 2015. Lingue e letterature Carocci 207.

---. "Barking (with) Dogs: The Grammar System of Transitivity in Munro's 'Save the Reaper' and 'Floating Bridge'." La question animale dans les nouvelles d'Alice Munro / *The Animal Question in Alice Munro's Stories*. Ed. Héliane Ventura. *Caliban: French Journal of English Studies* 57 (2017): 69-84.

---. "Dance of the Senses in 'Red Dress – 1946'." *"With a Roar from Underground": Alice Munro's* Dance of the Happy Shades. Ed. Corinne Bigot and Catherine Lanone. Paris: Presses Universitaires de Paris Ouest, 2015. 97-107.

---. "I and the Village: Locating Home and Self in Alice Munro's 'Soon'." *Reading Alice Munro in Italy*. Ed. Gianfranca Balestra, Laura Ferri, and Caterina Ricciardi. Toronto: The Frank Iacobucci Centre for Italian Canadian Studies, 2008. 71-81. Monograph Ser. 3.

---. "Memory and Desire in Alice Munro's Stories." *Memory and Desire: The Impossibility of the Archive and the Imperative To Remember*. Ed. Carla Locatelli and Ewa Ziarek. *Textus* 22 (2009): 341-59.

---. "Negotiation of Naming in Alice Munro's 'Meneseteung'." *The Short Stories of Alice Munro*. Ed. Héliane Ventura. *Journal of the Short Story in English / Les cahiers de la nouvelle* 55 (2010): 109-22.

---. "'Remember' in 'The Stone in the Field' by Alice Munro: A Qualitative and Quantitative Analysis." *Traduttrici: Female Voices Across Languages*. Ed. Oriana Palusci. Trento, It.: Tangram Edizioni Scientifiche, 2011. 161-73. Intersezioni/Intersections Collana di anglistica 4.

---. "Writing Secrets as 'Betraying the Past' in Alice Munro's 'What Is Remembered'." *Alice Munro: Writing Secrets*. Ed. Héliane Ventura and Mary Condé. *Open Letter* 11th ser., no. 9 - 12th ser., no. 1 (2003-04): 243-53.

Frazer, Sir James G. *The Golden Bough: A Study in Magic and Religion*. Abridged ed. New York: Macmillan, 1951.

Fremlin, Gerald, with Arthur H. Robinson. 2001. *Maps as Mediated Seeing: Fundamentals of Cartography*. Rev. ed. Victoria: Trafford, 2005.

Freud, Sigmund. *The Interpretation of Dreams*. 1900. Trans. James Strachey. Ed. Angela Richards. London: Penguin, 1991. Vol. 4 of *The Penguin Freud Library*. 15 vols. 1990-93.

Frye, Northrop. "Culture and Society in Ontario, 1784-1984." *On Education*. Markham, ON: Fitzhenry & Whiteside, 1988. 168-82. Rpt. in *Northrop Frye on Canada*. By Northrop Frye. Ed. Jean O'Grady and David Staines. Toronto: U of Toronto P, 2003. 614-28. Vol. 12 of *Collected Works of Northrop Frye*. 30 vols. 1996-2012.

Frye, Northrop, and Jay Macpherson. *Biblical and Classical Myths: The Mythological Framework of Western Culture*. Toronto: U of Toronto P, 2004.

Galbraith, John Kenneth. *The Scotch*. Illus. Samuel H. Bryant. Toronto: The Macmillan Company of Canada, 1964.

Gervais, Marty. *My Town: Faces of Windsor*. Windsor, ON: Biblioasis, 2006.

Gibson, Douglas. "Alice Munro: Not Bad Short Story Writer." *Stories about Storytellers: Publishing Alice Munro, Robertson Davies, Alistair MacLeod, Pierre Trudeau, and Others.* Illus. Anthony Jenkins. Toronto: ECW, 2011. 343-62. Rpt. (rev.) in *Stories about Storytellers: Publishing W.O. Mitchell, Mavis Gallant, Robertson Davies, Alice Munro, Pierre Trudeau, Hugh MacLennan, Barry Broadfoot, Jack Hodgins, Peter C. Newman, Brian Mulroney, Terry Fallis, Morley Callaghan, Alistair MacLeod, and Many More....* Illus. Anthony Jenkins. Toronto: ECW, 2014. 354-76. Rpt. (rev.) in *Alice Munro Country: Essays on Her Works I.* Ed. J.R. (Tim) Struthers. Toronto: Guernica Editions, 2020. Essential Writers Ser. 51.

---. "Alice Munro Country." *Across Canada by Story: A Coast-to-Coast Literary Adventure.* Illus. Anthony Jenkins. Toronto: ECW, 2015. 143-64.

Gillians, Dave. *For the Love of Bayfield: The Events and Special People Who Shaped This Village.* 2nd ed. Bayfield, ON: Bayfield Historical Society, 2012.

Gittings, Christopher E. "Constructing a Scots-Canadian Ground: Family History and Cultural Translation in Alice Munro." *Studies in Short Fiction* 34 (1997): 27-37.

Glazebrook, G.P. deT. *Life in Ontario: A Social History.* Illus. Adrian Dingle. Toronto: U of Toronto P, 1968.

Glover, Douglas. "Alice Munro's 'Meneseteung' – How To Read It (with Diagrams)." *Numero Cinq* 9 Oct. 2012. <numerocinqmagazine.com/2012/10/09/alice-munros-meneseteung-how-to-read-it-with-diagrams>.

---. "The Mind of Alice Munro." *CNQ: Canadian Notes and Queries* 79 (2010): 30-37. Rpt. in *Attack of the Copula Spiders and Other Essays on Writing.* By Douglas Glover. Windsor, ON: Biblioasis, 2012. 83-104.

---. "The Style of Alice Munro." *The Cambridge Companion to Alice Munro.* Ed. David Staines. Cambridge, Eng.: Cambridge UP, 2016. 45-59. Rpt. in *The Erotics of Restraint: Essays on Literary Form.* By Douglas Glover. Windsor, ON: Biblioasis, 2019. 1-22.

Grafe, Adrian. "The Unreal Material." *"With a Roar from Underground": Alice Munro's* Dance of the Happy Shades. Ed. Corinne Bigot and Catherine Lanone. Paris: Presses Universitaires de Paris Ouest, 2015. 165-76.

Graves, Robert. *The White Goddess: A Historical Grammar of Poetic Myth.* Amended and enlarged ed. New York: Farrar, Straus & Giroux, 1966.

Grimm, Jacob, and Wilhelm Grimm. *The Complete Grimm's Fairy Tales.* Trans. Margaret Hunt. Rev. James Stern. Introd. Padraic Colum. Folkloristic Commentary by Joseph Campbell. Illus. Josef Scharl. New York: Pantheon, 1972.

Guignery, Vanessa. "Introduction: The Balance of Opposites in Alice Munro's *Dance of the Happy Shades.*" *The Inside of a Shell: Alice Munro's* Dance of the Happy Shades. Ed. Vanessa Guignery. Newcastle upon Tyne, Eng.: Cambridge Scholars, 2015. 1-24.

---. "'Where Is the Voice Coming From?': A Question of Origins in Alice Munro's *Dance of the Happy Shades.*" *"With a Roar from Underground": Alice Munro's* Dance of the Happy Shades. Ed. Corinne Bigot and Catherine Lanone. Paris: Presses Universitaires de Paris Ouest, 2015. 19-33.

Guignery, Vanessa, ed. *The Inside of a Shell: Alice Munro's* Dance of the Happy Shades. Newcastle upon Tyne, Eng.: Cambridge Scholars, 2015.

Guth, Gwendolyn. "Class Act?: Status, Disability, and Tolerance in Alice Munro's 'Dance of the Happy Shades'." *Alice Munro Everlasting: Essays on Her Works II.* Ed. J.R. (Tim) Struthers. Toronto: Guernica Editions, 2020. Essential Writers Ser. 52.

Hanson, Clare. *Short Stories and Short Fictions, 1880-1980.* London: Macmillan, 1985. Macmillan Studies in Twentieth-Century Literature.

Heble, Ajay. *The Tumble of Reason: Alice Munro's Discourse of Absence.* Toronto: U of Toronto P, 1994.

Hill, Nicholas. *Historic Streetscapes of Huron County.* Illus. Nicholas Hill. Goderich, ON: n.p., 1981.

Hodgins, Jack. "Looking, Imagining." *Alice Munro Country: Essays on Her Works I.* Ed. J.R. (Tim) Struthers. Toronto: Guernica Editions, 2020. Essential Writers Ser. 51.

---. *A Passion for Narrative: A Guide for Writing Fiction.* 1993. Rev. ed. Toronto: McClelland & Stewart, 2001.

The Holy Bible. Cambridge, Eng.: Cambridge UP, n.d. Authorized King James Vers.

Hopper, Edward. *The Complete Oil Paintings by Edward Hopper.* Commentary by Gail Levin. New York: W.W. Norton, 2000.

Houle, Karen. "Ending Things Well: Alice Munro's 'White Dump'." *Alice Munro Everlasting: Essays on Her Works II.* Ed. J.R. (Tim) Struthers. Toronto: Guernica Editions, 2020. Essential Writers Ser. 52.

Houston, Pam. "A Hopeful Sign: The Making of Metonymic Meaning in Munro's 'Meneseteung'." *The Kenyon Review* ns 14.4 (1992): 79-92.

Howells, Coral Ann. *Alice Munro*. Manchester, Eng.: Manchester UP, 1998. Contemporary World Writers.

---. "Alice Munro and Her Life Writing." *The Cambridge Companion to Alice Munro*. Ed. David Staines. Cambridge, Eng.: Cambridge UP, 2016. 79-95.

---. "Alice Munro's Heritage Narratives." *Where Are the Voices Coming From?: Canadian Culture and the Legacies of History*. Ed. Coral Ann Howells. Amsterdam-New York: Rodopi, 2004. 5-14. Cross/Cultures: Readings in the Post/Colonial Literatures in English 73.

---. "Intimate Dislocations: Alice Munro, *Hateship, Friendship, Courtship, Loveship, Marriage*." *Contemporary Canadian Women's Fiction: Refiguring Identities*. By Coral Ann Howells. New York: Palgrave Macmillan, 2003. 53-78, 210-12. Rpt. in *Alice Munro*. Ed. and introd. Harold Bloom. New York: Bloom's Literary Criticism-Infobase, 2009. 167-92. Bloom's Modern Critical Views.

---. "Intimate Dislocations: Buried History and Geography in Alice Munro's So[u]westo Stories." *Dislocations: Changing Conceptions of Space and Time*. Ed. Danielle Fuller. *British Journal of Canadian Studies* 14 (1999): 7-16. Rpt. as "Intimate Dislocations: Buried History and Geography in Alice Munro's Souwesto Stories" in *Alice Munro Country: Essays on Her Works I*. Ed. J.R. (Tim) Struthers. Toronto: Guernica Editions, 2020. Essential Writers Ser. 51.

---. "The Telling of Secrets / The Secrets of Telling: An Overview of Alice Munro's Enigma Variations from *Dance of the Happy Shades* to *Hateship, Friendship, Courtship, Loveship, Marriage*." *Alice Munro: Writing Secrets*. Ed. Héliane Ventura and Mary Condé. *Open Letter* 11th ser., no. 9 - 12th ser., no. 1 (2003-04): 39-54.

Hoy, Helen. "Alice Munro: 'Unforgettable, Indigestible Messages'." *Journal of Canadian Studies / Revue d'études canadiennes* 26.1 (1991): 5-21.

---. "'Dull, Simple, Amazing, and Unfathomable': Paradox and Double Vision in Alice Munro's Fiction." *Studies in Canadian Literature* 5 (1980): 100-15.

---. "'Rose and Janet': Alice Munro's Metafiction." *Canadian Literature* 121 (1989): 59-83.

Hulan, Shelley. "Not for Entertainment Purposes Only: Ethnicity and Alice Munro's 'Powers'." *Alice Munro Country: Essays on Her Works I*. Ed. J.R. (Tim) Struthers. Toronto: Guernica Editions, 2020. Essential Writers Ser. 51.

---. "Yours To Recover: Mound Burial in Alice Munro's 'What Do You Want To Know For?'." *Canadian Literature and Cultural Memory*. Ed. Cynthia Sugars and Eleanor Ty. Toronto: Oxford UP, 2014. 260-73, 445-74 passim.

Hunter, Adrian. *The Cambridge Introduction to the Short Story in English*. Cambridge, Eng.: Cambridge UP, 2007. Cambridge Introductions to Literature.

---. "Story into History: Alice Munro's Minor Literature." *English: Journal of the English Association* 53 (2004): 219-38. Rpt. (rev. and abridged) as "Alice Munro" in *The Cambridge Introduction to the Short Story in English*. By Adrian Hunter. Cambridge, Eng.: Cambridge UP, 2007. 165-76, 187. Cambridge Introductions to Literature.

---. "Taking Possession: Alice Munro's 'A Wilderness Station' and James Hogg's *Justified Sinner*." *Studies in Canadian Literature / Études en littérature canadienne* 35.2 (2010): 114-28.

Hurley, Michael. "The Shadow Cast by Southern Ontario Gothic." *The Borders of Nightmare: The Fiction of John Richardson*. Toronto: U of Toronto P, 1992. 156-201, 219-24.

Illustrated Historical Atlas of the County of Huron Ont. Toronto: H. Belden, 1879. Offset ed. Owen Sound, ON: Richardson, Bond & Wright, 1972. Reprint ed. Rev. Goderich, ON: Huron Branch, Ontario Genealogical Society, 1996.

Jamieson, Sara. "Ethics and Infant Feeding in Alice Munro's Stories." *Ethics and Affects in the Fiction of Alice Munro*. Ed. Amelia DeFalco and Lorraine York. Cham, Switz.: Palgrave Macmillan, 2018. 13-33. Palgrave Studies in Affect Theory and Literary Criticism.

---. "The Fiction of Agelessness: Work, Leisure, and Aging in Alice Munro's 'Pictures of the Ice'." *Studies in Canadian Literature / Études en littérature canadienne* 29.1 (2004): 106-26.

---. "'The Stuff They Put in the Old Readers': Remembered and Recited Poetry in the Stories of Alice Munro." *Alice Munro's Miraculous Art: Critical Essays*. Ed. Janice Fiamengo and Gerald Lynch. Ottawa: U of Ottawa P, 2017. 79-95. Reappraisals: Canadian Writers 38.

Jernigan, Kim. "Narrative Hauntings in Alice Munro's 'Meneseteung'." *Alice Munro and the Souwesto Story*. Ed. J.R. (Tim) Struthers. *Short Story* ns 21.1 (2013 [2015]): 44-69.

Jobert, Manuel, and Michael Toolan, eds. *Stylistic Perspectives on Alice Munro's* Dance of the Happy Shades. *Études de Stylistique Anglais* 8 (2015): 3-242.

Johnston, Basil H. *Think Indian: Languages Are Beyond Price.* Cape Croker
Reserve, Wiarton, ON: Kegedonce, 2011.

Jones, Robert Leslie. *History of Agriculture in Ontario 1613-1880.* Toronto:
U of Toronto P, 1946.

Keith, W.J. "Alice Munro." *A Sense of Style: Studies in the Art of Fiction in
English-Speaking Canada.* Toronto: ECW, 1989. 155-74.

---. *Literary Images of Ontario.* Toronto: U of Toronto P, 1992. Ontario
Historical Studies Ser.

Klinck, Carl F., sel. and ed. *William "Tiger" Dunlop: "Backwoodian
Backwoodsman": Essays by and about Dunlop.* Toronto: Ryerson, 1958.

Knelman, Martin. "The Past, the Present, and Alice Munro." *Saturday
Night* Nov. 1979: 16-18, 20, 22.

Laidlaw, Robert. *The McGregors: A Novel of an Ontario Pioneer Family.*
Toronto: Macmillan of Canada, 1979.

Landon, Fred. *Lake Huron.* Indianapolis: Bobbs-Merrill, 1944. The American Lakes Ser.

Lanone, Catherine. "Clarity of Insight and Commonplaces: Alice Munro,
James Joyce and Alex Colville." *The Inside of a Shell: Alice Munro's
Dance of the Happy Shades.* Ed. Vanessa Guignery. Newcastle upon
Tyne, Eng.: Cambridge Scholars, 2015. 169-85.

LaPierre, Megan. "'The Music Itself': Musical Representation and Musi-
cality in the Short Stories of Alice Munro." *Alice Munro Everlasting:
Essays on Her Works II.* Ed. J.R. (Tim) Struthers. Toronto: Guernica
Editions, 2020. Essential Writers Ser. 52.

Lecercle, Jean-Jacques. "Alice Munro's Two Secrets." *Alice Munro: Writing
Secrets.* Ed. Héliane Ventura and Mary Condé. *Open Letter* 11th ser.,
no. 9 - 12th ser., no. 1 (2003-04): 23-37.

---. "'Pride' and Discretion." La question animale dans les nouvelles d'Alice
Munro / *The Animal Question in Alice Munro's Stories.* Ed. Héliane
Ventura. *Caliban: French Journal of English Studies* 57 (2017): 151-64.

Lee, John B. "Einstein's Hammer and the Painting Pachyderm: Reading
Alice Munro in the Digital Age (every day is trying to teach us some-
thing)." *Alice Munro Country: Essays on Her Works I.* Ed. J.R. (Tim)
Struthers. Toronto: Guernica Editions, 2020. Essential Writers Ser. 51.

Lee, Monika. "An Eerie and Numinous Place of Quiet Unknowing: Alice
Munro's 'The Love of a Good Woman' in Context." *Alice Munro:
A Souwesto Celebration.* Ed. J.R. (Tim) Struthers and John B. Lee. *The
Windsor Review* 47.2 (2014): 102-23.

---. "Fractal Fiction in Alice Munro's 'Too Much Happiness'." *Alice Munro Everlasting: Essays on Her Works II*. Ed. J.R. (Tim) Struthers. Toronto: Guernica Editions, 2020. Essential Writers Ser. 52.

Lee, Robert C. *The Canada Company and the Huron Tract, 1826-1853: Personalities, Profits and Politics*. Toronto: Natural Heritage, 2004.

Le Guin, Ursula K. *Steering the Craft: Exercises and Discussions on Story Writing for the Lone Navigator or the Mutinous Crew*. Portland, OR: Eighth Mountain, 1998. Rpt. (rev.) as *Steering the Craft: A Twenty-First-Century Guide to Sailing the Sea of Story*. Boston: Mariner-Houghton Mifflin Harcourt, 2015.

Leitch, Adelaide. *Floodtides of Fortune: The Story of Stratford and the Progress of the City Through Two Centuries*. Stratford, ON: The Corporation of the City of Stratford, 1980.

Le Jeune, Françoise, ed. [*Alice Munro's Short Fiction Writing*.] *Études Canadiennes / Canadian Studies* 77 (2014): 3, 5-6, 7-109.

Lizars, Robina, and Kathleen MacFarlane Lizars. *In the Days of the Canada Company: The Story of the Settlement of the Huron Tract and a View of the Social Life of the Period. 1825-1850*. Introd. G.M. Grant. Toronto: William Briggs, 1896. Toronto: Coles, 1972. Coles Canadiana Collection.

Lohafer, Susan. *Coming to Terms with the Short Story*. Baton Rouge: Louisiana State UP, 1983.

---. *Reading for Storyness: Preclosure Theory, Empirical Poetics, and Culture in the Short Story*. Baltimore: The Johns Hopkins UP, 2003.

---. "The Stories of 'Passion': An Empirical Study." [*Theoretical Approaches to Alice Munro's "Passion."*] Ed. Susan Lohafer. *Narrative* 20 (2012): 226-38.

Lohafer, Susan, ed. [*Theoretical Approaches to Alice Munro's "Passion."*] *Narrative* 20 (2012): 133-253.

Lorre-Johnston, Christine. "Down the Rabbit Hole: Revisiting the Topos of the Cave in Alice Munro's Short Stories." *Space and Place in Alice Munro's Fiction: "A Book with Maps in It"*. Ed. Christine Lorre-Johnston and Eleonora Rao. Rochester, NY: Camden House, 2018. 133-55.

---. "Imagined Geographies and the Memory of Nature in Three Stories by Alice Munro." *The Memory of Nature in Aboriginal, Canadian and American Contexts*. Ed. Françoise Besson, Claire Omhovère, and Héliane Ventura. Newcastle upon Tyne, Eng.: Cambridge Scholars, 2014. 73-86.

---. "Pictures of the Imagination: A Study of the Drafts of 'Images'." *The Inside of a Shell: Alice Munro's* Dance of the Happy Shades. Ed. Vanessa Guignery. Newcastle upon Tyne, Eng.: Cambridge Scholars, 2015. 226-43. Rpt. (abridged) as "'Images'" in "Chapter Four: Growing Up" in *The Mind's Eye: Alice Munro's* Dance of the Happy Shades. By Ailsa Cox and Christine Lorre-Johnston. Paris: Éditions Fahrenheit, 2015. 88-104.

---. "Remembering and Forgetting: Imagining Home in Alice Munro's *The View from Castle Rock*." *Re/membering Place*. Ed. Catherine Delmas and André Dodeman. Bern: Peter Lang, 2013. 49-62.

---. "Teenage in the Ironic Mode: A Study of the Drafts of 'Red Dress – 1946' by Alice Munro." *Stylistic Perspectives on Alice Munro's* Dance of the Happy Shades. Ed. Manuel Jobert and Michael Toolan. *Études de Stylistique Anglais* 8 (2015): 121-34. Rpt. (abridged) as "'Red Dress – 1946'" in "Chapter Four: Growing Up" in *The Mind's Eye: Alice Munro's* Dance of the Happy Shades. By Ailsa Cox and Christine Lorre-Johnston. Paris: Éditions Fahrenheit, 2015. 104-17.

Lorre-Johnston, Christine, and Eleonora Rao. Introduction. *Space and Place in Alice Munro's Fiction: "A Book with Maps in It"*. Rochester, NY: Camden House, 2018. 1-24.

Lorre-Johnston, Christine, and Eleonora Rao, eds. *Space and Place in Alice Munro's Fiction: "A Book with Maps in It"*. Rochester, NY: Camden House, 2018.

Löschnigg, Maria. "Carried Away by Letters: Alice Munro and the Epistolary Mode." *Alice Munro's Miraculous Art: Critical Essays*. Ed. Janice Fiamengo and Gerald Lynch. Ottawa: U of Ottawa P, 2017. 97-113. Reappraisals: Canadian Writers 38.

---. *The Contemporary Canadian Short Story in English: Continuity and Change*. Trier, Ger.: WVT Wissenschaftlicher Verlag Tier, 2014. CAT: Cultures in America in Transition 7.

Lynch, Gerald. "No Honey, I'm Home: Place Over Love in Alice Munro's Short Story Cycle, *Who Do You Think You Are?*." *Canadian Literature* 160 (1999): 73-98. Rpt. as "No Honey, I'm Home: Alice Munro's *Who Do You Think You Are?*" in *The One and the Many: English Canadian Short Story Cycles*. By Gerald Lynch. Toronto: U of Toronto P, 2001. 159-81.

---. "Three Encounters with Alice Munro." *Alice Munro: Reminiscence, Interpretation, Adaptation and Comparison*. Ed. Mirosława Buchholtz and Eugenia Sojka. Frankfurt am Main, Ger.: Peter Lang, 2015. 21-31. Dis/Continuities: Toruń Studies in Language, Literature and Culture 8.

Macfarlane, David. "Writer in Residence." *Saturday Night* Dec. 1986: 51-52, 54, 56.

MacKendrick, Louis K. "Giving Tongue: Scorings of Voice, Verse, and Flesh in Alice Munro's 'Meneseteung'." *Alice Munro and the Souwesto Story*. Ed. J.R. (Tim) Struthers. *Short Story* ns 21.1 (2013 [2015]): 70-87. Rpt. in *Alice Munro Country: Essays on Her Works I*. Ed. J.R. (Tim) Struthers. Toronto: Guernica Editions, 2020. Essential Writers Ser. 51.

---. *Some Other Reality: Alice Munro's* Something I've Been Meaning To Tell You. Toronto: ECW, 1993. Canadian Fiction Studies 25. Rpt. (excerpted) as "A Series of Metaphorical Epitaphs: Alice Munro's 'The Ottawa Valley'" in *Alice Munro Everlasting: Essays on Her Works II*. Ed. J.R. (Tim) Struthers. Toronto: Guernica Editions, 2020. Essential Writers Ser. 52.

MacKendrick, Louis K., ed. *Probable Fictions: Alice Munro's Narrative Acts*. Downsview, ON: ECW, 1983.

MacLeod, Alexander. "The Canadian Short Story in English: Aesthetic Agency, Social Change, and the Shifting Canon." *The Oxford Handbook of Canadian Literature*. Ed. Cynthia Sugars. Toronto: Oxford UP, 2016. 426-47.

March-Russell, Paul. *The Short Story: An Introduction*. Edinburgh: Edinburgh UP, 2009.

Martin, W.R. *Alice Munro: Paradox and Parallel*. Edmonton, AB: U of Alberta P, 1987.

---. "Alice Munro and James Joyce." *Journal of Canadian Fiction* 24 (1979): 120-26. Rpt. in *Alice Munro Everlasting: Essays on Her Works II*. Ed. J.R. (Tim) Struthers. Toronto: Guernica Editions, 2020. Essential Writers Ser. 52.

Martin, W.R., and Warren U. Ober. "Alice Munro as Small-Town Historian: 'Spaceships Have Landed'." *Alice Munro Writing On....* Ed. Robert Thacker. *Essays on Canadian Writing* 66 (1998): 128-46. Rpt. in *The Rest of the Story: Critical Essays on Alice Munro*. Ed. Robert Thacker. Toronto: ECW, 1999. 128-46. Rpt. (abridged) in *Alice Munro Country: Essays on Her Works I*. Ed. J.R. (Tim) Struthers. Toronto: Guernica Editions, 2020. Essential Writers Ser. 51.

Mathews, Lawrence. "*Who Do You Think You Are?*: Alice Munro's Art of Disarrangement." *Probable Fictions: Alice Munro's Narrative Acts*. Ed. Louis K. MacKendrick. Downsview, ON: ECW, 1983. 181-93. Rpt. in *Alice Munro Everlasting: Essays on Her Works II*. Ed. J.R. (Tim) Struthers. Toronto: Guernica Editions, 2020. Essential Writers Ser. 52.

May, Charles E. *Edgar Allan Poe: A Study of the Short Fiction.* Boston: Twayne-G.K. Hall, 1991. Twayne's Studies in Short Fiction 28.

---. *"I Am Your Brother": Short Story Studies.* Garden Grove, CA: Amayzing Editions, 2013.

---. "'The Key to the Treasure': Sex and Storytelling in *Hateship, Friendship, Courtship, Loveship, Marriage.*" *Alice Munro:* Hateship, Friendship, Courtship, Loveship, Marriage; Runaway; Dear Life. Ed. Robert Thacker. London: Bloomsbury, 2016. 25-43, 231-44 passim.

---. "Living in the Story: Fictional Reality in the Stories of Alice Munro." *Alice Munro's Miraculous Art: Critical Essays.* Ed. Janice Fiamengo and Gerald Lynch. Ottawa: U of Ottawa P, 2017. 43-61. Reappraisals: Canadian Writers 38.

---. "On Alice Munro." *Critical Insights: Alice Munro.* Ed. Charles E. May. Ipswich, MA: Salem-EBSCO, 2013. 3-18.

---. "Returning to the Source: Alice Munro, Flannery O'Connor, and Eudora Welty." *Alice Munro Everlasting: Essays on Her Works II.* Ed. J.R. (Tim) Struthers. Toronto: Guernica Editions, 2020. Essential Writers Ser. 52.

---. *The Short Story: The Reality of Artifice.* 1995. New York: Routledge, 2002.

---. "The Short Story's Way of Meaning: Alice Munro's 'Passion'." [*Theoretical Approaches to Alice Munro's "Passion."*] Ed. Susan Lohafer. *Narrative* 20 (2012): 172-82. Rpt. (rev.) in "The Short Story Way of Meaning: Alice Munro" in *"I Am Your Brother": Short Story Studies.* By Charles E. May. Garden Grove, CA: Amayzing Editions, 2013. 235-57.

---. "Why Does Alice Munro Write Short Stories?" *The Contemporary Short Story.* Ed. Michael Trussler. *Wascana Review* 38.1 (2003 [2005]): 16-28. Rpt. (rev.) in "The Short Story Way of Meaning: Alice Munro" in *"I Am Your Brother": Short Story Studies.* By Charles E. May. Garden Grove, CA: Amayzing Editions, 2013. 235-57.

May, Charles E., ed. *Critical Insights: Alice Munro.* Ipswich, MA: Salem-EBSCO, 2013.

Mazur, Carol, comp. *Alice Munro: An Annotated Bibliography of Works and Criticism.* Ed. Cathy Moulder. Lanham, MD: Scarecrow, 2007.

McCaig, JoAnn. *Reading In: Alice Munro's Archives.* Waterloo, ON: Wilfrid Laurier UP, 2002.

McCarthy, Dermot. "The Woman Out Back: Alice Munro's 'Meneseteung'." *Studies in Canadian Literature / Études en littérature canadienne* 19.1 (1994): 1-19.

McGill, Robert. "Alice Munro and Personal Development." *The Cambridge Companion to Alice Munro*. Ed. David Staines. Cambridge, Eng.: Cambridge UP, 2016. 136-53.

---. "'Daringly Out in the Public Eye': Alice Munro and the Ethics of Writing Back." *The Ethical Turn in Canadian Literature and Criticism*. Ed. Marlene Goldman and Kristina Kyser. *University of Toronto Quarterly* 76.3 (2007): 874-89.

---. "Mistaken Identities in 'The Bear Came Over the Mountain'." *Alice Munro:* Hateship, Friendship, Courtship, Loveship, Marriage; Runaway; Dear Life. Ed. Robert Thacker. London: Bloomsbury, 2016. 65-85, 221-23, 231-44 passim.

---. "Somewhere I've Been Meaning To Tell You: Alice Munro's Fiction of Distance." *The Journal of Commonwealth Literature* 37.1 (2002): 9-29.

---. "Where Do You Think You Are?: Alice Munro's Open Houses." *Mosaic: A Journal for the Interdisciplinary Study of Literature* 35.4 (2002): 103-19. Rpt. (rev.) in *Space and Place in Alice Munro's Fiction: "A Book with Maps in It"*. Ed. Christine Lorre-Johnston and Eleonora Rao. Rochester, NY: Camden House, 2018. 27-40.

McIlwraith, Thomas F. *Looking for Old Ontario: Two Centuries of Landscape Change*. Toronto: U of Toronto P, 1997.

McIntyre, Timothy. "Doing Her Duty and Writing Her Life: Alice Munro's Cultural and Historical Context." *Critical Insights: Alice Munro*. Ed. Charles E. May. Ipswich, MA: Salem-EBSCO, 2013. 52-67.

---. "'This Is Not Enough': Gesturing Beyond the Aesthetics of Failure in Alice Munro's 'Material'." *The Genius of Alice Munro*. Ed Robert Thacker. *American Review of Canadian Studies* 45.2 (2015). 161-73.

---. "'The Way the Stars Really Do Come Out at Night': The Trick of Representation in Alice Munro's 'The Moons of Jupiter'." *Canadian Literature* 200 (2009): 73-88. Rpt. in *Alice Munro Everlasting: Essays on Her Works II*. Ed. J.R. (Tim) Struthers. Toronto: Guernica Editions, 2020. Essential Writers Ser. 52.

Metcalf, John. *The Canadian Short Story*. Windsor, ON: Biblioasis, 2018.

---. "Casting Sad Spells: Alice Munro's 'Walker Brothers Cowboy'." *Writers in Aspic*. Ed. John Metcalf. Montreal: Véhicule, 1988. 186-200. Rpt. in *Freedom from Culture: Selected Essays 1982-92*. By John Metcalf. Toronto: ECW, 1994. 173-87. Rpt. in *Shut Up He Explained: A Literary Memoir Vol. II*. By John Metcalf. Windsor, ON: Biblioasis, 2007. 85-99. Rpt. in *The Canadian Short Story*. By John Metcalf. Windsor, ON: Biblioasis, 2018. 506-22.

---. "The Signs of Invasion: Alice Munro's 'Images'." *The Canadian Short Story*. Windsor, ON: Biblioasis, 2018. 488-506.

Micros, Marianne. "Et in Ontario Ego: The Pastoral Ideal and the Blazon Tradition in Alice Munro's 'Lichen'." *Alice Munro Writing On....* Ed. Robert Thacker. *Essays on Canadian Writing* 66 (1998): 44-59. Rpt. in *The Rest of the Story: Critical Essays on Alice Munro*. Ed. Robert Thacker. Toronto: ECW, 1999. 44-59.

---. "'Pearl Street ... is another story': Poetry and Reality in Alice Munro's 'Meneseteung'." *Alice Munro Country: Essays on Her Works I*. Ed. J.R. (Tim) Struthers. Toronto: Guernica Editions, 2020. Essential Writers Ser. 51.

Miller, Judith, ed. *The Art of Alice Munro: Saying the Unsayable*. Waterloo, ON: U of Waterloo P, 1984.

Miller, Judith Maclean. "Deconstructing Silence: The Mystery of Alice Munro." *The Antigonish Review* 129 (2002): 43-52.

---. "An Inner Bell That Rings: The Craft of Alice Munro." *The Antigonish Review* 115 (1998): 157-76.

---. "On Looking into Rifts and Crannies: Alice Munro's *Friend of My Youth*." *The Antigonish Review* 120 (2000): 205-26.

Miller, Orlo. *A Century of Western Ontario: The Story of London, "The Free Press," and Western Ontario, 1849-1949*. Toronto: Ryerson, 1949.

---. *The Donnellys Must Die*. Toronto: Macmillan of Canada, 1962.

---. *London 200: An Illustrated History*. London, ON: London Chamber of Commerce, 1992.

Monture, Rick. *We Share Our Matters: Two Centuries of Writing and Resistance at Six Nations of the Grand River*. Winnipeg: U of Manitoba P, 2014.

Morgenstern, Naomi. "The Baby or the Violin?: Ethics and Femininity in the Fiction of Alice Munro." *LIT: Literature Interpretation Theory* 14.2 (2003): 69-97.

---. "Life after Life: Survival in the (Late) Fiction of Alice Munro." *Ethics and Affects in the Fiction of Alice Munro*. Ed. Amelia DeFalco and Lorraine York. Cham, Switz.: Palgrave Macmillan, 2018. 219-44. Palgrave Studies in Affect Theory and Literary Criticism.

---. "Seduction and Subjectivity: Psychoanalysis and the Fiction of Alice Munro." *Critical Insights: Alice Munro*. Ed. Charles E. May. Ipswich, MA: Salem-EBSCO, 2013. 68-86.

Munro, Alice. "About This Book." *Alice Munro: Selected Stories: A Tribute.* Toronto: McClelland & Stewart, 1996. 1-7. Rpt. as "Introduction to the Vintage Edition" in *Selected Stories.* By Alice Munro. New York: Vintage, 1997. xiii-xxi. Vintage Contemporaries. Rpt. as Introduction in *Selected Stories.* By Alice Munro. Toronto: Penguin, 1998. ix-xvii. Rpt. as Introduction in *A Wilderness Station: Selected Stories 1968-1994.* By Alice Munro. Toronto: Penguin: 2015. xiii-xxi.

---. "Everything Here Is Touchable and Mysterious." *Weekend Magazine* [*The Globe and Mail*] 11 May 1974: [33].

---. Introduction. *The Moons of Jupiter.* Markham, ON: Penguin, 1986. xiii-xvi. Toronto: Penguin, 1995. xiii-xvi.

---. "An Open Letter." *Jubilee* [Gorrie, ON] 1 (1974): 5-7.

---. *The View from Castle Rock.* Toronto: McClelland & Stewart, 2006.

---. "What Is Real?" *Making It New: Contemporary Canadian Stories.* Ed. John Metcalf. Photographs by Sam Tata. Toronto: Methuen, 1982. 223-26. Rpt. in *How Stories Mean.* Ed. John Metcalf and J.R. (Tim) Struthers. Erin, ON: The Porcupine's Quill, 1993. 331-34. Critical Directions 3.

Munro, Sheila. *Lives of Mothers & Daughters: Growing Up with Alice Munro.* Toronto: McClelland & Stewart, 2001.

Munson, Marit K., and Susan M. Jamieson, eds. *Before Ontario: The Archaeology of a Province.* Montreal, QC and Kingston, ON: McGill-Queens UP, 2013.

Murray, Jennifer. *Reading Alice Munro with Jacques Lacan.* Montreal, QC and Kingston, ON: McGill-Queen's UP, 2016.

New, W.H. *Dreams of Speech and Violence: The Art of the Short Story in Canada and New Zealand.* Toronto: U of Toronto P, 1987.

---. *Reading Mansfield and Metaphors of Form.* Montreal, QC and Kingston, ON: McGill-Queen's UP, 1999.

Nischik, Reingard M. "Alice Munro: Nobel Prize-Winning Master of the Contemporary Short Story." [*Alice Munro's Short Fiction Writing.*] Ed. Françoise Le Jeune. *Études Canadiennes / Canadian Studies* 77 (2014): 7-25.

---. "(Un-)Doing Gender: Alice Munro, 'Boys and Girls' (1964)." *The Canadian Short Story: Interpretations.* Ed. Reingard M. Nischik. Rochester, NY: Camden House, 2007. 203-18. European Studies in American Literature and Culture.

Norris, Margot. *Suspicious Readings of Joyce's* Dubliners. Philadelphia: U of Pennsylvania P, 2003.

North Huron Museum, Wingham, Ontario. "Facades of Wingham – Past and Present." "Community Stories." *Virtual Museum of Canada (VMC)*. <www.virtualmuseum.ca/>.

O'Connor, Frank. *The Lonely Voice: A Study of the Short Story*. Cleveland, OH: World, 1963. Introd. Russell Banks. Hoboken, NJ: Melville House, 2004.

Oddliefson, Edward W. *Corporation of the Village of Bayfield History 1876-1985*. Bayfield, ON: Bayfield Historical Society, 1987.

O'Faolain, Sean. *The Short Story*. New York: Devin-Adair, 1951.

Omhovère, Claire. "'For There Is No Easy Way To Get to Jubilee from Anywhere on Earth': Places in Alice Munro's *Dance of the Happy Shades*." *The Inside of a Shell: Alice Munro's* Dance of the Happy Shades. Ed. Vanessa Guignery. Newcastle upon Tyne, Eng.: Cambridge Scholars, 2015. 26-45.

---. "Gravel and Grief: Alice Munro's Vulnerable Landscapes." *Ethics and Affects in the Fiction of Alice Munro*. Ed. Amelia DeFalco and Lorraine York. Cham, Switz.: Palgrave Macmillan, 2018. 177-94. Palgrave Studies in Affect Theory and Literary Criticism.

---. "Stories in the Landscape Mode: A Reading of Alice Munro's 'Lives of Girls and Women,' 'Walker Brothers Cowboy,' and 'Lichen'." *Space and Place in Alice Munro's Fiction: "A Book with Maps in It"*. Ed. Christine Lorre-Johnston and Eleonora Rao. Rochester, NY: Camden House, 2018. 82-99.

Ovid. *Metamorphoses*. Trans. Mary M. Innes. Harmondsworth, Eng.: Penguin, 1955.

Palusci, Oriana. "Breathing and the Power of Evil in 'Dimensions'." *Alice Munro and the Anatomy of the Short Story*. Ed. Oriana Palusci. Newcastle upon Tyne, Eng.: Cambridge Scholars, 2017. 111-25.

---. "Introduction: Alice Munro's Short Stories in the Anatomy Theatre." *Alice Munro and the Anatomy of the Short Story*. Ed. Oriana Palusci. Newcastle upon Tyne, Eng.: Cambridge Scholars, 2017. 1-10.

---. "The Memory of Ghosts: Alice Munro's 'My Mother's Dream'." *Reading Alice Munro in Italy*. Ed. Gianfranca Balestra, Laura Ferri, and Caterina Ricciardi. Toronto: The Frank Iacobucci Centre for Italian Canadian Studies, 2008. 47-57. Monograph Ser. 3.

---. "Plymouth Rocks and Christmas Turkeys: From Ecology to Metafiction in Two Short Stories by Alice Munro." La question animale dans les nouvelles d'Alice Munro / *The Animal Question in Alice Munro's Stories*. Ed. Héliane Ventura. *Caliban: French Journal of English Studies* 57 (2017): 11-20.

---. "A 'Postcard' in the Hands of Alice Munro." *"With a Roar from Underground": Alice Munro's* Dance of the Happy Shades. Ed. Corinne Bigot and Catherine Lanone. Paris: Presses Universitaires de Paris Ouest, 2015. 45-54.

Palusci, Oriana, ed. *Alice Munro and the Anatomy of the Short Story*. Newcastle upon Tyne, Eng.: Cambridge Scholars, 2017.

Pattison, John W. *Museum Musings: Brief Glimpses of Wingham's Past*. Wingham, ON: n.p., [1982].

Pressault, Valerie. *Memories of Life on the Farm: Photos from the Reuben R. Sallows Collection*. Goderich, ON: n.p., 2010.

Prose, Francine. *Reading Like a Writer: A Guide for People Who Love Books and for Those Who Want To Write Them*. 2006. New York: Harper Perennial, 2007.

Rae, Ian. "Alice Munro and the Huron Tract as a Literary Project." *The Inside of a Shell: Alice Munro's* Dance of the Happy Shades. Ed. Vanessa Guignery. Newcastle upon Tyne, Eng.: Cambridge Scholars, 2015. 46-64. Rpt. (rev.) in *Alice Munro Country: Essays on Her Works I*. Ed. J.R. (Tim) Struthers. Toronto: Guernica Editions, 2020. Essential Writers Ser. 51.

Rao, Eleonora. "'Here Was No Open Straightforward Plan': Jumbled Space in 'The Shining Houses'." *Stylistic Perspectives on Alice Munro's* Dance of the Happy Shades. Ed. Manuel Jobert and Michael Toolan. *Études de Stylistique Anglais* 8 (2015): 71-82.

---. "'Home' and the Narrative of an Impossible *Nostos*." *Alice Munro: Writing for Dear Life*. Ed. Corinne Bigot. *Commonwealth Essays and Studies* 37.2 (2015): 27-34.

---. "The Stranger's Time Is a Moving Train, a Plane in Flight: Alice Munro's *étranger*." *Time and the Short Story*. Ed. Maria Teresa Chialant and Marina Lops. Bern: Peter Lang, 2012. 211-24.

---. "'Whose House Is That?': Spaces of Metamorphosis in Alice Munro's *Dance of the Happy Shades, Who Do You Think You Are?*, and *The View from Castle Rock*." *Space and Place in Alice Munro's Fiction: "A Book with Maps in It"*. Ed. Christine Lorre-Johnston and Eleonora Rao. Rochester, NY: Camden House, 2018. 41-62.

Rasporich, Beverly J. *Dance of the Sexes: Art and Gender in the Fiction of Alice Munro.* Edmonton, AB: U of Alberta P, 1990.

Raymond, Katrine. "'Deep, Deep into the River of Her Mind': 'Menese-teung' and the Archival Hysteric." *Hysteria Manifest: Cultural Lives of a Great Disorder.* Ed. Ela Przybylo and Derritt Mason. *English Studies in Canada* 40.1 (2014): 95-122.

Reaney, James. "An ABC to Ontario Literature and Culture." *Black Moss: A Semi-Annual of Ontario Literature and Culture* 2nd ser. 3 (1977): 2-6. Rpt. in *Alice Munro Country: Essays on Her Works I.* Ed. J.R. (Tim) Struthers. Toronto: Guernica Editions, 2020. Essential Writers Ser. 51.

---. "Myths in Some Nineteenth-Century Ontario Newspapers." *Aspects of Nineteenth-Century Ontario: Essays Presented to James J. Talman.* Ed. F.H. Armstrong, H.A. Stevenson, and J.D. Wilson. Toronto: U of Toronto P, 1974. 253-66.

---. "Ontario Culture and – What?" *Canadian Literature* 100 (1984): 252-57.

Redekop, Magdalene. "Alice Munro and the Scottish Nostalgic Grotesque." *Alice Munro Writing On....* Ed. Robert Thacker. *Essays on Canadian Writing* 66 (1998): 21-43. Rpt. in *The Rest of the Story: Critical Essays on Alice Munro.* Ed. Robert Thacker. Toronto: ECW, 1999. 21-43.

---. "Alice Munro's Tilting Fields." *New Worlds: Discovering and Constructing the Unknown in Anglophone Literature: Presented to Walter Pache on the Occasion of His 60th Birthday.* Ed. Martin Kuester, Gabriele Christ, and Rudolf Beck. München, Ger.: Ernst Vögel, 2000. 343-62. Schriften der Philosophischen Fakultäten der Universität Augsburg 59.

---. *Mothers and Other Clowns: The Stories of Alice Munro.* London: Routledge, 1992. Rpt. (excerpted) as "Alice Munro's 'Images': Don't Tell Momma" in *The Inside of a Shell: Alice Munro's Dance of the Happy Shades.* Ed. Vanessa Guignery. Newcastle upon Tyne, Eng.: Cambridge Scholars, 2015. 218-25.

---. "On Sitting Down To Read 'Lichen' Once Again." *Alice Munro's Miraculous Art: Critical Essays.* Ed. Janice Fiamengo and Gerald Lynch. Ottawa: U of Ottawa P, 2017. 289-305. Reappraisals: Canadian Writers 38.

Reid, Dennis, ed. *Jack Chambers: Light, Spirit, Time, Place and Life.* Fredericton and Toronto: Goose Lane Editions and Art Gallery of Ontario, 2011.

Reid, Dennis, and Matthew Teitelbaum, eds. *Greg Curnoe: Life and Stuff.* Toronto / Vancouver: The Art Gallery of Ontario / Douglas & McIntyre, 2001.

Reid, Ian. *The Short Story*. London: Methuen, 1977. The Critical Idiom 37.

The Reuben R. Sallows Gallery, Goderich Library, Goderich, ON. "Photographic Travels of Reuben R. Sallows." "Community Stories." *Virtual Museum of Canada (VMC)*. .

Ricou, Laurie. *Everyday Magic: Child Languages in Canadian Literature*. Vancouver, BC: The U of British Columbia P, 1987.

Riley, John L. *The Once and Future Great Lakes Country: An Ecological History*. Montreal, QC and Kingston, ON: McGill-Queen's UP, 2013.

Rohrberger, Mary. *Hawthorne and the Modern Short Story: A Study in Genre*. The Hague, Neth.: Mouton, 1966. Studies in Genre and Comparative Literature 2.

Ross, Catherine Sheldrick. *Alice Munro: A Double Life*. Toronto: ECW, 1992. Canadian Biography Ser. 1. Rpt. (excerpted) as "Alice Munro: A Double Life: An Excerpt from a New Biography of One of Canada's Finest Writers." *Books in Canada* Apr. 1992: 16-21.

---. "Alice Munro (10 July 1931)." *Canadian Writers Since 1960: First Series*. Ed. W.H. New. *Dictionary of Literary Biography*. Vol. 53. Detroit, MI: Gale Research, 1986. 295-307.

---. "'At Least Part Legend': The Fiction of Alice Munro." *Probable Fictions: Alice Munro's Narrative Acts*. Ed. Louis K. MacKendrick. Downsview, ON: ECW, 1983. 112-26.

---. "'At the End of a Long Road': Alice Munro's 'Dear Life'." *Alice Munro Everlasting: Essays on Her Works II*. Ed. J.R. (Tim) Struthers. Toronto: Guernica Editions, 2020. Essential Writers Ser. 52.

---. "Calling Back the Ghost of the Old-Time Heroine: Duncan, Montgomery, Atwood, Laurence, and Munro." *Studies in Canadian Literature* 4.1 (1979): 43-58.

---. "'Too Many Things': Reading Alice Munro's 'The Love of a Good Woman'." *University of Toronto Quarterly* 71 (2002): 786-810.

Sabatini, Sandra. "My Mother's Dream." *Alice Munro Everlasting: Essays on Her Works II*. Ed. J.R. (Tim) Struthers. Toronto: Guernica Editions, 2020. Essential Writers Ser. 52.

Schull, Joseph. *Ontario Since 1867*. Toronto: McClelland and Stewart, 1978. Ontario Historical Studies Ser.

Scott, James. *Ontario Scene*. Toronto: Ryerson, 1969.

---. *The Settlement of Huron County*. Toronto: Ryerson, 1966.

Scrivener, Leslie. "Where Alice Munro Found Her Stories." *Toronto Star* 20 Oct. 2013: E1, E4-E5.

Simonds, Merilyn. "Where Do You Think You Are?: Place in the Short Stories of Alice Munro." *The Cambridge Companion to Alice Munro.* Ed. David Staines. Cambridge, Eng.: Cambridge UP, 2016. 26-44.

Skagert, Ulrica. *Possibility-Space and Its Imaginative Variations in Alice Munro's Short Stories.* Stockholm: Stockholm U, 2008.

---. "The Rupture of the Ordinary as an 'Awkward Little Space': Evental Moments in Alice Munro's 'Dance of the Happy Shades'." *The Inside of a Shell: Alice Munro's* Dance of the Happy Shades. Ed. Vanessa Guignery. Newcastle upon Tyne, Eng.: Cambridge Scholars, 2015. 271-82.

Smith, Michael, and Larry Mohring. *The Reuben R. Sallows Picture Postcard Handbook 1900-1925: Gems from "A Canadian Photographic Genius".* Goderich, ON: n.p., 2016.

Smith, Rowland. "Rewriting the Frontier: Wilderness and Social Code in the Fiction of Alice Munro." *Telling Stories: Postcolonial Short Fiction in English.* Ed. Jacqueline Bardolph. Finalized for Publication by André Viola with Jean-Pierre Durix. Amsterdam-Atlanta: Rodopi, 2001. 77-90. Cross/Cultures: Readings in the Post/Colonial Literatures in English 47. Rpt. as "Wilderness and Social Code in the Fiction of Alice Munro" in *Bloom's Modern Critical Views: Alice Munro.* Ed. Harold Bloom. New York: Bloom's Literary Criticism-Infobase, 2009. 153-65.

Smythe, Karen E. *Figuring Grief: Gallant, Munro, and the Poetics of Elegy.* Montreal, QC and Kingston, ON: McGill-Queen's UP, 1992.

Somacarrera, Pilar. "Exploring the Impenetrability of Narrative: A Study of Linguistic Modality in Alice Munro's Early Fiction." *Studies in Canadian Literature / Études en littérature canadienne* 21.1 (1996): 79-91.

---. "Speech Presentation and 'Coloured' Narrative in Alice Munro's *Who Do You Think You Are?.*" *Textual Studies in Canada* 10/11 (1998): 69-79.

---. "'The Unavoidable Collision of Religion and Life': Scots Presbyterianism in Alice Munro's Fiction." *Studies in Canadian Literature / Études en littérature canadienne* 40.2 (2015): 88-107.

Southwestern Ontario. Photographs by John deVisser. Introd. Orlo Miller. Toronto: Oxford UP, 1982.

Staines, David. "From Wingham to Clinton: Alice Munro in Her Canadian Context." *The Cambridge Companion to Alice Munro.* Ed. David Staines. Cambridge, Eng.: Cambridge UP, 2016. 7-25.

Staines, David, ed. *The Cambridge Companion to Alice Munro*. Cambridge, Eng.: Cambridge UP, 2016.

Stelter, Gilbert A. "John Galt: The Writer as Town Booster and Builder." *John Galt: Reappraisals*. Ed. Elizabeth Waterston. Guelph, ON: U of Guelph, 1985. 17-43.

Stich, Klaus P. "Letting Go with the Mind: Dionysus and Medusa in Alice Munro's 'Meneseteung'." *Canadian Literature* 169 (2001): 106-25.

---. "Munro's Grail Quest: The Progress of Logos." *Studies in Canadian Literature / Études en littérature canadienne* 32.1 (2007): 120-40.

Street, Susan, gen. ed. *Blyth: A Village Portrait*. Blyth, ON: n.p., [1977].

Struthers, J.R. (Tim). "Alice Munro and the American South." *The Canadian Review of American Studies* 6 (1975): 196-204. Rpt. (rev.) in *The Canadian Novel: Here and Now*. Ed. and introd. John Moss. Toronto: NC, 1978. 121-33. Rev. and expanded in *Short Story Criticism: Criticism of the Works of Short Fiction Writers*. Vol. 208. Ed. Lawrence J. Trudeau. Farmington Hills, MI: Gale, Cengage Learning, 2015. 99-117.

---. "Alice Munro (July 10, 1931–)." *A Reader's Companion to the Short Story in English*. Ed. Erin Fallon, R.C. Feddersen, James Kurtzleben, Maurice A. Lee, and Susan Rochette-Crawley. Westport, CT: Greenwood, 2001. 288-99.

---. "A Bibliographical Tour of Alice Munro Country." *Alice Munro Country: Essays on Her Works I*. Ed. J.R. (Tim) Struthers. Toronto: Guernica Editions, 2020. Essential Writers Ser. 51.

---. "Book by Book: A Checklist of Alice Munro's 148 Collected Stories, 1968-2012." *Alice Munro and the Souwesto Story*. Ed. J.R. (Tim) Struthers. *Short Story* ns 21.1 (2013 [2015]): 139-43.

---. "Imagining Alice Munro's 'Meneseteung': The Dynamics of Co-Creation." *Alice Munro: A Souwesto Celebration*. Ed. J.R. (Tim) Struthers and John B. Lee. *The Windsor Review* 47.2 (2014): 68-91.

---. "In Search of the Perfect Metaphor: The Language of the Short Story and Alice Munro's 'Meneseteung'." *Critical Insights: Alice Munro*. Ed. Charles E. May. Ipswich, MA: Salem-EBSCO, 2013. 175-94.

---. "The Place of Wisdom, Divination, the Act of Reading, and Alice Munro's 'Powers'." *Alice Munro Everlasting: Essays on Her Works II*. Ed. J.R. (Tim) Struthers. Toronto: Guernica Editions, 2020. Essential Writers Ser. 52.

---. "The Real Material: An Interview with Alice Munro." *Probable Fictions: Alice Munro's Narrative Acts*. Ed. Louis K. MacKendrick. Downsview, ON: ECW, 1983. 5-36.

---. "Remembrance Day 1988: An Interview with Alice Munro." *Alice Munro Country: Essays on Her Works I*. Ed. J.R. (Tim) Struthers. Toronto: Guernica Editions, 2020. Essential Writers Ser. 51.

---. "Song for Alice Munro." *Alice Munro and the Souwesto Story*. Ed. J.R. (Tim) Struthers. *Short Story* ns 21.1 (2013 [2015]): 88-102.

---. "Souwesto Stories: An Interview with James Reaney." *Alice Munro and the Souwesto Story*. Ed. J.R. (Tim) Struthers. *Short Story* ns 21.1 (2013 [2015]): 111-36.

---. "Traveling with Munro: Reading 'To Reach Japan'." *Alice Munro: Hateship, Friendship, Courtship, Loveship, Marriage; Runaway; Dear Life*. Ed. Robert Thacker. London: Bloomsbury, 2016. 163-83, 231-44 passim.

Struthers, J.R. (Tim), ed. *Alice Munro and the Souwesto Story*. *Short Story* ns 21.1 (2013 [2015]): [i, iii-v], 1-148.

---, ed. *Alice Munro Country: Essays on Her Works I*. Toronto: Guernica Editions, 2020. Essential Writers Ser. 51.

---, ed. *Alice Munro Everlasting: Essays on Her Works II*. Toronto: Guernica Editions, 2020. Essential Writers Ser. 52.

Struthers, J.R. (Tim), and John B. Lee, eds. *Alice Munro: A Souwesto Celebration*. *The Windsor Review* 47.2 (2014): 1-137.

Tausky, Thomas E. "Biocritical Essay." *The Alice Munro Papers First Accession: An Inventory of the Archive at The University of Calgary Libraries*. Comp. Jean M. Moore and Jean F. Tener. Ed. Apollonia Steele and Jean F. Tener. Calgary: U of Calgary P, 1986. ix-xxiv.

---. "'What Happened to Marion?': Art and Reality in *Lives of Girls and Women*." *Studies in Canadian Literature* 11 (1986): 52-76.

Thacker, Robert. "Alice Munro: An Annotated Bibliography." *The Annotated Bibliography of Canada's Major Authors*. Ed. Robert Lecker and Jack David. Vol. 5. Downsview, ON: ECW, 1984. 354-414. 8 vols. 1979-94.

---. "Alice Munro: Biographical." Nobel Media. 2014. <https://www.nobelprize.org/prizes/literature/2013/munro/biographical/>. Rpt. as "Alice Munro" in *The Nobel Prizes: 2013*. Ed. Karl Grandin. Sagamore Beach, MA: Science History Publications/USA-Watson Publishing International, 2014. 310-22.

---. *Alice Munro: Writing Her Lives: A Biography*. Toronto: McClelland & Stewart, 2005. Updated ed. Toronto: Emblem-McClelland & Stewart, 2011.

---. "Alice Munro Country." *The Dalhouse Review* 98 (2018): 412-18.

---. "'The Art of Representation Which a Biography Must Be': Writing Alice Munro's Biography." *Reading Alice Munro in Italy*. Ed. Gianfranca Balestra, Laura Ferri, and Caterina Ricciardi. Toronto: The Frank Iacobucci Centre for Italian Canadian Studies, 2008. 25-34. Monograph Ser. 3.

---. "'Evocative and Luminous Phrases': Reading Alice Munro's *Hateship, Friendship, Courtship, Loveship, Marriage*." *The Genius of Alice Munro*. Ed. Robert Thacker. *American Review of Canadian Studies* 45 (2015): 187-95.

---. "Introduction: 'Durable and Freestanding': The Late Art of Munro." *Alice Munro*: Hateship, Friendship, Courtship, Loveship, Marriage; Runaway; Dear Life. Ed. Robert Thacker. London: Bloomsbury, 2016. 1-20, 217-18, 231-44 passim.

---. *Reading Alice Munro: 1973-2013*. Calgary: U of Calgary P, 2016.

---. "Select Bibliography." *Alice Munro: Writing Her Lives: A Biography*. Toronto: McClelland & Stewart, 2005. 565-86. Rev. and expanded in *Alice Munro: Writing Her Lives: A Biography*. Updated ed. Toronto: Emblem-McClelland & Stewart, 2011. 607-30.

---. "'Stabbed to the Heart ... By the Beauty of Our Lives Streaming By': Munro's Finale." *Alice Munro Everlasting: Essays on Her Works II*. Ed. J.R. (Tim) Struthers. Toronto: Guernica Editions, 2020. Essential Writers Ser. 52.

---. "'This Is Not a Story, Only Life': Wondering with Alice Munro." *Alice Munro's Miraculous Art: Critical Essays*. Ed. Janice Fiamengo and Gerald Lynch. Ottawa: U of Ottawa P, 2017. 15-40. Reappraisals: Canadian Writers 38.

Thacker, Robert, ed. *Alice Munro:* Hateship, Friendship, Courtship, Loveship, Marriage; Runaway; Dear Life. London: Bloomsbury, 2016.

---, ed. *Alice Munro Writing On.... Essays on Canadian Writing* 66 (1998): 1-232. Rpt. as *The Rest of the Story: Critical Essays on Alice Munro*. Ed. Robert Thacker. Toronto: ECW, 1999.

---, ed. *The Genius of Alice Munro. American Review of Canadian Studies* 45 (2015): 144-207.

Thompson, Judith. "The Boy with the Banana in His Mouth." *Alice Munro Country: Essays on Her Works I*. Ed. J.R. (Tim) Struthers. Toronto: Guernica Editions, 2020. Essential Writers Ser. 51.

Thompson, Reg. "All Things Considered: Alice Munro First and Last." *Alice Munro: A Souwesto Celebration*. Ed. J.R. (Tim) Struthers and John B. Lee. *The Windsor Review* 47.2 (2014): 5-9. Rpt. in *Alice Munro Country: Essays on Her Works I*. Ed. J.R. (Tim) Struthers. Toronto: Guernica Editions, 2020. Essential Writers Ser. 51.

---. "Cemetery Hunting with Alice Munro." *The Rural Voice* Dec. 2019: 42-45.

Toolan, Michael. "The Complex Tangle of Secrets in Alice Munro's *Open Secrets*." *Critical Insights: Alice Munro*. Ed. Charles E. May. Ipswich, MA: Salem-EBSCO, 2013. 195-211.

---. "Engagement via Emotional Heightening in 'Passion': On the Grammatical Texture of Emotionally-Immersive Passages in Short Fiction." [*Theoretical Approaches to Alice Munro's "Passion."*] Ed. Susan Lohafer. *Narrative* 20 (2012): 210-25.

---. "Girl Power in 'A Trip to the Coast'." *Stylistic Perspectives on Alice Munro's* Dance of the Happy Shades. Ed. Manuel Jobert and Michael Toolan. *Études de Stylistique Anglais* 8 (2015): 195-215.

---. *Narrative Progression in the Short Story: A Corpus Stylistic Approach*. Amsterdam / Philadelphia: John Benjamins, 2009. Linguistic Approaches to Literature (LAL) 6.

Trigger, Bruce G. *The Huron: Farmers of the North*. New York: Holt, Rinehart, and Winston, 1969. Case Studies in Cultural Anthropology.

Trumpener, Katie. "Annals of Ice: Formations of Empire, Place and History in John Galt and Alice Munro." *Scottish Literature and Postcolonial Literature: Comparative Texts and Critical Perspectives*. Ed. Michael Gardiner, Graeme Macdonald, and Niall O'Gallagher. Edinburgh: Edinburgh UP, 2011. 43-56, 250-73 passim.

Trussler, Michael. "Narrative, Memory, and Contingency in Alice Munro's *Runaway*." *Critical Insights: Alice Munro*. Ed. Charles E. May. Ipswich, MA: Salem-EBSCO, 2013. 242-58.

---. "Pockets of Nothingness: 'Metaphysical Solitude' in Alice Munro's 'Passion'." [*Theoretical Approaches to Alice Munro's "Passion."*] Ed. Susan Lohafer. *Narrative* 20 (2012): 183-97.

---. "Uncanny Tracks in the Snow; or, Alice Munro as Assemblage Artist." *Alice Munro Everlasting: Essays on Her Works II*. Ed. J.R. (Tim) Struthers. Toronto: Guernica Editions, 2020. Essential Writers Ser. 52.

Turbide, Diane. "The Incomparable Storyteller." *Maclean's* 17 Oct. 1994: 46-49.

Vauthier, Simone. "Visiting Alice Munro's 'Pictures of the Ice'." *Writing (on) Short Stories: A Tribute to Paulette Michel-Michot*. Ed. Christine Pagnoulle. Liège, Belg.: *L*³ – Liège Language and Literature, 1997. 101-16.

Ventura, Héliane. *Alice Munro:* Dance of the Happy Shades. Neuilly, Fr.: Atlande, 2015. Clefs concours Anglais – Littérature.

---. "Dance of Happy Polysemy: The Reverberations of Alice Munro's Language." *Alice Munro and the Anatomy of the Short Story*. Ed. Oriana Palusci. Newcastle upon Tyne, Eng.: Cambridge Scholars, 2017. 13-26.

---. "The Female Bard: Retrieving Greek Myths, Celtic Ballads, Norse Sagas, and Popular Songs." *The Cambridge Companion to Alice Munro*. Ed. David Staines. Cambridge, Eng.: Cambridge UP, 2016. 154-77.

---. "From Accident to Murder: The Ethics of Responsibility in Alice Munro's 'The Time of Death' and 'Child's Play'." *The Inside of a Shell: Alice Munro's* Dance of the Happy Shades. Ed. Vanessa Guignery. Newcastle upon Tyne, Eng.: Cambridge Scholars, 2015. 158-68.

---. "From Shame to 'Pride'." La question animale dans les nouvelles d'Alice Munro / *The Animal Question in Alice Munro's Stories*. Ed. Héliane Ventura. *Caliban: French Journal of English Studies* 57 (2017): 139-50.

---. "Portrait of Man as Dog: Species Trouble in Alice Munro's 'Bardon Bus'." La question animale dans les nouvelles d'Alice Munro / *The Animal Question in Alice Munro's Stories*. Ed. Héliane Ventura. *Caliban: French Journal of English Studies* 57 (2017): 57-67.

---. "The Skald and the Goddess: Reading 'The Bear Came Over the Mountain' by Alice Munro." *The Short Stories of Alice Munro*. Ed. Héliane Ventura. *Journal of the Short Story in English / Les cahiers de la nouvelle* 55 (2010): 173-85. Rpt. as "The Skald and the Goddess: A Reading of Alice Munro's 'The Bear Came Over the Mountain'" in *Alice Munro Everlasting: Essays on Her Works II*. Ed. J.R. (Tim) Struthers. Toronto: Guernica Editions, 2020. Essential Writers Ser. 52.

---. "The Strumpet of Jubilee: Tragi-Comedy, Burlesque and Charivari in 'Postcard'." *"With a Roar from Underground": Alice Munro's* Dance of the Happy Shades. Ed. Corinne Bigot and Catherine Lanone. Paris: Presses Universitaires de Paris Ouest, 2015. 35-44.

Ventura, Héliane, ed. La question animale dans les nouvelles d'Alice Munro / *The Animal Question in Alice Munro's Stories. Caliban: French Journal of English Studies* 57 (2017): 5-164.

---, ed. *The Short Stories of Alice Munro. Journal of the Short Story in English / Les cahiers de la nouvelle* 55 (2010): 7-217.

Ventura, Héliane, and Mary Condé, eds. *Alice Munro: Writing Secrets. Open Letter* 11th ser., no. 9 - 12th ser., no. 1 (2003-04): 1-275.

Walker, Bev, ed. *Folk Art Treasures of Huron County.* Dungannon, ON: Gunbyfield, 1991.

Wallace, Bronwen. "Women's Lives: Alice Munro." *The Human Elements: Critical Essays.* Ed. David Helwig. Ottawa: Oberon, 1978. 52-67.

Wallace, Dorothy, gen. ed. *Memories of Goderich: The Romance of the Prettiest Town in Canada.* Goderich, ON: Jubilee 3 / Intercollegiate, 1977.

Ware, Tracy. "'And They May Get It Wrong, After All': Reading Alice Munro's 'Meneseteung'." *National Plots: Historical Fiction and Changing Ideas of Canada.* Ed. Andrea Cabajsky and Brett Josef Grubisic. Waterloo, ON: Wilfrid Laurier UP, 2010. 67-79, 215-36 passim.

---. "A Comic Streak: The Two 'Fairly Happy' Heroines of Alice Munro's 'Wigtime'." *Alice Munro Everlasting: Essays on Her Works II.* Ed. J.R. (Tim) Struthers. Toronto: Guernica Editions, 2020. Essential Writers Ser. 52.

---. "Momentous Shifts and Unimagined Changes in 'Jakarta'." *Alice Munro's Miraculous Art: Critical Essays.* Ed. Janice Fiamengo and Gerald Lynch. Ottawa: U of Ottawa P, 2017. 159-75. Reappraisals: Canadian Writers 38.

---. "Teaching and Conflict in Munro from 'The Day of the Butterfly' to 'Comfort'." *Alice Munro:* Hateship, Friendship, Courtship, Loveship, Marriage; Runaway; Dear Life. Ed. Robert Thacker. London: Bloomsbury, 2016. 44-64, 218-21, 231-44 passim.

---. "Tricks with 'a Sad Ring': The Endings of Alice Munro's 'The Ottawa Valley'." *Studies in Canadian Literature / Études en littérature canadienne* 31.2 (2006): 126-41.

Warkentin, John. "Lower Great Lakes Region *(Abundance, Manufactur-ing, Cities)*." *A Regional Geography of Canada: Life, Land, and Space.* 2nd ed. Scarborough, ON: Prentice Hall Canada, 2000. 318-34.

Waterston, Elizabeth. *Rapt in Plaid: Canadian Literature and Scottish Tradition.* Toronto: U of Toronto P, 2001.

Wayne, Joyce. "Huron County Blues." *Books in Canada* Oct. 1982: 9-12.

Weaver, John. "Society and Culture in Rural and Small-Town Ontario: Alice Munro's Testimony on the Last Forty Years." *Patterns of the Past: Interpreting Ontario's History.* Ed. Roger Hall, William Westfall, and Laurel Sefton MacDowell. Toronto: Dundurn, 1988. 381-402. Rpt. as "Society and Culture in Rural and Small-Town Ontario: Alice Munro's Testimony on the Forty Years from 1945 to 1985" in *Alice Munro Country: Essays on Her Works I.* Ed. J.R. (Tim) Struthers. Toronto: Guernica Editions, 2020. Essential Writers Ser. 51.

Wegg, Teffler, David Bishop, and Bonnie Sitter. *The Beauty & Bounty of Huron County.* Neustadt, ON: T. Wegg Photography, 2013.

Winther, Per. "Munro's Handling of Description, Focalization, and Voice in 'Passion'." [*Theoretical Approaches to Alice Munro's "Passion."*] Ed. Susan Lohafer. *Narrative* 20 (2012): 198-209.

York, Lorraine M. "'The Delicate Moment of Exposure': Alice Munro and Photography." *"The Other Side of Dailiness": Photography in the Works of Alice Munro, Timothy Findley, Michael Ondaatje, and Margaret Laurence.* Toronto: ECW, 1988. 21-50, 167-72 passim.

Zehelein, Eva-Sabine, ed. *For (Dear) Life: Close Readings of Alice Munro's Ultimate Fiction.* Zurich, Switz. and Berlin, Ger.: LIT, 2014. masteR-Research 7.

About the Writer

What could I say about ALICE MUNRO, the first Canadian writer, the first short story writer, and only the thirteenth woman to win the Nobel Prize in Literature? Perhaps that this very morning, the 455th anniversary of the birth of William Shakespeare, I awoke joyfully from a dream of meeting her for the first time in many years – Alice now in old age yet continuing to look so radiant. I had been wondering what I could possibly write about her and thinking that I would like to adapt a line deeply entrenched in my mind but remaining just out of reach: a line beginning with a question something like "What could I say about...?" From Shakespeare, perhaps? – I considered. Then, just as I arrived downstairs to prepare breakfast, I remembered the source. Alice Munro, of course. It's the thought that goes through the mind of the actress Rose in the last sentence of the final, title story of *Who Do You Think You Are?* – a book to which, long ago, I had devoted a chapter of my Ph.D. dissertation on the Canadian story cycle. Rose has seen a story in her hometown newspaper reporting the death in middle age of a childhood schoolmate, a mimic, and responds, "What could she say about herself and Ralph Gillespie, except that she felt his life, close, closer than the lives of men she'd loved, one slot over from her own?" I cannot think of a declaration more fitting to describe the feelings of so many remarkable readers about the ever-mesmerizing work of Alice Munro.

About the Artist

RON SHUEBROOK is a Canadian artist who is Professor Emeritus at OCAD University in Toronto where he served as President from 2000 to 2005 and as Vice-President, Academic from 1998 to 2002. He has taught and been an administrator at six other Canadian universities and art schools and is a former President of the Royal Canadian Academy of Arts and a former President of the Universities Art Association of Canada. He received an Honorary Doctorate from OCAD in 2005 as well as a Queen Elizabeth II Diamond Jubilee Medal in 2012. He is currently Senior Artist in Residence at Boarding House Arts in Guelph, Ontario. Shuebrook exhibits nationally and internationally and is represented by Olga Korper Gallery as well as other galleries. His work is in more than sixty public and corporate collections, including the National Gallery of Canada and the Art Gallery of Ontario, and in numerous private collections. An image of an untitled painting of his from 1989 (in the Art Gallery of Guelph collection) is reproduced in *Abstract Painting in Canada* by Roald Nasgaard. And a pair of drawings of his from 2013 were used as the cover art for Guernica Editions' companion volumes *Clark Blaise: Essays on His Works* and *Clark Blaise: The Interviews*. He lives in Guelph, Ontario and Blandford, Nova Scotia.

About the Editor

Highly respected nationally and internationally by scholars and creative writers for his work as a bibliographer, an interviewer, a literary critic, an editor, and the publisher of Red Kite Press, J.R. (TIM) STRUTHERS has edited some thirty volumes of theory, criticism, autobiography, fiction, and poetry – including works in honour of, or by, such important writers as Clark Blaise, George Elliott, Jack Hodgins, Hugh Hood, John Metcalf, and Alice Munro. Among these titles are his earlier pair of Guernica Editions collections, *Clark Blaise: Essays on His Works* and *Clark Blaise: The Interviews*, published in 2016. For more than forty-five years Tim has been writing about Canadian literature, particularly the short story, including, in 1975, the first two scholarly articles published world-wide on Alice Munro. He has conducted some forty interviews with Canadian writers and has been described by W.J. Keith, FRSC, as "probably the best literary interviewer in Canada." An enthusiastic teacher, he has taught English full-time at the University of Guelph for thirty-five years. Tim lives in Guelph with his bride of now forty-five years, poet and short story writer and scholar Marianne Micros, inspired and delighted by the company of their two daughters, Eleni and Joy, and their four grandchildren, Matteo, Rowan, Asher, and Reed.

Contributor Biographies

WILLIAM BUTT has worked in seventeen different countries, and has published articles in Canada, the U.S.A., Europe, Africa, and Asia. He has written drama scripts produced for and broadcast on CBC television and other networks, and has had seven of his theatre scripts produced, all based on subjects from local histories. He was co-founder and for eight years artistic director of a music and video production studio in Quelimane, Mozambique, where he was based as communications consultant for the United Church of Canada. He has published criticism on individual Canadian writers including Margaret Avison, Clark Blaise, George Elliott, Robert Gourlay, Jack Hodgins, Eli Mandel, and Alice Munro, as well as *Behind Our Doors: A Memoir of Esther Warmerdam as Told to William Butt* (2011), reminiscences of World War Two in Holland by a woman who was then a teenage girl. He has a Ph.D. in English from The University of Western Ontario, where he wrote his dissertation on the social conflicts that resulted in the Donnelly mass murders and on the ensuing cultural legacy in legend, literature, and other popular art forms. He is based now in Southwestern Ontario.

The 4th Poet Laureate of Toronto (2012-15) and the 7th Canadian Parliamentary Poet Laureate (2016-17), GEORGE ELLIOTT CLARKE is a revered artist in song, drama, fiction, screenplay, opera, criticism, and poetry. Born in Windsor, Nova Scotia, in 1960, Clarke was educated at the University of Waterloo, Dalhousie University, and Queen's University. He is also a pioneering scholar of African-Canadian literature, the author of *Odysseys Home: Mapping African-Canadian Literature* (2002) and *Directions Home: Approaches to African-Canadian Literature* (2012). A professor of English at the University of Toronto, where he is the inaugural E.J. Pratt Professor of Canadian Literature, a position established specifically for a poet-professor, Clarke has taught at Duke, McGill, the

University of British Columbia, and Harvard. He holds eight honorary doctorates, plus appointments to the Order of Nova Scotia and the Order of Canada at the rank of Officer. He is also a Fellow of the Royal Canadian Geographical Society. His recognitions include the Pierre Elliott Trudeau Fellowship Prize, the Governor General's Award for Poetry, the National Magazine Gold Award for Poetry, the Premiul Poesis (Romania), the Dartmouth Book Award for Fiction, the Eric Hoffer Book Award for Poetry (U.S.A.), and the Dr. Martin Luther King Jr. Achievement Award. Clarke's work is the subject of *Africadian Atlantic: Essays on George Elliott Clarke* (2012), edited by Joseph Pivato, and includes the triumphant continuing poem *Canticles I (mmxvi)* (2016) and *Canticles I (mmxvii)* (2017) published by Guernica Editions. The father of Montreal-based filmmaker Aurélia Morin-Clarke, Clarke lives in Toronto, but still owns property in Nova Scotia, near Windsor. Finally, though Clarke is racialized "Black" and was socialized as an Africadian, he is a card-carrying member of the Eastland Woodland Métis Nation Nova Scotia, registered under Section 35 of the Charter of Rights and Freedoms. He is, at last, a proud Afro-Métis Africadian.

AILSA COX is now Professor Emerita at Edge Hill University in the United Kingdom, where she was until her retirement from full-time teaching in 2019 Professor of Short Fiction. She is the author of *Alice Munro* (2004), *Writing Short Stories* (2005; 2nd ed., 2016), and, with Christine Lorre-Johnston, *The Mind's Eye: Alice Munro's Dance of the Happy Shades* (2015). Her own short fiction has been widely published and collected as *The Real Louise and Other Stories* (2009). She has also published various book chapters focussing mostly on Alice Munro's later stories, including contributions to volumes edited by Jakob Lothe, Hans H. Skei, and Per Winther (2008), Maggie Awadalla and Paul March-Russell (2013), Charles E. May (2013), Jochen Achilles and Ina Bergmann (2015), Robert Thacker (2016), Janice Fiamengo and Gerald Lynch (2017), Christine Lorre-Johnston and Eleonora Rao (2018), and J.R. (Tim) Struthers (2020). And she has published essays on other authors including Malcolm Lowry, Katherine Mansfield, and Helen Simpson. From its inception in 2011, she has been the editor of the journal *Short Fiction in Theory and Practice* (Intellect Press). She has also edited the collections *The Short Story* (2008) and *Teaching the Short Story* (2011).

DENNIS DUFFY, now Professor Emeritus at the University of Toronto and formerly Principal of Innis College there, is the author of the monograph *Marshall McLuhan* (1969), the studies *Gardens, Covenants, Exiles: Loyalism in the Literature of Upper Canada/Ontario* (1982) and *Sounding the Iceberg: An Essay on Canadian Historical Novels* (1986), and three volumes focussing on nineteenth-century Southwestern Ontario writer Major John Richardson, including *A World Under Sentence: John Richardson and the Interior* (1996). He is the author, as well, of essays on numerous modern Canadian writers including Hugh Hood, Al Purdy, George Elliott, Timothy Findley, Robertson Davies, Rudy Wiebe (aka Ruby Weed, according to very young Jonathan Redekop, Dennis's beloved stepson), Michael Ondaatje, and, more recently, Alice Munro, along with articles on popular American writers such as L. Frank Baum and Annie Fellows Johnston and Edward Stratemeyer. He has also produced historical and cultural studies on topics ranging from the origins of Algonquin Park to the impact of the Vimy memorial to the preoccupations of William Lyon Mackenzie King. His reviews and commentaries have been appearing in various Toronto and national outlets over the last 50+ years. Dennis continues to live and write in Toronto.

ALEC FOLLETT is finishing a Ph.D. in English at the University of Guelph, where he is writing his dissertation on the role of politically engaged Indigenous and Canadian writers in contemporary environmental justice movements. Prior to undertaking doctoral work, he completed a B.A. (Hon.) in English at the University of Guelph and an M.A. at Ryerson University, where he studied the popular reading material of late-eighteenth-century Ireland. Alec's research regularly addresses literary responses to environmental issues. He has published an in-depth interview with poet-ecologist Madhur Anand in *The Goose: A Journal of Arts, Environment, and Culture in Canada*. His essay "'A life of dignity, joy and good relation': Water, Knowledge, and Environmental Justice in Rita Wong's *undercurrent*" has appeared in *Canadian Literature*. And he is currently a co-editor of the on-line creative/critical periodical *The Goose*. Alec's academic work is informed by his experiences working with various community organizations that support local literary activity and environmental research and by his experiences as a resident of southern Ontario who aims to build better relationships across cultures and with the land.

DOUGLAS MAITLAND GIBSON was born in Scotland in 1943 and came to Canada in 1967, armed with degrees from St. Andrews and Yale. From 1968, until he "retired" in 2007, he worked as an Editor, and then as a Publisher. He first encountered Alice Munro when he was the Editorial Director at Macmillan of Canada, persuading her to continue writing short stories when the literary world was advising her to abandon stories in favour of "more saleable" novels. The first of the many story collections they published together was *Who Do You Think You Are?* (1978). When, in 1986, he was given Canada's first editorial imprint, Alice Munro chose to follow him to McClelland and Stewart. He continued to edit all of her books, even after he became M&S's Publisher in 1988. He was among the Canadians who went to Stockholm to celebrate Alice Munro's Nobel Prize. He writes about her achievements in his books *Stories about Storytellers* (2011; rev. ed., 2014) and *Across Canada by Story* (2015).

JACK HODGINS' novels and story collections include *Spit Delaney's Island* (1976), *The Invention of the World* (1977), *Broken Ground* (1998), and *The Master of Happy Endings* (2010). His book on writing, *A Passion for Narrative* (1993; rev. ed., 2001), is often used in classrooms and in writing groups. Hodgins' fiction – usually (but not always) set on Vancouver Island – has won the Governor General's Award, the Canada-Australia Prize, the regional Commonwealth Prize, the Gibson Literary Award, and the Ethel Wilson Fiction Prize, amongst other awards. His nonfiction book *Over 40 in Broken Hill* (1992) is an account of his adventures while travelling in the Outback with Australian novelist Roger McDonald. Born and raised in the Comox Valley community of Merville, Hodgins attended the University of British Columbia's new Education Faculty where he met Dianne Child, who later became his wife. Both accepted teaching positions in Nanaimo where they built a house and raised three children (Shannon, Gavin, and Tyler). During holidays and other school breaks he wrote fiction, and eventually sold a story to an Oregon literary magazine – his first publication. Before joining the teaching faculty in the University of Victoria's Department of Writing, Hodgins had taught short-term writing workshops in Saskatchewan, Ottawa, and various other parts of Canada. He and Dianne now live in Victoria, with family (including grandchildren) living nearby. In 2009 he was appointed a Member of the Order of Canada.

CORAL ANN HOWELLS, FRSC, is Professor Emerita at the University of Reading and Senior Research Fellow at the Institute of English Studies, University of London. She taught at the University of Reading for thirty years, was Visiting Exchange Professor at the University of Guelph (1981-82), and has held Visiting Professorships in Europe and India. She has lectured and published extensively on English-Canadian women writers. Her publications include *Margaret Atwood* (1996; 2nd ed., 2005), *Alice Munro* (1998), and *Contemporary Canadian Women's Fiction: Refiguring Identities* (2003). She is editor of *The Cambridge Companion to Margaret Atwood* (2006; 2nd ed., forthcoming), co-editor with Eva-Marie Kröller of *The Cambridge History of Canadian Literature* (2009), and co-editor with Paul Sharrad and Gerry Turcotte of Vol. 12 of *The Oxford History of the Novel in English* (2017).

SHELLEY HULAN is an Associate Professor of Canadian literature and Chair of the Department of English Language and Literature at the University of Waterloo. Among other interests, she researches the literature and rhetoric of early Canadian diplomacy and the end of empire in relation to early Canadian women writers. Her articles have appeared in *Canadian Poetry: Studies, Documents, Reviews, Journal of Canadian Studies, Mosaic: An Interdisciplinary Critical Journal, Studies in Canadian Literature, University of Toronto Quarterly*, and in various peer-reviewed essay collections. Her book chapter on Alice Munro's short story "What Do You Want To Know For?" is included in Cynthia Sugars and Eleanor Ty's volume *Canadian Literature and Cultural Memory* (2014).

JOHN B. LEE is the author of more than seventy-five books of poetry or prose and has edited over a dozen critically acclaimed anthologies, including, with J.R. (Tim) Struthers, *Alice Munro: A Souwesto Celebration* (2014), a special issue of *The Windsor Review*. Appointed Poet Laureate of the City of Brantford for life in 2004 and Poet Laureate of Norfolk County for life in 2014 – and a winner of a Canada 150 Sesquicentennial Pin for his contribution to literary culture in Canada in 2017 – he is the recipient of over eighty national and international awards for his writing including being the only two-time winner of the prestigious People's Poetry Award. He has read his work in nations all over the world; it has appeared internationally in over five hundred publications; and it has been translated into French, Spanish, Bosnian, and Korean. Called the greatest living poet in English by Canadian poet George Whipple, he has received letters of commendation from Nelson Mandela and Desmond Tutu for his book of poems inspired by his travels in South Africa, while his co-translation of Cuban poetry along with Professor Manuel Léon has been praised as "the most significant book of translated Cuban poetry ever published." His many books include the family memoir *The Farm on the Hill He Calls Home* (2004), two volumes of selected poems, *The Half-Way Tree: Poems Selected and New: 1970-2000* (2001) and *Beautiful Stupid: Selected Poems: 2001-2018* (2018), and a book of poems *These Are the Words* (2018) in collaboration with Canada's 7th Canadian Parliamentary Poet Laureate George Elliott Clarke. John lives with his wife Cathy in a lake house overlooking Long Point Bay in Port Dover where he works as a full-time author.

LOUIS K. MacKENDRICK, now Professor Emeritus at the University of Windsor, edited the very first volume of criticism about Munro, *Probable Fictions: Alice Munro's Narrative Acts* (1983); he has also written a monograph on Munro, *Some Other Reality: Alice Munro's* Something I've Been Meaning To Tell You (1993), in addition to a monograph on poet Al Purdy, *Al Purdy and His Works* (1990). A critic or, rather, a writer who not only has contributed to the understanding of many aspects of Canadian (and American) literature but also has elevated readers' sense of the possibilities of language and style in the art – criticism – that he practises, Kim continues to live and laugh in Windsor, Ontario, where at one point in time he earned the nickname "Hole-in-One MacKendrick."

W.R. MARTIN, before his death in 2015, one day short of his ninety-fifth birthday, was Distinguished Professor Emeritus in the University of Waterloo Department of English, where he also received the coveted Distinguished Teacher Award. Born in South Africa, he received his doctorate from Natal University and taught at Stellenbosch University before coming to Canada with his family in 1961. After a year at the Agricultural College in Guelph, he came to the fledgling English Department at the University of Waterloo where he taught until his retirement. He was also very involved with starting the University of Waterloo Drama Department.

While writing *Alice Munro: Paradox and Parallel*, Walter and his wife Patricia, on a drive through "Alice Munro Country," decided to drop in on

Munro's father, still living in Wingham. Robert Laidlaw was surprised but also very welcoming when they explained their mission. It seems that nobody had ever come to see him about his famous daughter. Walter wrote to Alice Munro about the visit and she responded saying her father had mentioned it and had been very pleased. When Walter's book on Munro was published, he sent her a copy, not really expecting to hear anything about it. Months later, Munro sent a postcard (of Clinton) saying that although she felt uncomfortable being written about, she thought he had done "a fine job."

W.R. Martin's *Alice Munro: Paradox and Parallel* was published in 1987 – the first full-length study of her stories by an individual hand – and was followed by articles and notes on Munro mostly co-written with Warren U. Ober. The two were co-authors of *Henry James's Apprenticeship: The Tales: 1864-1882* (1994), co-editors of a facsimile reproduction of James's 1910 short story collection *The Finer Grain* (1986), and co-editors of *Trees: A Browser's Anthology* (1998). They also collaborated on a total of eighteen articles on Henry James.

MARIANNE MICROS was born in the small town of Cuba, New York, where her family owned an ice cream factory. She is proud of her Greek heritage and has travelled many times to Greece, renewing her family ties and her conversational Greek language. Her background and her travels continue to inspire much of her writing. Marianne earned degrees at Sweet Briar College, St. Bonaventure University, and The University of Western Ontario. She moved to Canada in 1974 for Ph.D. studies, got married here, and never left. She has worked in a variety of jobs: receptionist and secretary at *Look* and *Family Circle* magazines; secretary in a Greek travel agency in New York City; waitress in a Middle Eastern restaurant in Greenwich Village; high-school teacher; teaching assistant, contract teacher, and finally Associate Professor at the university level.

Her story collection *Eye* (2018) explores the mythology, folklore, Greek customs, and old-world cultures that have fascinated her all her life. These tales of myth and magic tell of evil-eye curses, women healers, ghosts, a changeling, and people struggling to retain or gain power in a world of changing beliefs. *Eye* was named one of five finalists nationally for the Danuta Gleed Literary Award presented by The Writers' Union of Canada for the best first collection of Canadian short fiction, then again named one of five finalists for the Governor General's Literary Award for Fiction. Her previous publications include: a book of poetry about her Greek family, *Upstairs Over the Ice Cream* (1979); a poetry collection that focusses primarily on her search for ancestors and family members in Greece, *Seventeen Trees* (2007); and poems and short fiction in anthologies and journals. She has published scholarly articles on Renaissance and contemporary subjects, including essays on the writings of Edmund Spenser, John Milton, Margaret Cavendish, Mary, Queen of Scots, Mary Wroth, Denise Levertov, Gwendolyn MacEwen, and Alice Munro. She has also published a bibliographical monograph on Al Purdy (1980). Her suite of poems "Demeter's Daughters" was shortlisted for the Gwendolyn MacEwen poetry competition in 2015 and published in *Exile: The Literary Quarterly*.

After some forty-five years of teaching, Marianne has now retired from her career as an English professor at the University of Guelph, where she worked for thirty years, teaching Renaissance literature, Scottish literature, folktales, and creative writing. She has completed a new book of poetry entitled *The Aphrodite Suite* and is working on a second collection of stories. Marianne also spends time enjoying her grandchildren, reading mysteries, and bellydancing. She still loves ice cream!

WARREN U. OBER is Distinguished Professor Emeritus at the University of Waterloo, where he received the Distinguished Teacher Award and served terms as Chair of the English Department and Acting Dean of the Arts Faculty. With W.K. Thomas, he is the co-author of *A Mind For Ever Voyaging: Wordsworth at Work Portraying Newton and Science* (1989). With W.R. Martin, he is the co-author of *Henry James's Apprenticeship: The Tales: 1864-1882* (1994), eighteen articles on Henry James, and four articles on Alice Munro, and is the co-editor of a facsimile reproduction of James's 1910 short story collection *The Finer Grain* (1986) and of *Trees: A Browser's Anthology* (1998). With Neil C. Hultin, he is the co-editor of four books by the pioneer Irish folklorist, Thomas Crofton Croker, and the co-author of three articles largely on Croker. With his brother, Kenneth H. Ober, he is the co-author of fourteen articles on the translation of English poetry into Russian or Russian poetry into English. With Paul S. Burtness, he is the co-editor of *The Puzzle of Pearl Harbor* (1962) and the co-author of seven articles on the background to the onset of World War Two in the Pacific. He is the editor of *The Story of the Three*

Bears: The Evolution of an International Classic (1981) and the author of "The Three Bears from Southey to Tolstoy." He is the author of additional articles or notes on William Blake, William Wordsworth, Samuel Taylor Coleridge, and Robert Southey.

IAN RAE is an Associate Professor in the Department of English, French, and Writing at King's University College at Western University in London, Ontario. He is the author of the monograph *From Cohen to Carson: The Poet's Novel in Canada* (2008) and editor of *George Bowering: Bridges to Elsewhere* (2010), a special issue of *Open Letter*. Rae returned to Southwestern Ontario after years of study at Queen's University (Hon. B.A.), the University of Oslo, the University of British Columbia (Governor General's Gold Medal for M.A. thesis, SSHRC and Killam doctoral fellowships), McGill University (SSHRC and Max Bell postdoctoral fellowships), the University of Bonn (Visiting Assistant Professor), and the McGill Institute for the Study of Canada (Visiting Assistant Professor, Acting Program Director). In 2012, he earned a SSHRC Insight Development Grant for his *Mapping Stratford Culture* project, which aims to develop an interdisciplinary cultural history of this Canadian arts hub. In 2016, he received a Moore Institute Fellowship at the University of Ireland, Galway, for his research into the Stratford Festival and the Irish Literary Revival.

JAMES REANEY's enduring reputation as one of Canada's greatest writers rests for many on his theatrically and historically groundbreaking epic trilogy *The Donnellys*, portraying the story of the nineteenth-century Southwestern Ontario family of that name and first produced at Tarragon Theatre in Toronto in 1973, 1974, and 1975. The trilogy then toured nation-wide, as Reaney records in his delightful book *14 Barrels from Sea to Sea* (1977).

Yet Reaney's accomplishments and influences were – are – multifarious. As playwright: celebrated for *Sticks & Stones* and *The St. Nicholas Hotel* and *Handcuffs*, the three plays that comprise *The Donnellys* (1975, 1976, 1977; 1983; 2008), and for other dramatic works, including those in *Reaney Days in the West Room: Plays of James Reaney* (2009), edited by David Ferry. As poet: author of volumes such as *The Red Heart* (1949), *Twelve Letters to a Small Town* (1962; 2nd ed., 2002), *The Dance of Death at London, Ontario* (1963), illustrated by Jack Chambers, *Performance*

Poems (1990), and *Souwesto Home* (2005). As short story writer: Margaret Atwood has said that the lyrical and fierce originality of his story "The Bully," written by Reaney in 1948 at the age of 21 and gathered in his fifty-year retrospective collection *The Box Social and Other Stories* (1996), "offered us a whole new way of looking at the possibilities of the world available to us. ... Without 'The Bully,' my fiction would have followed other paths." As children's writer: including *Apple Butter & Other Plays for Children* (1973) and two children's novels. As essayist: the author, amongst other personal and inventive works, of the ever-fertile "An ABC to Ontario Literature and Culture." As historian: painstakingly researching, making selections for, and writing a 130-page introduction to *The Donnelly Documents: An Ontario Vendetta* (2004). As editor of *Alphabet: A Journal Devoted to the Iconography of the Imagination* (1960-71).

Perhaps above all, however, at least for his many students both inside and outside the classroom, as a Teacher. For forty years full-time *in addition to* his extraordinarily full writing career. First at the University of Manitoba, where he taught from 1949 until 1960 – except for a leave taken in the late 1950s to do a Ph.D. in English at the University of Toronto, work including his dissertation "The Influence of Spenser on Yeats" (1958) supervised by Northrop Frye. Then at The University of Western Ontario, from 1960 until his retirement (from teaching) in 1989. Reaney died on 11 June 2008.

J.R. (TIM) STRUTHERS has been publishing on Alice Munro and the short story for over forty-five years. His recent critical work on Munro includes several seminal essays – among them, a greatly expanded version published in *Short Story Criticism*, Vol. 208 (2015) of his pioneering 1975 essay "Alice Munro and the American South"; two essays on "Meneseteung," one published in *Critical Insights: Alice Munro* (2013) edited by Charles E. May and one published in *Alice Munro: A Souwesto Celebration* (2014), a special issue that Tim and John B. Lee edited for *The Windsor Review*; an essay on "To Reach Japan" in *Alice Munro* (2016) edited by Robert Thacker; and a new essay on Munro's novella "Powers" in *Alice Munro Everlasting* (2020).

Other recent critical writing includes an essay on Clark Blaise's story "A Fish Like A Buzzard" featured in 2011 as the lead article in the inaugural issue of the British journal *Short Fiction in Theory and Practice* and an essay on Clark Blaise's story "The Birth of the Blues" in *Clark Blaise: Essays on His Works* (2016). He has in addition carried out some forty interviews with Canadian writers, including two with Alice Munro. An initial interview, conducted in 1981, was published in *Probable Fictions: Alice Munro's Narrative Acts* (1983), the very first volume of criticism about Munro, edited by Louis K. MacKendrick; the second, conducted in 1988, appears for the first time in *Alice Munro Country* (2020).

His extensive research has resulted in foundational bibliographical works by him on Clark Blaise, Jack Hodgins, Hugh Hood, John Metcalf, Alice Munro, and Leon Rooke, including two recent studies surveying critical, cultural, and theoretical readings he considers important to understanding Munro's world and style: the creative/critical essay "Song for Alice Munro" published in *Alice Munro and the Souwesto Story* (2013 [2015]), a special issue that Tim edited for the American journal *Short Story*, and his 401-item "A Bibliographical Tour of Alice Munro Country" published in *Alice Munro Country* (2020).

He views the companion volumes *Alice Munro Country* and *Alice Munro Everlasting* not as an end but as a beginning.

JUDITH THOMPSON is a playwright, director, artistic director, actor, and teacher. She is the author of more than twenty-five plays, two feature films, numerous radio dramas, and many essays that have been included in anthologies. She is the co-founder and artistic director of RARE Theatre, a theatre dedicated to giving theatrical experience and voice to marginalized communities who seek a theatrical platform. She has won the Governor General's Award for dramatic writing twice, the Toronto Arts Award, the Walter Carsen Prize for Excellence in the Performing Arts, the Nellie Award, and others. She has been appointed as Officer of the Order of Canada, and is a Fellow of the Royal Society of Canada. Her play *Palace of the End* was premièred by the Canadian Stage Company in 2008 and won both the Susan Smith Blackburn Prize and the Amnesty International Freedom of Expression Award. She recently developed her fifth project for RARE Theatre, *Welcome to My Underworld*, featuring nine blazing hot emerging writers and produced at Soulpepper Theatre in Toronto. She holds an honorary Doctor of Divinity from Thorneloe University and an honorary Doctor of Laws from her alma mater, Queen's University.

REG THOMPSON has long been friends with Alice Munro. They share enthusiasm for rural landscape, history, and culture. They have spent many hours rambling the back roads of their territory, investigating bypassed hamlets, remnants of ancient swamps, tiny pioneer cemeteries. Thompson's focus on the intensely discovered local grows from thirty years employment in the Huron County Library system. He has a reputation as the research specialist, helping countless researchers in history and genealogy, concentrating on the deep details, while always watching the shrubbery for overlooked clues. Appreciation for his research help has been expressed formally by authors in more books than he knows or remembers. One of the authors being Alice Munro. He wrote the essay in this collection, "All Things Considered: Alice Munro First and Last," after Alice won the Nobel Prize. It was his personal consideration after reading many critical and literary assessments of her work, and the post-Nobel comments and coverage – much of which he thought missed the point. Another essay, "Cemetery Hunting with Alice Munro," appeared in 2019 in the magazine *The Rural Voice*. He contemplates producing an exhausting study of Munro's *oeuvre*, titled *Meadow Fescue; or, Goosefoot and Old Man's Beard: An Examination of Traditional Flora and Deracination in the Work of Alice Munro*.

A Distinguished University Professor and former Dean of Graduate Studies at McMaster University, JOHN WEAVER attributes a long interest in social history to the formative influences of small town Ontario. Experiences and village tales understandably drew him to Alice Munro. Town life provoked his later interest in living conditions, law and order, prejudice, and mental health; they appear in many of his articles and several books. He is best known, however, for the multiple-award-winning *The Great Land Rush and the Making of the Modern World, 1650-1900* (2003), a book fulfilling an urge to leave small towns while valuing their life-lessons about decency, foibles, and unfairness. He teaches courses on empires, capitalism, and law. Any presumption of linkages among them is probably correct.

Acknowledgements

An earlier version of William Butt's "Killer OSPs and Style Munro in 'Open Secrets'" was published in *Alice Munro: A Souwesto Celebration*, a special issue of *The Windsor Review* co-edited by J.R. (Tim) Struthers and John B. Lee.

George Elliott Clarke's "Alice Munro's Black Bottom; or Black Tints and Euro Hints in *Lives of Girls and Women*" was first published in *Alice Munro: Reminiscence, Interpretation, Adaptation and Comparison*, co-edited by Mirosława Buchholtz and Eugenia Sojka.

Dennis Duffy's "Too Little Geography; Too Much History: Writing the Balance in Alice Munro" was first published as "Too Little Geography; Too Much History: Writing the Balance in 'Meneseteung'" in *National Plots: Historical Fiction and Changing Ideas of Canada*, co-edited by Andrea Cabajsky and Brett Josef Grubisic.

Douglas Gibson's "Alice Munro: Not Bad Short Story Writer" is excerpted from Douglas Gibson, *Stories about Storytellers* (rev. ed.), published by ECW Press Ltd., 2014, 978-1-77041-209-5.

Coral Ann Howells' "Intimate Dislocations: Buried History and Geography in Alice Munro's Souwesto Stories" was first published in *Dislocations: Changing Conceptions of Space and Time*, a special issue of the *British Journal of Canadian Studies* edited by Danielle Fuller.

Louis K. MacKendrick's "Giving Tongue: Scorings of Voice, Verse, and Flesh in Alice Munro's 'Meneseteung'" was first published in *Alice Munro and the Souwesto Story*, a special issue of *Short Story* edited by J.R. (Tim) Struthers.

W.R. Martin and Warren U. Ober's "Alice Munro as Small-Town Historian: 'Spaceships Have Landed'" was first published in *Alice Munro Writing On...*, a special issue of *Essays on Canadian Writing* edited by Robert Thacker. This essay is reproduced here in slightly abridged form with the permission of Mary Martin and Warren U. Ober.

An earlier version of Ian Rae's "Alice Munro and the Huron Tract as a Literary Project" was published in *The Inside of a Shell: Alice Munro's Dance of the Happy Shades*, edited by Vanessa Guignery.

James Reaney's "An ABC to Ontario Literature and Culture" was first published in *Black Moss: A Semi-Annual of Ontario Literature and Culture*.

Reg Thompson's "All Things Considered: Alice Munro First and Last" was first published in *Alice Munro: A Souwesto Celebration*, a special issue of *The Windsor Review* co-edited by J.R. (Tim) Struthers and John B. Lee.

John Weaver's "Society and Culture in Rural and Small-Town Ontario: Alice Munro's Testimony on the Forty Years from 1945 to 1985" was first published as "Society and Culture in Rural and Small-Town Ontario: Alice Munro's Testimony on the Last Forty Years" in *Patterns of the Past: Interpreting Ontario's History*, co-edited by Roger Hall, William Westfall, and Laurel Sefton MacDowell.

J.R. (Tim) Struthers wishes to offer his heart-felt appreciation to Alec Follett, Eleni Kapetanios, Kelsey McCallum, Marianne Micros, Joy Struthers, and in particular Elizabeth Standing for their generous, perceptive, and good-humoured editorial assistance and support while he prepared the companion volumes *Alice Munro Country: Essays on Her Works I* and *Alice Munro Everlasting: Essays on Her Works II*. He would also like to thank the many other kind souls who offered him such vital encouragement and inspiration during the four years he spent on these two volumes, including the very special dedicatees of his essay on Munro's novella "Powers," William Butt and Marianne Micros and Catherine Sheldrick Ross and Ron Shuebrook, including good friend and researcher *extraordinaire* of local history Reg Thompson, along with all the other distinguished contributors to these two volumes, most notably the twenty individuals who enthusiastically agreed to produce such bold new work in honour of Alice Munro. Finally, at the University of Guelph, Tim wishes to thank the ever-helpful InterLibrary Loan staff and the ever-courteous Circulation staff at the McLaughlin Library, the benevolent and personable Manager of Information Technology Systems for the College of Arts, Chris Lee, and Tim's constantly encouraging Director in the School of English and Theatre Studies, Ann Wilson.

This book is made of paper from well-managed FSC® - certified
forests, recycled materials, and other controlled sources.